CELEBRATING

A CENTURY OF THE

Prix de l'Arc de Triomphe

CELEBRATING

A CENTURY OF THE

Prix de l'Arc de Triomphe

MALCOLM PANNETT

First published by Pitch Publishing, 2020

Pitch Publishing
A2 Yeoman Gate
Yeoman Way
Worthing
Sussex
BN13 3QZ
www.pitchpublishing.co.uk
info@pitchpublishing.co.uk

© 2020, Malcolm Pannett

A CIP catalogue record is available for this book
from the British Library.

ISBN 978 1 78531 724 8

Typesetting and origination by Pitch Publishing
Printed and bound in India by Replika Press Pvt. Ltd.

Contents

Key

In the form line sections, Arc-runners are shown in **bold.**

In the breeding diagrams, fillies and mares are shown in *italics* with Arc-winners in **bold.**

Foreword

In 1970, as a young boy in England, I crossed the road to my best friend's house in order to watch the BBC's coverage of the Arc – and Nijinsky was going to win.

In those days, satellite links were fragile and could break down at any time. Even in bright sunlight the grainy black and white pictures often gave the impression of thick fog or heavy snow.

What I saw was unbelievable. Lester Piggott was a genius, Nijinsky was unbeatable, but Nijinsky didn't win. He emerged from the 'fog' to come to take the lead. But instead of sprinting away, he was repassed by Sassafras, who won by a head.

I now know that there were very good reasons why Nijinsky didn't win – impatient readers should skip to the 1970 essay now – but at the time I couldn't understand what I'd just seen.

A year later the next English superstar, Mill Reef, did win and so within 12 months I'd experienced the extremes the Arc had to offer. But, more importantly, in those races I'd been introduced to Yves Saint-Martin and Freddy Head, who were now on my list of favourite jockeys.

It didn't take long for me to become a confirmed Francophile and for the Prix de l'Arc de Triomphe to become my favourite race.

Since then I've been lucky enough to have a series of jobs where I've been required to watch French racing on a daily basis – as the old line goes, 'it's a tough job but someone has to do it'.

As a history geek, I couldn't help but research the subject ad infinitum and after setting out to document everything that had ever happened in French racing, it seemed more sensible to limit the scope to the greatest race.

So here it is. The history of the autumn clash of the generations that produces the champion of Europe. I hope you have an enjoyable canter through the decades and that the more recent years jog plenty of memories.

Acknowledgements

I'd like to give my thanks to the following who, in their different ways, have all helped in bringing this project to fruition.

Firstly my friends and family, primarily my father to whom I owe everything. To Immy, Mandy, Steve, Paul, Joanna, Russell, and Paula, who all gave their unstinting support.

Tremendous thanks to Jane at Pitch who saw the merit of the venture, and who with their colleagues Graham, Dean, and Duncan – made it happen.

To Graham Russel – for his proof-reading pointers and Laurent Barbarin, Sky's 'French racing guru', for his help in finding some of the missing data. Brough Scott and Tim Cox for their encouragement and comments when the project was in its early stages.

Thanks also to Getty Images, Alamy, and the Press Association for the pictures. Finally to my current and former colleagues, Daren Cheverton, Martin Pennington, Shabaz Rafiq, Paul Newton, Richard Coghill and Ian Holding et al, for their knowledge and help over the years. And, of course, all at Brighton, Fontwell, and Plumpton racecourses.

Introduction

How the seventh French Classic came into being

This is the history of the greatest horse race in France – arguably the world. In its centenary year, what better time to celebrate the heritage of the race that has evolved to become the undisputed horse racing championship of Europe.

The Prix de l'Arc de Triomphe has produced extraordinary drama, some huge shocks, and even some gut-wrenching lows, but above all – and on a regular basis – it has witnessed the exploits of truly great champions.

Before we come on to the inaugural running of the great race we need all the required ingredients to be in place. We need the sport of horse racing to exist in France, we need an organising body, we need a racecourse to run it on and, of course, a great race requires a suitably grandiose name.

A brief history of horse racing and the French-bred thoroughbred

Horse racing has existed in many different forms for hundreds of years; it even featured in the ancient Olympics. In northern Europe in the 17th century it was the Stuart kings of England who laid the foundations of the sport on Newmarket's heath, while not long after in France, Louis XIV staged racing at Versailles.

Modern racing started in earnest with the emergence of the thoroughbred at the start of the 18th century. The thoroughbred as a distinct breed came into being in England by crossing imported Arabian stallions with indigenous mares.

Many stallions were brought to England but in the end, three – the Byerley Turk, Godolphin Arabian and Darley Arabian – were the most successful and as such all racehorses can trace their heritage to one or more of them.

Incidentally the Godolphin Arabian was owned by Louis XV for a couple of years and, apparently, he put him to good use as a carthorse.

The Darley Arabian, though, through the line of Eclipse, is by far and away the most dominant of the foundation sires, with 95 per cent of all thoroughbreds being descended from him.

So the roots of our story date back to 1704, the year that the Darley Arabian arrived in England. If we spin forward a couple of centuries and pass through 18 generations we find Comrade, the first winner of the Prix de l'Arc de Triomphe, with only a further seven generations bringing us to Waldgeist, the winner in 2019.

However, that was all in the future when, in 1750, the sport in England moved on to a more permanent footing with the formation of the Jockey Club in London, which provided an effective administration, including a single set of rules and detailed record keeping.

The French equivalent – the Société d'Encouragement pour l'Amélioration des Races de Chevaux en France – would not arrive on the scene until 1833.

This was largely due to the turmoil caused by the French Revolution, which understandably set the development of French racing back a considerable time. In the end it was a case of playing catch-up, with each development in England being used as a template for the French authorities to copy.

The Comte d'Artois, who owned racehorses in France and England, was a major mover and shaker in the sport, championing and promoting racing in and around Paris including at Chantilly.

He regularly accompanied Marie Antoinette to the races, and although she was a famous casualty of the Revolution, he survived. Once the monarchy was reinstated after Waterloo, the Count followed his brother, Louis XVIII, to become king himself, as Charles X in 1824.

Six years later, after the second French Revolution, he was replaced by Louis-Philippe who became the inaugural patron of the Société d'Encouragement, which nowadays has been subsumed under the France Galop banner.

Its mission was, and still is, to improve the quality of French-bred racehorses.

By definition all breeding suffixes refer to the country in which the horse is born in. Thus, a horse with the suffix (FR) must be foaled, that is to say born, in France.

As the French were so far behind the English at that time, they operated a closed shop, meaning only French-breds could run in races staged in France, although French-breds could run in England but those that did were finding it hard to do so with any success.

Many stallions were imported, mainly from England, to strengthen the French stock of which Rainbow, Royal Oak, Gladiator, Sting, The Emperor, The Baron, The Flying Dutchman, West Australian and Flying Fox made significant impacts.

Their offspring, notably Felix, Franck, Poëtess, Monarque, La Toucques and Vermeille, were some of the first French-bred superstars on the track and in the breeding sheds in France. Meanwhile Jouvence, Hervine, Dollar and Fille de l'Air started making successful raids on England, with the latter the first to win a Classic in 1864.

A year later, Gladiateur swept the board *outre-Manche,* winning the Triple Crown, which he followed up the next season by storming home 40 lengths clear in the Ascot Gold Cup.

The French thoroughbreds had come of age and were as good as, and in some cases far better than, the English-breds.

Longchamp Racecourse

Meanwhile in the power stakes, Louis-Philippe's reign had ended with the third French Revolution in 1848, and he was followed by Louis Napoléon, firstly as president of the Second Republic and then as Emperor Napoléon III.

It was he who supported the Société d'Encouragement's hopes of building a racecourse on land that he'd requisitioned as part of his plan to transform the Bois de Boulogne into a Paris version of London's Hyde Park. Longchamp racecourse opened in 1857, taking over the existing programme that had been run at the Champs de Mars course in front of the military school in central Paris – where 30 years later the Eiffel Tower was built.

In 1863, the season prior to Fille de l'Air's Oaks win, the Grand Prix de Paris had been inaugurated at Longchamp. The race for three-year-olds was the first in France open to all countries and was framed to provide a chance for the winners of the Derby and Prix du Jockey Club, as well as the top fillies, to meet.

From its inception, the Grand Prix de Paris was the most prestigious race in the French calendar – only surpassed later by the Prix de l'Arc de Triomphe – and it was the first French Classic not to be a copy of a race in England.

The next development was the addition of the Prix du Conseil Municipal to the programme in October 1893, which was launched to celebrate the extension of the lease on Longchamp racecourse.

It was also open to all-comers but this time for the Classic generation and their elders. The prize money was second only to the Grand Prix de Paris and it immediately became the highlight of the autumn programme. However, the race couldn't qualify as a Classic due to its penalty system.

On the resumption of racing after the First World War the French racing authorities decided to be even more ambitious and inaugurate a strictly weight-for-age championship race. The new race would be run on the date of the Prix du Conseil Municipal, which was to be moved back a week.

A monumental name

The Arc de Triomphe, initiated by Napoléon Bonaparte in 1806 and inaugurated by Louis-Philippe 30 years later – in the same year the Prix du Jockey Club was first run – had become one of the leading iconic symbols of Paris. The arch had been, and continues to be, utilised in nearly all of the major events in the city. Therefore, using its name for such a prestigious race would be apt.

After rejigging the racing programme the name of the iconic monument, which had previously been used for a seller, was freed up and given to the race that would become of monumental importance to French racing. Thus in 1920 the seventh French Classic was born.

Darley Arabian 1700
|
Bartlett's Childers 1716
|
Squirt 1732
|
Marske 1750
|
Eclipse 1764
|
Pot8os 1773
|
Waxy 1790
|
Whalebone 1807
|
Sir Hercules 1826
|
Birdcatcher 1833
|
The Baron 1842
|
Stockwell 1849
|
Doncaster 1870
|
Bend Or 1877
|
|_____|
| |
Kendal 1883   Bona Vista 1889
| |
Tredennis 1898   Cyllene 1895
| |
Bachelor's Double 1906   Polymelus 1902
| |
Comrade 1917   Phalaris 1913
                           |
                           Pharos 1920
                           |
                           Nearco 1935
                           |
                           Nearctic 1954
                           |
                           Northern Dancer 1961
                           |
                           Sadler's Wells 1981
                           |
                           Galileo 1998
                           |
                           Waldgeist 2014

Timeline of events

1750	Jockey Club founded in London
1776	First running of the St Leger
1779	First running of The Oaks
1780	First running of the Derby
1789 to 1799	French Revolution I
1806	First running of the Grand Prix, France's oldest surviving race (now the Prix Gladiateur) and the building of the Arc de Triomphe monument commences
1809	First running of the 2000 Guineas Stakes
1814	First running of the 1000 Guineas Stakes
1830	French Revolution II
1833	Société d'Encouragement pour l'Amélioration des Races de Chevaux en France founded in Paris
1834	The permanent racecourse and training centre at Chantilly is ready for action
1836	First running of the Prix du Jockey Club and the inauguration of the Arc de Triomphe monument in Paris
1840	First running of the Poule d'Essai (French Guineas)
1843	First running of the Prix de Diane
1848	French Revolution III
1853	First French-bred winner of an English trophy when Jouvence takes the Goodwood Cup
1857	Longchamp opened – the future home of the Prix de l'Arc de Triomphe
1861	First running of the Grand Prix du Prince Impérial (French St Leger), from 1869 renamed as the Prix Royal-Oak
1863	Inaugural running of the Grand Prix de Paris, the first race open to all comers
1864	First French-bred winner of The Oaks: Fille de l'Air
1865	First French-bred winner of the 2000 Guineas, Epsom Derby and St Leger: Gladiateur
1872	First French-bred winner of the 1000 Guineas: Reine and the Grand Prix de Deauville is now open to all
1883	Poule d'Essai split, to create a race for colts, the Poule d'Essai des Poulains, and a race for fillies, the Poule d'Essai des Pouliches
1893	First running of the Prix du Conseil Municipal (open to all)
1914 to 1918	First World War
1920	First running of Prix de l'Arc de Triomphe (open to all)

Comrade commands respect

First honours to cheap purchase trained in Newmarket

Background and fancied horses

The desire to stage a truly international race was hampered somewhat by the practical problems of moving horses on a French railway system still damaged by war. The network was incomplete and unreliable often leading to long delays – not ideal for transporting potentially fractious thoroughbreds.

With the defection of the 1919 Oaks-winner Keysoe, owned by Lord Derby – the British Ambassador in Paris – there were only two raiders, one from England and one from Italy, to take on the 11-strong home team.

There were, however, several top-class contestants in the field, and a decent purse including 150,000 francs for the winner. The older horses were set to carry 5kg more than the Classic generation with 60kg and 55kg respectively, while fillies received a 1.5kg allowance carrying 58.5kg or 53.5kg.

Atanik Eknayan, a famous jeweller whose greatest work was cutting the Blue Heart Diamond, was double-handed in the inaugural Prix de l'Arc de Triomphe with Pleurs and Cid Campéador. They had been second and third respectively in the Prix Eugène Adam, with the latter arriving on the back of a two-length success over King's Cross and Tullamore in the Prix du Prince d'Orange.

Although neither individually would have been favourite, Cid Campéador and Pleurs coupled together on the Pari Mutuel Urbain (PMU) headed the market at 2/1. The practice of coupling horses in the same ownership, or sometimes in the care of the same trainer, was a feature of the PMU until very recently.

Next in the market, for the inaugural Arc, were Embry and Comrade, who'd fought out the finish of a fascinating renewal of the Grand Prix de Paris, at the time the most valuable race in France. England's main hope in that race was the Derby-winner Spion Kop, trained by Peter Gilpin, who'd made the arduous journey across the Channel to Longchamp accompanied by his stable companion Comrade.

The race was a tactical affair, with several of the runners seemingly more intent on boxing-in Spion Kop than racing. In the straight, the Prix du Jockey Club-winner Sourbier held sway but was being challenged by Embry, who'd been third at Chantilly.

They fought it out as Comrade, who'd had the benefit of a trouble-free run, waited in third. Embry started to get on top, only to be pounced on by Comrade in the last few strides. Comrade won by a short head, with Spion Cop back in fifth and The Oaks-winner Charlebelle finishing down the pack.

Many onlookers that day thought Embry would gain revenge on Comrade in the Prix de l'Arc de Triomphe, especially as he'd subsequently won the Prix Royal-Oak – the French version of the St Leger. As such, Embry was preferred over his rival, being sent off a 2.8/1 chance with Comrade, the sole English challenger, at 3.4/1.

Two more owners were doubly represented and between them they had some of the best fillies around. The American adventurer and businessman 'King' Macomber fielded Vermeille-victor Meddlesome Maid and Battersea, who'd taken the Prix Lupin, while Baron Édouard de Rothschild had Prix de Diane-winner, and Vermeille-second Flowershop, along with 1919 Vermeille and Royal-Oak winner Stéarine.

In addition to Comrade, the only other invader was the winner of the first two runnings of the Gran Premio de Madrid, Nouvel An. French-bred but trained in Italy, he was the rank outsider of the party at 50/1.

Betting

2/1 Cid Campéador & Pleurs (coupled), 2.8/1 Embry, 3.4/1 Comrade, 12.5/1 Meddlesome Maid & Battersea (coupled), 19/1 Flowershop & Stéarine (coupled), 19/1 Le Rapin, 23/1 BAR.

Three-year-old form lines (*Prix de l'Arc de Triomphe runners in* **bold**)
Prix du Jockey Club, run at Longchamp: 1st Sourbier, 2nd Odol, 3rd **Embry**
Grand Prix de Paris: 1st **Comrade**, 2nd **Embry**, 3rd Sourbier, 4th Blue Dun, 0th Spion Kop, 0th Charlebelle, 0th **Flowershop**
Prix Eugène Adam: 1st Petit Palais, 2nd **Pleurs**, 3rd **Cid Campéador**
Prix Royal-Oak: 1st **Embry**, 2nd Zagreus, 3rd As Des As

Fillies only
Prix de Diane, run at Longchamp: 1st **Flowershop**, 2nd Zilpa, 3rd Take A Step
Prix Vermeille: 1st **Meddlesome Maid**, 2nd **Flowershop**, 3rd Tic Tac

Older horses and inter-generational races
Prix du Président de la République: 1st **Eugène de Savoie**, 2nd Petit Palais, 3rd **Meddlesome Maid**
La Coupe d'Or, at Maisons-Laffitte: 1st **Le Rapin**, 2nd **Pleurs**, 3rd Imaginaire
Grand Prix de Deauville: 1st **Tullamore**, 2nd Juveigneur, 3rd Caroly
Prix du Prince d'Orange: 1st **Cid Campéador**, 2nd **King's Cross**, 3rd **Tullamore**

Abroad
In England
Derby Stakes: 1st Spion Kop, 2nd Archaic, 3rd Orpheus
The Oaks: 1st Charlebelle, 2nd Cinna, 3rd Roselet

The race

Longchamp may not have been as crowded as on Grand Prix de Paris day, however, with the sun in evidence the course took in excess of 300,000 francs on the door.

At the off, Nouvel An and Eugène de Savoie were fast away but were soon overtaken by Stéarine who led them up the hill.

On the descent, King's Cross, Cid Campéador and Comrade moved up the order. Approaching the home straight Stéarine dropped out and King's Cross took over in front, slipstreamed by Comrade, with Cid Campéador and Pleurs just behind and Embry showing up on the outside.

Then the drama unfolded as King's Cross, who was trying to give away 5kg to his immediate pursuers, wavered off a straight line. Frank Bullock took his chance pushing Comrade through on the rail arriving there ahead of Cid Campéador, who then had nowhere to go. Pleurs was also slightly hampered.

From then on the contest was over and the son of Bachelor's Double dominated his rivals cruising home, heavily eased down, to score by a length with plenty in hand. King's Cross – who was also a decent hurdler with some good form at Auteuil – held on for second place ahead of Pleurs, followed after a gap by Meddlesome Maid, the disappointing Embry, who flattered to deceive, and Battersea.

The hard-luck stories concerned Cid Campéador, who had been short of room on the rails, and Meddlesome Maid. Depending on which account you read, the latter may have been kicked by Comrade in the preliminaries and/or brought to her knees when crossed by a rival entering the straight. Whichever, she certainly didn't have the best of luck and deservedly gained some recompense in the Prix de Conseil Municipal seven days later.

Comrade was generally seen as a worthy winner. Undoubtedly he had received the breaks in running but Comrade had asserted with such superiority that no one could argue that he was a fortunate winner.

The underlying purpose of running an international race is to beat all-comers and be proclaimed overall champion. The downside is that an interloper might win. Luckily Comrade was partly owned by a Frenchman and so the home team gave Evremond de Saint-Alary's charge a rousing reception.

But a French-trained winner was the goal. In the very next race after the Arc a two-year-old called Ksar finished second in the Prix Saint-Roman. Ksar wouldn't finish second in the Arc.

Post-race

The enterprise shown by Peter Gilpin had paid off and his Grand Prix de Paris-winner had netted another worthwhile prize. But, then again, Gilpin had always been enterprising; his whole training empire had been built on the success of a horse called Clarehaven, who'd landed a massive gamble in the 1900 Cesarewitch for him and owner Ludwig Neumann.

Gilpin, who is best remembered for training Pretty Polly to win the Fillies' Triple Crown in 1904, named his stables situated on Newmarket's Bury Road after Clarehaven, and they are now home to a certain John Gosden.

In 1918, when one of Neumann's Irish-bred yearlings failed to raise a bid at the Newmarket Sales, Gilpin, through loyalty to his owner, raised his own hand to purchase the son of 1909 Irish Derby-winner Bachelor's Double for 26 guineas – and yes that horse became Comrade.

After winning all of his three outings as a two-year-old, Gilpin sold a half-share of Comrade to Evremond de Saint-Alary, who'd been a top owner in France for over 30 years. And the rest, as they say, is history.

Comrade had taken his unbeaten run to six but that sequence came to an end shortly afterwards in the Champion Stakes. Over a reduced trip that probably didn't suit him, Comrade finished ahead of Spion Kop but had to be content with second place behind Derby-third Orpheus.

Comrade wasn't a great success at stud and died prematurely in 1928, with Bonny Boy II, who won the Ebor Handicap the year after his sire's death, his best progeny.

The Prix Comrade, honouring his memory, which was run for many years at Maisons-Laffitte, now takes place at Saint-Cloud.

Result

1920 Prix de l'Arc de Triomphe

Longchamp. Sunday, 3 October 1920
Weights: 3yo c: 55kg, 3yo f: 53.5kg, 4yo+ c: 60kg, 4yo+ f: 58.5kg

1st Comrade (IRE)　　　3yo c　55kg　**3.4/1**
by Bachelor's Double out of Sourabaya (Spearmint). Evremond de Saint-Alary / Peter Gilpin / Frank Bullock

2nd King's Cross (FR)　　6yo h　60kg　**33/1**
by Alcantara II out of Kizil Sou (Omnium II). Charles Liénhart / Jean Lieux / Marcel Allemand

3rd Pleurs (FR)　　　　3yo c　55kg　**2/1 fav** (coupled with Cid Campéador)
by Prestige out of Idunno (Orme). Atanik Eknayan / Paul Pantall / E. Bouillon

Runners: 13 (FR 11, GB 1, ITY 1). Distances: 1, hd. Going: good. Time: 2m 39s

Also ran: 4th **Meddlesome Maid** (FR) 3yo f, 5th **Embry** (FR) 3yo c, 6th **Battersea** (FR) 3yo c, 7th **Le Rapin** (FR) 4yo c. Unplaced: **Nouvel An** (FR) 5yo c, **Tullamore** (FR) 4yo f, **Stéarine** (FR) 4yo f, **Cid Campéador** (FR) 3yo c, **Eugène de Savoie** (FR) 3yo c, **Flowershop** (FR) 3yo f (13th).

1921

France off the mark with super Ksar

Arc now the second richest race in France

Background and fancied horses

There may have only been two raiders in 1920, but one of them had taken the prize and the home team needed to get back on terms quickly. But the desire to attract more invaders remained unabated and, as such, the prize money was doubled. With a purse of 300,000 francs the Prix de l'Arc de Triomphe was now only second in value to the Grand Prix de Paris.

Two months after the inaugural Arc, the politician and businessman Edmond Blanc died aged 64. Blanc had been a major owner and breeder for 50 years, he'd imported Flying Fox, built Saint-Cloud Racecourse and won five runnings of the Prix du Jockey Club, four of the Prix de Diane and the Grand Prix de Paris on seven occasions. Unfortunately, he didn't live to see his greatest purchase, Ksar, fulfil his potential.

The first running of the Prix Edmond Blanc at Saint-Cloud took place in the spring and was fittingly won by his widow, Marthe, with Le Filon II, with all of the first three home having been bred by the great man.

After the devastation of the war the quality of French bloodstock appeared to be starting to recover and in Ksar, the home team had a potential champion.

Bred by Evremond de Saint-Alary, the part-owner of Comrade, Ksar was by the influential sire Brûleur out of Kizil Kourgan, who had won the Poule d'Essai des Pouliches, Prix de Diane and Grand Prix de Paris in 1902.

Ksar was purchased by Edmond Blanc at the Deauville sales for 151,000 francs, and as a two-year-old he won the Prix de la Salamandre and Prix de Sablonville, as well as finishing second on Arc day. The following year, now running for the widowed Madame Blanc, he won two classic trials before obliging with impressive ease in the Prix du Jockey Club. Ksar seemed to be the real deal.

But next came the Grand Prix de Paris, where Ksar was a short-priced favourite. Accounts vary but whether it was the hard ground, the extended trip or some other reason, he was never in with a chance and finished midfield. The race itself was won by the English-trained Lemonara, who'd been third in the Derby, with Flèchois at a big price in second.

Ksar redeemed himself when storming home by three lengths in the Prix Royal-Oak, in the process reversing the form with Flèchois. As a result, he was a warm order to take the Arc.

None of the four candidates sent over from England were top class. However, lesser horses had won some of the top prizes in France that year, so there was a confidence in England, and a dread in France, that they could add to Comrade's triumph.

Chief among the raiders were the 1920 Royal Hunt Cup-winner Square Measure, who was sent off second favourite, and the fourth best in the market, Pomme-de-Terre, who earlier in the year has landed the Prix du Président de la République at Saint-Cloud. The other English competitors were the only filly in the field, Blue Dun, along with the Jockey Club Stakes-winner Torelore.

Cid Campéador was back with Nouvel An – who'd won the Gran Premio de Madrid for the third year in a row. Henri Ternynck's pair, the stayer Odol and As Des As, who'd been second to Meddlesome Maid in the 1920 Prix de Conseil Municipal, were coupled as third favourites.

Betting
1.5/1 Ksar, 5.8/1 Square Measure, 7.3/1 Odol & As Des As (coupled), 8.1/1 Pomme-de-Terre, 12/1 Blue Dun, 17/1 Nouvel An, 21/1 Tacite, 33/1 BAR.

Three-year-old form lines
Prix du Jockey Club: 1st **Ksar**, 2nd Grazing, 3rd Shake Hand
Grand Prix de Paris: 1st Lemonara, 2nd **Flèchois**, 3rd Harpocrate, 4th **Tacite**, 0th **Ksar**
Prix Royal-Oak: 1st **Ksar**, 2nd **Flèchois**, 3rd Harpocrate

Fillies only
Prix de Diane: 1st Doniazade, 2nd Ad Gloriam, 3rd Guerriere
Prix Vermeille: 1st Durban, 2nd Adry, 3rd Guerriere

Older horses and inter-generational races
Prix du Président de la République: 1st **Pomme-de-Terre**, 2nd Binic, 3rd Sourbier
Grand Prix de Deauville: 1st **Zagreus**, 2nd Caroly, 3rd **Nouvel An**
Prix du Prince d'Orange: 1st Harpocrate, 2nd Abri, 3rd **Nouvel An**

Abroad
In England
Derby Stakes: 1st Humorist, 2nd Craig an Eran, 3rd Lemonora

The race
Blue Dun, who'd been keen to post, led from flag fall at a suicidal pace and had a 20-length advantage after 800 metres. The main group were headed by

Torelore, As Des As, Odol and Square Measure. On the descent Ksar, ridden by George Stern, started to make good headway. Racing round the final turn Blue Dun, not surprisingly, ran out of petrol and Ksar on the outside swept by on the bridle.

The Parisians went mad cheering ecstatically as he sauntered home unbothered by any of his rivals. At the line he had an easy two lengths to spare over Flèchois, who ran on well for second, with a further one and a half to Square Measure, followed by Odol, Cid Campéador and the *longtemps-animateur* Blue Dun.

Despite the mid-season jitters, the dread had turned to elation and the home team had their champion.

Post-race

Ksar ran again a month later in a three-horse contest at Le Tremblay – a course that will feature in our story in the 1940s – but at long odds-on he could only manage a dead-heat. All stakes were returned as the win dividend after deductions would have led to a negative return. As a result, Ksar was put away for the winter under a slight cloud.

Result

1921 Prix de l'Arc de Triomphe
Longchamp. Sunday, 9 October 1921
Weights: 3yo c: 55kg, 3yo f: 53.5kg, 4yo+ c: 60kg, 4yo+ f: 58.5kg

1st Ksar (FR)   3yo c   55kg   **1.5/1 fav**
by Brûleur out of Kizil Kourgan (Omnium II). Marthe Blanc / Walter Walton / George Stern

2nd Fléchois (FR)   3yo c   55kg   **33/1**
by Negofol out of Saint Cyrienne (Gardefeu). Mario Perrone / Henry Count / George Bellhouse

3rd Square Measure (GB)   6yo h   60kg   **5.8/1**
by Simon Square out of Tit for Tat (Right-Away). Reid Walker / John Rogers / Frank Bullock

Runners: 12 (FR 7, GB 4, ITY 1). Distances: 2, 1½. Going: good. Time: 2m 34.80s

Also ran: 4th **Odol** (FR) 4yo c, 5th **Cid Campéador** (FR) 4yo c, 6th **Blue Dun** (GB) 4yo f. Unplaced: **Pomme-de-Terre** (GB) 5yo c, **Torelore** (GB) 4yo c, **Nouvel An** (FR) 6yo c, **Zagreus** (FR) 4yo c, **As Des As** (FR) 4yo c, **Tacite** (FR) 3yo c (12th).

Double and quits for Ksar

Lap of honour for champion as overseas opposition evaporates

Background and fancied horses

Ksar returned having won the Prix des Sablons (now the Prix Ganay) and the Prix du Cadran before losing out by a short head to the 1921 Irish St Leger-winner Kircubbin in the Prix du Président de la République (now the Grand Prix de Saint-Cloud).

There is a slightly fanciful story that Ksar, who was trained adjacent to the back straight at Saint-Cloud, was more intent on getting home for his food than racing in earnest. Whatever, he was back to form in the Prix du Prince d'Orange at Longchamp in September, hacking up by four lengths, giving 5.5kg to the runner-up Bahadur, and in the process scaring off all remaining potential foreign-trained runners in the Arc.

Earlier in the year the two English raiders for the Grand Prix de Paris hadn't been able to live with the French three-year-olds, finishing out of the places behind the winner Kéfalin and runner-up Ramus. The last-named, who lost out by three parts of a length, had been very slow away that day evidently hating the starting gate.

Ramus had previously become the first notable winner for Marcel Boussac when landing the Prix du Jockey Club by two lengths from Kéfalin. He was sent to England for the St Leger, where he was made favourite, but disgraced himself again when refusing to race.

Kéror, who had recent form in the book after winning the Prix Royal-Oak – when Kéfalin was absent because of a cough – was sent off second favourite. However, it was 11/1 bar one – that one of course being Ksar.

Betting

0.3/1 Ksar, 11/1 Keror, 13/1 Kéfalin, 14/1 Ramus, 22/1 Mont Blanc, 23/1 Trévise, 23/1 Bahadur & Gaurisankar (coupled), 80/1 BAR.

Three-year-old form lines

Prix du Jockey Club: 1st **Ramus**, 2nd **Kéfalin**, 3rd Algérien

Grand Prix de Paris: 1st **Kéfalin**, 2nd **Ramus**, 3rd Algérien, 0th **Bahadur**, 0th **Mont Blanc**, 0th **Lamartine**, 0th **Kéror**

Prix Royal-Oak: 1st **Kéror**, 2nd Algérien, 3rd Tribord

Fillies only

Prix de Diane: 1st Pellsie, 2nd Zariba, 3rd Esmee

Prix Vermeille: 1st Sainte Ursule, 2nd **Relapse**, 3rd Honeysuckle

Older horses and inter-generational races
Prix du Président de la République: 1st Kircubbin, 2nd **Ksar**, 3rd Zagreus
La Coupe d'Or, at Maisons-Laffitte: 1st **Bahadur**, 2nd Harpocrate, 3rd **Gaurisankar**
Grand Prix de Deauville: 1st **Bahadur**, 2nd Grillemont, 3rd Algérien
Prix du Prince d'Orange: 1st **Ksar**, 2nd **Bahadur**, 3rd Haroun Al Rachid

The race

All the action in the race itself happened in the early stages. Ramus was recalcitrant again and once the tapes rose, he refused to race. One hundred metres later, Mont Blanc, exhibiting a wild streak, threw his jockey to the floor, and the field was down to nine.

Kéror led from the riderless Mont Blanc then Gaurisankar, Trévise III and Ksar. The order stayed more or less the same until approaching the final turn when Ksar, ridden this time by Frank Bullock, showed his class. He passed Kéror with ease and then strode away imperiously to secure a second victory, albeit preceded by the *cheval au liberté* Mont Blanc.

Two and a half lengths back in second was the staying-on Fléchois, he'd been 33/1 when runner-up last year and was sent off at treble those odds this time. Another outsider, Relapse, was a neck further back in third, followed by Bahadur, Kéfalin and Kéror.

Post-race

With Ksar winning again, trainer Walter Walton and owner Madame Blanc moved their Arc scores on to two. As did Comrade's jockey Frank Bullock, who had replaced George Stern on Ksar this time.

Fléchois gained revenge on Ksar later in the month in the Prix Gladiateur, which was run over 6,200 metres at the time. The trip was probably too far for Ksar, who was subsequently retired to stud. He became a top sire, including being champion in 1931, and many of his offspring – in particular Tourbillon, Djébel and Caracalla – went on to play major roles in Prix de l'Arc de Triomphe history.

Ksar was the first dual winner and a great champion on and off the track.

Result

1922 Prix de l'Arc de Triomphe
Longchamp. Sunday, 9 October 1922
Weights: 3yo c: 55kg, 3yo f: 53.5kg, 4yo+ c: 60kg, 4yo+ f: 58.5kg

1st Ksar (FR)   4yo c   60kg   **0.3/1 fav**
by Brûleur out of Kizil Kourgan (Omnium II). Marthe Blanc / Walter Walton / Frank Bullock

2nd Fléchois (FR)   4yo c   60kg   **99/1**
by Negofol out of Saint Cyrienne (Gardefeu). Mario Perrone / Henry Count / Jack Jennings

3rd Relapse (FR)   3yo f   53.5kg   **80/1**
by Romagny out of Rignac (Libaros). Achille Fould / George Cunnington jnr / A Cormack

Runners: 11 (FR 11). Distances: 2½, nk. Going: good. Time: 2m 38.78s

Also ran: 4th **Bahadur** (FR) 3yo c, 5th **Kéfalin** (FR) 3yo c, 6th **Kéror** (FR) 3yo c. Unplaced: **Gaurisankar** (FR) 3yo c, **Lamartine** (FR) 3yo c, **Trévise III** (FR) 3yo f, **Mont Blanc** (FR) 3yo c (unseated rider), **Ramus** (FR) 3yo c (left at the start).

Ksar's family tree

This simplified family tree illustrates that Ksar is related to all three of the main foundation thoroughbred stallions. All thoroughbreds can trace their lineage in this way and are related to many exalted forbears.

Kizil Kourgan, Ksar's dam, for example, has Gladiateur, Vermeille, Hermit (1st 1867 2000 Guineas and Derby), Wild Dayrell (1st 1855 Derby), Skirmisher (1st 1857 Ascot Gold Cup), Saunterer (1st 1858 Goodwood Cup), and The Nabob (a leading sire in France), as well as The Flying Dutchman, in her fourth generation – the one with 16 great-great-grandparents.

Byerley Turk 1680 approx
|
Jigg 1700 approx
|
Croft's Partner 1718
|
Tartar 1743
|
Herod 1758

Darley Arabian 1700
|
Bartlett's Childers 1716
|
Squirt 1732
|
Marske 1750
|
Eclipse 1764
|_____
| |
Pot8os 1773   Don Quixote 1784
| |
Waxy 1790   Amadis 1807
| |
Whalebone 1807   *Darioletta* 1822
| |
Sir Hercules 1826 *Barbelle* 1836
| |
Birdcatcher 1833   The Flying Dutchman 1846
| |
The Baron 1842   Dollar 1860
| |
Stockwell 1849   Upas 1883
| |
Doncaster 1870   Omnium 1892
| |
Thora 1878   *Kizil Kourgan 1899*
| |
Bijou 1890   **Ksar** 1918
|
Basse Terre 1899
|
Brûleur 1910
|
Ksar 1918

Godolphin Arabian 1724
|
Cade 1734
|
Miss Ramsden 1755
|_____
|
Woodpecker 1773
|
Buzzard 1787
|
Selim 1802
|
Sultan 1816
|
Bay Middleton 1833
|
The Flying Dutchman 1846
|
Dollar 1860
|
Androcles 1870
|
Cambyse 1884
|
Gardfeu 1895
|
Chouberski 1902
|
Brûleur 1910
|
Ksar 1918

Parth to glory

O'Neill makes amends for Doncaster error

Background and fancied horses

With Ksar out of the way, the 1923 running featured runners from England and Italy. French aspirations, though, rested on the shoulders of Cesare Rannuci's Filibert de Savoie, who'd won the Grand Prix de Paris – beating Checkmate by a length – and then the Prix Royal-Oak, with São Paulo back in fourth. It looked strong form and the dappled grey was a clear favourite.

Next in the market was Scopas, the Italian-wizard Federico Tesio's first runner in the Arc. Scopas had proven form in Milan, and had also put up an impressive display when coming out on top in La Coupe d'Or at Maisons-Laffitte in September.

Massine, another French prospect, hadn't been seen since winning the Prix Lupin in May after sustaining a leg injury in his box. However, the vibes were good and he was third best ahead of Parth, one of two English raiders.

Parth had won the Greenham Stakes and, after a slow start, finished a creditable third in the Derby. As a result, he was fancied for the St Leger but he finished fourth after hitting the front too early. Generally Parth came with a late burst but he was taken to the front with three furlongs to go by the Paris-based Frank O'Neill, who hadn't sat on him before mounting for the Doncaster Classic.

Amédée Sabathier, who was a director of sporting newspaper *Le Jockey*, was doubly represented with the Prix de Diane and Prix Vermeille-winner Quoi, and Mirebeau II who had been third to the very useful Epinard in the Prix d'Ispahan.

Last year's fifth, Kéfalin was back. The other English raider was Franklin, the winner of the 1922 Champion Stakes.

Betting

2.1/1 Filibert de Savoie, 4.3/1 Scopas, 6.3/1 Massine, 8.5/1 Parth, 10.5/1 Checkmate, 13/1 Quoi & Mirebeau II (coupled), 13.5/1 Kéfalin, 16/1 Grillemont, 21/1 BAR.

Three-year-old form lines
Prix du Jockey Club: 1st Le Capucin, 2nd Nicéas, 3rd Sir Gallahad
Grand Prix de Paris: 1st **Filibert de Savoie**, 2nd **Checkmate**, 3rd Le Capucin
Prix Royal-Oak: 1st **Filibert de Savoie**, 2nd Sir Gallahad, 3rd Rusa

Fillies only

Prix de Diane: 1st **Quoi**, 2nd Marotte, 3rd Fiasque

Prix Vermeille: 1st **Quoi**, 2nd L'Avalanche, 3rd Swansea

Older horses and inter-generational races

La Coupe d'Or, at Maisons-Laffitte: 1st **Scopas**, 2nd Mirobolant, 3rd Gaurisankar

Grand Prix de Deauville: 1st **São Paulo**, 2nd **Grillemont**, 3rd Premontre

Abroad

In England

Derby Stakes: 1st Papyrus, 2nd Pharos, 3rd **Parth**

St Leger: 1st Tranquil, 2nd Papyrus, 3rd Teresina, 4th **Parth**

The race

The weather was decidedly inclement and the ground heavy as Bou Jeloud and Filibert de Savoie made the early pace. Scopas was in third followed by São Paulo and Massine before Checkmate moved up to join the first two. The new order remained intact until Bou Jeloud faded on the final turn.

Filibert de Savoie straightened for home first, closely attended by Massine and Checkmate with Parth not too far behind. Massine started to get the better of the argument. However O'Neill had learnt from the St Leger and, after waiting in rear, pounced late on Parth.

Wresting the advantage from Massine with 50 metres to travel, he won by a neck with Filibert de Savoie the same distance back in third, followed by Checkmate, Scopas and Kéfalin.

Post-race

By comparison to Ksar's win last year in an all-French field, Parth represented several countries. The horse was born in Ireland, trained in England, and owned and ridden by Americans, albeit both living in Paris.

Trainer James Crawford plied his trade near Marlborough in Wiltshire, and had been the private trainer of Mathrodus Golculdas, a textile magnate in Bombay, until a few months before the Arc.

Unfortunately, the Golculdas empire had then found itself in deep financial trouble. So, before the St Leger, Parth was sold to the Paris-based American Abraham Kingsley Macomber. Known as 'King' Macomber, he'd made his name in mining and prospecting and had previously run Meddlesome Maid and Battersea in the inaugural Arc.

Jockey Frank O'Neill made his way to Europe as part of the American Invasion, along with Tod Sloan et al. They came because pari-mutuel betting had been banned in the US after pressure from the anti-betting lobby, which had resulted in several racetracks closing. O'Neill was champion jockey in France 11 times and on one of his forays to England won the Derby aboard Spion Kop when Gilpin's stable jockey Arthur Smith rode Sarchedon.

Parth wasn't quite as good as a four-year-old but still had enough ability to win the Jubilee Handicap at Kempton, as well as finishing runner-up in the Champion Stakes.

Although he didn't become a top sire, he did have a few decent winners, most notably Davout, who took the 1936 Poule d'Essai des Poulains, Tempest, the 1937 Queen Anne Stakes-winner, and Bengali, who won the 1933 Prix Noailles. He was also represented by the filly Parth For Ever in the 1930 Arc.

Result

1923 Prix de l'Arc de Triomphe
Longchamp. Sunday, 7 October 1923
Weights: 3yo c: 55kg, 3yo f: 53.5kg, 4yo+ c: 60kg, 4yo+ f: 58.5kg

1st Parth (IRE)   3yo c   55kg   **8.5/1**
by Polymelus out of Willia (William the Third). A. Kingsley Macomber / James Crawford / Frank O'Neill

2nd Massine (FR)   3yo c   55kg   **6.3/1**
by Consols out of Mauri (Ajax). Henri Ternynck / Elijah Cunnington / Fred Sharpe

3rd Filibert de Savoie (FR)   3yo c   55kg   **2.1/1 fav**
by Isard II out of Yolande (Gardefeu). Cesare Rannuci / Henry Count / Jack Jennings

Runners: 13 (FR 10, GB 2, ITY 1). Distances: nk, nk. Going: heavy. Time: 2m 38.26s

Also ran: 4th **Checkmate** (FR) 3yo c, 5th **Scopas** (FR) 4yo c, 6th **Kéfalin** (FR) 4yo c, 7th **Quoi** (FR) 3yo f. Unplaced: **Mirebeau II** (_) 5yo c, **Bou Jeloud** (FR) 4yo c, **Mazeppa II** (FR) 4yo c, **Franklin** (GB) 5yo c, **Grillemont** (FR) 4yo c, **São Paulo** (FR) 3yo c (13th).

Magnificent Massine

Cunnington first and second

Background and fancied horses

After such a long absence, Massine had run a great race in last year's Arc. This term he'd again shown his quality when leading home a one-two-four for French-trained horses at Royal Ascot in the Gold Cup, where he was followed home by 1923 Arc-favourite Filibert de Savoie and Le Capucin. That show of strength certainly contributed to the absence of English challengers in the Arc.

Le Capucin went on to gain revenge on both of his cohorts, firstly beating Filibert de Savoie in the Prix du Président de la République – although both of them were behind the Aga Khan III's Prix du Jockey Club-winner Pot au Feu.

Then Le Capucin accounted for Massine by a short head in the great Belgian race of the time, the Grand Prix International d'Ostende, which was run at the Hippodrome Wellington, named after the victor at Waterloo. It had been a good effort by Massine in defeat as the heavy ground and 2,200-metre trip were against him, and as such he was sent off at a very short price for the Arc with Le Capucin trading as third favourite.

Between the two came the favourite's stablemate, Isola Bella, an improving filly who had taken the scalp of Prix de Diane-winner Uganda in the Prix Vermeille. The only other horse at less than 10/1 was Prix du Prince d'Orange-winner Cadum.

Among the longshots were Transvaal – who'd caused a sensation when winning a rough running of the Grand Prix de Paris when sent off at 120/1 – and the first Arc runner for the Aga Khan III, Nicéas. The Imam of Nizari-Ismaili Shia Islam had been fêted by the English royal family and was now spending a good deal of his time in France and England.

Betting
1.15/1 Massine, 3.8/1 Isola Bella, 8/1 Le Capucin, 9.5/1 Cadum, 10.5/1 Uganda, 20/1 BAR.

> **Three-year-old form lines**
> Prix du Jockey Club: 1st Pot au Feu, 2nd Canapé, 3rd Shahabbas
> Grand Prix de Paris: 1st **Transvaal**, 2nd Le Gros Morne, 3rd **Uganda**, 0th **Isola Bella**
> Prix Royal-Oak: 1st **Uganda**, 2nd Seclin, 3rd **Cadum**

Fillies only
Prix de Diane: 1st **Uganda**, 2nd **Isola Bella**, 3rd Farizade
Prix Vermeille: 1st **Isola Bella**, 2nd **Uganda**, 3rd Eblouissante

Older horses and inter-generational races
Prix du Président de la République: 1st Pot Au Feu, 2nd **Le Capucin**, 3rd Filibert de Savoie
La Coupe d'Or, at Maisons-Laffitte: 1st Scaramouche, 2nd Eblouissante, 3rd **Optimist**
Grand Prix de Deauville: 1st Swansea, 2nd **Optimist**, 3rd Sang Froid
Prix du Prince d'Orange: 1st **Cadum**, 2nd Prince d'Orange, 3rd Le Gross Morne

Abroad
In England
Derby Stakes: 1st Sansovino, 2nd St Germans, 3rd Hurstwood
Ascot Gold Cup: 1st **Massine**, 2nd Filibert de Savoie, 3rd Inkerman, 4th **Le Capucin**

In Belgium
Grand International d'Ostende: 1st **Le Capucin**, 2nd **Massine**, 3rd Subaltern

The race

On an overcast day, Cadum and Nicéas set the early gallop, going on by a few lengths to the main group headed by Massine, Uganda and Transvaal.

The *peloton* gradually closed the gap approaching the straight where Cadum was still clinging on to a small advantage over Massine and Uganda.

Cadum was brave but when Fred Sharpe asked Massine to go he couldn't repel the sublime attack of the favourite, who easily held the late challenge of Isola Bella to score by one and a half lengths. A further length back Cadum held on for third, followed by Le Capucin, Uganda and Optimist.

Post-race

It was a notable one-two for Elijah Cunnington, who'd initially entered the training ranks in France as the private trainer for Jean Prat in 1899 – Prat was a leading figure in the Société d'Encouragement whose fortune was derived from his family's vermouth business, Noilly-Prat. Cunnington trained some good ones during his career, including Massine's sire, Consols, and son, Mieuxcé, as well as Prix Gladiateur-winner Odol, but he thought Massine was his best.

Massine was retired to stud, in the box next to Filibert de Savoie. After a rocky start to his career, when he was almost unmanageable for a while, he calmed down and turned out to be a great success and was champion sire in 1932.

Among his best offspring were the aforementioned Mieuxcé and Strip the Willow – who both won the Prix du Jockey Club and Grand Prix de Paris.

He also sired Prix de Diane-winner Féerie, and Marvedis who scored in the Prix Royal-Oak.

Result
1924 Prix de l'Arc de Triomphe
Longchamp. Sunday, 5 October 1924
Weights: 3yo c: 55kg, 3yo f: 53.5kg, 4yo+ c: 60kg, 4yo+ f: 58.5kg

1st Massine (FR)   4yo c   60kg   **1.15/1 fav**
by Consols out of Mauri (Ajax). Henri Ternynck / Elijah Cunnington / Albert 'Fred' Sharpe

2nd Isola Bella (FR)   3yo f   53.5kg   **3.8/1**
by Mesilim out of Isola Saint Jean (Gouvernant). Alexandre Aumont / Elijah Cunnington / Arthur Esling

3rd Cadum (FR)   3yo c   55kg   **9.5/1**
by Sans Souci II out of Spring Cleaning (Neil Gow). Baron Édouard de Rothschild / Clément Duval / Matthew MacGee

Runners: 9 (FR 9). Distances: 1½, 1. Going: good. Time: 2m 40.80s

Also ran: 4th **Le Capucin** (FR) 4yo c, 5th **Uganda** (FR) 3yo f, 6th **Optimist** (FR) 3yo c. Unplaced: **Grillemont** (FR) 5yo h, **Nicéas** (FR) 3yo c, **Transvaal** (FR) 3yo c (9th).

Rules given Priori-ty over Cadum

Outsider wins in the Stewards' Room

Background and fancied horses

After sauntering home ahead of a quality field for the Prix du Président de la République and then adding the Prix du Prince d'Orange, Baron Édouard de Rothschild's Cadum, who'd been third last year, was made a short order to go two places better this time.

There had been plenty of drama in the Grand Prix de Paris when four horses came down on the first bend. Prix de Diane-winner Aquatinte II became unbalanced and managed to trip over herself and while crashing to the deck brought down three others including Priori.

Aquatinte II was never able to recapture her best form after that incident, however Priori wasn't affected and went on to dead-heat in the Grand Prix International d'Ostende before winning the Prix Royal-Oak outright.

But back to the Grand Prix de Paris, where the business end was also eventful with Dark Diamond being hampered just as he was starting his run. He survived the incident and ran on but could only manage third place behind the 119/1-winner Reine Lumière.

However, after a winning campaign at Deauville in August culminating in the Grand Prix de Deauville, where he beat future Prix Vermeille-winner La Habanera, Dark Diamond was made a solid second favourite for the Arc.

Ptolemy had been a good two-year-old, winning the Grand Critérium (now the Prix Jean-Luc Lagardère). But this term he'd disappointed until recovering his form in the Prix Eugène Adam, a success he followed up with victory in La Coupe d'Or at Maisons-Laffitte. With renewed confidence his supporters backed him into third spot in the market.

The 1924 Prix du Conseil Municipal winner, Tricard, was coupled at 10/1 with his stablemate Lucide, who'd come out on top in the Prix Daru. The aforementioned La Habanera was next at 15/1 and it was 21/1 or more for the remainder.

Betting

1.1/1 Cadum, 3.8/1 Dark Diamond, 6.8/1 Ptolemy, 10/1 Tricard & Lucide (coupled), 15/1 La Habanera, 21/1 BAR.

Three-year-old form lines

Prix du Jockey Club: 1st Belfonds, 2nd Pitchoury, 3rd **The Sirdar**, 0th **Ptolemy**

Grand Prix de Paris: 1st Reine Lumière, 2nd Terre Neuvien, 3rd **Dark Diamond**, 0th **Ptolemy**, fell **Aquatinte II**, brought down **Priori**

Prix Royal-Oak: 1st **Priori**, 2nd Astéroïde, 3rd Erofite

Fillies only

Prix de Diane: 1st **Aquatinte II**, 2nd **Lucide**, 3rd Frisette

Prix Vermeille: 1st **La Habanera**, 2nd **Lucide**, 3rd **Aquatinte II**

Older horses and inter-generational races

Prix du Président de la République: 1st **Cadum**, 2nd Le Capucin, 3rd Chubasco, 0th **Transvaal**

La Coupe d'Or, at Maisons-Laffitte: 1st **Ptolemy**, 2nd Frisette, 3rd **Sous-Préfet**, 0th **Si Si**

Grand Prix de Deauville: 1st **Dark Diamond**, 2nd Nid d'Or, 3rd **La Habanera**

Prix du Prince d'Orange: 1st **Cadum**, 2nd Leviathan, 3rd Tras Los Montes

Abroad

In England

Derby Stakes: 1st Manna, 2nd Zionist, 3rd **The Sirdar**, 10th **Ptolemy**

In Belgium

Grand Prix International d'Ostende: DH1st **Priori**, DH1st Sang Froid, 3rd **Tomy II**

The race

It was a lovely day for what was being billed as a match between Cadum and Dark Diamond. But, with the perennial front-runner Cadum slow away, and therefore unable to dictate the pace, the advantage looked to be immediately with Dark Diamond.

Lucide and Tricard were prominent early on from Sous-Préfet, Ptolemy and Priori. It wasn't until the approach to the straight that Cadum finally struck the front after coming wide round the field. Entering the last 200 metres Priori along with Tras los Montes emerged as the only serious challengers as Dark Diamond had failed to pick up.

Cadum, racing in the middle of the track, was still going strongly and was reportedly the better part of two lengths clear when he drifted markedly right to take the rail, in the process crossing Priori. The latter closed the gap to an official length at the line, with Tras los Montes back in third then La Habenera, Masked Marvel and Dark Diamond a disappointing sixth.

A stewards' inquiry was called and the placings were reversed, much to the bewilderment of racing correspondent Henri Thétard writing in the following day's *Le Petit Parisien*. He reported that Cadum had won easily and that any interference suffered by Priori had not been enough to deprive him of victory.

However, he went on to describe how Cadum's rear end had come into contact with Priori's chest during the crossing manoeuvre. Additionally, the photo of the finish suggests that the winning distance was shorter than the official length and shows that Priori had been switched to the outside and had subsequently made up some ground.

This would not be the last time in Arc history that the nature of the rules and their interpretation would cause consternation. One thing is for sure, the 40/1 returned on Priori, who had won the Prix Royal-Oak in convincing style, was very generous.

Post-race

It was a great win for Comte Gérard de Chavagnac who was fairly new to the game, while Marcel Allemand went one better than his second on King's Cross in the inaugural running.

Trainer Percy Carter was the son of Richard Carter jnr, who'd won the Prix du Jockey Club with Perth in 1899. He in turn was related to Tom 'Genius' Carter, one of the original Englishmen to be invited to France by the first president of the Société d'Encouragement, Lord Henry Seymour, in 1831. He'd set up shop in Chantilly in 1835 training the first three winners of the Prix du Jockey Club – Frank, Lydia and Vendredi – eventually taking his tally in that race to nine.

Tom and his immediate and extended family – various Carters married into the Jennings and Cunnington clans – won bucket loads of prestigious races. Percy, though, was the first Carter to land an Arc but he wouldn't be the last. His other career highlight was to train Pearl Diver to win the 1947 Derby. That horse's mother, Pearl Cap, will feature shortly in our story.

Priori, who was the third winner of the Arc in six years for Brûleur, would be back to defend his crown.

Result

1925 Prix de l'Arc de Triomphe

Longchamp. Sunday, 4 October 1925
Weights: 3yo c: 55kg, 3yo f: 53.5kg, 4yo+ c: 60kg, 4yo+ f: 58.5kg

1st Priori (FR)   3yo c   55kg   **40/1** (coupled with Tomy II)
by Brûleur out of Prima Vista (St Bris). Comte Gérard de Chavagnac / Percy Carter / Marcel Allemand

2nd Cadum (FR)   4yo c   60kg   **1.1/1 fav**
by Sans Souci II out of Spring Cleaning (Neil Gow). Baron Édouard de Rothschild / Clément Duval /Matthew MacGee

3rd Tras los Montes (FR) 3yo f   53.5kg **66/1**
by Alcantara II out of Tregaron (Tredennis). F. Pellissier-Tanon / J. B. Bourdalle / André Rabbe

Runners: 15 (FR 15). Distances: 1, 1. Going: good. Time: 2m 33.80s

Stewards' Inquiry: Cadum, who had finished first, was demoted to second place for hampering Priori

Also ran: 4th **La Habanera** (FR) 3yo f, 5th **Masked Marvel** (FR) 3yo c, 6th **Dark Diamond** (FR) 3yo c. Unplaced: **Tricard** (FR) 4yo c, **Transvaal** (FR) 4yo c, **The Sirdar** (FR) 3yo c, **Tomy II** (FR) 3yo c, **Ptolemy** (FR) 3yo c, **Si Si** (FR) 3yo c, **Sous-Préfet** (FR) 3yo c, **Lucide** (FR) 3yo f, **Aquatinte II** (FR) 3yo f (15th).

1926

Biribi suprême for Torterolos

No game of chance for flashy grey

Background and fancied horses

This year's market leader, the Juan Torterolo-trained Biribi, didn't race as a two-year-old. He'd broken his duck at the second time of asking in the Prix Noailles, before running out an easy winner in the Prix Lupin.

Next up, the striking steel grey with a white blaze finished second on heavy ground to his stablemate, Madrigal, in the Prix du Jockey Club. He hadn't received the strongest of rides on that occasion as his jockey Domingo Torterolo, the trainer's brother, had been ill and left his sick-bed to take the ride.

After finishing in the frame in the Grand Prix de Paris, Prix du Président de la République and Grand Prix International d'Ostende, Biribi recorded his second success when taking the Prix Royal-Oak by three and a half lengths.

Behind him in the betting were the Boussac pairing of Astérus and Banstar. The former had split Ptolemy and Biribi in the Grand Prix International d'Ostende and the second had taken the Prix Eugène Adam.

The only foreign-trained horse was Federico Tesio's Apelle, who ended up being returned at the same price as the aforementioned duo. He had been well-beaten in the Prix du Président de la République but had subsequently scored in La Coupe d'Or at Maisons-Laffitte.

Masked Ruler, representing 'King' Macomber and coupled with War Mist, had finished fourth in the St Leger before obliging in the Prix du Prince d'Orange.

Dorina, a 500,000-franc purchase as a yearling, was the best filly in the field having scorched clear in both the Prix de Diane and Prix Vermeille.

Last year's winner Priori, who'd won the Prix du Cadran in the spring, hadn't been seen since finishing a creditable second to Solario in the Ascot Gold Cup.

Betting

2.5/1 Biribi, 3.3/1 Astérus & Banstar (coupled), 3.3/1 Apelle, 8.3/1 Masked Ruler & War Mist (coupled), 8.6/1 Dorina, 12/1 Priori & Tomy II (coupled), 12/1 Astéroïde, 15/1 Ptolemy, 21/1 BAR.

Three-year-old form lines

Prix du Jockey Club: 1st Madrigal, 2nd **Biribi**, 3rd Nino

Grand Prix de Paris: 1st Take My Tip, 2nd **Biribi**, 3rd Bois Josselyn, 4th **Masked Ruler**, 5th **Apelle**

Prix Royal-Oak: 1st **Biribi**, 2nd Bois Josselyn, 3rd Felton, 0th **Banstar**

Fillies only

Prix de Diane: 1st **Dorina**, 2nd Carissima, 3rd Serre Malice

Prix Vermeille: 1st **Dorina**, 2nd Gitane, 3rd Carissima, 0th **Cerulea**

Older horses and inter-generational races

Prix du Président de la République: 1st Nino, 2nd **Biribi**, 3rd **Cerulea**

La Coupe d'Or, at Maisons-Laffitte: 1st **Apelle**, 2nd Bad Leg, 3rd **Ptolemy**

Grand Prix de Deauville: 1st **Astéroïde**, 2nd Sang Froid, 3rd Sebecourt

Prix du Prince d'Orange: 1st **Masked Ruler**, 2nd Aethelstan, 3rd Cocange

Abroad

In England

Derby Stakes: 1st Coronach, 2nd Lancegaye, 3rd Colorado

Ascot Gold Cup: 1st Solario, 2nd **Priori**, 3rd Pons Asinorum

St Leger: 1st Coronach, 2nd Caissot, 3rd Foliation, 4th **Masked Ruler**

In Belgium

Grand Prix International d'Ostende: 1st **Ptolemy**, 2nd **Astérus**, 3rd **Biribi**

The race

With the sun shining, a huge crowd had assembled to watch the 16 runners, the biggest field in the Arc so far. Apelle and Masked Ruler were soon prominent at the head of the *peloton* with Biribi going easily further back.

On the descent, Biribi made eye-catching progress, tucking into second place, and entering the straight the magnificent grey struck for home. His long raking stride quickly took him clear of the others and it was immediately obvious that the only remaining race was for second place.

Biribi was simply a class better than his rivals and at the line he was two and a half lengths clear of Dorina, who won the race for second by a neck from Ptolemy. Masked Ruler stayed on for fourth followed by last year's winner Priori – who never looked dangerous – and Astéroïde. The race proved to be the swansong for Priori who was retired to stud, unfortunately producing nothing of note.

Post-race

Owned by Simon Guthmann, who had made his fortune in the grain markets, and trained in France by the Argentine Torterolo, Biribi had won in style and was kept in training in 1927, being aimed at the Ascot Gold Cup.

Unfortunately, he picked up a deep cut when only beaten a neck in the Prix du Cadran, which affected the preparation for his trip to England. He still ran at Ascot but turned out to be no match for Foxlaw, finishing fourth, and was retired afterwards.

Named after a game of chance similar to roulette – that was Casanova's preferred betting medium – Biribi became champion sire in 1941, the same year in which his son Le Pacha, won the Prix de l'Arc de Triomphe. His line produced two other Arc winners, but like many horses of this era it wouldn't all be plain sailing for Biribi and we will revisit him in 1940.

Biribi 1923

La Pacha 1938

Couleur 1939

Marmelade 1949

Sicalade 1956

Sea Bird 1962

Allez France 1970

Result
1926 Prix de l'Arc de Triomphe
Longchamp. Sunday, 3 October 1926
Weights: 3yo c: 55kg, 3yo f: 53.5kg, 4yo+ c: 60kg, 4yo+ f: 58.5kg

1st Biribi (FR)   3yo c   55kg   **2.5/1 fav**
by Rabelais out of La Bidouze (Chouberski). Simon Guthmann / Juan Torterolo / Domingo Torterolo

2nd Dorina (FR)   3yo f   53.5kg   **8.6/1**
by La Farina out of Dora Agnès (Roi Hérode). Edward Esmond / Frank Carter / Guy Garner

3rd Ptolemy (FR)   4yo c   60kg   **15/1**
by Teddy out of Macedonia (Sea Sick). Jefferson Davis Cohn / George Newton / Fred Sharpe

Runners: 16 (FR 15, ITY 1). Distances: 2½, nk. Going: good. Time: 2m 32.80s

Also ran: 4th **Masked Ruler** (FR) 3yo c, 5th **Priori** (FR) 4yo c, 6th **Astéroïde** (FR) 4yo c, 7th **Apelle** (ITY) 3yo c. Unplaced: **Warminster** (GB) 4yo c, **Take My Tip** (GB) 3yo c, **Tomy II** (FR) 4yo c, **King's Darling** (FR) 3yo c, **War Mist** (FR) 3yo c, **Soubadar** (FR) 3yo c, **Astérus** (FR) 3yo c, **Banstar** (FR) 3yo c, **Cerulea** (FR) 3yo f (16th).

Fourth time's the charm for Mon Talisman

Revenge is sweet as Semblat opens his account

Background and fancied horses

It was to be round four of Fiterari versus Mon Talisman, the two star three-year-olds of the season. The latter had won the Prix du Jockey Club with the former finishing as runner-up, only for Fiterari to reverse the placings on heavy ground in the Grand Prix de Paris and then confirm them in even more testing conditions in the Prix Royal-Oak.

Monsieur Moulines's Fiterari topped the market, coupled with the best of the older generation, Nino, who in the summer had won the Prix du Président de la République for the second time.

The runner-up and third in that race, Marcel Boussac's Banstar and Baron Édouard de Rothschild's Cerulea, who'd been last but one and last in the Arc 12 months ago were third and fourth favourites. The latter was coupled with Prix Hocquart-winner Flamant, who'd finished third in the Grand Prix de Paris.

Betting

1.75/1 Fiterari & Nino (coupled), 2.4/1 Mon Talisman, 3.4/1 Banstar, 9.2/1 Flamant & Cerulea (coupled), 18/1 BAR.

Three-year-old form lines
Prix du Jockey Club: 1st **Mon Talisman**, 2nd **Fiterari**, 3rd Basilisque
Grand Prix de Paris: 1st **Fiterari**, 2nd **Mon Talisman**, 3rd **Flamant**
Prix Royal-Oak: 1st **Fiterari**, 2nd **Mon Talisman**, 3rd Bouda

Fillies only
Prix de Diane: 1st Fairy Legend, 2nd Kitty Tchin, 3rd Impecuniouss
Prix Vermeille: 1st Samphire, 2nd Accalmie, 3rd Bellecour

Older horses and inter-generational races
Prix du Président de la République: 1st **Nino**, 2nd **Banstar**, 3rd **Cerulea**

Abroad
In England
Derby Stakes: 1st Call Boy, 2nd Hot Night, 3rd Shian Mor

In Belgium
Grand Prix International d'Ostende: 1st Embargo, 2nd **Felton**, 3rd **Nino**

The race

On good ground, Felton and Queen Iseult were quickly to the fore, Fiterari slotted into midfield while Mon Talisman was content to wait at the back of the pack.

Turning for home Fiterari improved his position, taking up the lead early in the straight. Mon Talisman was making ground on the outside of the leaders with Nino just behind.

What happened next was staggering. Given the office by Semblat, Mon Talisman unleashed a finishing effort that left the others for dead. Favoured by the firmer surface than in his last two races, he scooted away to score by two lengths at the line from Nino, who followed him through for second, with Felton grabbing third from Fiterari close home. They were followed by Flamant and Cerulea.

Post-race

Two years after Percy Carter, it was his older cousin Frank's turn to lift the Arc. The emphatic victory of Mon Talisman helped Carter beat his own record for prize money earned in a season and contributed to owner Edouard Martinez de Hoz, the son of the president of the Jockey Club of Argentina, becoming the year's leading owner.

It was also the start of a what would be a very long and successful association with the Arc for winning jockey Charles Semblat.

Mon Talisman was the first Prix du Jockey Club-victor to win the Arc since Ksar in 1921. He appeared just once more when winning the following year's Prix du Président de la République. However, while being trained for the Arc he became unmanageable and was retired.

Fourth-placed Fiterari was sent to stud immediately after the 1927 Arc. The great rivals both became champion sire, Fiterari in 1936 and Mon Talisman the year after.

Result

1927 Prix de l'Arc de Triomphe

Longchamp. Sunday, 9 October 1927
Weights: 3yo c: 55kg, 3yo f: 53.5kg, 4yo+ c: 60kg, 4yo+ f: 58.5kg

1st Mon Talisman (FR)   3yo c   55kg   **2.4/1**
by Craig an Eran out of Ruthene (Lemberg). Edouard Martinez de Hoz / Frank Carter / Charles Semblat

2nd Nino (FR)   4yo c   60kg   **1.75/1** fav (coupled with Fiterari)
by Clarissimus out of Azalee (Ajax). M. P. Moulines / William Hall / Guy Garner

3rd Felton (FR)   4yo c   60kg   **18/1**
by Nimbus II (FR) out of Fusee d'Or (Brûleur). Gustave Wattinne / William Hall / Arthur Esling

Runners: 10 (FR 10). Distances: 2, 2½. Going: good. Time: 2m 32.80s

Also ran: 4th **Fiterari** (FR) 3yo c, 5th **Flamant** (FR) 3yo c, 6th **Cerulea** (FR) 4yo f. Unplaced: **Banstar** (FR) 4yo c, **Concilliator** (FR) 3yo c, **Fortunio** (FR) 3yo c, **Queen Iseult** (FR) 3yo f (10th).

Kantar is turbo-charged

German challenger runs out of racing room

Background and fancied horses

The top two in the market, Finglas and Bubbles, couldn't be split and ended up as 3/1 joint-favourites. Evremond de Saint-Alary, who had part-owned Comrade and bred Ksar, was represented by the first-named.

Finglas had formerly been trained in England by Comrade's handler Peter Gilpin and boasted a good record at Royal Ascot. He'd won the King Edward VII stakes in 1927, the Queen Alexandra Stakes the following year and been second to Invershin in the Ascot Gold Cup this term. Now under the care of last year's winning trainer, Frank Carter, he'd completed his Arc preparation by scoring in the Prix du Prince d'Orange.

Bubbles, a highly strung type owned by Édouard de Rothschild, had been a decent juvenile and had registered a notable success this campaign when taking the Prix Lupin, beating Ivanhoe and Kantar, before finishing a creditable third in the Grand Prix de Paris.

The pair of runners owned by Ogden Mills, Kantar and Cri de Guerre, were only slightly longer than the joint-favourites.

Also bred by Evremond de Saint-Alary, Kantar had been the champion two-year-old of 1928. After finishing third to Bubbles in the Prix Lupin he was promoted to second in a rough running of the Prix du Jockey Club which culminated in a fight between the placed jockeys, Arthur Esling and Guy Garner, in the weighing room.

Kantar sustained a serious cut on his leg in that race and plans to run in the Grand Prix de Paris were immediately aborted. Mills won the race anyway with the able deputy and former pacemaker for Kantar, Cri de Guerre, with Bubbles in third. A recovered Kantar was back in action at the end of September, winning the Prix Henri Delamarre.

The only challenger from outside France was Oleander at 4.5/1. A promising two-year-old before he fractured his pelvis, George Arnull's charge wasn't seen until the following August when he proceeded to pick up four decent prizes including the Grosser Preis von Baden. This term he'd added a further seven wins, in most cases without being extended, including a second Grosser Preis von Baden.

With five horses at 4.5/1 or less there was inevitably a gap to the Prix Omnium II and Prix Eugène Adam-winner Guy Fawkes, who was a 16/1 chance.

Betting
3/1 Finglas, 3/1 Bubbles, 3.2/1 Kantar & Cri de Guerre (coupled), 4.5/1 Oleander, 16/1 Guy Fawkes, 22/1 BAR.

Three-year-old form lines
Prix du Jockey Club: 1st Le Corrège, 2nd (3rd ptp) **Kantar**, 3rd (2nd ptp) Ivanhoe
Grand Prix de Paris: 1st **Cri de Guerre**, 2nd **Pinceau**, 3rd **Bubbles**, 0th Le Corrège, 0th Motrico, 0th Mary Legend
Prix Royal-Oak: 1st Cacao, 2nd **Pinceau**, 3rd Ernagines

Fillies only
Prix de Diane: 1st Mary Legend, 2nd Merry Girl, 3rd Tanais
Prix Vermeille: 1st Merry Girl, 2nd Sainte Mandane, 3rd Bocchetta

Older horses and inter-generational races
Prix du Prince d'Orange: 1st **Finglas**, 2nd Licteur, 3rd Balmoral

Abroad
In England
Derby Stakes: 1st Felstead, 2nd Flamingo, 3rd Black Watch, 0th **Cri de Guerre**
Ascot Gold Cup: 1st Invershin, 2nd **Finglas**, 3rd Cinq à Sept
St Leger: 1st Fairway, 2nd Palais Royal, 3rd Cyclonic

In Germany
Grosser Preis von Baden: 1st **Oleander**, 2nd Lampos, 3rd Lupus

In Belgium
Grand Prix International d'Ostende: 1st **Rialto**, 2nd Beaumont, 3rd Ivanhoe

The race
Bubbles played up at the start, which unsettled Oleander and Rialto, who both missed the break. Bubbles himself, though, made a clean getaway and led them along from Cri de Guerre and Mourad.

Kantar, with Esling putting up half a kilo overweight, and Finglas were settled out the back. Both gradually took closer order and were in challenging positions on the turn for home, where Bubbles still held the advantage from Rialto, Motrico and Guy Fawkes.

Bubbles emptied early in the straight and started to backpedal as Oleander in sixth went for a daring run through a narrow gap that had appeared. But he found his path blocked as Semblat on Finglass, who was also making his move, legitimately closed the gap.

With 300 metres to run Finglas struck the front, only to be mown down by Kantar who found an extra gear in the final 100 metres. In the end Kantar won comfortably by three parts holding off the staying-on Rialto with Finglas fading back to third. Motrico, who was also motoring at the death, took fourth followed by the luckless Oleander and Pinceau.

Post-race

Kantar's success was a great triumph for the Chantilly-based Dick Carver, the son of William Carver, who'd been one of the first English jockeys to ride in France.

William had ridden Boïard to victory in the 1873 Prix du Jockey Club and Grand Prix de Paris, and the following year's Ascot Gold Cup, before setting up as a trainer. His son, Dick and his grandson Richard jnr will also feature in our story.

Kantar's Arc win was also a great achievement for jockey Arthur Esling who'd been runner-up on Isola Bella in 1924 and third on Felton last year.

The winning owner, Ogden Mills, had been US ambassador in London and Paris. Together with his sister, Gladys, he owned Wheatley Stable in Kentucky. This was the operation that down the road would produce Seabiscuit and Bold Ruler, the latter being the sire of Secretariat and grandsire of Seattle Slew.

However, Mills, along with Lord Derby – his racing partner, who had an interest in the horse – were both absentees for Kantar's great triumph. Mills died the following January and so also missed his charge's further exploits.

Both Kantar and Oleander, who had finished the Arc with a cut under his near fore knee, would be back at Longchamp the following autumn.

Result

1928 Prix de l'Arc de Triomphe
Longchamp. Sunday, 7 October 1928
Weights: 3yo c: 55kg, 3yo f: 53.5kg, 4yo+ c: 60kg, 4yo+ f: 58.5kg

1st Kantar (FR)   3yo c   55.5kg*   **3.2/1** (coupled with Cri de Guerre)
by Alcantara II out of Karabe (Chouberski). Ogden Mills / Richard Carver / Arthur Esling

2nd Rialto (FR)   5yo h   60kg   **22/1**
by Rabelais out of La Grelee (Helicon). Jean Stern / Arthur Watkins / W. Lister

3rd Finglas (FR)   5yo h   60kg   **3/1 jt fav** (coupled with Bubbles)
by Brûleur out of Fair Simone (Farman). Evremond de Saint-Alary / Frank Carter / Charles Semblat
*including 0.5kg overweight.

Runners: 11 (FR 10, GER 1). Distances: ¾, 1. Going: good. Time: 2m 38.80s

Also ran: 4th **Motrico** (FR) 3yo c, 5th **Oleander** (GER) 4yo c, 6th **Pinceau** (FR) 3yo c. Unplaced: **Guy Fawkes** (FR) 3yo c, **Mourad** (GB) 3yo c, **Cri de Guerre** (FR) 3yo c, **Bubbles** (FR) 3yo c, **Mondovi** (GB) 3yo c (11th).

Ortello opens account for Italy

Double-seeking Kantar leaves it too late

Background and fancied horses

Kantar arrived to defend his title with a seasonal record of three out of six. He'd been well-beaten in a falsely run Prix du Président de la République but arrived on the back of a three-length win over the useful Le Chatelet in the Prix du Prince d'Orange.

After Ogden Mills's death, Kantar was now running in the silks of Mills's daughter Lady Granard and, coupled with his pacemaker Montcalm, he was a short order to become the second dual winner.

Oleander, fully recovered from the injury sustained in last year's Arc, had again been in dazzling form winning all five starts. Most recently he'd completed a hat-trick in the Grosser Preis von Baden when beating German Derby-winner Graf Isolani by four lengths.

He was a 4.6/1-shot followed by Calandria, who'd been unlucky in the Grand Prix de Deauville – when stopped in her tracks just as she was challenging – but had subsequently taken the Prix Royal-Oak and Prix Vermeille.

Next, on 12/1, came Palais Royal who'd shown ability on his raids to England. He'd been runner-up in the 1928 St Leger before landing a massive gamble in the Cambridgeshire, and this term he'd finished third in the Ascot Gold Cup.

The Italian-trained Ortello was a point longer. A winner of ten of his 11 career starts, he'd been slow to stride in the Gran Premio di Milano but had still given weight and a beating to Pinceau.

Hotweed, winner of the Prix du Jockey Club and Grand Prix de Paris, was absent after picking up an injury in the St Leger – which was run on hard ground – and would have to wait another 12 months before taking his place in the Arc line-up.

Betting

1.2/1 Kantar & Montcalm (coupled), 4.6/1 Oleander, 6.7/1 Calandria, 12/1 Palais Royal, 13/1 Ortello, 20/1 BAR.

Three-year-old form lines

Prix du Jockey Club: 1st Hotweed, 2nd **Charlemagne**, 3rd Cordial

Grand Prix de Paris: 1st Hotweed, 2nd Buland Bala, 3rd **Calandria**

Prix Royal-Oak: 1st **Calandria**, 2nd Cabire, 3rd Grock

Fillies only

Prix de Diane: 1st **Ukrania**, 2nd **Calandria**, 3rd Queskella

Prix Vermeille: 1st **Calandria**, 2nd Skyrame, 3rd Fête Royale

Older horses and inter-generational races

Prix du Président de la République: 1st Bubbles, 2nd **Vatout**, 3rd **Pinceau**, 4th **Kantar**

La Coupe de Maisons-Laffitte: 1st Kantara, 2nd Marot, 3rd Areska, 4th **Palais Royal**

Grand Prix de Deauville: 1st **Charlemagne**, 2nd Kantara, 3rd Skyrame, 4th **Calandria**

Prix du Prince d'Orange: 1st **Kantar**, 2nd Le Chatelet, 3rd Double Dutch

Abroad

In England

Derby Stakes: 1st Trigo, 2nd Walter Gay, 3rd Brienz

Ascot Gold Cup: 1st Invershin, 2nd Reigh Count, 3rd **Palais Royal**

In Germany

Grosser Preis von Baden: 1st **Oleander**, 2nd Graf Isolani, 3rd Daphnis

In Italy

Gran Premio di Milano: 1st **Ortello**, 2nd **Pinceau**, 3rd Erba

The race

It had been a dry summer and the track had been thoroughly watered. However heavy rain overnight and throughout the morning meant the ground was now heavy.

At the off, Montcalm, Kantar's pacemaker, went straight to the front, followed through by Pinceau. They were clear of the main body of the field, where Oleander, Ortello, Calandria and Charlemagne were prominent.

Down the side of the track the pacesetters started to come back to the pack. Joe Childs, who had replaced Lajos Varga on Oleander, was mindful of what had happened to his predecessor last year. So, he took the opportunity to make his move, pushing Oleander into the lead with fully 800 metres to go.

Ortello, who was second entering the straight, gradually started to eat into Oleander's advantage. Meanwhile, towards the back, Kantar was under pressure. At the 200-metre pole Ortello mastered Oleander. The German horse was game but Ortello was just too strong.

But the action wasn't over as Kantar, finally answering his jockey's frantic urgings, charged through the field in the last 100 metres and got to within half a length of the winner at the line. It was the same distance back to

Oleander. Vatout in fourth, was five lengths behind, followed by the Prix de Diane-winner Ukrania and then Palais Royal in sixth.

Post-race
Spectators and pundits alike were asking the perennial questions: had Childs gone too soon on Oleander? Had Esling left it too late on Kanter?

The answer may have been 'yes' on both counts; however, it was the Italian chestnut who was first past the post to record a first win for Italy. In doing so he may have landed a hefty wager for Mussolini, as a man placing a large bet on Ortello claimed to be Il Duce's representative.

Owned by Guiseppe del Montel, Ortello was handled by his private trainer Willy Carter, another cousin of Percy (Priori) and Frank (Mon Talisman). Before taking the contract with del Montel he'd had a public yard and had tasted success with Or du Rhin in the 1910 Prix du Jockey Club, and with Germaine and Alerte in the 1899 and 1914 runnings of the Prix de Diane.

Jockey Paolo Caprioli had been champion in Italy since 1924, and his Arc story wasn't finished. Neither was Ortello's – but Kantar's was. At stud he sired the useful Victrix who won the 1937 Prix Royal-Oak and the Prix du Président de la République the following year.

Result
1929 Prix de l'Arc de Triomphe
Longchamp. Sunday, 6 October 1929
Weights: 3yo c: 55kg, 3yo f: 53.5kg, 4yo+ c: 60kg, 4yo+ f: 58.5kg

1st Ortello (ITY)   3yo c   55.5kg   **13/1**
by Teddy out of Hollebeck (Gorgos). Guiseppe del Montel / Willy Carter / Paolo Caprioli

2nd Kantar (FR)   4yo c   60kg   **1.2/1 fav** (coupled with Montcalm)
by Alcantara II out of Karabe (Chouberski). Lady Granard / Richard Carver / Arthur Esling

3rd Oleander (FR)   5yo h   60kg   **4.6/1**
by Prunus out of Orchidee II (Galtee More). Baron S. A. von Oppenheim / George Arnull / Joe Childs

Runners: 13 (FR 11, GER 1, ITY1). Distances: ½, ½. Going: heavy. Time: 2m 42.80s

Also ran: 4th **Vatout** (FR) 3yo c, 5th **Ukrania** (FR) 3yo f, 6th **Palais Royal** (FR) 4yo c. Unplaced: **Guy Fawkes** (FR) 4yo c, **Pinceau** (FR) 4yo c, **Montcalm** (FR) 3yo c, **Arbalétrier** (FR) 3yo c, **Charlemagne** (FR) 3yo c, **Amorina** (FR) 3yo f, **Calandria** (FR) 3yo f (13th).

1930
Motrico jumps to it
on rain-sodden ground

Favourite bogged down while Hotweed is irresolute

Background and fancied horses

There had been appalling storms the night before the race. The terrible weather was a key factor in the tragic crash of the British R101 airship which came down near Beauvais, to the north of Paris, with the loss of nearly 50 lives. It also meant that the ground at Longchamp would be hock-deep and the mood sombre.

The grey filly, Commanderie, was all the rage after picking up the Prix de Diane – beating the Poule d'Essai des Pouliches-winner Rose Thé – followed by the Grand Prix de Paris at the expense of Prix du Jockey Club-victor Château Bouscaut, who admittedly hadn't found the clearest of runs. Commanderie then waltzed home by five lengths in the Prix Vermeille; the only doubt was whether she would handle the heavy ground.

Last year's winner, Ortello, had picked up an injury in early summer during his preparation for the Ascot Gold Cup, a race he had subsequently missed. However, he'd recently hacked up by six lengths in the Premio Laveno at San Siro, and seemed like he might be back to his best.

The 1929 winner of the Prix du Jockey Club and Grand Prix de Paris, Hotweed, had run in the Ascot showpiece, finishing runner-up to Bosworth. He hadn't been suited by the hard ground in the previous year's St Leger, so the prevailing conditions at Longchamp were likely to be in his favour. In the betting he was second best coupled with his pacemaker Lovelace, who'd finished second to Château Bouscaut in the Prix du Jockey Club.

The heavy ground would also suit Motrico, fourth in the 1928 Arc and a successful hurdler at Auteuil and Nice, who needed soft underfoot conditions due to his badly conformed hocks. He arrived on the back of an impressive success in the Prix du Prince d'Orange.

Ortello was joined by another Italian challenger in the form of Gran Premio di Milano runner-up Filarete. Previous-winner Parth was represented by Parth For Ever, who'd finished third in the Poule d'Essai des Pouliches and fifth in The Oaks.

There had been a change to the conditions for the race since last year, with the weights being slightly altered to reduce the gap between the older and younger horses to 4.5kg.

Betting

2.6/1 Commanderie, 3.5/1 Ortello, 3.7/1 Hotweed & Lovelace (coupled), 4.5/1 Château Bouscaut, 8.3/1 Motrico, 14/1 Parth For Ever & Arques la Bataille (coupled), 31/1 BAR.

Three-year-old form lines
Prix du Jockey Club: 1st **Château Bouscaut**, 2nd **Lovelace**, 3rd Fizy Pop
Grand Prix de Paris: 1st **Commanderie**, 2nd **Château Bouscaut**, DH3rd Godiche, DH3rd Veloucreme
Prix Royal-Oak: 1st Taicoun, 2nd **Château Bouscaut**, 3rd Rieur

Fillies only
Prix de Diane: 1st **Commanderie**, 2nd Rose Thé, 3rd La Savoyarde
Prix Vermeille: 1st **Commanderie**, 2nd Kill Lady, 3rd Aude

Older horses and inter-generational races
Prix du Président de la République: 1st Feb, 2nd **Le Chatelet**, 3rd **Château Bouscaut**
La Coupe d'Or, at Maisons-Laffitte: 1st **Parth For Ever**, 2nd Finsovino, 3rd **Filarete**
Grand Prix de Deauville: 1st Rieur, 2nd **Motrico**, 3rd **Le Chatelet**
Prix du Prince d'Orange: 1st **Motrico**, 2nd Vatout, 3rd Godiche

Abroad
In England
Derby Stakes: 1st Blenheim, 2nd Iliad, 3rd Diolite
Oaks Stakes: 1st Rose of England, 2nd Wedding Favour, 3rd Micmac, 5th **Parth For Ever**
Ascot Gold Cup: 1st Bosworth, 2nd **Hotweed**, 3rd The Bastard

In Italy
Gran Premio di Milano: 1st Cavaliere d'Arpino, 2nd **Filarete**, 3rd Emanuele Filiberto

The race

Lovelace led from flag fall, followed by Arques la Bataille, Filarete, Ortello and Commanderie, who was pulling for her head.

Down the hill Motrico, under Marcel Fruhinsholtz, made rapid progress and took the lead just before they entered the straight. Only the blinkered Hotweed looked capable of pegging him back.

During the preliminaries Hotweed had played up, and after getting to within a length of Motrico he started to show signs of temperament again. Putting his head in the air, Hotweed looked to be ducking the issue. Motrico on the other hand was totally resolute and stayed on doggedly to prevail by two lengths.

Despite not putting it all in, Hotweed still had three lengths to spare over Filarete in third, followed by Ortello and Commanderie – who didn't act on the surface – and then Château Bouscaut.

Post-race

It was a first Arc winner for owner Vicomte Max de Rivaud, trainer Maurice d'Okhuysen and jockey Marcel Fruhinsholtz. In fact, it was only the 27th ride on the flat for Fruhinsholtz who normally plied his trade over jumps.

Motrico had loved the conditions and, as it remained wet, he turned out again in the Prix du Conseil Municipal. But he finished unplaced after receiving a hefty bump just as he was starting his challenge. Motrico was then sent to stud. However, as it turned out, he would be back at Longchamp in 1932.

Last year's winner Ortello, on the other hand, went to stud and stayed there, becoming the champion sire in Italy on six occasions. His best progeny included the very useful Zuccarello, and in 1944 his sons Macherio and Torbido between them won the Italian versions of the 2000 Guineas, Derby and St Leger, as well as several other prestigious prizes.

Result

1930 Prix de l'Arc de Triomphe
Longchamp. Sunday, 5 October 1930
Weights: 3yo c: 55.5kg, 3yo f: 54kg, 4yo+ c: 60kg, 4yo+ f: 58.5kg

1st Motrico (FR)   5yo h   60kg   **8.3/1**
by Radames out of Martigues (Doricles). Vicomte Max de Rivaud / Maurice d'Okhuysen / Marcel Fruhinsholtz

2nd Hotweed (FR)   4yo c   60kg   **3.7/1** (coupled with Lovelace)
by Brûleur out of Seaweed (Spearmint). Edward Esmond / Frank Carter / Guy Garner

3rd Filarete (ITY)   3yo c   55.5kg **31/1**
by Blandford out of Pommade Divine (Pommern). Comte P. A. Guazzone / Domingo Torterolo / Charles Bouillon

Runners: 10 (FR 8, ITY 2). Distances: 2, 3. Going: heavy. Time: 2m 44.80s

Also ran: 4th **Ortello** (ITY) 4yo c, 5th **Commanderie** (FR) 3yo f, 6th **Château Bouscaut** (FR) 3yo c. Unplaced: **Le Chatelet** (FR) 4yo c, **Lovelace** (FR) 3yo c, **Arques la Bataille** (FR) 3yo c, **Parth For Ever** (FR) 3yo f (10th).

Pearl Cap asserts
as Tourbillon fails to ignite

Gift horse is the first filly to win the Arc

Background and fancied horses

Marcel Boussac's Tourbillon, coupled with his pacemaker Erain, headed the market at 2/1. He'd won the Prix du Jockey Club but had suffered some reverses after that, notably in the Grand Prix de Paris where it seemed like he didn't stay. However, Tourbillon arrived on the back of a decent second in the Prix Royal-Oak and headed most shortlists.

The filly Pearl Cap was second favourite; she'd been a very good two-year-old but wasn't expected to shine in her Classic year due to her diminutive frame – so much so that Edward Esmond had given her away to his daughter. The assessment proved to be wholeheartedly incorrect as she skipped away with the Poule d'Essai des Pouliches, before overcoming quagmire conditions to land the Prix de Diane.

Next she went to Belgium to take on the local-superstar Prince Rose in the Grand Prix International d'Ostende. She lost out by a length, which was probably a good effort taking into account her frenzied behaviour on the day. She'd sweated profusely and played up throughout the proceedings and even reared up and fell over twice after the race.

Normal service was resumed back in France where Pearl Cap beat her stable companion, the Oaks-winner Brûlette, by three lengths in the Prix Vermeille. The second favourite would be on home soil for the rematch with Prince Rose, who goes down as the first Belgian-trained runner in the Arc. He'd extended his unbeaten run to 11 when beating Pearl Cap in the Grand Prix International d'Ostende, a race that would shortly to be renamed in his honour.

Édouard de Rothschild's Taxodium, who'd been runner-up in both the Grand Prix de Paris and Prix du Prince d'Orange, was next best, followed by the horse that had beaten him in the Prix du Prince d'Orange, Lovelace, then another Boussac runner, Brûledur, and Taxodium's pacemaker Ski.

Betting

2/1 Tourbillon & Erain (coupled), 3.2/1 Pearl Cap, 3.7/1 Prince Rose, 7.5/1 Taxodium, 10/1 Lovelace, 14/1 Brûledur, 17.5/1 Ski, 24/1 BAR.

Three-year-old form lines

Prix du Jockey Club: 1st **Tourbillon**, 2nd **Brûledur**, 3rd Barneveldt

Grand Prix de Paris: 1st Barneveldt, 2nd **Taxodium**, 3rd **Tourbillon**, 4th Deiri

Prix Royal-Oak: 1st Deiri, 2nd **Tourbillon**, 3rd **Brûledur**

Fillies only

Prix de Diane: 1st **Pearl Cap**, 2nd Confidence, 3rd Celerina

Prix Vermeille: 1st **Pearl Cap**, 2nd **Brûlette**, 3rd Confidence

Older horses and inter-generational races

Prix du Président de la République: 1st Barneveldt, 2nd **Tourbillon**, 3rd Roi de Trefle

Grand Prix de Deauville: 1st Celerina, 2nd Confidence, 3rd **Brûledur**

Prix du Prince d'Orange: 1st **Lovelace**, 2nd **Taxodium**, 3rd Angelico

Abroad

In England

Derby Stakes: 1st Cameronian, 2nd Orpen, 3rd Sandwich

Oaks Stakes: 1st **Brûlette**, 2nd Four Course, 3rd Links Tor

In Belgium

Grand Prix International d'Ostende: 1st **Prince Rose**, 2nd **Pearl Cap**, 3rd **Amfortas**

The race

Erain, the pacemaker for Tourbillon, was very smartly away. Ski, who was undertaking the same role for Taxodium, wasn't and had to be rushed through the field after his tardy departure, but soon joined Erain up front.

Amfortas, an outsider but a course specialist, and Taxodium followed them through with Prince Rose. However, as they started the descent, the latter became unbalanced, changing legs several times, and as a result dropped back through the field.

On the other hand, Lovelace was making good ground from midfield and took up the running rounding the home turn. Amfortas was still prominent, followed by Pearl Cap, who had appeared menacingly on the outside.

Amfortas challenged and passed Lovelace at the 400-metre pole, but Pearl Cap was only cantering in behind, and when Semblat let her go she produced a sublime burst of speed to score by one and a half lengths.

After recovering his action back on the level, Prince Rose made up a lot of ground to finish third, followed by Brûlette, Taxodium and the disappointing favourite Tourbillon, who was never going.

Post-race

Pearl Cap had written her own entry in the history of the Arc, becoming the first filly to win the race. It was a fantastic success for both the current owner Diana, who was a top golfer, and her father Edward, the breeder and former owner, who'd been second with Dorina in 1926 and Hotweed in 1930.

Trainer Frank Carter and jockey Charles Semblat were adding to their win with Mon Talisman in 1927, which for the latter meant equalling Frank Bullock as the only other two-time winning jockey.

Pearl Cap was retired and sent to be covered by Hotweed. But that didn't work out and she struggled to get in-foal at the start of her career at stud, and the offspring she did produce were disappointing. However, in 1944 she excelled herself, producing Pearl Diver who went on to win the Derby.

The runner-up Amfortas, by Ksar, became the first offspring of a former winner to make the frame. Ksar's other representative in the race, the favourite Tourbillon, may have failed to fire on that occasion but he went on to become one of Marcel Boussac's most influential sires in his own right, and his offspring would win the Arc twice.

Ksar's own sire, Brûleur, had also been doubly represented in this year's Arc with the clue-is-in-the-name pairing of Brûledur and Brûlette.

Result
1931 Prix de l'Arc de Triomphe
Longchamp. Sunday, 4 October 1931
Weights: 3yo c: 55.5kg, 3yo f: 54kg, 4yo+ c: 60kg, 4yo+ f: 58.5kg

1st Pearl Cap (FR)   3yo f   55.5kg   **3.2/1**
by Le Capucin out of Pearl Maiden (Phaleron). Diana Esmond / Frank Carter / Charles Semblat

2nd Amfortas (FR)   4yo c   60kg   **25.5/1**
by Ksar out of Persephone (Teddy). Jefferson Davis Cohn / George Newton / Wally Sibbritt

3rd Prince Rose (GB)   3yo c   55.5kg   **3.7/1**
by Rose Prince out of Indolence (Gay Crusader). Henri Coppez / G. Charlton / Hervé Denaigre

Runners: 10 (FR 9, BEL 1). Distances: 1½, 1. Going: good. Time: 2m 38.80s

Also ran: 4th **Brûlette** (FR) 3yo f, 5th **Taxodium** (FR) 3yo c, 6th **Tourbillon** (FR) 3yo c. Unplaced: **Lovelace** (FR) 4yo c, **Ski** (FR) 3yo c, **Brûledur** (FR) 3yo c, **Erain** (FR) 3yo c (10th).

Back from stud Motrico wins again

Heavy-ground specialist is the oldest winner

Background and fancied horses

At the age of seven, Motrico was back. He'd sired 17 foals since being retired to stud after his win in 1930 and one of those, Vulgate, would in turn produce the great jumps sire Vulgan. But at the time, Motrico's output was seen as less than satisfactory and so he was returned to the track.

After a couple of outings on fast ground, conditions changed in his favour and on heavy going at Longchamp he obliged in the Prix du Prince d'Orange. The going remained testing and Motrico, with Charles Semblat in the plate this time, was made favourite to recapture the Arc.

Second favourite Macaroni, owned by Jean Prat, hadn't been entered in the Classics but had run up a series of wins, producing collateral form that suggested he was as good, if not better, than any of the other three-year-olds who were running.

Le Bécau finished down the field in the Prix du Prince d'Orange, but it was his first run since winning the Poule d'Essai des Poulains in the spring. Supporters who thought that he would come on for that run, backed him into third spot in the market.

Next came the Marcel Boussac-owned trio of Goyescas, Pancho and Thaouka, with the first-named being the pick of the bunch. Trained in Newmarket by Basil Jarvis, he'd won last year's Champion Stakes after finishing second in the 2000 Guineas and fourth in the Derby.

This term Goyescas had taken the Hardwicke Stakes at Royal Ascot and had also been a fast-finishing fourth in the Grand Prix International d'Ostende after being boxed-in. That race had gone to Sanzio, one of the two Italian-trained runners in the Arc. He'd won six of his nine races but had unfortunately been out of sorts since arriving in Paris. The other Italian was Fenolo, who'd won the Italian St Leger by eight lengths.

Others that could be given an outside chance included Grand Prix de Paris-second Satrap, coupled with the Poule d'Essai des Pouliches runner-up Disguise, and the first two in the Prix Royal-Oak, namely Laeken and Bosphore.

Betting

3.8/1 Motrico, 4.2/1 Macaroni, 6.8/1 Le Bécau, 7.6/1 Goyescas & Thaouka

& Pancho (all coupled), 11/1 Satrap & Disguise (coupled), 11/1 Laeken, 12/1 Bosphore, 17/1 BAR.

Three-year-old form lines
Prix du Jockey Club: 1st Strip the Willow, 2nd Shred, 3rd **Gris Perle**
Grand Prix de Paris: 1st Strip the Willow, 2nd **Satrap**, 3rd Fog Horn, 0th **Hénin**, 0th **Bosphore**
Prix Royal-Oak: 1st **Laeken**, 2nd **Bosphore**, 3rd **Gris Perle**, 0th Strip the Willow

Fillies only
Prix de Diane: 1st Perruche Bleue, 2nd Ligne de Fond, 3rd La Bourrasque
Prix Vermeille: 1st Kiddie, 2nd Nanaia, 3rd Malina, 4th **Thaouka**

Older horses and inter-generational races
Prix du Président de la République: 1st Prince Rose, 2nd Taxodium, 3rd **Gris Perle**
La Coupe de Maisons-Laffitte: DH1st (won the run-off) Jus De Raisin, DH1st **Fenolo**, 3rd Bievres
Prix du Prince d'Orange: 1st **Motrico**, 2nd Courageux, 3rd Agnello, 0th **Le Bécau**

Abroad
In England
Derby Stakes: 1st April the Fifth, 2nd Dastur, 3rd Miracle

In Germany
Grosser Preis von Baden: 1st Widerhall, 2nd **Hénin**, 3rd Lord Nelson

In Belgium
Grand Prix International d'Ostende: 1st **Sanzio**, 2nd **Bosphore**, 3rd Casteau, 4th **Goyescas**

In Italy
Gran Premio di Milano: 1st **Sanzio**, 2nd **Fenolo**, 3rd Guernanville

The race
Laeken led early but moved off the rails going up the hill. In doing so, he made contact with another runner and dropped back. That left Le Bécau in the lead, and he was still at the head of affairs entering the straight, followed by Goyescas, Macaroni and Motrico

Goyescas soon overhauled Le Bécau but then had to fend off Motrico and Macaroni. A tremendous battle ensued with Goyescas refusing to cave in. However, Motrico was relentless and used all his power and experience to close the gap and then move alongside.

In the last few strides, Motrico finally got the better of the argument, forcing his nose in front to secure victory in what had been a thrilling finish. The winning distance was half a length in the end, with the same to Macaroni in third. After a gap of two lengths, Le Bécau came through in fourth, followed by Fenolo and Bosphore.

Post-race

It was a second Arc for the Vicomte Max de Rivaud and Maurice d'Okhuysen combination which would be represented by Assuérus in the next three runnings.

For Charles Semblat it was two in a row and three in all, making him the winning-most rider in the race.

A fortnight later Macaroni, on more favourable terms than in the Arc, reversed the form when winning the Prix du Conseil Municipal, with Motrico finishing unplaced. It proved to be Motrico's farewell performance and he returned to stud with a racing record that boasted 14 wins on the flat and several more over hurdles.

Motrico was the second horse to win the Arc twice, after Ksar, and to date remains the only successful seven-year-old.

Result

1932 Prix de l'Arc de Triomphe
Longchamp. Sunday, 9 October 1932
Weights: 3yo c: 55.5kg, 3yo f: 54kg, 4yo+ c: 60kg, 4yo+ f: 58.5kg

1st Motrico (FR)　　　　7yo h　60kg　　**3.8/1 fav**
by Radames out of Martigues (Doricles). Vicomte Max de Rivaud / Maurice d'Okhuysen/ Charles Semblat

2nd Goyescas (FR)　　　4yo c　60kg　　**7.6/1**
by Gainsborough out of Zariba (Sardanapale). Marcel Boussac / Basil Jarvis / Charlie Elliott

3rd Macaroni (FR)　　　3yo c　55.5kg　**4.2/1**
by Passebreul out of Monnaie (Montmartin). Jean Prat / Henri Harper / André Rabbe

Runners: 15 (FR 12, ITY 2, GB 1). Distances: ½, ½. Going: heavy. Time: 2m 44.60s

Also ran: 4th **Le Bécau** (FR) 3yo c, 5th **Fenolo** (ITY) 3yo c, 6th **Bosphore** (FR) 3yo c. Unplaced: **Amfortas** (FR) 5yo h, **Sanzio** (GB) 4yo c, **Pancho** (FR) 3yo c, **Laeken** (FR) 3yo c, **Hénin** (FR) 3yo c, **Gris Perle** (FR) 3yo c, **Satrap** (FR) 3yo c, **Disguise** (FR) 3yo f, **Thaouka** (FR) 3yo f (15th).

1933
Gap comes in time for Crapom
Great performance by Italian-trained favourite

Background and fancied horses

The effects of the economic downturn which became known as the Great Depression were reaching Europe and the prize money for the Arc was reduced by 20 per cent. On the technical side this was the first year that a public address system was set up on the course so that a running commentary could be given.

No older horses took up the challenge and a field comprised of 15 three-year-olds went to post with Crapom, one of the Italian raiders, trading as favourite.

He'd won the Premio Parioli (Italian 2000 Guineas) before finishing second to his stablemate Pilade in the Derby Italiano. After disappointing in the Premio d'Italia he recaptured his form in the Gran Premio di Milano, this time beating Pilade by eight lengths.

Further wins in the Grand Prix International d'Ostende and Italian St Leger secured his place as a serious challenger for the Arc.

The horse he was coupled with, Sans Souci, was an enigma typifying the phrase 'morning glory'. He'd had a leg problem after winning on debut, but although he repeatedly beat Crapom and Pilade on the home gallops he couldn't repeat the form on the track.

Next best was Marcel Boussac's Negundo, who'd won the Prix Eugène Adam from Assuérus, who was representing last year's winning owner, the now Comte de Rivaud.

Others worthy of consideration included Pantalon, who'd started as a selling plater before rising through the ranks to become a decent two-year-old. This year he'd won the Prix Omnium II in March but hadn't shown much since.

Showman and entrepreneur Léon Volterra had two runners in the shape of Prix du Jockey Club-third Casterari and Jumbo. The latter had won the Prix Royal-Oak by 20 lengths when running as a pacemaker for Casterari, in a classic case of a front runner being given too long a lead before anyone reacted.

Édouard de Rothschild was represented by Camping, who had form on a par with Casterari. The Prix Hocquart-winner Le Grand Cyrus and the Prix du Président de la République runner-up Généralissime were both owned officially by Señor E. Dorn y de Alsúa, the Ecuadorian Ambassador for France. However, that turned out to be a front, as will be revealed.

Betting

2.2/1 Crapom & Sans Souci (coupled), 6.3/1 Negundo, 7.7/1 Assuérus, 8.1/1 Pantalon, 8.7/1 Casterari & Jumbo (coupled), 13/1 Généralissime, 13/1 Le Grand Cyrus, 14/1 Camping, 15/1 Minestrone, 22.5/1 BAR.

Three-year-old form lines
Prix du Jockey Club: 1st Thor, 2nd **Camping**, 3rd **Casterari**
Grand Prix de Paris: 1st Cappiello, 2nd Thor, 3rd **Assuérus**, 0th **Rodosto**
Prix Royal-Oak: 1st **Jumbo**, 2nd **Minestrone**, 3rd **Camping**, 4th **Casterari**

Fillies only
Prix de Diane: 1st Vendange, 2nd La Souriciere, 3rd Pampilhosa
Prix Vermeille: 1st La Circe, 2nd Armoise, 3rd Vendange

Older horses and inter-generational races
Prix du Président de la République: 1st Macaroni, 2nd **Généralissime**, 3rd Taxodium, 0th **Rodosto**
La Coupe de Maisons-Laffitte: 1st Magnus, 2nd **Assuérus**, 3rd Quartz
Grand Prix de Deauville: 1st Queen Of Scots, 2nd Pick-Up, 3rd **Assuérus**

Abroad
In England
Derby Stakes: 1st Hyperion, 2nd King Salmon, 3rd Statesman

In Germany
Grosser Preis von Baden: 1st Alchimist, 2nd **Negundo**, 3rd Janitor, 0th **Sans Souci**

In Belgium
Grand Prix International d'Ostende: 1st **Crapom**, 2nd Nitsichin, 3rd Gris Perle

In Italy
Gran Premio di Milano: 1st **Crapom**, 2nd Pilade, 3rd Ello

The race

Dual Guineas-winner Rodosto played up at the start, delaying the despatch. When they finally got away, Jumbo was first to show but was overtaken by Sans Souci just after the Petit Bois, who in turn was overhauled by Généralissime on the run to the top turn.

Rodosto took over on the downhill run to become the race's fourth leader. He led them to the straight followed by Assuérus, Camping and Pantalon. When Rodosto capitulated, they became the first three. Meanwhile Casterari looked menacing on the outside and was making progress. The favourite Crapom, though, was stuck in a pocket behind the leaders.

Pantalon proved to be stronger than Camping and Assuérus, but in the final 200 metres was joined by Casterari. The pair engaged in a tremendous duel until Crapom, who'd finally found some racing room, engaged turbocharge.

The turn of foot he produced was decisive. Passing Casterari and Pantalon as though they were standing still, Crapom scored, going away by half a length. Casterari short-headed Pantalon for second, followed by Assuérus, Camping and Rodosto.

Post-race

Owned by newspaper proprietor Mario Crespi, Crapom's name – which has unintended connotations in English – was formed by adding the first three letters of his dam's name, Pompea, to the first three of his sire, dual Premio di Milano-winner Cranach.

Trainer Federico Regoli had been a top jockey and still holds the record for most victories in the Derby Italiano with eight wins between 1917 and 1926. Jockey Paolo Caprioli was adding to his win aboard Ortello in 1929.

Crapom was aimed at the following year's Ascot Gold Cup but finished fifth after sweating up badly in the preliminaries. He was retired and stood at stud in Italy and then Germany but didn't made a big impact in either.

It later emerged that Le Grand Cyrus and Généralissime, who had run in the name of Señor E Dorn y de Alsúa, were actually the property of the notorious nightclub owner, swindler, drug-runner and police informant Serge Alexandre Stavisky.

His scheme to buy shares with fraudulent money, before laundering the profits from below market-price sales of those shares, produced a small fortune. However, he was exposed when government officials, including a minister, became embroiled in the plot and life insurance companies, and therefore the public, started to bear the brunt of the deception.

Initially Stavisky escaped, but in January 1934 he shot himself when police surrounded the chalet in Chamonix where he'd taken refuge. The apparent distance the shot had travelled led one satirical newspaper to muse that he must have had a very long arm.

The huge amount of public money that was lost, the involvement of politicians, members of high society and celebrities – including the actress and singer Mistinguett, whose namesake would win the Cleeve Hurdle at Cheltenham in 1998 – made this one of the biggest scandals in French history and was a contributory factor in the build-up to the following month's riot aimed at taking down the government, which left 15 demonstrators dead.

Result

1933 Prix de l'Arc de Triomphe
Longchamp. Sunday, 8 October 1933
Weights: 3yo c: 55.5kg, 3yo f: 54kg, 4yo+ c: 60kg, 4yo+ f: 58.5kg

1st Crapom (ITY)　　　3yo c　55.5kg　**2.2/1 fav** (coupled with Sans Souci)
by Cranach out of Pompea (Adam). Mario Crespi / Federico Regoli / Paolo Caprioli

2nd Casterari (FR)　　　3yo c　55.5kg　**8.7/1**
by Fiterari out of Castleline (Son-in-Law). Léon Volterra / Emile Charlier / Georges Bridgeland

3rd Pantalon (FR)　　　3yo c　55.5kg　**8.1/1**
by Scaramouche out of La Traviata (Alcantara II). Henri Cottevieille / D. Englander / Rae Johnstone

Runners: 15 (FR 13, ITY 2). Distances: ½, sh. Going: good. Time: 2m 41.60s

Also ran: 4th **Assuérus** (IRE) 3yo c, 5th **Camping** (FR) 3yo c, 6th **Rodosto** (FR) 3yo c. Unplaced: **Sans Souci** (FR/GB) 3yo c, **Jumbo** (FR) 3yo c, **Le Grand Cyrus** (FR) 3yo c, **Généralissime** (FR) 3yo c, **Pick-Up** (FR) 3yo c, **Minestrone** (FR) 3yo c, **Negundo** (FR) 3yo c, **Anténor** (FR) 3yo c, **Revery** (FR) 3yo f (15th).

Brilliant Brantôme flashes home

Class act overcomes interrupted preparation

Background and fancied horses

Édouard de Rothschild's Brantôme had been the top two-year-old of 1933 and confirmed his superiority over the second best, Admiral Drake, when hosing home in the Poule d'Essai de Poulains by an unextended three lengths.

He followed that by hacking up in the Prix Lupin, but unfortunately couldn't contest the Prix du Jockey Club or Grand Prix de Paris as Lucien Robert's stable was hit by a severe bout of coughing.

On his reappearance in September, despite being rusty and still showing some of the effects of the cough, Brantôme maintained his unbeaten record when producing an exhilarating burst of speed to reel in Astronomer in the Prix Royal-Oak.

In the process he convincingly beat Prix Hocquart and Prix Greffulhe-winner Maravédis (by Massine), Admiral Drake – who'd won the Grand Prix de Paris after finishing last in the Derby when badly hampered – and Morvillars, the son of Mon Talisman, who won the Grand Prix de Deauville. As a result, Brantôme was a skinny price to add the Arc.

The Aga Khan III's English-trained Felicitation, who'd finished runner-up to Hyperion in the previous year's St Leger, was second favourite. He'd categorically turned that form around in this term's Ascot Gold Cup when sauntering home eight lengths to the good over Thor, with Hyperion only third, and last year's Arc-winner Crapom in fifth.

Assuérus, who'd utilised exaggerated waiting tactics when landing the Prix du Président de la République, had probably needed the race when beaten by Negundo in the Prix du Prince d'Orange. The Comte de Rivaud's charge, who had been fourth last year, traded as third best in the market for this year's contest.

As well as Admiral Drake, Léon Volterra had Prix du Jockey Club-winner Duplex, while Marcel Boussac was triple-handed with Antiochus and Denver in addition to the aforementioned Negundo.

PRIX DE L'ARC DE TRIOMPHE

Betting

1.1/1 Brantôme, 2.9/1 Felicitation, 7.5/1 Assuérus, 12.5/1 Admiral Drake &
Duplex (coupled), 13/1 Maravédis, 15.5/1 Negundo & Antiochus & Denver
(all coupled), 28/1 BAR.

Three-year-old form lines

Prix du Jockey Club: 1st **Duplex**, 2nd Pons Legend, 3rd **Admiral Drake**

Grand Prix de Paris: 1st **Admiral Drake**, 2nd Foulaubin, 3rd Easton

Prix Royal-Oak: 1st **Brantôme**, 2nd Astronomer, 3rd **Maravédis**, 4th **Admiral
Drake**, 0th **Morvillars**, 0th **Antiochus**

Fillies only

Prix de Diane: 1st Adargatis, 2nd Mary Tudor, 3rd Rarity

Prix Vermeille: 1st Mary Tudor, 2nd Reine Isaure, 3rd **Sa Parade**

Older horses and inter-generational races

Prix du Président de la République: 1st **Assuérus**, 2nd Mas d'Antibes, 3rd **Morvillars**,
0th **Negundo**, 0th **Antiochus**

La Coupe d'Or, at Maisons-Laffitte: 1st **Sa Parade**, 2nd Astronomer, 3rd **Silver Plated**

Grand Prix de Deauville: 1st **Morvillars**, 2nd Formasterus, 3rd Foulaubin

Prix du Prince d'Orange: 1st **Negundo**, 2nd **Assuérus**, 3rd Taxodium

Abroad

In England

Derby Stakes: 1st Windsor Lad, 2nd Easton, 3rd Colombo, 0th/last **Admiral Drake**

Ascot Gold Cup: 1st **Felicitation**, 2nd Thor, 3rd Hyperion, 5th Crapom

In Belgium

Grand International d'Ostende/Grand Prix Prince Rose: 1st Easton, 2nd **Admiral
Drake**, 3rd Rentenmark

The race

Heavy downpours in the morning meant that the ground was heavy
underfoot, but the rain had stopped by the start of the meeting.

The blinkered English raider, Felicitation, was pushed to the front by
Gordon Richards to make the running with Negundo and Astrophel in close
attendance. The favourite, Brantôme, who'd sweated in the preliminaries and
had been a little slow away, was back in touch as they emerged from the Petit
Bois. Meanwhile Assuérus, who'd kicked out at the start, had been settled
in rear.

Down the hill, Negundo dropped back, while at the same time Brantôme
steadily improved his position, moving firstly into fourth and then third
as they entered the straight. Admiral Drake and Duplex were also taking
closer order.

On the run for home Felicitation was stronger than Astrophel. However, neither had a chance as Brantôme, in the manner of his Prix Royal-Oak success, unleashed a staggering burst of acceleration to cut them down in double-quick time.

According to *Le Petit Parisien*, Brantôme had dismissed the best opposition as though they were claiming class and his acceleration would never be forgotten by those who had seen it.

Assuérus, who had used the same exaggerated waiting tactics that had worked so well in the Prix du Président de la République, came from miles back to collar Felicitation entering the final 200 metres.

Assuérus even started to reduce the gap to Brantôme, who, with the race won, was idling. Sensing his rival, Brantôme lengthened away again to record a two and a half-length success, with a further one and a half to Felicitation, followed after a gap of three lengths by Silver Plated, Sa Parade – the only filly in the field – and Morvillars.

Post-race

It was a first success in the Arc for Baron Édouard de Rothschild, whose Cadum had been third to Massine in 1924 and a demoted-second to Priori the following year. Édouard was the son of Alphonse de Rothschild who'd won nine French Classics and founded the Haras de Meautry, near Deauville, from where he bred many winners.

It was also a first win in the race for jockey Charles Bouillon, whose best position to date had been a third on Filarete behind Motrico in 1930. Much credit must also go to trainer Lucien Robert who had nursed the son of Blandford back to health.

Brantôme had maintained his unbeaten record, which now extended to nine races, and was proclaimed a phenomenon being compared to Monarque, Gladiateur, Boïard and Ajax. He was retired for the season but kept in training.

Result

1934 Prix de l'Arc de Triomphe

Longchamp. Sunday, 7 October 1934
Weights: 3yo c: 55.5kg, 3yo f: 54kg, 4yo+ c: 60kg, 4yo+ f: 58.5kg

1st Brantôme (FR)   3yo c   55.5kg   **1.1/1 fav**

by Blandford out of Vitamine (Clarissimus). Baron Édouard de Rothschild / Lucien Robert / Charles Bouillon

2nd Assuérus (FR)   4yo c   60kg   **7.5/1**

by Astérus out of Slip Along (Hurry On). Comte Max de Rivaud / Maurice d'Okhuysen / Rae Johnstone

3rd Felicitation (GB)   4yo c   60kg   **2.9/1**

by Colorado out of Felicita (Cantilever). HH Aga Khan III / Frank Butters / Gordon Richards

Runners: 13 (FR 12, GB 1). Distances: 2½, 1½. Going: heavy. Time: 2m 41.82s

Also ran: 4th **Silver Plated** 3yo c, 5th **Sa Parade** 3yo f, 6th **Morvillars** (FR) 3yo c. Unplaced: **Negundo** (FR) 4yo c, **Antiochus** (FR) 3yo c, **Denver** (FR) 3yo c, **Admiral Drake** (FR) 3yo c, **Duplex** (FR) 3yo c, **Astrophel** (FR) 3yo c, **Maravédis** (FR) 3yo c (13th).

Samos is a great spare ride for Sibbritt

Brantôme fails as fillies fill the frame

Background and fancied horses

The big change this year was that the Société d'Encouragement had been given government permission for the first time to run a sweepstake on the Grand Prix de Paris and the Prix de l'Arc de Triomphe, which helped to boost the finances.

Reigning champion, Brantôme, was back and favourite to win again. However, he'd become somewhat of an escape artist during the season and on the second occasion he got loose, on the way to the start for the Prix Dangu at Chantilly, was free for over an hour and proceeded to dice with the traffic on the roads near the track. When he was finally caught he was not only in a frantic state but had also sustained a cut to a joint.

A mere ten days later he lined up for the Ascot Gold Cup but ran way below his best finishing down the field. He lost his unbeaten record in the process, with the exertions at Chantilly having apparently taken their toll.

After a considerable rest he won the Prix du Prince d'Orange on his return, albeit not as easily as he might have in his pomp. Nevertheless, coupled with Édouard de Rothschild's other runner the Prix de Diane-winner Péniche, Brantôme was odds-on to lift a second Arc.

It was double figures bar the pair bringing in the Marcel Boussac-owned Corrida. The chestnut filly had been a leading fancy for the 1000 Guineas but had finished last. She'd shown something more like her true running when a half-length second to Admiral Drake in the Grand Prix International d'Ostende.

The English-trained William of Valence, a 12/1-shot, was making his first appearance since finishing a close second in the Grand Prix de Paris. In one of two late jockey changes he would now be ridden by Brownie Carslake, replacing Steve Donoghue who'd been injured the previous afternoon at Kempton Park.

Of the others, Pampeiro, who'd been good at two but hadn't trained on, was a couple of points shorter than the aforementioned Admiral Drake, and the same price as last year's runner-up Assuérus, who had become difficult to train.

Evremond de Saint-Alary's Samos was the only other horse under 20/1. The Prix de Malleret-winner had a big home reputation but finished behind Péniche in both the Prix de Diane and Prix Vermeille. Samos would now be partnered by Wally Sibbritt as Charles Semblatt had broken his leg in a fall during the first race on the card.

Betting

1/2 Brantôme & Péniche (coupled), 11.5/1 Corrida, 12/1 William of Valence, 14/1 Pampeiro 16/1 Admiral Drake, 16/1 Assuérus, 19/1 Samos, 20/1 BAR.

Three-year-old form lines

Prix du Jockey Club: 1st Pearlweed, 2nd **Ping Pong**, 3rd Mansur

Grand Prix de Paris: 1st Crudité, 2nd **William of Valence**, 3rd Louqsor, 4th **Samos**, 0th **Kant**

Fillies only

Prix de Diane: 1st **Péniche**, 2nd **Samos**, 3rd Clairvoyante, 0th Crudité

Prix Vermeille: 1st Crisa, 2nd The Nile, 3rd **Péniche**, 0th **Samos**

Older horses and inter-generational races

Prix du Président de la République: 1st Louqsor, 2nd Mesa, 3rd **Ping Pong**, 0th **Admiral Drake**, 0th **Kant**

La Coupe de Maisons-Laffitte: 1st Rarity, 2nd **Sa Parade**, 3rd Roi Mage

Grand Prix de Deauville: 1st **Ping Pong**, 2nd Nicophana, 3rd Will Of The Wisp

Prix du Prince d'Orange: 1st **Brantôme**, 2nd Arkina, 3rd Vanda Teres

Abroad

In England

Derby Stakes: 1st Bahram, 2nd Robin Goodfellow, 3rd Field Trial

Ascot Gold Cup: 1st Tiberius, 2nd Alcazar, 3rd Denver, 0th **Brantôme**

In Belgium

Grand Prix International d'Ostende: 1st **Admiral Drake**, 2nd **Corrida**, 3rd Theft, 4th **Péniche**

In Italy

Gran Premio di Milano: 1st Partenio, 2nd Osimo, 3rd Grand Marnier, 0th **Assuérus**

The race

William of Valence sweated up badly in the build-up and, as had become usual, Assuérus played up at the start, impeding Samos and costing her a few lengths. Péniche set the early pace from Poule d'Essai des Poulains-winner Kant as they made their way up the hill.

On the descent Ping Pong received a knock that effectively ended his chances while Brantôme and Samos moved into contention. Switched to the outside by Bouillon entering the *ligne d'arrivée*, Brantôme was ideally placed to unleash his finishing run.

But when asked to do so, the answer was zero. Meanwhile, on the rails, Samos made ground behind Péniche who still led. But then Péniche wobbled, maybe unbalanced when jockey Villecourt turned around to look for stable-companion Brantôme.

Whatever the reason, Sibbritt quickly accepted the invitation, pushing Samos through the gap between the rails and Péniche to take the lead and win by a neck on the line. Corrida, came wide, fast and late to secure third spot, a similar neck behind Péniche to complete a one-two-three for the fillies. There was then one and a half lengths to last year's winner Brantôme who plugged on for fourth. He was followed by Admiral Drake and Pampeiro.

Post-race

Evremond de Saint-Alary, who'd won the inaugural running of the Arc as well as breeding the winner of the next two, was back in the winner's enclosure and this time he owned and bred the winner. For Frank Carter it was a third success after Mon Talisman and Pearl Cap. The last-named had been the first filly to win the race; Samos was the second.

She was another winner for Brûleur, and a fortuitous spare ride for substitute jockey Wally Sibbritt, who'd been second on Amfortas behind Pearl Cap. The Australian had a link to Saint-Alary's other successes as his father-in-law, Frank Bullock, had ridden Comrade and partnered Ksar to his 1921 success.

Sibbritt had been based in France for ten years but the following year left for England, where he would ride for Bullock. Sibbritt wouldn't be back but Samos would.

Brûleur 1910

Ksar 1918   **Priori** 1922   Palais Royal 1925   **Samos** 1932

Niki 1935

Nikellora 1942

Result
1935 Prix de l'Arc de Triomphe
Longchamp. Sunday, 6 October 1935
Weights: 3yo c: 55.5kg, 3yo f: 54kg, 4yo+ c: 60kg, 4yo+ f: 58.5kg

1st Samos (FR)   3yo f   54kg   **19/1**
by Brûleur out of Samya (Nimbus II [FR]). Evremond de Saint-Alary / Frank Carter / Wally Sibbritt

2nd Péniche (FR)   3yo f   54kg   **1/2 fav** (coupled with Brantôme)
by Belfonds out of Caravelle (Sans Souci II). Baron Édouard de Rothschild / Lucien Robert / P. Villecourt

3rd Corrida (FR)   3yo f   54kg   **11.5/1**
by Coronach out of Zariba (Sardanapale). Marcel Boussac / William Hall / Charlie Elliott

Runners: 12 (FR 11, GB 1). Distances: nk, nk. Going: good. Time: 2m 42.60s

Also ran: 4th **Brantôme** (FR) 4yo c, 5th **Admiral Drake** (FR) 4yo c, 6th **Pampeiro** (FR) 3yo c. Unplaced: **Assuérus** (IRE) 5yo h, **Astrophel** (FR) 4yo c, **Sa Parade** (FR) 4yo f, **Kant** (FR) 3yo c, **William of Valence** (FR) 3yo c, **Ping Pong** (FR) 3yo c (12th).

Boussac off the mark with Corrida

Favourite saunters home under Elliott

Background and fancied horses

There was unrest and strikes on many fronts, racing and non-racing, in 1936. One of the main issues to affect the horse racing industry was the proposed minimum wage for stable staff. This was opposed by trainers as they thought the increased costs that would be incurred were likely to scare owners away from the sport. However, the staff not surprisingly wanted a fair day's pay for what was quite often a very long day's work. This led to a stable lads' strike.

The tension in Paris caused by other non-racing related strikes was high and so moving police to Chantilly for the Prix de Diane was thought to be unwise. Therefore the race was transferred to Longchamp. There was no betting across the country for the Grand Prix de Paris due to the staff of the PMU taking industrial action, and at the meeting itself a loud protest by suffragettes was staged in front of the President's box.

On the day of the Prix de l'Arc de Triomphe there was a Communist demonstration at the Parc des Princes stadium just down the road from Longchamp, while back in central Paris the army had joined the police on the Champs-Élysées to see off the expected fascist response to that rally.

Nevertheless there were some uplifting notes. Racegoers arriving at Longchamp were greeted for the first time by the magnificent statue of a horse labelled as Gladiateur, and the prize money had returned to 1932 levels with 500,000 francs to the winner. This was partly due to the sweepstake which was now being organised by the Loterie Nationale.

After finishing third in last year's race, Corrida had then been beaten a short head in the Prix du Conseil Municipal before winning the Grand Prix de Marseille.

This year, after a slow start in the spring, she'd warmed up to win the Hardwicke Stakes at Royal Ascot and the Prix du Président de la République, before losing nothing in defeat to Nereide, who'd won the German Derby and Oaks, in a valuable race in Munich.

Most recently Corrida had convincingly beaten Derby-second Taj Akbar in the Grand Prix International d'Ostende. Her form was strong and it was no surprise that Corrida was odds-on to add the Arc to her haul.

Second favourite Fantastic was no slouch, though, having won, among other races, the Grand Prix de Deauville, before completing a nap hand in the Prix Royal-Oak.

Last year's heroine, Samos, was third best after a disappointing campaign. She'd won the Prix la Rochette against inferior opposition but could only manage fifth in the Ascot Gold Cup. In her latest outing she'd been third in La Coupe d'Or at Maisons-Laffitte when attempting to give away lumps of weight.

Others of note included Prix du Jockey Club-second Vatellor – who'd finished third to Corrida in Ostend – and Blue Bear, the winner of the Poule d'Essai des Pouliches and runner-up in the Prix Vermeille.

Mieuxcé, the winner of the Prix du Jockey Club and Grand Prix de Paris, had been an intended runner but injured a leg during his preparation and was retired to stud.

Betting
0.8/1 Corrida, 4.8/1 Fantastic, 8.2/1 Samos, 11/1 Vatellor, 12/1 Blue Bear, 26/1 BAR.

Three-year-old form lines
Prix du Jockey Club: 1st Mieuxcé, 2nd **Vatellor**, 3rd Génetout
Grand Prix de Paris: 1st Mieuxcé, 2nd Sind, 3rd Alcali
Prix Royal-Oak: 1st **Fantastic**, 2nd Turbotin, 3rd Alcali

Fillies only
Prix de Diane, at Longchamp: 1st Mistress Ford, 2nd Dorinda, 3rd Royalebuchy
Prix Vermeille: 1st Mistress Ford, 2nd **Blue Bear**, 3rd **Love Call**

Older horses and inter-generational races
Prix du Président de la République: 1st **Corrida**, 2nd **Vatellor**, 3rd Bouillon
La Coupe d'Or at Maisons-Laffitte: 1st Davout, 2nd **Cousine**, 3rd **Samos**
Grand Prix de Deauville: 1st **Fantastic**, 2nd El Mers, 3rd **Cousine**

Abroad
In England
Derby Stakes: 1st Mahmoud, 2nd Taj Akbar, 3rd Thankerton
Ascot Gold Cup: 1st Quashed, 2nd Omaha, 3rd Bokbul, 5th **Samos**

In Belgium
Grand Prix International d'Ostende: 1st **Corrida**, 2nd Taj Akbar, 3rd **Vatellor**

The race

Corrida played up at the start, delaying the *grand départ* by several minutes, and when they did get going she was slow to stride. The sun was out as Kant led at a modest pace from Love Call and Fantastic.

Corrida had moved up into the first half-dozen by the time they reached the top of the hill and was third, behind Fantastic and the weakening Kant, as they entered the straight.

When Elliot asked Corrida to go, she went, quickly passing Fantastic and striding on to win by a comfortable length and a half. On the outside, Cousine found overdrive to take a never-threatening second a neck ahead of Fantastic, Blue Bear, Samos and Astrophel.

Post-race

This was the first win in the Prix de l'Arc de Triomphe for textile magnate Marcel Boussac who'd had runners in the race as far back as 1921. Boussac would continue to be a major figure in French and English racing for the next two decades.

John E. Watts, better known as 'Jack', had taken over from William Hall as Boussac's private trainer at the end of the previous year. He'd already tasted big race success when Call Boy won the 1927 Derby. Call Boy, like Corrida, had been ridden by Charlie Elliott.

Elliot, who tied with Steve Donoghue in the 1923 English jockeys championship before winning it outright the following year, had become Boussac's stable jockey in 1929.

Corrida's next outing was in the Champion Stakes, but the race was run at a dawdle which didn't suit her and she had to be content with third in the sprint for glory. As a result Dadji was utilised as a pacemaker in the Grand Prix de Marseille which she took for the second year.

Corrida would be back at Longchamp the following autumn, but Samos was off to stud where her best offspring was Prix Jean Prat-winner Marveil who also took the 1947 running of the King George VI Stakes-winner at Ascot. That race would shortly be amalgamated with the Queen Elizabeth Stakes to create what the French now call *l'arc anglaise*.

Result

1936 Prix de l'Arc de Triomphe
Longchamp. Sunday, 4 October 1936
Weights: 3yo c: 55.5kg, 3yo f: 54kg, 4yo+ c: 60kg, 4yo+ f: 58.5kg

1st Corrida (FR)　　　　4yo f　58.5kg　**0.8/1 fav**
by Coronach out of Zariba (Sardanapale). Marcel Boussac / Jack Watts / Charlie Elliott

2nd Cousine (FR)　　　　3yo f　54kg　**27/1**
by Deiri out of Jennie (Sunningdale). Princesse de Faucigny-Lucinge / Henry Count / Roger Brethès

3rd Fantastic (FR)　　　　3yo c　54kg　**4.8/1**
by Aethelstan out of Fanatic (Durbar II). Jean Stern / A. Roberts / Guy Duforez

Runners: 10 (FR 10). Distances: 1½, nk. Going: good. Time: 2m 38.60s

Also ran: 4th **Blue Bear** (FR) 3yo f, 5th **Samos** (FR) 4yo f, 6th **Astrophel** (FR) 5yo h. Unplaced: **Lorenzo de Medici** (FR) 4yo c, **Kant** (FR) 4yo c, **Vatellor** (FR) 3yo c, **Love Call** (FR) 3yo f (10th).

Corrida comes wide
to collect a million francs

Boussac's charge emulates Ksar and Motrico with second win

Background and fancied horses

The prize money was doubled and now the winner would collect one million francs. The reigning champion, Corrida, once again took a few races to warm up, finally showing the first hint of rejuvenation in the Prix du Président de la République. Off a funereal pace, she made up a huge amount of ground to finish fourth behind Vatellor, her supposed pacemaker Dadji and Édouard de Rothschild's Mousson.

In her next outing she reversed the form with Mousson when easily winning the Grand Prix International d'Ostende for the second time.

Corrida followed that by beating a high-class field, including the 1935 German Derby-winner Sturmvogel, in the Grosser Preis der Reichshaupstadt at Hoppegarten – the race formerly known as the Grosser Preis von Berlin and which reverted to that title in 2011. Coupled with her sometime pacemaker and winner of the Grosser Preis von Baden, Dadji, Corrida was even money to take a second Arc.

In addition to the aforementioned Mousson, Édouard de Rothschild also ran the Prix Vermeille-winner Tonnelle, and they came next in the betting at 4.3/1.

At nearly double that price were 2000 Guineas-winner Le Ksar along with Princess Aly Khan's pair Le Duc – runner-up in the Prix du Prince d'Orange – and Grand Prix de Paris-fourth Sultan Mahomed, who'd had a luckless run in the St Leger being baulked twice when sent off second favourite.

Princess Aly Khan was married to the Aga Khan III's son, Prince Aly. She was born Joan Yarde-Buller and is best known as one of the Bright Young Things. The previous December she had given birth to her first son, Karim, who in years to come would make his mark on Arc history.

Sultan Mahomed, who was trained in England by Frank Butters, was one of two raiders, the other being Corrida's Grosser Preis der Reichshaupstadt victim, Sturmvogel.

Betting

1/1 Corrida & Dadji (coupled), 4.3/1 Mousson & Tonnelle (coupled), 8/1 Le Ksar, 8.5/1 Le Duc & Sultan Mahomed (coupled), 14/1 BAR.

Three-year-old form lines

Prix du Jockey Club: 1st Clairvoyant, 2nd Actor, 3rd Galloway

Grand Prix de Paris: 1st Clairvoyant, 2nd Donatello II, 3rd Gonfalonier, 4th **Sultan Mahomed**, 5th **Tonnelle**, 0th **En Fraude**

Fillies only

Prix de Diane: 1st **En Fraude**, 2nd Sylvanire, 3rd **Tonnelle**

Prix Vermeille: 1st **Tonnelle**, 2nd **En Fraude**, 3rd Sylvanire

Older horses and inter-generational races

Prix du Président de la République: 1st **Vatellor**, 2nd **Dadji**, 3rd **Mousson**, 4th **Corrida**

La Coupe de Maisons-Laffitte: 1st Frexo, 2nd **Khasnadar**, 3rd Solmint

Grand Prix de Deauville: 1st Saint Preux, 2nd Cosquilla, 3rd **Khasnadar**

Prix du Prince d'Orange: 1st Gonfalonier, 2nd **Le Duc**, 3rd Trapolin

Abroad

In England

Derby Stakes: 1st Midday Sun, 2nd Sandsprite, 3rd Le Grand Duc, 13th **Le Ksar**

St Leger: 1st Chulmleigh, 2nd Fair Copy, 3rd Midday Sun, 11th **Sultan Mahomed**

In Germany

Grosser Preis von Baden: 1st **Dadji**, 2nd Gaio, 3rd Ricardo

In Belgium

Grand Prix International d'Ostende: 1st **Corrida**, 2nd **Mousson**, 3rd **Sanquinetto**

The race

On a damp and foggy afternoon the start was delayed momentarily by Sanguinetto, who was playing up. Once he settled, they were on their way but at a very leisurely stroll with Le Duc, Mousson, Dadji and Sturmvogel all prominent.

Eventually the pace quickened at the top of the hill. However there were still eight in the leading line as they fanned out in the straight, at which point the Rothschild pair, Mousson and Tonnelle, pushed on with the latter holding the advantage.

Meanwhile, Corrida faced a wall of horses and Elliot had to steer a very wide passage to find room for a run.

It looked an impossible task, but the acceleration Corrida mustered was simply phenomenal. Even so, it wasn't until the final stride that she collared Tonnelle, winning by a short head with Mousson a further one and a half lengths back in third. He was followed by En Fraude, Sturmvogel and Sultan Mahomed.

Post-race

A delighted Marcel Boussac was in the winner's enclosure again, and not for the last time. Charlie Elliot became the first jockey to win consecutive renewals on the same horse, while it was job done for Jack Watts, who returned to England to be replaced by Albert Swann.

Corrida, the third dual winner after Ksar and Motrico, had been brilliant again and was immediately retired, taking up residence at Boussac's Haras de Fresnay-le-Buffard operation in Normandy. Her second offspring, Coaraze, won the Prix du Jockey Club and Grand Prix de Saint-Cloud (formerly the Prix du Président de la République).

What might or might not have happened to Corrida next is documented in the 1940 essay. She is commemorated by the Prix Corrida, the current incarnation of which is run at Saint-Cloud in May.

Result

1937 Prix de l'Arc de Triomphe
Longchamp. Sunday, 3 October 1937
Weights: 3yo c: 55.5kg, 3yo f: 54kg, 4yo+ c: 60kg, 4yo+ f: 58.5kg

1st Corrida (FR)   5yo m 58.5kg **1/1 fav** (coupled with Dadji)
by Coronach out of Zariba (Sardanapale). Marcel Boussac / Jack Watts / Charlie Elliott

2nd Tonnelle (FR)   3yo f 54kg **4.3/1** (coupled with Mousson)
by Bubbles out of Bow Window (Grand Parade). Baron Édouard de Rothschild / Lucien Robert / P. Villecourt

3rd Mousson (FR)   3yo c 55.5kg **4.3/1** (coupled with Tonnelle)
by Rose Prince out of Spring Tide (Sans Souci II). Baron Édouard de Rothschild / Lucien Robert / Charles Bouillon

Runners: 12 (FR 10, GB 1, GER 1). Distances: sh, 1½. Going: good. Time: 2m 33.90s

Also ran: 4th **En Fraude** (FR) 3yo f, 5th **Sturmvogel** (GER) 5yo h, 6th **Sultan Mahomed** (FR) 3yo c. Unplaced: **Sanguinetto** (FR) 4yo c, **Vatellor** (FR) 4yo c, **Le Duc** (FR) 4yo c, **Dadji** (FR) 4yo c, **Le Ksar** (FR) 3yo c, **Khasnadar** (FR) 3yo c (12th).

Rothschild scores again with Éclair au Chocolat

A tasty treat before the peace evaporates

Background and fancied horses

Nazi Germany had annexed Austria in March and the Munich agreement, granting them Sudetenland in return for peace, was signed at the end of September. Unfortunately that peace would be short lived.

Nine days later the ten runners for what would turn out to be the last Prix de l'Arc de Triomphe for three years went to post.

Éclair au Chocolat was a late developing sort who had been used as a pacemaker for his stablemates Royal Gift and Bougainville in the Prix du Jockey Club. Running on his own merits he scored in the Prix Royal-Oak, despite swerving when coming under pressure close home. Now he was favourite for the Arc at 2.6/1, accompanied by Bougainville who hadn't lived up to his early promise.

Marcel Boussac's hard-pulling Prix du Jockey Club-victor Cillas, and his pacemaker Chesham, were half a point longer, followed by Prix Lupin-winner Castel Fusano, who'd been runner-up in the Prix Royal-Oak. Then came Canot, who'd made the frame in the Prix du Jockey Club, the Grand Prix de Paris – behind Federico Tesio's latest superstar Nearco – and the Prix Royal-Oak.

Next best were Prix du Prince d'Orange-winner Vatellor and Antonym. The latter had been beaten out of sight when favourite for the Prix du Président de la République but had made amends when lifting the Grosser Preis der Reichshauptstadt in mid-September.

Because of the uncertainty caused by the ongoing political situation, several potential runners stayed at home or were retired to stud early, including Prix du Président de la République-winner Victrix and the Italian-trained Procle, the winner of the Grosser Preis von Baden.

Betting

2.6/1 Éclair au Chocolat & Bougainville (coupled), 3.1/1 Cillas & Chesham (coupled), 4/1 Castel Fusano, 5.5/1 Canot, 9/1 Vatellor, 9.2/1 Antonym, 24/1 BAR.

Three-year-old form lines

Prix du Jockey Club: 1st **Cillas**, 2nd **Canot**, 3rd **Antonym**, 0th **Castel Fusano**, 0th **Bougainville**, 0th Éclair au Chocolat

Grand Prix de Paris: 1st Nearco, 2nd **Canot**, 3rd Bois Roussel

Prix Royal-Oak: 1st **Éclair au Chocolat**, 2nd **Castel Fusano**, 3rd **Canot**, 0th **Bougainville**, 0th **L'Ouragan III**

Fillies only

Prix de Diane: 1st Féerie, 2nd Ad Astra II, 3rd Gossip

Prix Vermeille: 1st Ma Normandie, 2nd Argolide, 3rd Terre Rose

Older horses and inter-generational races

Prix du Président de la République: 1st Victrix, 2nd Dadji, 3rd Asheratt, 0th **Vatellor**, 0th **Antonym**

La Coupe d'Or, at Maisons-Laffitte: 1st Khasnadar, 2nd **Castel Fusano**, 3rd Love Secret

Prix du Prince d'Orange: 1st **Vatellor**, 2nd Yoshiwara, 3rd Dilemne

Abroad

In England

Derby Stakes: 1st Bois Roussel, 2nd Scottish Union, 3rd Pasch

In Germany

Grosser Preis von Baden: 1st Procle, 2nd **Vatellor**, 3rd Dadji

The race

In mild but overcast conditions Éclair au Chocolat broke well but Bouillon soon took a pull and allowed Chesham, the Boussac second string, to take over from the hard-pulling Cillas.

The order then stayed roughly the same from the Petit Bois to the top of the hill. On the descent Cillas started to struggle and dropped back a few places. Then, when Chesham also tired, Bouillon asked Éclair au Chocolat to extend as they started to approach the turn-in.

He did as he was asked – and in style – quickly opening up a substantial advantage which he never relinquished. Castel Fusano chased after Éclair au Chocolat but in vain, and that effort may have cost him a place.

He was eventually passed by Antonym, who found plenty after being boxed-in, and on the line was short-headed by Canot who also flew at the death. Vatellor came home fifth, followed by Cillas.

None of them, though, could live with Éclair au Chocolat who had romped home two lengths clear of the battle for the places.

Post-race

The team responsible for Brantôme in 1934 had done it again. The victory helped decide several titles with Édouard de Rothschild becoming the champion owner, Lucien Robert the champion trainer based on prize money, and Bubbles the leading sire. Éclair au Chocolat retired joining Bubbles at Rothschild's Haras de Meautry.

Result

1938 Prix de l'Arc de Triomphe
Longchamp. Sunday, 9 October 1938
Weights: 3yo c: 55.5kg, 3yo f: 54kg, 4yo+ c: 60kg, 4yo+ f: 58.5kg

1st Éclair au Chocolat (FR) 3yo c   55.5kg **2.6/1 fav** (coupled with Bougainville)
by Bubbles out of Honey Sweet (Kircubbin). Baron Édouard de Rothschild / Lucien Robert / Charles Bouillon

2nd Antonym (FR)   3yo c   55.5kg **9.2/1**
by Vatout out of Antonine (Belfonds). H. M. Holdert / Henry Count / Arthur Tucker

3rd Canot (FR)   3yo c   55.5kg **5.5/1**
by Nino out of Canalette (Cannobie). Robert Lazard / William Cunnington / Rae Johnstone

Runners: 10 (FR 10). Distances: 2, ½. Going: heavy. Time: 2m 39.82s

Also ran: 4th **Castel Fusano** (FR) 3yo c, 5th **Vatellor** (FR) 5yo h, 6th **Cillas** (FR) 3yo c. Unplaced: **Lorenzo de Medici** (FR) 6yo h, **Chesham** (FR) 4yo c, **L'Ouragan III** (FR) 3yo c, **Bougainville** (FR) 3yo c (10th).

Prix de l'Arc de Triomphe cancelled

Pharis stars before racing is suspended in early September

The Munich agreement had just postponed the inevitable, and the situation escalated quickly from the end of August when the Nazi–Soviet pact, which took Russia out of the equation, was signed.

The race meeting at Clairefontaine on 30th August turned out to be the last before racing was suspended on 2nd September – a day after the Nazi invasion of Poland, and a day before Britain declared war after the deadline for Germany to withdraw had passed.

Before the suspension of racing, two potential greats had emerged, one on either side of the Channel. Marcel Boussac's Pharis had overcome a rough passage in the Prix du Jockey Club – where he was knocked back to last place entering the straight – to score emphatically by two and a half lengths.

He was also short of racing room in the Grand Prix de Paris, but again showed electric speed to steamroller his rivals once racing room appeared.

Unfortunately, the planned meeting in the St Leger with Blue Peter – the winner of the 2000 Guineas, Derby and the Eclipse – was doomed never to happen. Both Pharis and Blue Peter were retired soon after the declaration of war. Pharis in particular sired some useful sorts including Ardan, who will play his part in our story.

Three-year-old form lines
Prix du Jockey Club: 1st Pharis, 2nd Galérien, 3rd Bacchus
Grand Prix de Paris: 1st Pharis, 2nd Tricaméron, 3rd Etalon Or
Prix Royal-Oak: no race

Fillies only
Prix de Diane: 1st Lysistrata, 2nd Dream Girl, 3rd Kaligoussa
Prix Vermeille: no race

Older horses and inter-generational races
Prix du Président de la République: 1st Genievre, 2nd Military, 3rd Accord Parfait
La Coupe d'Or, at Maisons-Laffitte: no race
Grand Prix de Deauville: 1st Birikil, 2nd Dixiana, 3rd Peau Dane
Prix du Prince d'Orange: no race

Abroad
In England
Derby Stakes: 1st Blue Peter, 2nd Fox Cub, 3rd Heliopolis
St Leger: no race

In Germany

Grosser Preis von Baden: 1st Trollius, 2nd Organdy, 3rd Canzoni

In Belgium

Grand Prix International d'Ostende: 1st Mon Tresor, 2nd Goya, 3rd Vezzano

In Italy

Gran Premio di Milano: 1st Vezzano, 2nd Ursone, 3rd Acquaforte

Nazi occupation of France begins

Several Arc winners meet an untimely fate

After several months of what became known as the Phoney War, when there was no major military action, racing resumed in February. However, after France along with Holland and Belgium were attacked in early May, racing was suspended again, with the last meeting taking place at Auteuil on 9th May.

From then on it got much worse. In mid-May Chantilly was bombed and by early June was almost completely evacuated. A few days later, on 14th June, the occupation of Paris began.

In July, the Nazis presented a list of 27 horses in training, together with five stallions and 21 mares, they wanted to 'buy' for their Heeresgestüt Altefeld breeding operation. The fees to be paid were only available if the owners were French or Aryan, otherwise they paid nothing. Several owners who did qualify refused the payments.

The compulsorily purchased stallions were Brantôme, Pharis, Bubbles, Antonym and Mirza, while some of the mares came from the stock of the Aga Khan III and Édouard de Rothschild. This was just the first wave, as in the end more than 600 horses were officially deported to Germany and Hungary.

The Nazis liked racing and so an autumn calendar was put together to include a condensed season of substitute races, moving from the combined Poule d'Essai, through the Prix du Jockey Club to culminate with the Grand Prix de Paris.

As Longchamp was out of action, the races took place at Auteuil. There wouldn't be time to run the normal season finales, so once again the Prix de l'Arc de Triomphe was shelved. However, a full programme was pencilled in for 1941.

Three-year-old form lines

Poule d'Essai, combined substitute run at Auteuil in the autumn: 1st Djébel, 2nd Maurepas, 3rd Beaux Arts

Prix de Chantilly*, substitute for Prix du Jockey Club run at Auteuil in the autumn: 1st Quicko, 2nd Raffaello, 3rd Djébel

* the race title Prix de Chantilly has been utilised several times over the years. One version morphed into the Prix Niel, while the current Grand Prix de Chantilly started in 1997 as a replacement for the Grand Prix d'Évry.

Grand Prix de Paris, run at Auteuil in the autumn: 1st Maurepas, 2nd Quicko, 3rd Raffaello

Prix Royal-Oak: no race

Fillies only

Prix de Diane: no race

Prix Vermeille: no race

Older horses and inter-generational races

Prix du Président de la République: no race

La Coupe d'Or, at Maisons-Laffitte: no race

Grand Prix de Deauville: no race

Prix du Prince d'Orange: no race

Abroad

In England

New Derby Stakes, substitute race run at Newmarket July Course: 1st Pont l'Evêque, 2nd Turkhan, 3rd Lighthouse II

Ascot Gold Cup: no race

Yorkshire St Leger, substitute race run at Thirsk: 1st Turkhan, 2nd Stardust, 3rd Hippius

In Germany

Grosser Preis von Baden: no race

In Italy

Gran Premio di Milano: 1st Sirte, 2nd Bellini, 3rd Moroni

Horse deaths and disappearances

Many racehorses, including all of Marcel Boussac's, were evacuated to the south of France, but others were not so lucky.

Some were requisitioned to be used in the war effort, others were eaten – or abandoned to starve – by the invading Nazis or French refugees during the invasion, with more meeting the same fate at the end of the occupation during the Nazi retreat.

Among them were Arc heroes like **Mon Talisman** who starved to death alongside his son Clairvoyant, who'd won the 1937 Prix du Jockey Club. They were in the group of 100 or so horses left behind when Chantilly was evacuated.

Biribi was one of those compulsorily purchased. He did make it back but was in a poor state and died prematurely in early 1946.

There are two reports concerning dual-winner **Corrida**; one points to her being shot by a German soldier who tried to ride her into battle; the other suggests that she disappeared from Haras de Fresnay-le-Buffard during the Battle of Normandy.

The most recent winner of the Arc, **Éclair au Chocolat**, was also never seen again.

All of the five original stallions demanded by the Nazis made it back to France, although **Brantôme** returned with an injured eye.

Le Pacha scores in smallest Arc field

Son of Biribi wins Prix Royal-Oak replay

Background and fancied horses

The main races of the season were to be shared among Longchamp, Auteuil and Maisons-Laffitte. Public transport was limited but racegoers arrived by all sorts of improvised means.

The Société d'Encouragement was obliged to remove all Jewish members from the club but came up with various subversive means to protect them and also the interests of foreign-owned stables, which included running their horses under other people's names.

As the Third Republic was now over, the Prix du Président de la République was renamed as the Grand Prix de Saint-Cloud. In addition, La Coupe d'Or run at Maisons-Laffitte was also retitled as La Coupe de Maisons-Laffitte.

Not surprisingly the prize money for the Prix de l'Arc de Triomphe took a downturn, being reduced to 600,000 francs to the winner, and there was no sweepstake.

Marcel Boussac owned the market leaders, Djébel and Jock, who were returned at 0.8/1. The first-named had won the 1939 Middle Park Stakes and returned to England the following season to cruise home in the 2000 Guineas. He was favourite for the Derby but, as the Germans advanced, instead of going to Epsom he was evacuated to the south of France.

Djébel returned to Paris in October, where he won the substitute Poule d'Essai at Auteuil but disappointingly could only manage third in the Prix de Chantilly, the replacement race for the Prix du Jockey Club.

This year he'd won three times before finishing second twice to Maurepas – the winner of the substitute Grand Prix de Paris of 1940.

Jock was a late starter due to an injury and the war. But he'd won twice as a four-year-old in 1940 and was unbeaten in three appearances this term, including winning the Grand Prix de Deauville which was held at Longchamp.

Philippe Gund's Le Pacha, who liked to be prominent in his races, had won all of his six outings, including impressive successes in the Prix du Jockey Club and Grand Prix de Paris. He'd also shown his mettle with a hard-fought victory over Nepenthe in the Prix Royal-Oak. In a sensationally overround book he, together with his pacemaker Le Flutian, traded at 1.8/1.

Owned by Lord Derby, but running through necessity in the colours of his racing manager the Marquis de Saint-Sauveur, Nepenthe was 5.3/1. He'd finished runner-up to Le Pacha in both the Grand Prix de Paris and Prix Royal-Oak. In the latter he collared Le Pacha in the last 50 metres only for Le Pacha to fight back and score by a short head, albeit aided by the fact that Guy Duforez, Nepenthe's jockey, had dropped his whip.

The only filly running, Longthanh, had won the Poule d'Essai des Pouliches and Prix Vermeille, after only finding one too good in the Prix de Diane.

Completing the septet in the smallest field in the history of the Arc was Lorenzo de Medici. The nine-year-old had first run in the Arc as long ago as 1936 and was making his third appearance.

Betting

0.8/1 Djébel & Jock (coupled), 1.8/1 Le Pacha & Le Flutian (coupled), 5.3/1 Nepenthe, 15/1 Longthanh, 50/1 Lorenzo de Medici

Three-year-old form lines

Prix du Jockey Club, at Longchamp: 1st **Le Pacha**, DH2nd Pizzicato, DH2nd Le Pampre

Grand Prix de Paris: 1st **Le Pacha**, 2nd **Nepenthe**, 3rd Pizzicato

Prix Royal-Oak: 1st **Le Pacha**, 2nd **Nepenthe**, 3rd Clodoche

Fillies only

Prix de Diane, at Longchamp: 1st Sapotille II, 2nd **Longthanh**, 3rd Mzimba

Prix Vermeille: 1st **Longthanh**, 2nd Mascotte, 3rd Dauphine

Older horses and inter-generational races

Grand Prix de Saint-Cloud, at Longchamp: 1st Maurepas, 2nd **Djébel**, 3rd Majano

Grand Prix de Deauville, at Longchamp: 1st **Jock**, 2nd Majano, 3rd Adaris

The race

As expected, Le Flutian went off in front with his stablemate Le Pacha tucking in behind, followed by Nepenthe and then the Boussac pair, Djébel and Jock.

Le Flutian led to the entrance of the straight, when, job done, he dropped back, leaving Le Pacha in the lead. Jockey Paul Francolon pushed his mount on and Nepenthe went with him, but there was no response from either Djébel or Jock.

The one-two in the Prix Royal-Oak again settled down to fight it out. Le Pacha, who was always seemingly just going a bit stronger than his rival, won the battle royal, prevailing by a short head with two lengths back to Djébel, followed by Jock, Longthanh and Le Flutian.

Post-race

In becoming the third horse to win both the Prix du Jockey Club and the Arc, Le Pacha had more than repaid owner Philippe Gund, who had shelled out 500,000 francs for the then unraced colt at the dispersal sale of the late Hippolyte Randon in April.

It was the second win for the Cunningtons, with John's Le Pacha adding to his uncle Elijah's win with Massine in 1924.

This was the highlight of jockey Paul Francolon's career; five years later he suffered a career-ending fall in which his legs were paralysed. Using pioneering techniques, a doctor in America helped him to walk again using braces and crutches, his fare to the USA having been raised by racing charities.

After seven wins in a row, Le Pacha, who was by 1926-winner Biribi out of a mare sired by Ksar, was retired for the year.

Result

1941 Prix de l'Arc de Triomphe
Longchamp. Sunday, 5 October 1941
Weights: 3yo c: 55.5kg, 3yo f: 54kg, 4yo+ c: 60kg, 4yo+ f: 58.5kg

1st Le Pacha (FR)   3yo c   55.5kg   **1.8/1** (coupled with Le Flutian)
by Biribi out of Advertencia (Ksar). Philippe Gund / John Cunnington snr / Paul Francolon

2nd Nepenthe (FR)   3yo c   55.5kg   **5.3/1**
by Plassy out of Frisky (Isard II). Marquis de Saint-Sauveur (for Lord Derby) / Richard Carver / Guy Duforez

3rd Djébel (FR)   4yo c   60kg   **0.8/1 fav** (coupled with Jock)
by Tourbillon out of Loika (Gay Crusader). Marcel Boussac / Percy Carter / Jacques Doyasbère

Runners: 7 (FR 7). Distances: sh, 2. Going: good. Time: 2m 36.26s

Also ran: 4th **Jock** (FR) 5yo h, 5th **Longthanh** (FR) 3yo f, 6th **Le Flutian** (FR) 3yo c, 7th **Lorenzo de Medici** (FR) 9yo h.

1942
Devastating Djébel
scores with authority

Third success for Boussac; winner becomes a great sire

Background and fancied horses

Times continued to be hard under the German occupation. Due to the continuing severe shortage of food for horses in training, and those at stud, there was a strict limit on the racehorse population, who were each issued with a ration card.

The total number allowed was 2,100. Therefore, if a horse proved to be short of top class it would be retired at the end of its three-year-old career in order that others could have a chance.

Under the prevailing conditions it was a triumph over adversity that racing took place at all. That the Arc was again an all-French affair was inevitable.

Last year's winner and third returned and were faced by seven three-year-olds including one filly. Le Pacha was having a fairly light campaign, as he suffered from occasional rheumatism, but was fit enough when losing his unbeaten record in the Grand Prix de Saint-Cloud which was again run at Longchamp.

He'd taken over from his pacemaker with 800 metres to run but was then dominated by Djébel, who delivered a spectacular burst of acceleration in the last 100 metres.

Back to winning ways next time when securing the Prix du Prince d'Orange, Le Pacha, coupled with his pacemaker Massinor, was sent off favourite at 0.8/1 for his bid to gain revenge on Djébel and repeat last year's Arc triumph.

While Le Pacha's training regime had been made easier, Djébel's had been made tougher. He had always appeared as though he only needed light work, but after his disappointments last backend he was subjected to a much more strenuous training scheme.

It seemed to be working, as evidenced by the amazing turn of foot he'd shown in cutting down Le Pacha in the Grand Prix de Saint-Cloud. However, the real test would be whether his level of form would hold up during the autumn campaign.

He arrived on Arc day having won his prep race, and coupled with the Prix Royal-Oak victor, Tifinar, was joint second best in the market at 1.8/1.

It was double figures bar the coupled horses bringing in Vigilance – the top three-year-old filly of the campaign – Prix Hocquart-winner Hern the Hunter, and Tornado, who'd been placed in the Prix du Jockey Club, Grand Prix de Paris and Prix Royal-Oak.

Betting

0.8/1 Le Pacha & Massinor (coupled), 1.8/1 Djébel & Tifinar (coupled), 11/1 Vigilance, 14/1 Hern the Hunter, 16/1 Tornado, 64/1 BAR

Three-year-old form lines
Prix du Jockey Club, at Longchamp: 1st Magister, 2nd **Tornado**, 3rd **Hern the Hunter**
Grand Prix de Paris: 1st Magister, 2nd **Tifinar**, 3rd **Tornado**
Prix Royal-Oak: 1st **Tifinar**, 2nd **Tornado**, 3rd Magister

Fillies only
Prix de Diane, at Longchamp: 1st **Vigilance**, 2nd Esméralda, 3rd Monnaie d'Or
Prix Vermeille: 1st **Vigilance**, 2nd Guirlande, 3rd Esméralda

Older horses and inter-generational races
Grand Prix de Saint-Cloud, at Longchamp: 1st **Djébel**, 2nd **Le Pacha**, 3rd Porphyros
Prix du Prince d'Orange: 1st **Le Pacha**, 2nd Nabah, 3rd Tranquil

The race

Racegoers' loyalties were split between last year's winner and the horse that had beaten him in the Grand Prix de Saint-Cloud. Unfortunately, the eagerly anticipated rematch between Le Pacha and Djébel never materialised.

All looked to be going well as Le Pacha bowled along in the lead on what was holding ground. He galloped strongly until approaching the straight when disaster struck as he broke down and immediately dropped back through the field.

The stunned crowd had only just taken in what they had witnessed when Djébel appeared on the scene. He was full of running and, in a manner that showed he was clearly superior to the remaining challengers, simply scampered away to win completely unchallenged by an easy two lengths.

Tornado took second, with another one and a half lengths back to Prix de Nice-winner Breughel, who just got the better of Hern the Hunter by a head for third. Further back came Vigilance followed by Le Pacha, who limped home in sixth.

Post-race

The team responsible for Djébel was comprised of some of the most successful individuals in the history of the Arc. After Corrida in 1936 and 1937, this was a third win for owner Marcel Boussac, who was now two years into what would turn out to be a run of nine podium finishes.

Charles Semblat also added to his strong record in the Arc, notching up the first of what would be four wins as a trainer after his successes as a jockey on Mon Talisman, Pearl Cap and Motrico.

For jockey Jacques Doyasbère, who had been third on Djébel last year, it was a first win. However, he would be in the frame again for the next three years, and would partner a dual-winner in the 1950s.

Whether or not Le Pacha could have given Djébel a run for his money is a matter of conjecture. However, off the course Djébel turned out to be in a different league to his rival.

Both retired after the Arc with Le Pacha, whose best offspring was the 1950 Italian Oaks-winner La Cadette, being completely eclipsed at stud by Djébel's multitude of big race winners, which included the likes of My Babu (1948 2000 Guineas), Arbar (1948 Prix du Cadran and Ascot Gold Cup), Galcador (1950 Epsom Derby) and Hugh Lupus (1955 Irish 2000 Guineas).

Djébel was champion sire in France in 1949 and 1956 and made the top ten on five other occasions. He also had a big impact on the Arc, siring 1949-victor Coronation, with a further six of his descendants also going on to win the Longchamp showpiece.

The Group 3 Prix Djébel, a trial for the Poule d'Essai des Poulains and 2000 Guineas, which started in 1949, was run at Maisons-Laffitte until 2019 and now takes place at Deauville.

Result
1942 Prix de l'Arc de Triomphe
Longchamp. Sunday, 4 October 1942
Weights: 3yo c: 55.5kg, 3yo f: 54kg, 4yo+ c: 60kg, 4yo+ f: 58.5kg

1st Djébel (FR)　　　　　5yo h　60kg　　**1.8/1** (coupled with Tifinar)
by Tourbillon out of Loika (Gay Crusader). Marcel Boussac / Charles Semblat / Jacques Doyasbère

2nd Tornado (FR)　　　　3yo c　55.5kg　**16/1**
by Tourbillon out of Roseola (Swynford). Jean Couturié / A. Duvivier / Charles Bouillon

3rd Breughel (FR)　　　　3yo c　55.5kg　**73/1**
by Brantôme out of Buchanite (Son-in-Law). Madame M. Anguenot / __ / René Bertiglia

Runners: 9 (FR 9). Distances: 2, 1½. Going: holding. Time: 2m 37.96s

Also ran: 4th **Hern the Hunter** (FR) 3yo c, 5th **Vigilance** (_) 3yo f, 6th **Le Pacha** (FR) 4yo c. Unplaced: **Massinor** (FR) 3yo c, **Tifinar** (FR) 3yo c, **Châteauroux** (FR) 3yo c (9th).

Verso II is victorious at Le Tremblay

Race moved after the back straight at Longchamp is blown up

Background and fancied horses

As the German occupation continued there was the real danger that racing might be forced to stop through a lack of staff in stables and at the racecourse. There was some relief when the Société d'Encouragement managed to secure a conscription amnesty for jockeys and stable lads. This was partly due to the Nazis wanting to try and maintain morale by keeping life as normal as possible in Paris, where going racing was part of the fabric of life.

On 4 April at Longchamp an American air raid, probably targeting the Renault factory at nearby Bilancourt, started as the runners for the first race were on their way to post. The warning sirens wailed and were followed by the American bombs and accompanying German anti-aircraft fire.

The explosions started near the windmill at the start of the Arc course, and proceeded in a straight line to the Petit Bois. Seven spectators who'd gone to view the racing from near the wood were killed. There were no further casualties as none of the 14 bombs landed near the grandstands.

In the spirit of the age, the meeting went ahead after the course was repaired, with the first race being run about 90 minutes late. Afterwards, though, the Germans decided that future racing at Longchamp would be suspended in case there was another raid. The programme was rejigged and weekday races were run at Maisons-Laffitte with the weekend action taking place at Auteuil and Le Tremblay.

The latter had been inaugurated in 1906 and was situated in the south east of Paris, adjacent to the Bois de Vincennes and in fact only 2km east of the Vincennes trotting hippodrome. Le Tremblay had a wide straight and was easier to access than the other tracks, so all the top races were to take place there including the Arc, which was to be run over the slightly reduced distance of 2,300 metres.

Hubert de Chambure's Verso II had been green as a two-year-old but finished the year with a stunning eight-length success over the useful Atilla II. He beat Pensbury in the Prix du Jockey Club but succumbed to that rival in the Grand Prix de Paris, before finishing his preparation when scoring in the Prix Royal-Oak. Coupled with his inferior stablemate Astérian, he was 1.2/1 favourite to lift the Arc.

Pensbury, a nervous sort, had tried to make up ground too quickly in the Prix du Jockey Club before winning the Grand Prix de Paris in grand style. However, he boiled over in the Prix du Prince d'Orange, finishing last behind his useful pacemaker Norseman, who dead-heated with Guirlande. Pensbury and Norseman were coupled at 3.8/1.

Esméralda was probably the best of Marcel Boussac's pair. She'd taken the Poule d'Essai des Pouliches in 1942 before finishing second in the Prix de Diane. Esméralda was priced at 6/1 along with the returning Tifinar, who'd been sent off favourite when third home in the Grand Prix de Saint-Cloud.

Prix Vermeille-winner Folle Nuit at 9/1 was the only three-year-old filly present. She looked held on her fourth in the Grand Prix de Paris. Of the others, Cordon Rouge III arrived on the back of wins in La Coupe de Maisons-Laffitte and the Grand Prix de Deauville. While Grand Prix de Saint-Cloud-victor Escamillo was coupled with the aforementioned Guirlande, who'd dead-heated with Norseman in the Prix du Prince d'Orange.

Betting

1.2/1 Verso II & Astérian (coupled), 3.8/1 Norseman & Pensbury (coupled), 6/1 Esméralda & Tifinar (coupled), 9/1 Folle Nuit, 9.5/1 Cordon Rouge III, 15/1 Escamillo & Guirlande (coupled), 28/1 BAR.

Three-year-old form lines

Prix du Jockey Club, at Le Tremblay: 1st **Verso II**, 2nd **Pensbury**, 3rd Aristocrate, 4th **Norseman**

Grand Prix de Paris, at Le Tremblay: 1st **Pensbury**, 2nd **Verso II**, 3rd Marsyas, 4th **Folle Nuit**

Prix Royal-Oak, at Le Tremblay: 1st **Verso II**, 2nd Marsyas, 3rd **Norseman**

Fillies only

Prix de Diane, at Le Tremblay: 1st Caravelle, 2nd Buena Vista, 3rd La Chatoulue, 5th **Folle Nuit**

Prix Vermeille, at Le Tremblay: 1st **Folle Nuit**, 2nd Caravelle, 3rd La Chatoulue

Older horses and inter-generational races

Grand Prix de Saint-Cloud, at Maisons-Laffitte: 1st **Escamillo**, 2nd Un Gaillard, 3rd **Tifinar**

La Coupe de Maisons-Laffitte: 1st **Cordon Rouge III**, 2nd **Ace Card**, 3rd **Châteauroux**

Grand Prix de Deauville, at Maisons-Laffitte: 1st **Cordon Rouge III**, 2nd Esméralda, 3rd Seraphin

Prix du Prince d'Orange, at Le Tremblay: DH1st **Guirlande**, DH1st **Norseman**, 3rd Lackland, 6th/last **Pensbury**

The race

The third meeting of Pensbury and Verso II was quickly underway, with Norseman going straight into the lead. He set a testing pace for Verso II, who was more than content to slipstream in behind Pensbury's pacemaker.

As the race went on, the order stayed the same with Verso II looking as though he was just biding his time, while fans of Pensbury were already looking worried as he wasn't travelling well. Entering the straight the vibes given off by Verso II proved to be correct as he lengthened in style putting the race to bed in just a few strides.

In the end he ambled home three lengths clear of Esméralda, who collared Norseman in the last few metres. Two lengths further back came Cordon Rouge III, Châteauroux and Sir Fellah. As in the Prix du Prince d'Orange, Pensbury's suspect temperament had got the better of him; he ran no race at all, finishing in rear.

Post-race

After coming third on Fantastic in 1936 and second on Nepenthe in 1941, jockey Guy Duforez finally broke his Arc duck, as did owner Hubert de Chambure – a banker and rubber tree planter – and Chantilly-based trainer Charles Clout. Verso II, the fourth Prix du Jockey Club-winner to take the Arc, had won with assuredness and was kept in training.

Result

1943 Prix de l'Arc de Triomphe
Le Tremblay. Sunday, 3 October 1943
Weights: 3yo c: 55.5kg, 3yo f: 54kg, 4yo+ c: 60kg, 4yo+ f: 58.5kg

1st Verso II (FR)   3yo c   55.5kg   **1.2/1 fav** (coupled with Astérian)
by Pinceau out of Variete (La Farina). Comte Hubert de Chambure / Charles Clout / Guy Duforez

2nd Esméralda (FR)   4yo f   58.5kg   **6/1** (coupled with Tifinar)
by Tourbillon out of Sanaa (Asterus). Marcel Boussac / Charles Semblat / Jacques Doyasbère

3rd Norseman (FR)   3yo c   55.5kg   **3.8/1** (coupled with Pensbury)
by Umidwar out of Tara (Teddy). Madame René de Bonnand / John Cunnington snr / Henri Signoret

Runners: 13 (FR 13). Distances: 3, sh nk. Going: holding. Time: 2m 33.40s

Also ran: 4th **Cordon Rouge III** (FR) 6yo h, 5th **Châteauroux** (FR) 4yo c, 6th **Sir Fellah** (FR) 3yo c. Unplaced: **Ace Card** (FR) 4yo c, **Escamillo** (FR) 4yo c, **Tifinar** (FR) 4yo c, **Guirlande** (FR) 4yo f, **Astérian** (FR) 3yo c, **Pensbury** (FR) 3yo c, **Folle Nuit** (FR) 3yo f (13th).

1944

Ardan wins first Arc after the liberation of Paris

Second running at Le Tremblay

Background and fancied horses

In their bid to overcome the Nazis, the British air force tried to knock out strategic targets in Paris. They attacked the railway bridge linking Maisons-Laffitte with Satrouville in May on the day before the Prix Lupin. Satrouville bore the brunt of the first raid but two other attacks followed, with trainer Roch Fillipi being killed at his stables in Maisons-Laffitte and several horses being injured. A bomb also landed at the entrance to the racecourse, leading to the temporary closure of the track.

However, the tide was starting to turn, though, and a few days later the allies landed in Normandy on what is known as D-Day in English and J-Jour in French. The racing community was on the one hand delighted that the allies were on their way, but on the other concerned about the fate of the many studs in Normandy.

There were more bombs in Chantilly in early August, which landed on the famous Les Aigles gallops, but luckily missed the town itself. A couple of weeks after that, the French Resistance rose up and a week later the allies arrived to complete the liberation on 25 August.

Racing, which had understandably been suspended during the liberation, resumed on 6 October at Le Tremblay, where Verso II won the featured Grand Prix de Deauville. It proved to be Verso II's swansong as he finished lame, with what looked to be a recurrence of the tendon injury that had kept him on the sidelines since last year's Arc.

To make up for lost ground the flat season continued into December, with the Arc pushed back to 22 October and set to be run again at Le Tremblay. Longchamp had been back in action temporarily but was then requisitioned as a base for American soldiers.

Marcel Boussac was triple-handed with Ardan, who won the Prix du Jockey Club from the front, probably his best chance. Ardan had tried to repeat the tactics in the longer Grand Prix de Paris but hadn't settled and, although first past the post, was demoted to third after leaning into Sampiero who couldn't avoid bumping into the eventual runner-up Deux-Pour-Cent.

After a break, Ardan finished third in the Prix Royal-Oak, being beaten a head and a short head when looking like he needed the race.

He was coupled with Esméralda – second to Un Gaillard in the Grand Prix de Saint-Cloud and to Verso II in the Grand Prix de Deauville – and the easy Prix Kergorlay-winner Marsyas, and they were 1.5/1 shots.

Next came Norseman, who preferred cut in the ground and had not been suited by the prevailing firm conditions. He had, though, beaten Un Gaillard in a stirring finish to the Prix des Sablons and with the ground now heavy, found plenty of takers and ended up at 3.5/1.

Un Gaillard had been in good form, winning several races including the Grand Prix de Saint-Cloud and La Coupe de Maisons-Laffitte, but had suffered one off-day when down the field in the Prix de Bois Roussel. Prix du Prince d'Orange-winner Folle Nuit was the last horse in single figures, followed by the aforementioned Sampiero, and Lazare, whose best form looked to be behind him.

Betting

1.5/1 Ardan & Esméralda & Marsyas (all coupled), 3.5/1 Norseman, 5/1 Un Gaillard, 6.3/1 Folle Nuit, 13/1 Lazare, 13/1 Sampiero, 27/1 BAR.

Three-year-old form lines

Prix du Jockey Club, at Le Tremblay: 1st **Ardan**, 2nd **Sampiero**, 3rd Laborde
Grand Prix de Paris, at Le Tremblay: 1st (2nd ptp) **Deux-Pour-Cent**, 2nd (3rd ptp) **Sampiero**, 3rd (1st ptp) **Ardan**, 5th **Samaritain**
Prix Royal-Oak, at Le Tremblay: 1st **Samaritain**, 2nd Brazza, 3rd **Ardan**

Fillies only

Prix de Diane, at Le Tremblay: 1st Pointe à Pitre, 2nd La Belle du Canet, 3rd Oalgabla
Prix Vermeille, at Le Tremblay: 1st La Belle du Canet, 2nd Algat, 3rd Pointre à Pitre

Older horses and inter-generational races

Grand Prix de Saint-Cloud, at Le Tremblay: 1st **Un Gaillard**, 2nd **Esméralda**, 3rd **Marsyas**
La Coupe de Maisons-Laffitte, at Le Tremblay: 1st **Un Gaillard**, 2nd Galène, 3rd Tifinar
Grand Prix de Deauville, at Le Tremblay: 1st Verso II, 2nd **Esméralda**, 3rd Galène
Prix du Prince d'Orange, at Le Tremblay: 1st **Folle Nuit**, 2nd Galène, 3rd **Guirlande**

The race

The front-running Norseman was soon to the fore, followed by Esméralda and Un Gaillard ahead of Ardan, who'd been settled by Jacques Doyasbère, with Lazare in last place. The order remained the same until Norseman started to drop back on the home turn. Then Un Gaillard went on, but Ardan was swinging off the bit and at the 100-metre pole he swept by majestically to claim the prize by an easy length and in doing so became the fifth Prix du Jockey Club-victor to win the Arc.

There was another one and a half lengths back to Deux-Pour-Cent, who had struggled to keep up in the early stages but ran on late to take third ahead of Esméralda and Samaritain, with Lazare, who made some progress in the straight, finishing sixth.

Post-race

Ardan was a winner for Pharis, who'd been the best horse in France in 1939. After Corrida's two wins, plus Djébel's victory two years ago, it was a fourth success for Marcel Boussac.

Charles Semblat, who'd won three times as a jockey, doubled his training tally, and Jacques Doyasbère the rider of Semblat's first winner as a trainer, Djébel, recorded his second success.

Ardan was kept in training, but last year's winner Verso II had gone to stud after his Grand Prix de Deauville victory. He produced a few decent types, of which Lavandin, who won the Derby in 1956, was the standout.

Result

1944 Prix de l'Arc de Triomphe
Le Tremblay. Sunday, 22 October 1944
Weights: 3yo c: 55.5kg, 3yo f: 54kg, 4yo+ c: 60kg, 4yo+ f: 58.5kg

1st Ardan (FR)   3yo c   55.5kg   **1.5/1 fav**
by Pharis out of Adargatis (Astérus). Marcel Boussac / Charles Semblat / Jacques Doyasbère

2nd Un Gaillard (FR)   6yo h   60kg   **5/1**
by Biribi out of Undies (Jaeger). Julien Décrion / Maurice d'Okhuysen / Roger Poincelet

3rd Deux-Pour-Cent (FR) 3yo c   55.5kg   **27/1**
by Deiri out of Dix Pour Cent (Feridoon). J. M. Sion / Maurice Adele / G. Delaurie

Runners: 11 (FR 11). Distances: 1, 1½. Going: heavy. Time: 2m 35.00s

Also ran: 4th **Esméralda** (FR) 5yo m, 5th **Samaritain** (FR) 3yo c, 6th **Lazare** (FR) 6yo h. Unplaced: **Norseman** (FR) 4yo c, **Marsyas** (FR) 4yo c, **Guirlande** (FR) 5yo m, **Folle Nuit** (FR) 4yo f, **Sampiero** (FR) 3yo c (11th).

Nikellora has her day in the sun

In-and-out performer becomes third filly to win the Arc

Background and fancied horses

The return of the requisitioned horses from Germany, although welcomed, caused problems as it was impossible to tell who the in-foal mares had been covered by. To start with all horses exported after June 1940 and their offspring were banned from racing. A case-by-case reinstatement process was then put in place.

Deauville was still out of action and Saint-Cloud would not resume until October. However, Longchamp returned to action in early summer. A stable lads' strike for more pay and a guaranteed day off led to the Prix du Jockey Club and Prix de Diane being postponed for two weeks and moved to Longchamp.

A shortage of coal meant that the pumps for the water tanks at Chantilly couldn't be used so the gallops were rock hard, which delayed the appearance of many horses. It didn't stop the dominance of Marcel Boussac's horses, who were mopping up all and sundry in France.

Boussac was also responsible for the first French runner to race in England since the War, when Priam only lost out by a short head to 2000 Guineas-winner Court Martial in the Champion Stakes. And with Ardan, Coaraze and Micipsa he had an extremely strong hand for the Arc, which was back at Longchamp and over the full distance of 2,400 metres.

Reigning champion Ardan, had been in sparkling form, racking up six successes including the Grand Prix de Saint-Cloud. Coaraze, who was Corrida's only offspring to race, had won the last Prix du Jockey Club confined to French-breds, while Micipsa, who was often used as a pacemaker, was good enough to land the Prix du Prince d'Orange. Together they were 0.1/1-shots – 1/10 in old money.

Also coupled were Jean Couturié's Basileus and Galène. The former had finished runner-up on several occasions, including in the Prix du Jockey Club and Prix Royal-Oak, but did come out on top in the Grand Prix de Deauville. Galène, who won the 1944 Prix Conseil Municipal, was there to make the pace.

Nikellora, the only filly to line up, had won the Poule d'Essai des Pouliches and Prix de Diane before disappointing in the Grand Prix de Paris. She also lost out by a length to Coaraze in the Prix Jacques Le Marois before winning the Prix Vermeille.

Betting

0.1/1 Ardan & Coaraze & Micipsa (all coupled), 9.3/1 Basileus & Galène (coupled), 10/1 Nikellora, 33/1 BAR.

Three-year-old form lines

Prix du Jockey Club, at Longchamp: 1st **Coaraze**, 2nd **Basileus**, 3rd **His Eminence**, 4th **Chanteur**

Grand Prix de Paris: 1st Caracalla, 2nd **Chanteur**, 3rd Mistral, 4th **Coaraze**, 0th **Nikellora**

Prix Royal-Oak: 1st Caracalla, 2nd **Basileus**, 3rd **Chanteur**

Fillies only

Prix de Diane, at Longchamp: 1st **Nikellora**, 2nd Raïta, 3rd Blue Top
Prix Vermeille: 1st **Nikellora**, 2nd Raïta, 3rd Blue Top

Older horses and inter-generational races

Grand Prix de Saint-Cloud, at Maisons-Laffitte: 1st **Ardan**, 2nd Priam, 3rd **Samaritain**

La Coupe de Maisons-Laffitte, at Longchamp: 1st Priam, 2nd _, 3rd **Tribi**

Grand Prix de Deauville, at Longchamp: 1st **Basileus**, 2nd **Micipsa**, 3rd _

Prix du Prince d'Orange: 1st **Micipsa**, 2nd **Samaritain**, 3rd **Galène**

The race

As expected, Galène set off in front at a lively pace, followed by last year's winner Ardan, and they maintained their stations until entering the home straight. There, Galène dropped away, leaving Ardan in the lead. Roger Brethès moved Chanteur up alongside Ardan, and the two of them engaged in an elongated duel.

Behind them, though, Rae Johnstone on Nikellora was sitting motionless. When asked at the 200-metre pole, the Prix Vermeille-winner quickly accelerated, producing a fine turn of speed. She easily overhauled Ardan and Chanteur to secure victory by three parts of a length at the line.

Ardan just won the battle for second place by a short neck from Chanteur. They in turn were followed through by the fast-finishing Basileus, just a further neck behind, with a length to Samaritain and His Eminence in fifth and sixth. Coaraze, who'd beaten Nikellora in the Prix Jacques Le Marois, was last.

Post-race

Although Nikellora was clearly the best filly around, she had looked to have it all to do after the reverses against the colts. But this was her day and she performed to her best while others didn't, and she was a deserved winner for Madame Robert Patureau, who had leased her for her three-year-old career.

It was the first win in the race for trainer René Pelat and jockey Rae Johnstone, but it wouldn't be the pair's last. In fact, it was a great spare ride for Johnstone, who'd finished in the frame three times before the war, as he'd taken over from her usual rider Marcel Lollièrou, who'd been claimed for Samaritain.

Two weeks later Nikellora reappeared, only to finish third to Basileus and Micipsa, when not getting a clear run, in the Prix du Conseil Municipal. She was kept in training but didn't reproduce her best efforts and was retired to the paddocks. Her most talented offspring was Chief, who won the Prix d'Isapahan and Prix Caracalla in 1957. The latter race bears the name of a horse that will figure in our story sooner than soon. Ardan, who'd won last year and been second this time, was put away for the winter and would be back.

Result

1945 Prix de l'Arc de Triomphe
Longchamp. Sunday, 30 October 1945
Weights: 3yo c: 55.5kg, 3yo f: 54kg, 4yo+ c: 60kg, 4yo+ f: 58.5kg

1st Nikellora (FR) 3yo f 54kg **10/1**
by Vatellor out of Niki (Palais Royal). Madame Robert Patureau / René Pelat / Rae Johnstone

2nd Ardan (FR) 4yo c 60kg **0.1/1 fav** (coupled with Coaraze & Micipsa)
by Pharis out of Adargatis (Astérus). Marcel Boussac / Charles Semblat / Jacques Doyasbère

3rd Chanteur (FR) 3yo c 55.5kg **47/1**
by Château Bouscaut out of La Diva (Blue Skies). Pierre Magot / Henry Count / Roger Brethès

Runners: 11 (FR 11). Distances: ¾, sh nk. Going: good. Time: 2m 34.82s

Also ran: 4th **Basileus** (FR) 3yo c, 5th **Samaritain** (FR) 4yo c, 6th **His Eminence** (FR) 3yo c. Unplaced: **Seer** (FR) 5yo h, **Tribi** (FR) 5yo h, **Galène** (FR) 6yo h, **Micipsa** (FR) 5yo h, **Coaraze** (FR) 3yo c (11th).

Caracalla gives Boussac a fifth Arc

First foreign runner since 1937.
King George VI Stakes clashes with the Arc

Background and fancied horses

Marcel Boussac had such an embarrassment of riches in 1945 that his unbeaten Grand Prix de Paris and Prix Royal-Oak-winner, Caracalla, was surplus to requirements with regards to his Arc team. This year the son of Tourbillon had overcome the effects of a virus to win on seasonal debut and seemed to be back to his best when winning the Prix du Dangu at the start of June.

He then joined the Boussac raiding party headed for Royal Ascot, which produced three winners: Priam took the Hardwicke Stakes; Marsyas the Queen Alexandra Stakes; and most importantly for our story, Caracalla hacked up in the Gold Cup.

Back in France he picked up a slight injury in training, so went to the Arc without a prep race but was given the amazing compliment of having Ardan, first and second in the last two Arcs, as his pacemaker. Ardan had also been successful in England, winning the Coronation Cup before finishing second to the on-song Coaraze in the Grand Prix de Saint-Cloud. Caracalla and Ardan were odds-on to win the Arc, for which the first prize had risen from 1.2 million francs to two million francs.

Prince Chevalier, returned at 6.8/1, had won the Prix du Jockey Club which was open to all-comers for the first time. He'd subsequently been just touched off by Souverain in a photo for the Grand Prix de Paris, before going down by two lengths to the same horse in the Prix Royal-Oak.

The Italian-trained Fante was the first raider since 1937. The third favourite had won last year's Gran Premio di Milano and finished second to the Italian Derby-winner Gladiolo in the same race this term. Since then he'd convincingly reversed placings with that horse when they were first and third in the Premio del Jockey Club.

The best three-year-old filly in France, Pirette, had won the Prix de Diane and Prix Vermeille, and finished third in the Grand Prix de Paris, and was a 10.5/1 chance.

The aforementioned Souverain, the Prix du Jockey Club-second Elseneur and also the useful Nirgal, were being aimed at the inaugural running of the King George VI Stakes at Ascot the following Saturday.

In 1951 that contest would evolve into the race known in France as *l'arc anglaise,* which on its new date in July would augment the international programme. Until then it would do the opposite – watering down the Arc by diverting to Berkshire some of the horses that would otherwise have gone to Longchamp.

Betting
0.3/1 Ardan & Caracalla (coupled), 6.8/1 Prince Chevalier, 7.3/1 Fante, 10.5/1 Pirette, 21/1 BAR.

Three-year-old form lines
Prix du Jockey Club, at Longchamp: 1st **Prince Chevalier**, 2nd Elseneur, 3rd **Pactole**, 4th Yong Lo
Grand Prix de Paris: 1st Souverain, 2nd **Prince Chevalier**, 3rd **Pirette**
Prix Royal-Oak: 1st Souverain, 2nd **Prince Chevalier**, 3rd Goyama

Fillies only
Prix de Diane, at Longchamp: 1st **Pirette**, 2nd Rimsy, 3rd Ephese
Prix Vermeille: 1st **Pirette**, 2nd Pastourelle, 3rd Alborado

Older horses and inter-generational races
Grand Prix de Saint-Cloud: 1st Coaraze, 2nd **Ardan**, 3rd Basileus
Prix du Prince d'Orange: 1st Achille, 2nd **Chanteur**, 3rd _

Abroad
In England
Derby Stakes: 1st Airborne, 2nd Gulf Stream, 3rd Radiotherapy
Ascot Gold Cup: 1st **Caracalla**, 2nd **Chanteur**, 3rd Basileus

In Italy
Gran Premio di Milano: 1st Gladiolo, 2nd **Fante**, 3rd Campiello, 0th Micipsa

The race
At the first attempt there was a *faux depart* as the tapes only rose halfway, prompting Ardan to lunge under the gate and Jacques Doyasbère did well to stay on board. A few minutes later take two was successful and the 25th Arc was underway with Ardan quick to stride, leading from Fante, Fine Lad and Prince Chevalier.

Ardan was still there as they entered the straight followed by Pirette and Prince Chevalier. Caracalla, who'd been outpaced early on, was gradually moving into contention. In the final 100 metres Prince Chevalier crept up the rails as Ardan drifted left. Pirette looked held in third but Caracalla was far from done.

He accelerated hard, passing his rivals one by one, finally getting up close home to prevail by a head on the line from Prince Chevalier, with one and a half lengths to Pirette in third. The long-time leader Ardan came home in fourth ahead of Fine Lad and Fante.

Post-race

The crowd had witnessed a staggering performance, made more memorable by the fact that Caracalla hadn't run since winning the Ascot Gold Cup in June, and that the Arc trip was probably on the short side for him. It was the fifth win for Marcel Boussac in the last nine runnings, and in that time he'd also had two seconds and a third.

Jockey Charlie Elliot was winning for the third time, equalling the record of Charles Semblat in the saddle, and it was a third for Semblat himself in his role as trainer.

Unbeaten in eight races, Caracalla was retired to stud but was not a great success. Stable companion Ardan, who contributed to Caracalla's win and had won the Arc himself in 1944, also retired. He sired Hard Sauce who in turn produced 1958 Irish 2000 Guineas and Derby-winner Hard Ridden. The latter's son, Hard To Beat, will feature in our story in the 1970s.

Result
1946 Prix de l'Arc de Triomphe
Longchamp. Sunday, 6 October 1946
Weights: 3yo c: 55.5kg, 3yo f: 54kg, 4yo+ c: 60kg, 4yo+ f: 58.5kg

1st Caracalla (FR)   4yo c   60kg   **0.3/1 fav** (coupled with Ardan)
by Tourbillon out of Astronomie (Astérus). Marcel Boussac / Charles Semblat / Charlie Elliott

2nd Prince Chevalier (FR) 3yo c   55.5kg **6.8/1**
by Prince Rose out of Chevalerie (Abbot's Speed). Paul Boyriven / Edmond Boullenger / Roger Poincelet

3rd Pirette (FR)   3yo f   54kg   **10.5/1**
by Deiri out of Pimpette (Town Guard). Marcel le Baron /_/ Henri Signoret

Runners: 9 (FR 8, ITY 1). Distances: hd, 1½. Going: good. Time: 2m 33.30s

Also ran: 4th **Ardan** (FR) 5yo h, 5th **Fine Lad** (IRE) 3yo c, 6th **Fante** (ITY) 4yo c. Unplaced: **Royal Hunter** (FR) 6yo h, **Chanteur** (FR) 4yo c, **Pactole** (_) 3yo c (9th).

Le Paillon adds Arc to French Champion Hurdle

First win for the Head family as prize money soars

Background and fancied horses

The Arc prize money more than doubled this year, rising from two million francs to five million francs to the winner. The odds-on favourite to win the purse was Tourment.

He'd survived the Battle of Normandy due to the quick actions of the owner of the stud he'd been taken from, who sent his manager out with an armful of cash which helped persuade the German soldier, who was guarding the son of Tourbillon, to return him.

That cash proved to be a sound investment as Tourment won the Poule d'Essai des Poulains. He was then just beaten by Sandjar in the Prix du Jockey Club after an epic duel up the straight. Next, Tourment just failed to reel in the enterprisingly ridden Avenger in the Grand Prix de Paris before easily winning the Prix Royal-Oak.

It was 9.3/1 bar one, which brought in Marcel Boussac's sole runner Goyama. He'd often been used as a pacemaker for Coaraze, but the second favourite for the Arc had been good enough to finish third in the 1946 Prix Royal-Oak. He'd taken the same berth this year in the Rous Memorial at Royal Ascot and the Princess of Wales's Stakes at Newmarket.

The Italian-raider Fante, at 11/1, was back and had finished ten lengths clear of the rest when second in the Gran Premio di Milano to the very talented Tenerani.

Fante was the same price as Monténica. Runner-up to Imprudence in the Poule d'Essai des Pouliches, she'd won the Prix de Diane. In the Prix Vermeille, Monténica had tracked Imprudence, who ran badly, and was left with too much to do, finishing fast to take third behind Procureuse. The latter was also in the Arc line-up, trading at a point longer on 12/1.

Sandwiched between them on 11.5/1 was Le Paillon, who had developed into a very useful dual-purpose sort. Runner-up at Cheltenham to National Spirit in the Champion Hurdle, when taken wide, he'd won the French equivalent, the Grand Course de Haies d'Auteuil, in June. Reverting to the flat after a break, he'd been successful in two of his three outings, most recently scoring in the Grand Prix de Deauville.

Next at 13/1 came the previously mentioned Imprudence, the winner of the 1000 Guineas and Poule d'Essai des Pouliches, who had taken her Classic tally to three in The Oaks before being rested.

She disappointed on her second run back in the Prix Vermeille, and jockey Roger Brethès was slated in the press, with one correspondent saying he was past it. A few days later Brethès pushed said journalist to the floor when they clashed at the races and started a slander suit against him. The net result was that Jacques Doyasbère was in the saddle aboard Imprudence in the Arc.

Betting
0.7/1 Tourment, 9.3/1 Goyama, 11/1 Fante, 11/1 Monténica, 11.5/1 Le Paillon, 12/1 Procureuse, 13/1 Imprudence, 22/1 Madelon & Bibi (coupled), 34/1 BAR.

Three-year-old form lines
Prix du Jockey Club, at Longchamp: 1st Sandjar, 2nd **Tourment**, 3rd Giafar
Grand Prix de Paris: 1st Avenger, 2nd **Tourment**, 3rd Giafar, 4th Sandjar, 5th **Cappielluca**, 0th Pearl Diver
Prix Royal-Oak: 1st **Tourment**, 2nd L'Impérial, 3rd Cadir

Fillies only
Prix de Diane, at Longchamp: 1st **Monténica**, 2nd Apostille, 3rd Sikoussa
Prix Vermeille: 1st **Procureuse**, 2nd Danaë, 3rd **Monténica**, 0th **Imprudence**

Older horses and inter-generational races
Grand Prix de Deauville: 1st **Le Paillon**, 2nd Elseneur, 3rd Platiname, last **Madelon**
Prix du Prince d'Orange: 1st Oviedo, 2nd **Madelon**, 3rd _

Abroad
In England
Derby Stakes: 1st Pearl Diver, 2nd Migoli, 3rd Sayajirao
Oaks Stakes: 1st **Imprudence**, 2nd Netherton Maid, 3rd Mermaid

In Italy
Gran Premio di Milano: 1st Tenerani, 2nd **Fante**, 3rd _

The race
Bibi, the pacemaker for Prix Malleret-winner Madelon, together with Carassin were the first to show. Fante, though, was slow away and lost about half-a-dozen lengths. Imprudence, who was initially in the midfield, gradually improved her position to take up third approaching halfway.

Into the straight Bibi and Carassin both folded, followed soon after by Imprudence. There wasn't much to choose between Tourment on the rails and Madelon, but then Tourment also reached the end of his tether and dropped back, seriously interfering with Goyama, who also tangled with Madelon.

Meanwhile Le Paillon, who had been in rear with Fante, appeared on the scene, steering a passage through beaten horses. He quickly reached Madelon and mastered her and then pushed on to open up what proved to be a race-winning gap.

At the line Le Paillon had a length and a half to spare over Goyama, who made up lots of ground at the death, once recovered from the barging he received at the hands of Tourment. Madelon was three parts of a length back in third. Fante finished fastest of all, from an impossible position, to take fourth, with Tourment fifth and Cappielluca sixth.

Post-race

Goyama's rider, Roger Poincelet, lodged an objection against those that had hampered him and although Bridgland, who rode Tourment, and Thirion, aboard Madelon, were given warnings the result stood as Goyama had finished ahead of both of them.

Goyama gained some recompense when winning the Prix du Conseil Municipal, with Madelon coming home third; he also won the Coronation Cup the following year. Le Paillon, though, had kept out of trouble, under Fernand Rochetti, providing a memorable win for Madame Lucienne Aurousseau.

More significantly it was the first success for one of the great French racing dynasties. Le Paillon's handler, Willie Head, was the son of William Head snr a successful jockey and trainer who came over from England in the 1870s.

William junior, aka Willie, joined another of the most influential families in French racing when marrying Henrietta Jennings, and their son Jacques-Alexandre, known as Alec, who had ridden Le Paillon in the Champion Hurdle, would go on to play his own role in Arc history. As would his children.

It was job done for Le Paillon, who retired to stud where he produced a few winners, including two of the Spanish Derby, Caporal and El Santo, but no superstars.

Result
1947 Prix de l'Arc de Triomphe
Longchamp. Sunday, 5 October 1947
Weights: 3yo c: 55.5kg, 3yo f: 54kg, 4yo+ c: 60kg, 4yo+ f: 58.5kg

1st Le Paillon (FR)   5yo h   60kg   **11.5/1**
by Fastnet out of Blue Bear (Blenheim). Madame Lucienne Aurousseau / Willie Head / Fernand Rochetti

2nd Goyama (FR)   4yo c   60kg   **9.3/1**
by Goya out of Devineress (Finglas). Marcel Boussac / Charles Semblat / Roger Poincelet

3rd Madelon (GER)   3yo f   54kg   **22/1**
by Trollius out of La Pawlova (Papyrus). André Lombard / Georges Pelat / F. Thirion

Runners: 12 (FR 11, ITY 1). Distances: 1½, ¾. Going: firm. Time: 2m 33.42s

Result stood after an objection by Poincelet against the riders of Tourment and Madelon

Also ran: 4th **Fante** (ITY) 5yo h, 5th **Tourment** (FR) 3yo c, 6th **Cappielluca** (FR) 3yo c. Unplaced: **Imprudence** (FR) 3yo f, **Monténica** (FR) 3yo f, **Carassin** (IRE) 4yo c, **Bibi** (GER) 4yo c, **Revigny** (FR) 4yo c, **Procureuse** (FR) 3yo f (12th).

1948

Migoli the first winner for the Aga Khan III

Dappled grey scores as Italy's fancied fillies fail

Background and fancied horses

Federico Tesio had two strong candidates in the form of Astolfina and Trevisana. The first-named had won the Italian versions of the 1000 Guineas, 2000 Guineas and The Oaks before beating the latter in the Gran Premio di Milano.

Trevisana, who'd previously won the Gran Premio d'Italia, gained her revenge in the Premio Besana – although that may have been on team orders – before adding the Italian St Leger. Coupled at 1.4/1 the Italian raiders headed the market.

Yong Lo, fourth in the 1946 Prix du Jockey Club and the winner of last year's Grand Prix de Saint-Cloud, had only reappeared in September when winning the Prix de Bois Roussel in fine style. He then made all to land the Prix du Prince d'Orange and was next best for the Arc at 4.8/1.

Then came Prix du Jockey Club-winner Bey at 7/1. Beaten by his stable companion, the Derby-winner My Love, in the Grand Prix de Paris, he was back to winning ways in the Prix Kergorlay where he beat Rigolo. In his latest outing, the Prix Royal-Oak, he'd been caught by Spooney after being left in the lead too early.

Rigolo was a very good two-year-old and showed he had trained on when scoring by two lengths in the Poule d'Essai des Poulains. That race was watched by England's future queen, Princess Elizabeth, who was there with the Duke of Edinburgh. An avid racing fan, like many of her predecessors including her mother and father, she would put her own imprint on the Arc in due course.

Rigolo wasn't entered for the Prix du Jockey Club or Grand Prix de Paris, so was next seen in the Prix Lupin, which he won before contracting a cough that ruled him out of the Grand Prix de Saint-Cloud. He was beaten by Bey in the Prix Kergorlay on his reappearance, and then failed to give weight away in the Prix du Prince d'Orange, but he still had plenty of support at Longchamp, being returned at 7.3/1.

The English-trained Migoli at 10/1 had finished second to Pearl Diver in last year's Derby before winning the King Edward VII Stakes at Royal Ascot, the Eclipse Stakes and Champion Stakes. This term, after losing out by a neck to Goyama in the Coronation Cup, the dappled grey, who inherited his colour from The Tetrarch line, had not been suited by the slow pace in the Eclipse Stakes and could only manage to finish fourth. However, his battling success at the end of August in the Rose of York Stakes showed he was back to his best.

Marcel Boussac's Nirgal had won the Hardwicke Stakes at Royal Ascot last year, and had followed up in the Princess of Wales's Stakes at Newmarket before finishing second to Migoli in the Champion Stakes. This year Nirgal had won three times but found one too good in the Hardwicke Stakes when bidding for a repeat win. He was an 11/1-chance coupled with his pacemaker Iror.

Betting

1.4/1 Astolfina & Trevisana (coupled), 4.8/1 Yong Lo, 7/1 Bey, 7.3/1 Rigolo, 10/1 Migoli, 11/1 Nirgal & Iror (coupled), 13/1 Spooney, 35/1 BAR.

Three-year-old form lines
Prix du Jockey Club: 1st **Bey**, 2nd Tanagrello, 3rd Flush Royal
Grand Prix de Paris: 1st My Love, 2nd Flush Royal, 3rd **Bey**, 4th **Spooney**, 0th **Balsamine**
Prix Royal-Oak: 1st **Spooney**, 2nd **Bey**, 3rd **Turmoil**

Fillies only
Prix de Diane: 1st Corteira, 2nd Doria, 3rd Cozina, 0th **Balsamine**
Prix Vermeille: 1st Corteira, 2nd Doria, 3rd Combinaison, 0th **Balsamine**

Older horses and inter-generational races
Grand Prix de Saint-Cloud: 1st **Goyama**, 2nd Rigoletto, 3rd Boby III
La Coupe de Maisons-Laffitte: 1st **Jocker**, 2nd Quessant, 3rd Golestan
Grand Prix de Deauville: 1st **Turmoil**, 2nd Baroque, 3rd Tanagrello
Prix du Prince d'Orange: 1st **Yong Lo**, 2nd Djéfou, 3rd **Pearl Diver**, 4th/last **Rigolo**

Abroad
In England
Derby Stakes: 1st My Love, 2nd Royal Drake, 3rd Noor

In Italy
Gran Premio di Milano: 1st **Astolfina**, 2nd Tenerani, 3rd **Trevisana**

The race

From the get-go it was Nirgal's pacemaker, Iror, who made the running. Nirgal himself settled into second place followed by Trevisana, Quatrain and Migoli. At the other end of the field Bey was waited with in last place.

Iror ran out of petrol at the 1,000-metre mark leaving Nirgal in front with Migoli two lengths behind in second. The same distance separated the pair as they entered the straight with a further two back to the others. It looked to be a straight match.

Smike, aboard Migoli, was oozing confidence and delayed his challenge until the last 300 metres. The dappled grey readily went on but veered to the rail and Poincelet had to stop riding for a stride. Nirgal battled gamely but at the line Migoli had pulled one and a half lengths clear with the same to Bey, who ran on for third.

A neck further back Spooney was fourth ahead of Turmoil and Quatrain who dead-heated for fifth. The Italian fillies, who were never in the hunt in the straight, finished last and last but one.

Post-race

This victory capped a great season for the Aga Khan III and his son Prince Aly Khan, who was very much involved in his father's racing empire and was a decent amateur jockey. As well as Migoli's great triumph, they had won the Derby and Grand Prix de Paris with My Love, The Oaks and Irish Oaks with Masaka, and the Irish Derby with Nathoo.

Trained by Frank Butters, who plied his trade at Newmarket, Migoli was the first foreign-trained winner since Crapom in 1933 and the first ever British-bred winner – the previous English-trained winners, Comrade and Parth, had both been born in Ireland.

A couple of weeks later Migoli finished fourth in the Champion Stakes and was then retired to stud. He had some success in the USA, where his Gallant Man won the 1957 Belmont Stakes and Jockey Club Cup as well as finishing runner-up in the Kentucky Derby.

Six days after the Arc, Alycidon won the King George VI Stakes at Ascot, taking home a bigger purse than Migoli. If the top horses in Europe were to be lured to Longchamp the Arc needed more prize money. To that end negotiations started with the Loterie Nationale, which had arranged sweepstakes on the race up until 1938.

The Tetrach 1911

|

Mumtaz Mahal 1921

|

Mah Mahal 1928

|

Mah Iran 1939

|

Migoli 1944

Result
1948 Prix de l'Arc de Triomphe
Longchamp. Sunday, 3 October 1948
Weights: 3yo c: 55.5kg, 3yo f: 54kg, 4yo+ c: 60kg, 4yo+ f: 58.5kg

1st Migoli (GB)   4yo c   60kg   **10/1**
by Bois Roussel out of Mah Iran (Bahram). HH Aga Khan III / Frank Butters / Charlie Smirke

2nd Nirgal (FR)   5yo h   60kg   **11/1** (coupled with Iror)
by Goya out of Castillane (Cameronian). Marcel Boussac / Charles Semblat / Roger Poincelet

3rd Bey (FR)   3yo f   55.5kg   **7/1**
by Deiri out of Bourgogne (Blandford). Constant Vandamme / Richard Carver / Rae Johnstone

Runners: 14 (FR 11, ITY 2, GB 1). Distances: 1½, 1½. Going: good. Time: 2m 31.60s

Also ran: 4th **Spooney** (FR) 3yo c, DH5th **Turmoil** (FR) 3yo c, DH5th **Quatrain** (FR) 5yo h, 7th **Rigolo** (FR) 3yo c, 8th **Yong Lo** (FR) 5yo h. Unplaced: **Pearl Diver** (FR) 4yo c, **Iror** (FR) 3yo c, **Jocker** (FR) 3yo c, **Balsamine** (FR) 3yo f, **Astolfina** (ITY) 3yo f, **Trevisana** (ITY) 3yo f (14th).

Coronation reigns in Europe's richest race

Quintupled prize money attracts record field

Background and fancied horses

The negotiations with the Loterie Nationale proved to be fruitful and on Bastille Day an agreement between the Société d'Encouragement pour l'Amélioration des Races de Chevaux and the Loterie Nationale was signed.

The deal meant that the prize money for the Arc increased fivefold, from five million francs to 25 million francs. The Arc was now the richest race in Europe and attracted a record field of 28, a number that wouldn't be topped until 1967.

It was tight at the head of the market with six horses under 4/1, albeit one of those was a pacemaker. Amour Drake and Val Drake, respectively a son and grandson of Admiral Drake, shared favouritism with Bagheera.

After finishing fourth in the 2000 Guineas and then winning the Poule d'Essai des Poulains, Amour Drake had been unlucky in the Derby. With his path suddenly blocked 400 metres from home, he'd been switched out wide and only lost out by a head to Nimbus on the line.

Sadly, the next evening his owner Léon Volterra, who'd been ill for several months, died. He'd run the Lido on the Champs-Élysées and had been a successful owner and breeder for 30 years. His horses would now run in the silks of his widow, Suzy.

Amour Drake's stamina was found out in the Grand Prix de Paris where he came home fifth, but back over a shorter trip he obliged with ease in the Prix Jacques Le Marois. In the Arc he was accompanied to post by Val Drake who'd finished third in the Prix Royal-Oak.

Returned at the same price as that duo was Bagheera. The best filly of the year, she'd not only won the Prix de Diane and Prix Vermeille but had stayed the extended distance when taking the Grand Prix de Paris.

Marcel Boussac's trio included Djeddah, who'd finished out of the frame in three Classics last year. However, he'd improved as a four-year-old and was unbeaten, having taken his sequence to four in the Eclipse Stakes.

Coronation had been a brilliant two-year-old to start with, but her form had tailed off at the end of the season. This year she'd just lost out to Musidora after a battle royal in The Oaks, before finishing second again in the Irish version.

However, in the latter she was clearly feeling the effects of the cough that had swept through Boussac's yard and wasn't seen again until the Arc. Her home reports, though, were very encouraging. Coronation and Djeddah were joined by Norval, who would act as a pacemaker.

The Irish-trained Beau Sabreur was the first horse in double figures. Last year he'd won the Irish 2000 Guineas and Irish St Leger but had missed the Irish Derby due to a cough. This term he'd come out on top in the Coronation Cup before taking second place behind Lone Eagle in the Queen Elizabeth Stakes at Ascot in June.

Others at the same sort of price included returnee Rigolo, who hadn't shown much on the track this year, and the Prix du Prince d'Orange-winner Oghio. Among the longer shots was the best Belgian filly for a while, Frinette, but her form had been put into context when she was well-beaten in the Prix Vermeille.

There were also four English-trained runners but they were all outsiders: Grand Prix de Paris-second Royal Empire at 33/1; dual Jockey Club Cup-winner Vic Day 60/1; 1948 Prix du Jockey Club-third Flush Royal 80/1; and Tsaoko at 160/1.

Betting
3.5/1 Amour Drake & Val Drake (coupled), 3.5/1 Bagheera, 3.7/1 Coronation & Djeddah & Norval (all coupled), 10/1 Beau Sabreur, 10/1 Rigolo, 11/1 Oghio, 30/1 BAR.

Three-year-old form lines
Prix du Jockey Club: 1st **Good Luck**, 2nd Ambiorix, 3rd Violoncelle
Grand Prix de Paris: 1st **Bagheera**, 2nd **Royal Empire**, 3rd Springfield, 5th **Amour Drake**, 0th **Double Rose**, 0th **Good Luck**, 0th **Goody**, 0th **Rantzau**
Prix Royal-Oak: 1st Ciel Etoilé, 2nd **Rantzau**, 3rd **Val Drake**

Fillies only
Prix de Diane: 1st **Bagheera**, 2nd Dona Mencia, 3rd Musette
Prix Vermeille: 1st **Bagheera**, 2nd **Vela**, 3rd Tagala, 5th **Double Rose**, 7th **Frinette**

Older horses and inter-generational races
Grand Prix de Saint-Cloud: 1st **Médium**, 2nd Ricquebourg, 3rd **Goody**
Prix du Prince d'Orange: 1st **Oghio**, 2nd **Ménétrier**, 3rd **Kerlan**, 4th **Good Luck**

Abroad
In England
Derby Stakes: 1st Nimbus (GB), 2nd **Amour Drake**, 3rd Swallow Tail, 14th **Val Drake**
Oaks Stakes: 1st Musidora, 2nd **Coronation**, 3rd Vice Versa II

The race

A huge crowd saw Norvel take the lead in the early stages from Astramgram and Royal Empire. Djeddah was close behind, followed by a group that included the sweating Coast Guard, Armour Drake and Coronation.

Outsider Double Rose, owned by film star Rita Hayworth in her incarnation as the second wife of Prince Aly Khan, started to make a move as they turned downhill. With 900 metres to run, Norval capitulated leaving Coast Guard in front.

Entering the straight Coast Guard himself tired and Beau Sabreur and Amour Drake tussled for the lead. On the outside Double Rose and Coronation appeared on the scene, and at the 400-metre pole Double Rose challenged Amour Drake.

However, Coronation in third place looked to be going exceedingly easily. When Poincelet let her loose she settled the issue in a few strides, quickly passing the others and pulling away to score by four lengths.

Double Rose came home in second with a length to spare over Amour Drake. They were followed home by Rantzau, Médium and Tanagrello. Djeddah, who'd been baulked several times but would gain some recompense when winning the Champion Stakes, came in ninth ahead of Oghio, who hit the rails, while the fancied Bagheera finished in the pack.

Post-race

Marcel Boussac was not renowned for his ability to smile, but he couldn't resist when greeting Coronation who was his sixth Arc winner after Corrida twice, Djébel, Ardan, and Caracalla. Boussac's ownership achievement was to stand as an outright record until 2018.

Charles Semblat, who had been victorious three times as a jockey, had now won a record-breaking four times as a trainer. Jockey Roger Poincelet, who'd been runner-up in four of the last five races, had finally got the monkey off his back.

Coronation was retired for the year but kept in training. The daughter of Djébel was the second winner to be sired by a previous victor.

Result

1949 Prix de l'Arc de Triomphe
Longchamp. Sunday, 9 October 1949
Weights: 3yo c: 55.5kg, 3yo f: 54kg, 4yo+ c: 60kg, 4yo+ f: 58.5kg

1st Coronation (FR)   3yo f   54kg   **3.7/1** (coupled with Djeddah & Norval)
by Djébel out of Esméralda (Tourbillon). Marcel Boussac / Charles Semblat / Roger Poincelet

2nd Double Rose (FR)   3yo f   54kg   **60/1**
by Macaron out of Double Call (Colorado Kid). Princesse Rita Khan / Richard Carver / Bill Rickaby

3rd Amour Drake (FR)   3yo c   55.5kg   **3.5/1 fav** (coupled with Val Drake)
by Admiral Drake out of Vers Laurore (Vatout). Suzy Volterra / Richard Carver / Rae Johnstone

Runners: 28 (FR 22, GB 4, BEL 1, IRE 1). Distances: 4, 1. Going: good. Time: 2m 33.30s

Also ran: 4th **Rantzau** (FR) 3yo c, 5th **Médium** (FR) 3yo c, 6th **Tanagrello** (FR) 4yo h, 7th **Beau Sabreur** (GB) 4yo c, 8th **Ménétrier** (FR) 5yo h, 9th **Djeddah** (FR) 4yo c, 10th **Flush Royal** (FR) 4yo c. Unplaced: **Goody** (FR) 7yo h, **Val Drake** (FR) 3yo c, **Oghio** (FR) 3yo c, **Rigoletto** (FR) 4yo c, **Vic Day** (FR) 4yo c, **Bagheera** (FR) 3yo f, **Good Luck** (FR) 3yo c, **Vela** (FR) 3yo f, **Royal Empire** (FR) 3yo c, **Flocon** (FR) 3yo c, **Rigolo** (FR) 4yo c, **Frinette** (BEL) 3yo f, **Astramgram** (FR) 3yo c, **Quatrain** (FR) 6yo h, **Kerlor** (FR) 4yo c, **Coast Guard** (IRE) 3yo c, **Norval** (GB) 3yo c, **Tsaoko** (FR) 4yo c.

1950

Tantième trounces opposition

Unlucky Prix du Jockey Club-second squelches home

Background and fancied horses

It had been an exceptional year for French horses in England where they had taken most of the main prizes. Indeed, Marcel Boussac had won three Classics in England with Galcador taking the Derby, Asmena The Oaks, and Scratch the St Leger, which helped him to the first of two consecutive English champion owner titles.

Prior to his success at Doncaster, Scratch had fought out a very close finish with Tantième in the Prix du Jockey Club. In a decision that sparked controversy, the judge bravely gave it as an outright win to Scratch. At the time Chantilly was the only Paris racecourse that didn't have a photo finish – that would be rectified by the end of 1950.

François Dupré's Tantième also had form with another Boussac runner, last year's winner Coronation. She hadn't really sparkled and it was her best effort of the season so far when she only went down by a head to Tantième in the Queen Elizabeth Stakes, in what was the last running of that race before its amalgamation with the King George VI Stakes.

Scratch and Coronation, together with their pacemaker Astella, were coupled at 1.9/1. Poule d'Essai des Poulains-winner Tantième, who was unbeaten this season barring that decision at Chantilly was 2.5/1.

Alizier, running for Édouard de Rothschild's son Guy, had been second to Vieux Manoir, another horse in his ownership, in the Grand Prix de Paris. Subsequently he'd won the Grand Prix de Deauville with last year's Arc runner-up Double Rose in second place. Alizier was a 4.3/1-shot for the Arc.

The only non-French participant was the Irish Derby-winner Dark Warrior. However, he hadn't acted on the soft ground when down the field in the Irish St Leger and, at 35/1, was the rank outsider of the field.

Betting

1.9/1 Coronation & Scratch & Astella (all coupled), 2.5/1 Tantième, 4.3/1 Alizier, 15/1 Fort Napoléon, 16/1 Pan, 17/1 Médium, 19/1 L'Amiral, 23/1 BAR.

> **Three-year-old form lines**
> Prix du Jockey Club: 1st **Scratch**, 2nd **Tantième**, 3rd Lacaduv, 4th **Fort Napoléon**
> Grand Prix de Paris: 1st Vieux Manoir, 2nd **Alizier**, 3rd Lacaduv, 4th **Scratch**, 5th **L'Amiral**, 0th **Pan**

Prix Royal-Oak: 1st **Pan**, 2nd Anubis, 3rd Fast Fox

Fillies only

Prix de Diane: 1st Aglaé Grâce, 2nd Corejada, 3rd Aïn el Chams

Prix Vermeille: 1st Kilette, 2nd Nuit de Folies, 3rd Asmena

Older horses and inter-generational races

Grand Prix de Saint-Cloud: 1st Ocarina, 2nd Amour Drake, 3rd **Médium**

Grand Prix de Deauville: 1st **Alizier**, 2nd **Double Rose**, 3rd Coast Guard

Prix du Prince d'Orange: 1st **Médium**, 2nd **Bagheera**, 3rd _

Abroad

In England

Derby Stakes: 1st Galcador, 2nd Prince Simon, 3rd Double Eclipse, 10th **L'Amiral**

Ascot Gold Cup: 1st Supertello, 2nd **Bagheera**, 3rd Alindrake

St Leger: 1st **Scratch**, 2nd Vieux Manoir, 3rd Sanlinea, 9th **L'Amiral**

In Ireland

Irish Derby: 1st **Dark Warrior**, 2nd Eclat, 3rd Pardal

The race

It rained for several hours before the race, which softened the ground to heavy. The eagerly awaited rematch between Scratch and Tantième was to be run in humid conditions and the last-named was sweating up badly.

As soon as the tapes rose, the Boussac pacemaker, Astella, set a fast pace with Coronation, Dark Warrior and Médium also to the fore. Starting the descent, Astella still had the advantage with Coronation cruising in second. Others including Bagheera were starting to struggle.

With 900 metres to run, Coronation and Médium were on terms with the pacesetters and Alizier was starting to close in along with L'Amiral, Tantième and Scratch.

Rounding the final bend, Alizier collared the leaders followed by Tantième, who was going easily, and L'Amiral. Scratch, though, couldn't respond. At the 300-metre mark Doyasbère finally pressed the button and Tantième readily passed Alizier to score in dominant style by one and a half lengths, with L'Amiral another two lengths behind.

Scratch was only three parts further back in fourth, but then there was a yawning gap of four lengths to Fort Napoléon and Pan to complete a first six which was comprised entirely of three-year-olds.

With all the success in England, and the fact that last year's winner and runner-up were only able to beat the Boussac's pacemaker home, it tended to confirm that this year's French Classic generation were indeed a classic generation.

Post-race

Tantième, sporting grey silks with a pink cap, was bred as well as owned by hotel magnate François Dupré, who finished second in the list of leading owners behind Guy de Rothschild.

The winner was trained by François Mathet, who was to become a legend in the sport and will feature many times in our story. For jockey Jacques Doyasbère it was a third victory, after Djébel and Ardan, equalling Semblat and Elliott's record.

Last year's winner, Coronation, retired to the paddocks but was barren every year from 1952 to 1961. This may have been due to her in-breeding to Tourbillon, the grandsire of both her parents, which was a controversial experiment at the time and would be unlikely to be repeated nowadays.

What can't be taken away is that she was a spectacular three-year-old who was the apple of Marcel Boussac's eye. The *restaurant panoramique* in the grandstand at Maisons-Laffitte was named in her honour.

Coronation may have left the scene but Tantième would be back to defend his title.

Result

1950 Prix de l'Arc de Triomphe
Longchamp. Sunday, 8 October 1950
Weights: 3yo c: 55.5kg, 3yo f: 54kg, 4yo+ c: 60kg, 4yo+ f: 58.5kg

1st Tantième (FR)　　　　3yo c　55.5kg　**2.5/1**
by Deux-Pour-Cent out of Terka (Indus) François Dupré / François Mathet / Jacques Doyasbère

2nd Alizier (FR)　　　　3yo c　55.5kg　**4.3/1**
by Téléférique out of Alizarine (Coronach) Baron Guy de Rothschild / Geoff Watson / Freddie Palmer

3rd L'Amiral (FR)　　　　3yo c　55.5kg　**19/1**
by Admiral Drake out of Hurrylor (Vatellor) Suzy Volterra / Richard Carver / Roger Poincelet

Runners: 12 (FR 11, IRE 1). Distances: 1½, 2. Going: heavy. Time: 2m 34.22s

Also ran: 4th **Scratch** (FR) 3yo c, 5th **Fort Napoléon** (FR) 3yo c, 6th **Pan** (FR) 3yo c, 7th **Bagheera** (FR) 4yo f, 8th **Dark Warrior** (IRE) 3yo c. Unplaced: **Médium** (FR) 4yo c, **Coronation** (FR) 4yo f, **Double Rose** (FR) 4yo f, **Astella** (FR) 3yo f.

1951
Terrific Tantième does it again

Dupré star equals feats of Ksar, Motrico, and Corrida

Background and fancied horses

After being an irritant to the Arc in its October berth, the King George VI Stakes became a positive boon to the international programme this year, once amalgamated with the Queen Elizabeth Stakes and moved to July.

Run initially as the Festival of Britain Stakes, to coincide with the 100-year anniversary of the Great Exhibition, it became the King George VI and Queen Elizabeth Stakes from 1952. This new clash of the generations over 2,400 metres complimented rather than clashed with the Arc.

With prize money second only to the Derby it was no surprise that Tantième was aimed at the new event. By July he'd already picked up the Prix Ganay and Coronation Cup, but unfortunately his flight to Ascot on the morning of the race met with turbulence, which may have accounted for his inability to find his normal change of gear in the closing stages.

In the end Tantième finished third to Supreme Court and Zucchero. However, back on home soil he was favourite to retain his Arc title.

Tantième faced a four-strong Boussac posse headed by Dynamiter. He'd won the Prix d'Ispahan before disappointing in the Festival of Britain Stakes, but had a big home reputation. Dynamiter was joined by Prix Vermeille-third Djelfa, Pharsale – runner-up in the Grand Prix de Deauville – and pacemaker Phare.

They were followed by Guy de Rothschild's Grand Prix de Saint-Cloud victor Violoncelle, Prix du Jockey Club runner-up Free Man, and Pan, who'd notched up high-profile successes in the Prix du Cadran, Ascot Gold Cup and Goodwood Cup.

Sussex Stakes-winner Le Sage was the shortest of the three English-trained runners. The others being the Irish Derby-hero Fraise du Bois II, and Saturn who'd taken the Hardwicke Stakes at Royal Ascot.

Vincent O'Brien's 1950 Ormonde Stakes-winner Olein's Grace represented Ireland, with Nuccio, the winner of the Premio Presidente della Repubblica and Gran Premio d'Italia, doing the same for Italy, albeit he was temporarily lodging with Alec Head at Chantilly.

Betting

1.7/1 Tantième, 6/1 Djelfa & Dynamiter & Phare & Pharsale (all coupled), 7.5/1 Violoncelle, 10/1 Free Man, 11/1 Le Sage, 13/1 Pan, 23/1 BAR.

Three-year-old form lines

Prix du Jockey Club: 1st Sicambre, 2nd **Free Man**, 3rd, Lavarède, 5th **Mât de Cocagne**, 9th **Florian IV**

Grand Prix de Paris: 1st Sicambre, 2nd Lavarède, 3rd Aquino, 4th **Mât de Cocagne**, 0th **Free Man**

Prix Royal-Oak: 1st Stymphale, 2nd Romney, 3rd **Mât de Cocagne**

Fillies only

Prix de Diane: 1st Stratonice, 2nd Santa Bella, 3rd Maitrise, 0th **Djelfa**

Prix Vermeille: 1st Orberose, 2nd Satinette, 3rd **Djelfa**

Older horses and inter-generational races

Grand Prix de Saint-Cloud: 1st **Violoncelle**, 2nd **Florian IV**, 3rd Sahib, 4th **L'Amiral**, 0th **Nuccio**, 0th **Le Tyrol**, last **Pharsale**

La Coupe de Maisons-Laffitte: 1st **Pharsale**, 2nd _, 3rd _

Grand Prix de Deauville: 1st Coast Guard, 2nd **Pharsale**, 3rd **L'Amiral**, 4th **Florian IV**

Prix du Prince d'Orange: 1st **Florian IV** , 2nd _, 3rd _, last **Nuccio**

Abroad

In England

Derby Stakes: 1st Arctic Prince, 2nd Sybil's Nephew, 3rd Signal Box, 4th **Le Tyrol**, 0th **Fraise du Bois II**

Ascot Gold Cup: 1st **Pan**, 2nd Colonist II, 3rd Alizier

Festival of Britain Stakes: 1st Supreme Court, 2nd Zucchero, 3rd **Tantième**, 5th **Olein's Grace**, 12th **Le Tyrol**, 15th **Dynamiter**

St Leger: 1st Talma, 2nd **Fraise du Bois II**, 3rd Medway

In Ireland

Irish Derby: 1st **Fraise du Bois II**, 2nd Signal Box, 3rd Bolivar

The race

The going was soft but the weather *parfait* as they got underway. Phare led with Olein's Grace, Fraise du Bois II and Le Tyrol all well-placed, but Mât de Cocagne had dwelt at the start, losing four lengths.

Pan and Saturn moved up behind Phare as he started the descent. Le Tyrol was still prominent while L'Amiral and Tantième were taking closer order as the field turned for home.

Round the final bend, Phare dropped away and Pan took over in front. Le Sage made rapid progress into second while Tantième continued to close in. Le Sage made it to the front for a couple of strides before running out of steam, Tantième on the other hand was still cantering.

Pan had the lead again, but not for long. With 400 metres to go, Doyasbère asked Tantième to quicken and he answered in the best possible fashion, striding clear under a hands and heels ride to leave the Ascot Gold Cup-winner for dead, at the line winning by two lengths.

Pan kept going at one pace but had no answer to the acceleration shown by the fast-finishing Nuccio, Le Tyrol and Djelfa, who engulfed him close home. Mât de Cocagne was next past the post in sixth.

Post-race

Tantième's success was even easier than last year, and in the process he emulated Ksar, Corrida and Motrico to become the fourth dual winner. François Dupré and François Mathet doubled their scores while Jacques Doyasbère, having equalled Semblat and Elliott's record last year now surpassed them becoming the winning-most jockey with four wins.

Tantième was retired to stud and was very successful. He was champion sire in 1962 and 1965, with his standouts being Reliance and Match, who will both feature in our story.

Result

1951 Prix de l'Arc de Triomphe
Longchamp. Sunday, 7 October 1951
Weights: 3yo c: 55.5kg, 3yo f: 54kg, 4yo+ c: 60kg, 4yo+ f: 58.5kg

1st Tantième (FR)   4yo c   60kg   **1.7/1 fav**
by Deux Pour Cent out of Terka (Indus). François Dupré / François Mathet / Jacques Doyasbère

2nd Nuccio (ITY)   3yo c   55.5kg   **25/1**
by Traghetto out of Nuvoletta (Muzio). Dr Guido Beradelli / Alec Head / Fernand Rochetti

3rd Le Tyrol (FR)   3yo c   55.5kg   **30/1**
by Verso II out of Princesse Lointaine (Prince Rose). Ralph Strassburger / Henri Delavaud / Marcel Lollièrou

Runners: 19 (FR 14, ENG 3, ITY 1, IRE 1). Distances: 2, 1. Going: soft. Time: 2m 32.84s

Also ran: 4th **Djelfa** (FR) 3yo f, 5th **Pan** (FR) 4yo c, 6th **Mât de Cocagne** (FR) 3yo c, 7th **Florian IV** (FR) 3yo c, 8th **Free Man** (FR) 3yo c, 9th **Fast Fox** (FR) 4yo c, 10th **Fraise du Bois II** (FR) 3yo c. Unplaced: **Le Sage** (GB) 3yo c, **Violoncelle** (GER) 5yo h, **Hero** (FR) 4yo f, **Dynamiter** (GB) 3yo c, **Pharsale** (FR) 3yo c, **L'Amiral** (FR) 4yo c, **Olein's Grace** (GB) 5yo h, **Phare** (FR) 3yo c, **Saturn** (GB) 4yo c.

Nuccio wins Head-to-Head

Last year's second goes one place better as son beats father

Background and fancied horses

Maurice Hennessy's filly La Mirambule, trained by Willie Head, was the leading fancy for this year's renewal at 2.25/1. Heavily supported in the 1000 Guineas and Prix de Diane, she'd finished second in both – in the latter being short-headed by outsider Seria. After that, though, La Mirambule hit her stride winning twice at Deauville before scooting home eight lengths clear in the Prix Vermeille.

Dynamiter was back captaining Team Boussac. He'd enhanced his reputation soon after last season's Arc disappointment by winning the Champion Stakes. This term he'd sluiced up in the Hardwicke Stakes at Royal Ascot and finished second to the enigmatic Zucchero in the Rose of York Stakes.

Boussac's top filly, Arbèle, had run prominently in The Oaks until fading, and gained some recompense in the Prix d'Ispahan before adding to her haul with an impressive win in the Prix Jacques Le Marois. Dynamiter and Arbèle, together with St Leger-third Alcinus and pacemaker Amphis, were bundled together at 5.5/1.

Next came Grand Prix de Saint-Cloud-winner Fast Fox, followed by last year's runner-up Nuccio, whose temporary stay with Alec Head had been extended indefinitely after he was purchased by the Aga Khan III.

Nuccio opened his 1952 account in England taking the Coronation Cup. A couple of reverses followed when he finished ninth on unsuitably fast ground in the King George VI and Queen Elizabeth Stakes and then second in the Prix du Prince d'Orange, eight lengths behind Silnet.

But now with the ground continuing to ease at Longchamp his chances were improving by the minute. Nuccio and his pacemaker Néarque II were at 7.4/1 with Silnet a fraction longer at 7.5/1.

Others to consider included Grand Prix de Paris-winner Orfeo, also at 7.5/1, and the 9/1 Ralph Strassburger duo of Worden, third in the King George VI and Queen Elizabeth Stakes; and Seria, the surprise winner of the Prix de Diane.

The only raider was Italy's Oise, a 60/1-shot who'd been runner-up in the Derby Italiano, Premio Presidente della Republique, Gran Premio di

Milano and St Leger Italiano. He was to be the first Arc ride for 16-year-old wonderkid Lester Piggott.

Betting

2.25/1 La Mirambule, 5.5/1 Dynamiter & Arbèle & Alcinus & Amphis (all coupled), 6/1 Fast Fox, 7.4/1 Nuccio & Néarque II (coupled), 7.5/1 Silnet, 7.5/1 Orfeo, 9/1 Worden & Seria (coupled), 24/1 BAR.

Three-year-old form lines

Prix du Jockey Club: 1st Auriban, 2nd Corindon, 3rd **Silnet**, 4th **Ararat**
Grand Prix de Paris: 1st **Orfeo**, 2nd Auriban, 3rd Epicea
Prix Royal-Oak: 1st Feu du Diable, 2nd **Vamos**, 3rd Aram

Fillies only

Prix de Diane: 1st **Seria**, 2nd **La Mirambule**, 3rd **Pomaré**
Prix Vermeille: 1st **La Mirambule**, 2nd Khadidja, 3rd Canova

Older horses and inter-generational races

Grand Prix de Saint-Cloud: 1st **Fast Fox**, 2nd **Silnet**, 3rd Mât de Cocagne, 4th **Alcinus**
Prix du Prince d'Orange: 1st **Silnet**, 2nd **Nuccio**, 3rd Fedala

Abroad

In England
Derby Stakes: 1st Tulyar, 2nd Gay Time, 3rd Faubourg II, 6th **Silnet**, 0th **Worden**, 0th **Ararat**
Oaks Stakes: 1st Frieze, 2nd Zabara, 3rd Moon Star, 0th **Arbèle**
King George VI and Queen Elizabeth Stakes: 1st Tulyar, 2nd Gay Time, 3rd **Worden**, 6th **Arbèle**, 9th **Nuccio**
St Leger: 1st Tulyar, 2nd **Vamos**, 3rd **Alcinus**, last **Magnific**

In Italy
Gran Premio di Milano: 1st Neebisch, 2nd Oise, 3rd _

The race

In the preliminaries, Silnet was sweating profusely while Pomaré kicked a spectator on the way from the paddock to the track. Once away, Néarque II fulfilled his role by setting the pace from Pomaré, but Dynamiter was slow to stride. In the second group Nuccio was prominent along with Magnific and Lamirault.

The Boussac pacemaker, Amphis, took over at halfway with Nuccio going ominously well just behind. With 1,000 metres to travel, Nuccio overhauled Amphis as Worden, Dynamiter and Silnet made progress from the rear.

At the approach to the straight it was the favourite, La Mirambule, who challenged Nuccio first, and the pair came clear of the others. Willie Head's La Mirambule tried hard but couldn't get on terms with his son's charge and in the end Nuccio had the greater stamina and pulled away to secure victory by three lengths.

Dynamiter made up a lot of ground and in the end only failed by a head to collar La Mirambule. Four lengths away Silnet took fourth followed by Worden and Lamirault.

Post-race

Nuccio received a good reception from the crowd as he was led in by the Begum Aga Khan, the Aga Khan's fourth wife and former Miss France, Yvette Labrousse. The Aga Khan was adding to Migoli in 1948, while Roger Poincelet also doubled his tally having scored with Coronation in 1949.

Willie Head had played second fiddle to his son on another red-letter occasion for the Head family, and both were destined to win again.

Third-placed Dynamiter went on to win the Champion Stakes for the second time, while Nuccio retired for the season but was kept in training.

Result

1952 Prix de l'Arc de Triomphe
Longchamp. Sunday, 5 October 1952
Weights: 3yo c: 55.5kg, 3yo f: 54kg, 4yo+ c: 60kg, 4yo+ f: 58.5kg

1st Nuccio (ITY)   4yo c 60kg **7.4/1** (coupled with Néarque II)
by Traghetto out of Nuvoletta (Muzio). HH Aga Khan III / Alec Head / Roger Poincelet

2nd La Mirambule (FR) 3yo f 54kg **2.25/1 fav**
by Coaraze out of La Futaie (Gris Perle). Maurice Hennessy / William Head / Claudius Lalanne

3rd Dynamiter (GB)   4yo c 60kg **5.5/1** (coupled with Arbèle & Alcinus & Amphis)
by Pharis out of Pretty Lady (Umidwar). Marcel Boussac / Charles Semblat / Charlie Elliott

Runners: 18 (FR 17, ITY 1). Distances: 3, hd. Going: soft. Time: 2m 39.84s

Also ran: 4th **Silnet** (FR) 3yo c, 5th **Worden** (FR) 3yo c, 6th **Lamirault** (_) 3yo c, 7th **Vamos** (FR) 3yo c, 8th **Amphis** (FR) 3yo c, 9th **Fast Fox** (FR) 5yo h, 10th **Oise** (FR) 3yo c. Unplaced: **Arbèle** (FR) 3yo f, **Orfeo** (FR) 3yo c, **Ararat** (FR) 3yo c, **Alcinus** (FR) 3yo c, **Néarque II** (GB) 3yo c, **Seria** (FR) 3yo f, **Pomaré** (FR) 3yo f, **Magnific** (FR) 3yo c.

La Sorellina and Silnet give Étienne Pollet a one-two

Silver Jill's pair clear of the third in a rough race

Background and fancied horses

Between them Team Aga Khan and Marcel Boussac had seven of the 25-strong field. However, Nuccio apart, none of them were champions.

Nuccio, last year's winner and one of five of the 1952 runners to return, had run boldly in the King George VI and Queen Elizabeth Stakes. He'd taken the race to the opposition and still led entering the closing stages but was overhauled by Epsom Derby-first and-second, Pinza and Aureole, eventually coming home fifth.

Most recently he'd finished second to the useful Worden in the Prix du Prince d'Orange with the pair five lengths clear of the third. With the ground easing overnight Nuccio's connections were full of hope.

Shikampur, who had been fourth in the Derby and the Grand Prix de Paris in the summer and third to art dealer Georges Wildenstein's Buisson d'Or in the Prix Royal-Oak, represented the Aga Khan's three-year-olds along with his son's Skyraider.

The latter had taken the King Edward VII Stakes at Royal Ascot but was down the field in the Grand Prix de Paris. Pacemaker Nemrod II completed the quartet who were returned at 3.25/1.

Pole position in the Boussac trio belonged to Janitor. He'd had an enforced break due to an injury picked up when finishing third in the Prix Jean Prat in April. But when returning in mid-September he'd hacked up in eye-catching fashion in the Prix de Saint Fargeau.

Arbèle, who'd been placed behind Cosmos in the Rous Memorial at Royal Ascot and La Coupe de Maisons-Laffitte, was back and together with the mare, Damaka, winner of the Prix de Pomone at Deauville in August, completed the Boussac team who were priced at 5.8/1.

The English raiding party did include a champion in the form of the Cecil Boyd-Rochfort's St Leger-winner Premonition, who'd beaten Grand Prix de Paris-victor Northern Light to land the Doncaster Classic.

The 6/1-chance for the Arc had also been first past the post in the Irish Derby but had interfered with the winner and lost out in the Stewards' Room. Premonition was joined by the enigmatic Zucchero, who'd taken the Coronation Cup and Rose of York Stakes but had also refused to race on three occasions.

The only other overseas runner was Niederländer, the first German representative since his grandsire Oleander finished third to Ortello in 1929. Baron Heinrich von Thyssen's six-year-old had won the Deutsches Derby in 1950 and had beaten the French-trained Fauberg in the Grosser Preis von Baden this term. But the German form was generally seen as being weak and he was available at 50/1.

Paul Duboscq had two useful sorts in the shape of last year's fourth Silnet and his half-sister La Sorellina, who were coupled at 16.3/1. La Sorellina had just got the better of Banassa and Poule d'Essai des Pouliches-winner Hurnli when landing the Prix de Diane.

Subsequently she'd been unlucky in the Prix Vermeille, losing all chance when being blocked in just as she was starting her run. The race eventually went to the rank outsider Radio.

Betting
3.25/1 Nuccio & Shikampur & Skyraider & Nemrod II (all coupled), 5.8/1 Janitor & Arbèle & Damaka (all coupled), 6/1 Premonition, 6.8/1 Northern Light, 8/1 Buisson d'Or, 16/1 Worden, 16.3/1 Silnet & La Sorellina (coupled), 18/1 Marley Knowe, 25/1 BAR.

Three-year-old form lines
Prix du Jockey Club: 1st Chamant, 2nd Sériphos, 3rd Marley Knowe
Grand Prix de Paris: 1st Northern Light, 2nd Flûte Enchantée, 3rd Buisson d'Or, 4th Shikampur, 0th Skyraider
Prix Royal-Oak: 1st Buisson d'Or, 2nd Coquelin, 3rd Shikampur, 4th Sériphos,

Fillies only
Prix de Diane: 1st La Sorellina, 2nd Banassa, 3rd Hurnli
Prix Vermeille: 1st Radio, 2nd Gourabe, 3rd Banassa, 4th Noémi, 6th La Sorellina,

Older horses and inter-generational races
Grand Prix de Saint-Cloud: 1st Magnific, 2nd Nordiste, 3rd Vamos
La Coupe de Maisons-Laffitte: 1st Cosmos, 2nd Arbèle, 3rd _
Prix du Prince d'Orange: 1st Worden, 2nd Nuccio, 3rd Sénégal, 5th Cosmos

Abroad
In England
Derby Stakes: 1st Pinza, 2nd Aureole, 3rd Pink Horse, 4th Shikampur, 5th Premonition
Oaks Stakes: 1st Ambiguity, 2nd Kerkeb, 3rd Noémi
King George VI and Queen Elizabeth Stakes: 1st Pinza, 2nd Aureole, 3rd Worden, 5th Nuccio, 0th Silnet, refused to race Zucchero

St Leger: 1st **Premonition**, 2nd **Northern Light**, 3rd Aureole

In Ireland
Irish Derby: 1st Chamier, 2nd Sea Charger, 3rd Clonleason, disq (1st ptp) **Premonition**

In Germany
Grosser Preis von Baden: 1st **Niederländer**, 2nd Fauberg, 3rd Salut

The race

It was a bright sunny day and after a clean break Nemrod II, as expected, made the pace followed by Skyraider, Shikampur and Worden. After 100 metres, Zucchero, with Lester Piggott in the saddle, decided enough was enough and pulled himself up.

However, Zucchero being Zucchero he changed his mind again and, despite being about 200 metres behind, decided to set off after the field and actually managed to catch and pass a few of the stragglers in the straight.

The order at the front was maintained until they started down the hill where Worden pushed on, with Northern Light and La Sorellina starting to move nearer. Further back in what was a tightly bunched field, Janitor and Niederländer got in each other's way effectively ending both of their chances, with the former receiving a cut behind his off-fore knee.

Worden entered the straight three lengths clear of Northern Light, who had moved into second, with La Sorellina on his tail followed by Silnet, Nuccio and Buisson d'Or. Premonition, who was also in the chasing group, was severely hampered as runners jostled for racing room and dropped out of contention. Later he was found to have received a significant injury to his off-hind leg.

Meanwhile La Sorellina first mastered Northern Light and then Worden to take the lead with 200 metres to go. She looked to have the prize in the bag until her half-brother, Silnet, produced an amazing late charge and at the line La Sorellina only had a head to spare in a thrilling finish to give Étienne Pollet a fantastic one-two.

Three lengths behind the Pollet pair came Worden, who just held on for third from the fast-finishing Buisson d'Or. They were followed by Northern Light and the two hard-luck stories, Premonition and Janitor, who both finished with deep cuts.

Post-race

The day belonged to owner Paul Duboscq who bred the winner and the runner-up from his mare Silver Jill. She had been a decent sort on the track but, due to the occupation, had mainly run in the south-west of the country.

It was more dangerous in the north, which Silver Jill found out when transferred to stud in Normandy where, like so many other horses, she was taken by the Nazis. Once returned to France she passed through several hands before being picked up for a song by Duboscq.

Based near Bordeaux, where he was a major figure in the organisation of racing in the area, Duboscq was well aware of Silver Jill's form on the track, and her children's one-two in the Arc played a major part in him claiming the 1953 crown of champion owner in France.

It was also a tremendous training feat by Étienne Pollet, who was to taste Arc glory twice more, but it was the only win in the race for jockey Maurice Larraun, although he would take minor honours three times in the early in 1960s.

There were inquiries into the injuries to Premonition and Janitor, but they were deemed to be racing incidents with no clear blame being apportioned. As a result, the decision was made to introduce patrol cameras as soon as possible, in order to give the stewards more angles from which to review the action.

Another talking point was whether or not Worden had gone too soon. Those who thought he might have were given further impetuous to their argument when he went on to win the Washington DC International by six lengths.

It was the end of the Arc story for last year's winner Nuccio, who'd finished in midfield.

After a winless season in 1954 he was retired. He didn't produce much of note and his best progeny were fillies or broodmares including Ivresse, who won the Preis der Diana (German Oaks) in 1958. Silnet also retired to stud, but La Sorellina would return.

Result
1953 Prix de l'Arc de Triomphe
Longchamp. Sunday, 4 October 1953
Weights: 3yo c: 55.5kg, 3yo f: 54kg, 4yo+ c: 60kg, 4yo+ f: 58.5kg

1st La Sorellina (FR)　　3yo f　54kg　　**16.3/1** (coupled with Silnet)
by Sayani out of Silver Jill (King Salmon). Paul Duboscq / Étienne Pollet / Maurice Larraun

2nd Silnet (FR)　　　4yo c　61kg*　**16.3/1** (coupled with La Sorellina)
by Fastnet out of Silver Jill (King Salmon). Paul Duboscq / Étienne Pollet / C. Mère

3rd Worden (FR)　　　4yo c　60kg　　**16/1**
by Wild Risk out of Sans Tares (Sind). Ralph Strassburger / George Bridgland / Claudius Lalanne

*including 1kg overweight

Runners: 25 (FR 22, GB 2, GER 1). Distances: hd, 3. Going: good. Time: 2m 31.82s

Also ran: 4th **Buisson d'Or** (FR) 3yo c, 5th **Northern Light** (FR) 3yo c, 6th **Premonition** (GB) 3yo c, 7th **Janitor** (GB) 3yo c, 8th **Etrier Royal** (FR) 4yo c, 9th **Cosmos** (FR) 4yo c, 10th **Radio** (FR) 3yo f. Unplaced: **Shikampur** (IRE) 3yo c, **Nuccio** (ITY) 5yo h, **Nemrod II** 4yo c, **Sénégal** (_) 4yo c, **Château d'If** 4yo c, **Zucchero** (GB) 4yo c, **Niederländer** (GER) 6yo h, **Vamos** (FR) 4yo c, **Arbèle** (FR) 4yo f, **Damaka** (FR) 5yo m, **Skyraider** (GB) 3yo c, **Marly Knowe** (FR) 3yo c, **Seriphos** (FR) 3yo c, **Gourabe** (FR) 3yo f, **Noémi** (FR) 3yo f.

Silky smooth Sica Boy sluices in

Like father like son for Pelat

Background and fancied horses

Sica Boy headed the betting after posting two excellent performances in the autumn. Beforehand, on the basis of his win in the Prix Lupin, he was sent off favourite for the Prix du Jockey Club which was run in torrential rain. He squelched his way to third place but then appeared to really let the side down when only beating one home in the Grand Prix de Paris.

Subsequently he was found to have a physical problem which inhibited him from galloping at full tilt. Once recovered he returned to action at Chantilly, beating the Prix de Diane-winner Tahiti by half a length.

The market suggested that the runner-up that day would be his main opposition again in the Arc as they were returned at 4.1/1 and 4.3/1 respectively – the latter coupled with her pacemaker Bastia. A week after his successful return, Sica Boy further enhanced his reputation when handsomely winning the Prix Royal-Oak from Grand Prix de Paris runner-up Yorick.

Marcel Boussac's Cordova, along with her pacesetter Almaos, was only slightly longer at 4.5/1. Cordova had been a very useful two-year-old but had been under the weather when only managing seventh place in the 1000 Guineas. Back in France and rested until mid-July, she won the Prix Eugène Adam by four lengths, and in her final prep was only beaten by Philante in the Prix Vermeille.

Next up was Vamos at 7/1, who was having a third Arc foray after finishing seventh in 1952 and even further down the field last year. His second to Aureole in the King George VI and Queen Elizabeth Stakes in the summer was his best effort for a while.

Last year's winner, La Sorellina, ran deplorably in the Grand Prix de Saint-Cloud and as a result was taken out of *l'arc anglaise*. However, she did give her supporters a glimmer of hope when winning the Prix Vermout in early September. Paul Duboscq also ran Philante, who'd been third in The Oaks before disappointing on a couple of occasions. But she was back on song when beating Cordova in the Prix Vermeille.

Banassa boasted some of the best form in the line-up after winning the Grand Prix de Saint-Cloud, beating seven who were to re-oppose, and more recently the Prix du Prince d'Orange.

Among the outsiders were Sun Cap, a surprise but decisive winner of The Oaks, and the only foreign-trained runner, By Thunder!.

Trained by Sam Armstrong in Newmarket, By Thunder! had routed the opposition in the Ebor Handicap, coming home 12 lengths clear. He'd then finished fourth to Derby-winner Never Say Die in the St Leger. By Thunder! was accompanied to Longchamp by a pony called Smokey who belonged to the trainer's daughter Susan – the future Mrs Lester Piggott.

Betting

4.1/1 Sica Boy, 4.3/1 Tahiti & Bastia (coupled), 4.5/1 Cordova & Almaos (coupled), 7/1 Vamos, 9/1 Philante & La Sorellina (coupled), 9/1 Banassa, 12/1 Yorick, 25/1 BAR.

Three-year-old form lines
Prix du Jockey Club: 1st Le Petit Prince, 2nd Antarès, 3rd **Sica Boy**, 0th **Yorick**, 0th **Tribord**
Grand Prix de Paris: 1st Popof, 2nd **Yorick**, 3rd Alcara, 0th **Sun Cap**, 0th **Altana**, 0th **Sica Boy**
Prix Royal-Oak: 1st **Sica Boy**, 2nd **Yorick**, 3rd **Soleil Levant**

Fillies only
Prix de Diane: 1st **Tahiti**, 2nd Baghicheh, 3rd Uptala
Prix Vermeille: 1st **Philante**, 2nd **Cordova**, 3rd Reine d'Atout

Older horses and inter-generational races
Grand Prix de Saint-Cloud: 1st **Banassa**, 2nd **Savoyard**, 3rd **Vamos**, 0th **Norman**, 0th **Prince Rouge**, 0th **Romantisme**, 0th **La Sorellina**, 0th **Soleil Levant**
Grand Prix de Deauville: 1st Doux Vert, 2nd Gourabe, 3rd _, 0th **Philante**
Prix du Prince d'Orange: 1st **Banassa**, 2nd Batailleur IV, 3rd Radio, 4th Elu, 5th/last **Otto**

Abroad
In England
Derby Stakes: 1st Never Say Die, 2nd Arabian Night, 3rd Darius, 4th Elopement
Oaks Stakes: 1st **Sun Cap**, 2nd Altana, 3rd **Philante**
King George VI and Queen Elizabeth Stakes: 1st Aureole, 2nd **Vamos**, 3rd Darius, 5th Elopement
St Leger: 1st Never Say Die, 2nd Elopement, 3rd Estremadur, 4th **By Thunder!**

The race

On soft going the three pacemakers, Bastia, Almaos and Rabella, were all prominent early on followed by a group that included By Thunder!, Philante and Sica Boy. Meanwhile, Tahiti, La Sorellina and Cordova were in rear, along with Vamos, who'd created problems at the start and lost several lengths as the tapes rose.

After 1,000 metres Bastia called enough while Philante was asked to take closer order, and after joining Almaos and Rabella, the trio opened up a gap of six lengths to the pursuers.

With 800 metres to travel, Philante led on his own as the pacemakers dropped out. By Thunder!, Sica Boy and Romantisme where all well-placed while Banassa had made some good progress down the hill.

Sica Boy easily moved into second place as they entered the straight, and it just looked like a matter of time before he would pass Philante as Johnstone was still on the bridle. He waited until the final 100 metres before pressing the accelerator, to which Sica Boy responded instantly and the race was won.

Banassa finished best of the rest to take second place – a length behind the eased-down Sica Boy – with the game Philante holding on for third ahead of Norman, Cordova and Romantisme. Sadly Almaos broke a leg entering the straight and had to be put down.

Post-race

Sica Boy's facile victory was a second success in the race for the veteran jockey Rae Johnstone, who'd also won on Nikellora in 1945. The last-named had been conditioned by René Pelat, the father of this year's trainer, Pierre Pelat, who was based at Maisons-Laffitte.

While Sica Boy was retired for the season but kept in training, last year's winner La Sorellina had raced for the last time. She produced nine foals of which three won, albeit nothing of any great note.

Result

1954 Prix de l'Arc de Triomphe
Longchamp. Sunday, 3 October 1954
Weights: 3yo c: 55.5kg, 3yo f: 54kg, 4yo+ c: 60kg, 4yo+ f: 58.5kg

1st Sica Boy (FR)   3yo c   55.5kg   **4.1/1 fav**
by Sunny Boy out of Sica (Meridien). Madame Jean Cochery / Pierre Pelat / Rae Johnstone

2nd Banassa (FR)   4yo f   58.5kg   **9/1**
by Un Gaillard out of Fatou Gaye (Fair Copy). Julien Décrion / William Head / Claudius Lalanne

3rd Philante (FR)   3yo f   54kg   **9/1** (coupled with La Sorellina)
by Sayani out of Philaminte (Mon Trésor). Ralph Strassburger / Étienne Pollet / Guy Lequeux

Runners: 21 (FR 20, GB 1). Distances: 1, 1. Going: soft. Time: 2m 36.34s

Also ran: 4th **Norman** (FR) 6yo h, 5th **Cordova** (FR) 3yo f, 6th **Romantisme** (FR) 4yo c, 7th **Clochard** (FR) 4yo c, 8th **Tahiti** (GB) 3yo f, 9th **By Thunder!** (GB) 3yo c, 10th **Soleil Levant** (FR) 3yo c. Unplaced: **Elu** (GB) 5yo h, **Otto** (FR) 4yo c, **Vamos** (FR) 5yo h, **La Sorellina** (FR) 4yo c, **Prince Rouge** (FR) 3yo c, **Yorick** (FR) 3yo c, **Tribord** (FR) 3yo c, **Rabella** (GB) 3yo f, **Bastia** (ARG) 3yo f, **Sun Cap** (FR) 3yo f, **Almaos** (FR) 3yo f (PU).

Tesio scores posthumously with Ribot

First Italian winner since Crapom

Background and fancied horses

This year saw the first running of the Prix Henri Foy. The race, whose title was shortened to Prix Foy in 1969, would in time replace the Prix du Prince d'Orange as the major Arc trial for older horses run in France.

In the meantime, the horse that had won the latter race topped the betting for this year's race. Cordova, the only returnee from last year's Arc, had accounted for seven who were to run again in what, despite her being favoured by the weights, looked like a strong piece of form.

Cordova was accompanied by the winner of the Prix Royal-Oak, Macip, Prix du Jockey Club-fourth Kurun, and pacemaker Mercedial, to make up a Boussac quartet returned at 1.25/1. Fans of the new jockey sensation Serge Boullenger, who took the mount on Cordova, may have contributed to what was quite a skinny price.

It was 8/1 bar, which brought in the Prix du Jockey Club-winner Rapace, who was followed by Ribot at 8.8/1. One of four foreign-trained horses, Ribot had been bred by Federico Tesio who'd died the previous year in May, and therefore hadn't seen Ribot's two-year-old campaign.

The compact son of Tenerani won on all three appearances and had extended that unbeaten run to nine this term, despite injuring a fetlock in one race and missing some time due to a cough. He hadn't been entered in the Italian Classics but the collateral form indicated that he was superior to his contemporaries.

Georges Wildenstein's Beau Prince II, who'd been third home in both the Grand Prix de Paris and St Leger, was next. He would now be ridden by Jacques Fabre after Maxime Garcia broke his collar bone in the paddock before the previous race. Beau Prince II was followed in the betting by Prix du Prince d'Orange runner-up Savoyard, and Walhalla, who arrived on the back of wins in the Prix de Chantilly and Prix Henry Delamarre.

The rest of the overseas contingent were comprised of: last year's Irish Derby-winner and this season's runner-up, Zarathustra and Hugh Lupus, representing the Emerald Isle; and England's Hardwicke Stakes-winner Elopement, who'd been delayed on the trip over.

Betting

1.25/1 Cordova & Macip & Kurun & Mercedial (all coupled), 8/1 Rapace, 8.8/1 Ribot, 16/1 Beau Prince II, 17/1 Savoyard, 18/1 Walhalla, 20/1 BAR.

Three-year-old form lines

Prix du Jockey Club: 1st **Rapace**, 2nd Vimy, 3rd **Beignet**, 4th **Kurun**, 6th **Bewitched**, 0th, **Beau Prince II**, 0th **Fric**, 0th **Norfolk**, 0th **Tragedian**

Grand Prix de Paris: 1st Phil Drake, 2nd **Bewitched**, 3rd **Beau Prince II**, 4th **Rapace**, 0th **Kurun**, 0th **Douve**

Prix Royal-Oak: 1st **Macip**, 2nd **Bewitched**, 3rd Dhanous

Fillies only

Prix de Diane: 1st **Douve**, 2nd **Picounda**, 3rd Myriade

Prix Vermeille: 1st Wild Miss, 2nd **Picounda**, 3rd **Douve**

Older horses and inter-generational races

Grand Prix de Saint-Cloud: 1st **Chingacgook**, 2nd **Mahan**, 3rd Prince Rouge, 5th **Cordova**

Prix du Prince d'Orange: 1st **Cordova,** 2nd **Savoyard**, 3rd **Mahan**, 4th **Norfolk**, 0th **Hidalgo**, 0th **Kurun**, 0th **Rapace**, 0th **Fric**

Prix Henri Foy, inaugural race: 1st Norman, 2nd **Fauchelevent**, 3rd Rosa Bonheur, 0th **Savoyard**

Abroad

In England

Derby Stakes: 1st Phil Drake, 2nd Panaslipper, 3rd Acropolis

King George VI and Queen Elizabeth Stakes: 1st Vimy, 2nd Acropolis, 3rd **Elopement**, 5th **Hugh Lupus**, 7th **Zarathustra**, 9th **Darius**, last **Cordova**

St Leger: 1st Meld, 2nd Nucleus, 3rd **Beau Prince II**

In Ireland

Irish Derby: 1st Panaslipper, 2nd **Hugh Lupus**, 3rd Anns Kuda

The race

Picounda, Fric and Macip all broke fast. Macip was immediately restrained and once the runners on the inner settled down it was Mahan who went on from Ribot, Picounda, Zarathustra and Beau Prince II. However, as the horses drawn wide moved across Rapace, Cordova and Bewitched were squeezed out while Hidalgo fared worst of all, losing his jockey in the process.

At the top of the hill the riderless Hidalgo preceded Mahan, who still led, with Ribot and Beau Prince II not far behind as Zarathustra started to back pedal. Meanwhile Hugh Lupus and Rapace both started to make some progress from the rear.

On the final bend, though, Ribot cruised into the lead accompanied by the loose horse and had the race won bar interference entering the straight. Hidalgo didn't cause any problems and Ribot passed the post three lengths to the good over Beau Prince II – a great spare ride for Jacques Fabre – with a margin of two and a half lengths to Picounda in third.

The first of the Boussac quartet was Kurun in fourth followed by the first older horse, Savoyard, and then Macip. After looking dangerous, Rapace finished lame, while Hugh Lupus was found to be coughing once home in Ireland. Elopement, unsuited by the ground, skulked around in rear.

Post-race

It was a formidable performance by Ribot, who became the first Italian-trained winner since Crapom in 1934. Ribot was sired by the Italian-champion Tenerani, who was by then standing at the English National Stud in West Grinstead, where Ribot himself was foaled.

Named after Théodule Augustin Ribot, a nineteenth century painter of the Realist school, he was owned in partnership by Tesio's widow, Lydia, and Marchese Mario Incisa della Rocchetta. He was trained at their Razza Dormello Olgiata estate by Ugo Penco.

After the Arc, Ribot returned to Italy, where two weeks later he won the Premio del Jockey Club by 15 lengths. As always, he was ridden by the gifted veteran jockey Enrico Camici, who was 43 at the time. It was another brilliant exhibition and it wouldn't be his last.

Result

1955 Prix de l'Arc de Triomphe
Longchamp. Sunday, 9 October 1955
Weights: 3yo c: 55.5kg, 3yo f: 54kg, 4yo+ c: 60kg, 4yo+ f: 58.5kg

1st Ribot (GB)   3yo c   55.5kg   **8.8/1**
by Tenerani out of Romanella (El Greco). Marchese Mario Incisa della Rocchetta / Ugo Penco / Enrico Camici

2nd Beau Prince II (GB)   3yo c   55.5kg   **16/1**
by Prince Chevalier out of Isabelle Brand (Black Devil). Georges Wildenstein / Edmond Boullenger / Jacques Fabre

3rd Picounda (FR)   3yo f   54kg   **60/1**
by Oubanghi out of Nikitina (Tourbillon). Comte Roland de Chambure / _ / Maurice Larraun

Runners: 23 (FR 19, IRE 2, GB 1, ITY 1). Distances: 3, 2½. Going: soft. Time: 2m 35.68s

Also ran: 4th **Kurun** (FR) 3yo c, 5th **Savoyard** (GB) 5yo h, 6th **Macip** (FR) 3yo c, 7th **Cordova** (FR) 4yo f, 8th **Bewitched** (FR) 3yo c, 9th **Fric** (FR) 3yo c, 10th **Mahan** (GB) 4yo c. Unplaced: **Zarathustra** (GB) 4yo c, **Elopement** (GB) 4yo c, **Mistralor** (FR) 4yo c, **Mercedial** (_) 3yo c, **Hugh Lupus** (FR) 3yo c (previously called Amortisseur), **Walhalla** (FR) 3yo c, **Rapace** (FR) 3yo c, **Norfolk** (FR) 3yo c, **Tragedien** (FR) 3yo c, **Beignet** (FR) 3yo c, **Fauchelevent** (FR) 3yo c, **Douve** (FR) 3yo f, **Hidalgo** (FR) 4yo c (UR).

Ribot all class as he extends unbeaten run to 16

First runners from the USA

Background and fancied horses

Ribot was back, and after five wide-margin victories in Italy, he'd returned to his country of origin to contest the King George VI and Queen Elizabeth Stakes at Ascot. The ground was heavy and he'd had to be rousted along at certain stages but eventually Ribot pulled five lengths clear to take his unbeaten run to 14.

Rightly or wrongly some observers were disparaging about this performance. However, back in Italy, and on a firmer surface, Ribot showed he still possessed an electrifying turn of foot when scorching home eight lengths to the good in the Premio del Piazzale. His fans stayed loyal and at 0.6/1 he was a warm order to retain his Arc crown.

Marcel Boussac's filly Apollonia, who'd won the Poule d'Essai des Pouliches and the Prix de Diane, was second favourite at 6.8/1. On the negative side she'd only managed sixth place in the Grand Prix de Saint-Cloud, and hadn't had a prep race after missing the Prix Vermeille due to the soft ground.

As a result of winning the Prix Juigné, Prix Noialles and Prix Lupin, Arc third-favourite Tanerko was sent off at odds-on in the Prix du Jockey Club. But on heavy ground he couldn't accelerate and finished third. After a three-month break, François Dupré's charge had returned in style to take the Prix du Prince d'Orange.

The Oaks-winner Sicarelle, who suffered interference in the Grand Prix de Paris before running inexplicably badly in the Prix Vermeille, and her stable companion Vattel were joint-fourth favourites. The last-named had won what was a strong renewal of the Grand Prix de Paris, only for her newly elevated reputation to be tarnished when she was trounced by the outsider Arabian in the Prix Royal-Oak.

Career Boy and Fisherman were the first USA-trained horses to run in Europe since Omaha was just beaten by Quashed in the legendary duel for the 1936 Ascot Gold Cup. Career Boy suffered a setback before the Kentucky Derby and only managed sixth place. After missing the Preakness Stakes he returned to action, finishing a creditable second in the Belmont Stakes.

Since then he'd given weight and a beating to some decent sorts in the United Nations Handicap. Fisherman, who'd won the 1954 Washington DC International Stakes, was in as Career Boy's pacemaker.

In addition to Ribot and the duo from the USA, Zarathustra was back after winning the Goodwood Cup, and now under the aegis of Cecil Boyd-Rochfort was representing England. As was the Harry Wragg-trained Irish Derby-winner Talga.

Betting

0.6/1 Ribot, 6.8/1 Apollonia, 8/1 Tanerko, 11/1 Sicarelle & Vattel (coupled), 19/1 Arabian, 21/1 Career Boy & Fisherman (coupled), 32/1 BAR.

Three-year-old form lines
Prix du Jockey Club: 1st Philius, 2nd **Saint Raphael**, 3rd **Tanerko**, 0th **Ambiax**
Grand Prix de Paris: 1st **Vattel**, 2nd Floriados, 3rd Aztèque, 0th **Ambiax**, 0th (finished injured) Lavandin, last **Sicarelle**
Prix Royal-Oak: 1st **Arabian**, 2nd **Vattel**, 3rd The Kite

Fillies only
Prix de Diane: 1st **Apollonia**, 2nd Tour de Londres, 3rd Midget
Prix Vermeille: 1st Janiari, 2nd Yasmin, 3rd Ad Altiora, 6th **Sicarelle**

Older horses and inter-generational races
Grand Prix de Saint-Cloud: DH1st **Burgos**, DH1st **Oroso**, 3rd Beau Prince II, 6th **Apollonia**, last **Sicarelle**
La Coupe de Maisons-Laffitte: 1st **Cobetto**, 2nd _, 3rd _
Prix du Prince d'Orange: 1st **Tanerko**, 2nd **Tenareze**, 3rd Saint Raphael, 0th **Ambiax**
Prix Henri Foy: 1st **Fric**, 2nd **Master Boing**, 3rd _, 0th **Oroso**

Abroad
In England
Derby Stakes: 1st Lavandin, 2nd Montaval, 3rd Roistar, 7th **Tenareze**
Oaks Stakes: 1st **Sicarelle**, 2nd Janiari, 3rd Yasmin
King George VI and Queen Elizabeth Stakes: 1st **Ribot**, 2nd High Veldt, 3rd Kurun
St Leger: 1st Cambremer, 2nd Hornbeam, 3rd French Beige, 4th **Talgo**,

In Ireland
Irish Derby: 1st **Talgo**, 2nd Roistar, 3rd No Comment

In Italy
Gran Premio di Milano: 1st **Ribot**, 2nd Tissot, 3rd Murano II

The race

It had rained during the week and the ground was heavy. Fisherman broke well and quickly built up a five-length advantage over Norfolk, Ribot and Master Boing, while Vattel and Talgo were in rear.

Tanerko and Apollonia moved into the first half-dozen after 400 metres, with Master Boing and Fric just behind. Zarathustra, who'd been at the back, started to make a few places as they reached the top of the hill, and Talgo could also be seen closing in on the inside.

On the descent, Fisherman still led from the under-pressure Norfolk. Ominously for his rivals, Ribot was still going very easily and approaching the straight Camici made his move and quickly passed Fisherman.

Shifting through the gears, Ribot quickly put the race beyond doubt and cleared away to win by six lengths in what was a dazzling performance. Talgo won the race for second place with Tanerko third and the first American home, Career Boy, in fourth. Master Boing and Oroso were next past the post.

Post-race

The Ascot doubters had been well and truly silenced, and through the collateral form with the USA runners it looked as though Ribot could be hailed as the best racehorse in the world. Indeed, Timeform gave him a higher rating than any previous Arc winner.

It was a glorious swansong for the now fifth dual winner of the Arc and he was sent to stud. He stood in Newmarket for a couple of years before returning to Italy for another two and then on to the USA. He sired some magnificent racehorses, including two winners of our race as well as horses of the stature of Ragusa, Ribocco, Ribero and Tom Wolfe. His extended line has produced at least another seven Arc winners.

Federico Tesio, Ribot's breeder, had famously said that: 'The thoroughbred exists because its selection has depended not on experts, technicians or zoologists, but on a piece of wood – the winning post of the Epsom Derby.' Although the importance of Epsom – and Chantilly – should never be underestimated, arguably the winning post on the Bois de Boulogne has subsequently superseded them in importance – especially as the Prix de l'Arc de Triomphe can be won more than once.

Ribot was unbeaten in 16 races and one of the greatest racehorses of all time.

Result

1956 Prix de l'Arc de Triomphe
Longchamp. Sunday, 7 October 1956
Weights: 3yo c: 55.5kg, 3yo f: 54kg, 4yo+ c: 60kg, 4yo+ f: 58.5kg

1st Ribot (GB)   4yo c   60kg   **0.6/1 fav**
by Tenerani out of Romanella (El Greco). Marchese Mario Incisa della Rocchetta / Ugo Penco / Enrico Camici

2nd Talgo (IRE)   3yo c   55.5kg   **100/1**
by Krakatao out of Miss France (Jock). Gerry Oldham / Harry Wragg / Manny Mercer

3rd Tanerko (FR)   3yo c   55.5kg   **8/1**
by Tantième out of La Divine (Fair Copy). François Dupré / François Mathet / Jacques Doyasbère

Runners: 20 (FR 15, GB 2, USA 2, ITY 1). Distances: 6, 2. Going: heavy. Time: 2m 34.76s

Also ran: 4th **Career Boy** (USA) 3yo c, 5th **Master Boing** (GB) 3yo c, 6th **Oroso** (FR) 3yo c, 7th **Fric** (FR) 4yo c, 8th **Burgos** (FR) 4yo c, 9th **Fisherman** (USA) 5yo h, 10th **Arabian** (FR) 3yo c. Unplaced: **Zarathustra** (GB) 5yo h, **Norfolk** (FR) 4yo c, **Flying Flag** (FR) 3yo c, **Saint Raphael** (FR) 3yo c, **Ambiax** (FR) 3yo c, **Cobetto** (GB) 4yo c, **Tenareze** (FR) 3yo c, **Vattel** (FR) 3yo c, **Apollonia** (FR) 3yo f, **Sicarelle** (FR) 3yo f.

Serge Boullenger steers home longshot Oroso

Prize money raised dramatically

Background and fancied horses

To celebrate the centenary of the opening of Longchamp racecourse, the prize money was raised again from 25 million francs to 40 million francs and two new races, the Prix de l'Abbaye de Longchamp and Prix du Moulin de Longchamp, were inaugurated.

In the absence of Ribot, last year's third Tanerko was favourite after a campaign highlighted by successes in the Prix Ganay, Grand Prix de Saint-Cloud and Prix du Prince d'Orange. In the latter he beat the Prix Jean Prat-winner Oroso by six lengths with a further four back to the third. Joined by Poisson Volant to force the pace, he was returned at 1.4/1.

The opposition was headed by the Grand Prix de Paris-victor Altipan at 6.8/1, followed by the Vincent O'Brien-trained Gladness at 9/1. She'd won the Sunninghill Park Stakes at Ascot in July and had beaten her stable companion Derby-second Ballymoss in a pre-Arc gallop.

The first runners in double figures were Marcel Boussac's Arbencia, the winner of the Prix Vermeille, and Prince Aly Khan's trio, the King George VI and Queen Elizabeth Stakes-second Al Mabsoot, Magic North, and Prince Taj, who'd whipped round at the start of the Derby. In the summer Prince Aly's father, the Aga Khan III, who had owned Migolo and Nuccio, had died. Aly was bypassed for the Aga Khan title which instead went to his 20-year-old son Karim.

Others with a shout included Guy de Rothschild's Prix Hocquart-winner Argel at 14/1, the returning USA-challenger Career Boy at 18/1, and Derby-third Pipe of Peace at the same price. The last-named, like last year's runner-up Talgo, who was back, was trained in England.

Betting

1.4/1 Tanerko & Poisson Volant (coupled), 6.8/1 Altipan, 9/1 Gladness, 10/1 Arbencia, 12/1 Al Mabsoot & Magic North & Prince Taj (all coupled), 14/1 Argel, 18/1 Career Boy, 18/1 Pipe of Peace, 25/1 BAR.

Three-year-old form lines

Prix du Jockey Club: 1st Amber, 2nd Guard's Tie, 3rd Le Haar, 5th **Al Mabsoot**, 7th **Altipan**, 8th **Argel**

Grand Prix de Paris: 1st **Altipan**, 2nd Guard's Tie, 3rd **Magic North**

Prix Royal-Oak: 1st Scot, 2nd **Argel**, 3rd **Altipan**, 4th **Magic North**, 5th **Flying Relic**

Fillies only

Prix de Diane: 1st Cerisoles, 2nd Kalitka, 3rd Toro, 4th **Denisy**, 0th **Arbencia** (fav, left at start)

Prix Vermeille: 1st **Arbencia**, 2nd **Denisy**, 3rd **Great Success**

Older horses and inter-generational races

Grand Prix de Saint-Cloud: 1st **Tanerko**, 2nd Franc Luron, 3rd Haut Brion, 4th **Oroso**, 7th **Al Mabsoot**, 9th **Flying Relic**

Prix du Prince d'Orange: 1st **Tanerko**, 2nd **Oroso**, 3rd Tapioca

Prix Henri Foy: 1st **Blockhaus**, 2nd Tapioca, 3rd **Flying Relic**, 0th **Al Mabsoot**

Abroad

In England

Derby Stakes: 1st Crepello, 2nd Ballymoss, 3rd **Pipe of Peace**, 9th **Prince Taj** (whipped round start)

King George VI and Queen Elizabeth Stakes: 1st Montavel, 2nd **Al Mabsoot**, 5th **Talgo**, 6th **Fric**, 0th **Oroso**

The race

There had been heavy rain during the week and on the night before, but it was a sunny afternoon as Tanerko's pacemaker, Poisson Volant, led them away, from Ambiax, Oroso, Tanerko and Balbo.

The order at the front remained pretty much the same until the final turn, when Poisson Volant stalled, which allowed Tanerko, Oroso and Ambiax, all abreast, to go on, with Balbo, Prince Taj and Denisy in the second rank. Ambiax cracked next, followed by favourite Tanerko, much to the consternation of the crowd.

Inside the last 400 metres it was Oroso and Denisy at the head of affairs. They were at it hammer and tongs with the former a nose to the good. Try as she might, Denisy just couldn't quite get on terms and eventually Oroso extended the lead to half a length as they passed the post.

There was two and a half lengths further to Balbo in third followed, after a yawning gap, by Prince Taj, the fast-finishing Al Mabsoot and Tanerko, who was later found to have injured his off-hind leg.

Post-race

It was a shock result, to say the very least. Unfancied at 52/1, Oroso had finished behind Tanerko in their four previous meetings during the season, and in the Arc last year. It wasn't that Oroso had no talent, more that he was quirky and needed everything to go his way, which it had on that October afternoon. He retired a short while later but didn't make a great mark at stud and was exported to Denmark in 1967.

Delighted owner Raoul Meyer, who'd also bred Oroso in partnership with René Leroy, was the president of the famous department store Galeries Lafayette, situated on Boulevard Haussmann in Paris.

Trainer Daniel Lescalle ran a mixed yard and had tasted many successes at Auteuil, most memorably when Bouzoulou won the Grand Steeple-Chase de Paris. Jockey Serge Boullenger had started his obligatory three-months military service four weeks before the race, but fortunately the Minister of War allowed him the day off to take the ride.

Result
1957 Prix de l'Arc de Triomphe
Longchamp. Sunday, 6 October 1957
Weights: 3yo c: 55.5kg, 3yo f: 54kg, 4yo+ c: 60kg, 4yo+ f: 58.5kg

1st Oroso (FR)　　　　　4yo c　60kg　**52/1**
by Tifinar out of Eos (Solferino). Raoul Meyer / Daniel Lescalle / Serge Boullenger

2nd Denisy (FR)　　　　　3yo f　54kg　**45/1**
by Pan out of Sainte Mesme (Le Pacha). Roger Saint / Georges Pelat / Guy Chancelier

3rd Balbo (FR)　　　　　3yo c　55.5kg　**8/1**
by Apple Pie out of Blue Bottle (Blue Moon). Georges Wildenstein / Percy Carter / Jacques Fabre

Runners: 24 (FR 20, GB 2, USA 1, IRE 1). Distances: ½, 2½. Going: good. Time: 2m 33.42s

Also ran: 4th **Prince Taj** (FR) 3yo c, 5th **Al Mabsoot** (FR) 3yo c, 6th **Tanerko** (FR) 4yo c, 7th **Great Success** (FR) 3yo f, 8th **Fric** (FR) 5yo h, 9th **Altipan** (FR) 3yo c, 10th **Arbencia** (FR) 3yo f. Unplaced: **Gladness** (IRE) 4yo f, **Pipe of Peace** (FR) 3yo c, **Mr Pickwick** (FR) 3yo c, **Rumesnil** (FR) 4yo c, **Argel** (FR) 3yo c, **Yellowstone** (GB) 4yo c, **Magic North** (FR) 3yo c, **Career Boy** (USA) 4yo c, **Ambiax** (FR) 4yo c, **Blockhaus** (FR) 4yo c, **Flying Relic** (FR) 3yo c, **Talgo** (IRE) 4yo c, **Poisson Volant** (FR) 4yo c, **Flying Flag** (FR) 4yo c.

1958

Ballymoss the first winner for Ireland

Vincent O'Brien's Longchamp legend begins

Background

François Dupré's Bella Paola was the filly of the year and, along with hardy-perennial Tanerko, topped the market at 1.75/1. Bella Paola's list of achievements was pretty extensive. She'd won the 1000 Guineas, The Oaks and the Prix Vermeille and had been unlucky when runner-up in the Prix du Jockey Club.

Tanerko, third to Ribot in 1956 and favourite last year, had confirmed his wellbeing in the summer when winning a second Grand Prix de Saint-Cloud.

Next in the betting was Ballymoss at 3.9/1. Last season he'd become the first ever Irish-trained horse to win the St Leger. This term, with Scobie Breasley riding, replacing the injured Tommy Burns, he'd beaten Fric when winning the Coronation Cup. The new pairing added emphatic victories in the Eclipse Stakes and King George VI and Queen Elizabeth Stakes before Ballymoss was put away for the Arc.

The Italian representative Sedan, at 4.3/1, had been in excellent form, winning, among other races, the Derby Italiano, Gran Premio d'Italia and Gran Premio di Milano.

The last two winners of the Prix Royal-Oak, Wallaby and Scot, together with the latter's stablemate Cherasco, were the only other horses under 20/1.

In addition to Ballymoss and Sedan there was one more raider in the form of the German-trained Nogaro II, who'd been fourth to Prix de Diane-winner Dushka in the Grosser Preis von Baden.

Betting

1.75/1 Bella Paola & Tanerko (coupled), 3.9/1 Ballymoss, 4.3/1 Sedan, 10/1 Wallaby, 14/1 Scot & Cherasco (coupled), 20/1 BAR.

Three-year-old form lines
Prix du Jockey Club: 1st Tamanar, 2nd **Bella Paola**, 3rd Pepin le Bref, 4th **San Roman**, 5th **Wallaby**, 0th **Cherasco**, 0th **Malefaim**
Grand Prix de Paris: 1st **San Roman**, 2nd Pépin le Bref, 3rd Love Boy, 5th **Upstart**
Prix Royal-Oak: 1st **Wallaby**, 2nd **Upstart**, 3rd Tello, 0th **San Roman**,

Fillies only

Prix de Diane: 1st **Dushka**, 2nd Cataracte, 3rd Djelouba, 7th **Pharstella**

Prix Vermeille: 1st **Bella Paola**, 2nd **V.I.P.**, 3rd Djelouba 4th **Dushka**

Older horses and inter-generational races

Grand Prix de Saint-Cloud: 1st **Tanerko**, 2nd Denisy, 3rd Flying Relic, 4th **Fric**, 5th **Al Mabsoot**, 7th **V.I.P.**, 8th **Malefaim**

La Coupe de Maisons-Laffitte: 1st **Fric**, 2nd Franc Luron, 3rd Tapioca

Grand Prix de Deauville: 1st Chippendale, 2nd **Cherasco**, 3rd Fils de Roi, 4th **Fric**

Prix du Prince d'Orange: 1st Chief, 2nd _, 3rd **Malefaim**, 4th **Scot**

Prix Henri Foy: 1st Primesautier, 2nd _, 3rd _, 0th **Al Mabsoot**

Abroad

In England

Derby Stakes: 1st Hard Ridden, 2nd Paddy's Point, 3rd Nagami, 0th **Wallaby**

Oaks Stakes: 1st **Bella Paola**, 2nd Mother Goose, 3rd None Nicer, 0th **V.I.P.**

Ascot Gold Cup: 1st Gladness, 2nd Hornbeam, 3rd Doutelle, 4th **Scot**

King George VI and Queen Elizabeth Stakes: 1st **Ballymoss**, 2nd Almeria, 3rd Doutelle

In Germany

Grosser Preis von Baden: 1st **Dushka**, 2nd Aletsch, 3rd Agio, 4th **Nogaro II**

In Italy

Gran Premio di Milano: 1st **Sedan**, 2nd Tiepolo, 3rd Malhoa

The race

There was a torrential downpour while the horses were in the paddock but it stopped just as the runners were led out for the parade, and in the end the race was run under a cloudless sky.

But the ground was now softer than predicted as Nogaro II, under Lester Piggott, flew at the start and led the way from Bella Paola, Sedan and Tombeur. The other Dupré runner, Tanerko, was in midfield, while Ballymoss was having to be pushed along to maintain his position.

Nogaro II had a clear advantage as they reached the summit of the hill, where Wallaby dropped back suddenly and Cherasco took closer order. Bella Paola and Tombeur were still prominent and Ballymoss was starting to improve up the inside.

Rounding the final turn, Nogaro II and Cherasco still had the lead. However, Bella Paola, Tanerko and Fric were all close behind. Then on the inner, after securing a dream passage, Ballymoss breezed into contention looking full of running.

The Irish colt passed everything in double-quick time and sailed away to score by two lengths from Fric, who ran on well but never looked like catching the winner. Cherasco was a further two and a half lengths back in third with another three to V.I.P. in fourth, then Tanerko and Malefaim.

Post-race

Ballymoss had been all quality on a surface that his trainer didn't think would suit. In fact, after the storm Vincent O'Brien wanted to withdraw Ballymoss but had been persuaded to run by an official. Many fans had made their way across from Ireland and he received a tremendous reception, especially from those who remembered the Coronation Cup and had backed him in a forecast with Fric.

Owner John McShain's construction firm worked on over 100 buildings in and around Washington DC, notably The Pentagon and the Jefferson Memorial, as well as the post-war reconstruction of the White House.

The man on board, who was about to win the first of what would be four jockeys' championships in England, had been born Arthur Edward Breasley, but while still very young was given the nickname 'Scobie' after the famous Australian trainer and jockey James Scobie.

Vincent O'Brien had always been a canny trainer of flat horses, but his exploits in the jump world in the late 1940s and 50s were of a stellar nature. They included handling Cottage Rake, the winner of three Cheltenham Gold Cups, and the triple-Champion Hurdler Hatton's Grace before notching up a hat-trick in the Grand National with Early Mist, Royal Tan and Quare Times.

He'd won the 1953 Irish Derby with Chamier and had concentrated on the flat from 1956. Ballymoss's win in the Prix de l'Arc de Triomphe was just the start of the legend, and the name M. V. O'Brien will figure many more times in our story.

Ballymoss went to America for his last appearance, running third in a rough house renewal of the Washington DC International Stakes. Hampered on several occasions, and unsuited by the tight turning track, he did well to make the frame at all. He was then syndicated at stud producing among others the brilliant Royal Palace who in turn sired Dunfermline. Ballymoss was also the grandsire of Levmoss and dual Ascot Gold Cup-winner Le Moss.

Result

1958 Prix de l'Arc de Triomphe

Longchamp. Sunday, 5 October 1958
Weights: 3yo c: 55.5kg, 3yo f: 54kg, 4yo+ c: 60kg, 4yo+ f: 58.5kg

1st Ballymoss (GB)   4yo c   60kg   **3.9/1**
by Mossborough out of Indian Call (Singapore). John McShain / Vincent O'Brien / Scobie Breasley

2nd Fric (FR)   6yo h   60kg   **37/1**
by Vandale out of Fripe (Mehemet Ali). Michel Calmann / Philippe Lallie / B. Margueritte

3rd Cherasco (FR)   3yo c   55.5kg   **14/1** (coupled with Scot)
by Vieux Manoir out of Cannelle (Biribi). Simone del Duca / Pierre Pelat / Jean Massard

Runners: 17 (FR 14, GER 1, IRE 1, ITY 1). Distances: 2, 2½. Going: soft. Time: 2m 37.91s

Also ran: 4th **V.I.P.** (FR) 3yo f, 5th **Tanerko** (FR) 5yo h, 6th **Malefaim** (FR) 3yo c, 7th **Scot** (FR) 4yo c, 8th **Bella Paola** (FR) 3yo f, 9th **Upstart** (FR) 3yo c, 10th **Nogaro II** (GER) 4yo c. Unplaced: **San Roman** (FR) 3yo c, **Tombeur** (FR) 3yo c, **Pharstella** (FR) 3yo f, **Sedan** (FR) 3yo c, **Al Mabsoot** (FR) 4yo c, **Wallaby** (FR) 3yo c, **Balbo** (FR) 4yo c.

Saint Crespin – it's close, very close

A sensational finish that ends up in the Stewards' Room

Background and fancied horses

The home team couldn't see beyond the Simone del Duca-owned Herbager. After winning the Prix du Jockey Club he'd beaten the unlucky Derby-third Shantung when landing the Grand Prix de Saint-Cloud. And then, after a break, he'd cantered home unchallenged in the Prix du Prince d'Orange. Coupled with pacemaker L'Aymé, Herbager was odds-on to add the Arc.

The English-trained Primera, who'd won the Prince of Wales's Stakes and had then given away lumps of weight when scoring in the Ebor Handicap, was next at 9/1.

Vamour, at 12/1, had a huge home reputation but disappointed when favourite for the Prix Noailles and the Grand Prix de Paris. He'd finally started to deliver when taking the Prix Royal-Oak.

Last year's Prix Royal-Oak-victor Wallaby was back and, in the meantime, he'd won the Ascot Gold Cup. He was returned at 16/1, a point shorter than Prince Aly Khan's Saint Crespin who'd been antepost favourite for the Derby.

As it turned out, Saint Crespin finished fourth at Epsom after being held up in his work with a stomach problem. He'd made amends in the Eclipse Stakes. However, four days before the Arc he'd injured a leg but was running after passing a veterinary inspection.

Dr Carlo Vittadini's Gran Premio d'Italia and Gran Premio di Milano-winner Exar was the same price and the best of the three-strong Italian challenge. The others, Toukaram, who'd beaten Exar in receipt of 4kg in the Premio Boschetti, and Derby Italiano-winner Marino, were 85/1 and 42/1 respectively.

The fifth and final foreign challenger was Brita Strokirk's filly Lycaste II – the first Swedish-trained horse to line up in the Arc – who'd finished second in the Stockholm Cup.

Betting

1.75/1 Herbager & L'Aymé (coupled), 9/1 Primera, 12/1 Vamour, 16/1 Wallaby, 17/1 Exar, 17/1 Saint Crespin, 32/1 BAR.

Three-year-old form lines

Prix du Jockey Club: 1st **Herbager**, 2nd Dan Cupid, 3rd **Midnight Sun**, 6th **Le Loup Garou**, 7th **Montrouge**, 0th **Minstrel**

Grand Prix de Paris: 1st Birum, 2nd **Le Loup Garou**, 3rd **Apollo**, 5th **Fatrolo**, 9th **Vamour**

Prix Royal-Oak: 1st **Vamour**, 2nd Gric, 3rd **Minstrel**, 4th **Le Loup Garou**

Fillies only

Prix de Diane: 1st **Barquette**, 2nd **Fiorenza**, 3rd La Coquenne

Prix Vermeille: 1st **Mi Carina**, 2nd Favréale, 3rd Sabre Jet, 5th **Fiorenza**, 0th **Barquette**

Older horses and inter-generational races

Grand Prix de Saint-Cloud: 1st **Herbager**, 2nd Shantung, 3rd Noelor, 5th **Malefaim**, 9th **Djesak**

Prix du Prince d'Orange: 1st **Herbager**, 2nd **Marino**, 3rd **Balbo**, 0th **Midnight Sun**,

Abroad

In England

Derby Stakes: 1st Parthia, 2nd Fidalgo, 3rd Shantung, 4th **Saint Crespin**, 10th Dan Cupid

Ascot Gold Cup: 1st **Wallaby**, 2nd Alcide, 3rd French Beige

King George VI and Queen Elizabeth Stakes: 1st Alcide, 2nd Gladness, 3rd **Balbo**, 0th **Wallaby**

In Germany

Grosser Preis von Baden: 1st **Malefaim**, 2nd Turkrano, 3rd Orsini

In Italy

Gran Premio di Milano: 1st **Exar**, 2nd Feria, 3rd Surdi, 4th **Marino**, 5th Rio Marin

The race

On a very hot day in front of a huge crowd, the majority of whom were there to see Herbager, Marcel Boussac-representative Djesak immediately set off in front. He was followed by Midnight Sun, Marino and Vieux Château, with Saint Crespin in the next group.

Down the hill, Lester Piggott on Primera took closer order. However, favourite Herbager was still at the back. At the turn-in Midnight Sun took over from the tiring Djesak closely followed by Primera and Saint Crespin, while Mi Carina and Le Loup Garou were making ground in the middle of the track. Exar and Fatrolo also had chances, but it was looking ominous for Herbager.

Midnight Sun was resolute on the inside as first Primera and then Saint Crespin challenged. All the time Mi Carina and Le Loup Garou were creeping closer and closer. A battle royal ensued between Midnight Sun and Saint Crespin. Primera was also still there as Mi Carina and Le Loup Garou joined them on the line and the quintet whizzed past together in one of the closest finishes ever seen.

Unfortunately Saint Crespin finished lame, presumably due to a recurrence of his recent leg injury.

It took 12 minutes to sort out the photo, with Midnight Sun and Saint Crespin adjudged to have dead-heated, with Le Loup Garou a short head back in third and then a short neck and the same to Mi Carina in fourth and Primera in fifth. Half a length back there was another dead-heat for sixth place between Exar and Fatrolo. Herbager could only manage 10th but like Saint Crespin he was found to be lame having strained a ligament in the early stages.

The drama was not over as Saint Crespin's jockey, George Moore, lodged an objection against Midnight Sun for bumping him on several occasions. Predictably a counter objection was made against Saint Crespin by Midnight Sun's trainer François Mathet.

After 20 minutes of deliberations the stewards gave their verdict. The camera patrol film supported the view that Midnight Sun was to blame and the outright victory was awarded to Saint Crespin, with Midnight Sun demoted to second and his jockey, Jacques Fabre, given a week's ban.

Post-race

Saint Crespin's owner, Prince Aly Khan, who ended the year as leading owner in France and England, joined his father on the Arc roll of honour. He'd been successful with Migoli in 1948 and Nuccio in 1952; the latter, like Saint Crespin, had been trained by Alec Head, who now moved his score on to two.

It was the first win for Prince Aly's stable jockey, the Australian George Moore. Saint Crespin was retired for the season, but that became permanent after a freak accident. One day during training his work rider was knocked out of the saddle by a falling branch and a scared Saint Crespin ran full tilt into another tree sustaining a career-ending shoulder injury.

Retired to Aly Khan's Gilltown Stud in Ireland, his best progeny were fillies, including the 1971 1000 Guineas, Oaks and Irish Oaks-winner Altesse Royal, the 1967 Prix Vermeille-victor Casaque Grise, and Alvertona the dam of 1979 Cheltenham Gold Cup-winner Alverton.

Result

1959 Prix de l'Arc de Triomphe
Longchamp. Sunday, 4 October 1959
Weights: 3yo c: 55.5kg, 3yo f: 54kg, 4yo+ c: 60kg, 4yo+ f: 58.5kg

1st Saint Crespin (GB)　　3yo c　55.5kg　**17/1**
by Aureole out of Neocracy (Nearco). Prince Aly Khan / Alec Head / George Moore

2nd Midnight Sun (FR)　　3yo c　55.5kg　**50/1**
by Sunny Boy out of Polaire (Le Volcan). François Dupré / François Mathet / Jacques Fabre

3rd Le Loup Garou (FR)　　3yo c　55.5kg　**45/1**
by Prince Bio out of Roxelane (Foxhunter). Comte d'Audiffret-Pasquier / Richard Carver / B. Margueritte

Runners: 25 (FR 20, ITY 3, GB 1, SWE 1). Distances: DH, sh hd. Going: good. Time: 2m 33.30s

Stewards' Inquiry: Midnight Sun, who'd dead-heated with Saint Crespin, was adjudged to have interfered with Saint Crespin on more than one occasion in the straight and was placed second.

Also ran: 4th **Mi Carina** (FR) 3yo f, 5th **Primera** (GB) 5yo h, DH6th **Exar** (FR) 3yo c, DH6th **Fatralo** (FR) 3yo c, 8th **Vamour** (FR) 3yo c, 9th **Djesak** (FR) 4yo c, 10th **Herbager** (FR) 3yo c. Unplaced: **Minstrel** (GB) 3yo c, **Malefaim** (FR) 4yo c, **L'Aymé** (FR) 5yo h, **San Roman** (FR) 4yo c, **Tapioca** (FR) 6yo h, **Wallaby** (FR) 4yo c, **Balbo** (FR) 5yo h, **Lycaste II** (SWE) 4yo f, **Marino** (FR) 3yo c, **Montrouge** (FR) 3yo c **Vieux Château** (FR) 3yo c, **Toukaram** (FR) 3yo c, **Apollo** (FR) 3yo c, **Fiorenza** (GB) 3yo f, **Barquette** (FR) 3yo f.

A powerful performance by Puissant Chef

Owner's decision not to sell vindicated

Background and fancied horses

The entrance to the straight at Longchamp had been redesigned since the last Arc to make it 600 metres long and also wider, in the hope that it would make it unnecessary to jostle for positions on the final bend.

The prize money for the winner changed from 40 million francs to 500,000 nouveau francs, which was an increase as each new franc was worth 100 of the old variety.

Prince Aly Khan had been riding the crest of a wave in 1959 but unfortunately it was all about to unravel. His Venture II was narrowly beaten in the 2000 Guineas, and then, when Sheshoon lost out in the Prix du Cadran at the start of May, after stumbling in the last 50 metres when victory had looked assured, he said in jest: 'I'm afraid my luck is beginning to run out.'

Unfortunately, four days later that prophecy came true when he was killed in a car crash not far from Saint-Cloud Racecourse. His son Karim, the Aga Khan IV, would take up the equine mantle and equal his father's and grandfather's horse racing accomplishments, and, in terms of the Prix de l'Arc de Triomphe, far exceed them.

Karim made an immediate impact when Charlottesville easily won the Prix du Jockey Club before adding the Grand Prix de Paris and Prix du Prince d'Orange in equally convincing style. If that wasn't enough, he also had another potent weapon in his armoury in the shape of Sheshoon, who, after the Prix du Cadran *débâcle*, won the Grand Prix de Saint-Cloud, Ascot Gold Cup and Grosser Preis von Baden. The Aga Khan's Arc team was completed by pacemaker Princillon, and together they were favourites at 0.4/1.

Next in the market was the known-mudlark Hautain who'd won the Prix Greffulhe, but had missed the Classics after throwing a splint. He'd eventually returned with a two-length success in the Prix de la Côte Normande and was an 11/1 chance.

Three horses were returned at 14/1: the late-maturing Esquimau, who won the Prix Vermout on his second outing before finishing runner-up in the Prix du Prince d'Orange; the Prix Royal-Oak victor, Puissant Chef, who the ill-fated Aly Khan offered to buy after he won the Prix La Force but was turned down; and Guy de Rothschild's filly Timandra, the winner of the Poule d'Essai des Pouliches and Prix de Diane.

The only non-French runners were from Italy, the 1959 Derby Italiano-winner Rio Marin and the useful filly Santa Severa.

Betting

0.4/1 Charlottesville & Sheshoon & Princillon (all coupled), 11/1 Hautain, 14/1 Esquimau, 14/1 Puissant Chef, 14/1 Timandra, 29/1 BAR.

Three-year-old form lines
Prix du Jockey Club: 1st **Charlottesville**, 2nd Night and Day, 3rd Bonjour, 4th **Puissant Chef**, 5th Wordpam, 0th **Flores**
Grand Prix de Paris: 1st **Charlottesville**, 2nd Kirkes, 3rd Eranhild, 6th **Flores**, 0th **Puissant Chef**, 0th **Or du Rhin**
Prix Royal-Oak: 1st **Puissant Chef**, 2nd **Wordpam** 3rd **Or du Rhin**

Fillies only
Prix de Diane: 1st **Timandra**, 2nd Notch, 3rd Noves
Prix Vermeille: 1st Lezghinka, 2nd Marella, 3rd **Dalama**

Older horses and inter-generational races
Grand Prix de Saint-Cloud: 1st **Sheshoon**, 2nd **Tiepoletto**, 3rd Malefaim
La Coupe de Maisons-Laffitte: 1st **Point d'Amour III**, 2nd Escart, 3rd Bosalino
Grand Prix de Deauville: 1st **Wordpam**, 2nd Rose de Picardie, 3rd Nelson
Prix du Prince d'Orange: 1st **Charlottesville**, 2nd **Esquimau**, 3rd King Size, 5th **Tiepoletto**

Abroad
In England
Derby Stakes: 1st St Paddy, 2nd Alcaeus, 3rd Kythnos
Ascot Gold Cup: 1st **Sheshoon**, 2nd Exar, 3rd Le Loup Garou
King George VI and Queen Elizabeth Stakes: 1st Aggressor, 2nd Petite Etoile, 3rd Kythnos, 5th **Flores**

In Germany
Grosser Preis von Baden: 1st **Sheshoon**, 2nd Agio, 3rd Mohikaner, 6th Malefaim

The race

In driving rain and strong winds, the Aga Khan's hare, Princillon, scampered off in front while Sheshoon, who received a bump, was last away. After 800 metres, Princillon gave way and Rio Marin and Tiepoletto took over followed by Point d'Amour III and Timandra. Charlottesville was on the inner in about seventh or eighth position.

After Rio Marin and Tiepoletto dropped back approaching the final turn, it was Point d'Amour III who led them into the straight. Hautain and Puissant Chef had both made good ground coming down the hill and now moved into second and third followed by Charlottesville and Esquimau, the first Arc ride for Yves Saint-Martin. Point d'Amour III appeared to be going strongly, but Charlottesville was under pressure.

It looked to be between the leader, Puissant Chef, and Hautain, but once Maxime Garcia pressed the button Puissant Chef settled the issue in a moment, powering away to score by three lengths. Hautain mastered Point d'Amour III to take the runner's up spot. Next were Esquimau and Santa Severa, with Charlottesville only managing sixth.

Post-race

The prevailing conditions had suited Puissant Chef who, like the runner-up, had relished the deep ground. Owner and breeder Henri Aubert's decision not to sell Puissant Chef had been justified and allowed trainer Mick Bartholomew, who was based at Chantilly, to open his Arc account. Jockey Maxime Garcia was winning on what was only his second appearance in the race.

Puissant Chef went to the USA for the Washington DC International, but as the tapes rose he ducked sharply right unshipping his jockey. He returned to France and would be campaigned in 1961.

Result

1960 Prix de l'Arc de Triomphe
Longchamp. Sunday, 9 October 1960
Weights: 3yo c: 55.5kg, 3yo f: 54kg, 4yo+ c: 60kg, 4yo+ f: 58.5kg

1st Puissant Chef (FR)   3yo c   55.5kg   **14/1**
by Djéfou out of La Sirene (Astrophel). Henri Aubert / Mick Bartholomew / Maxime Garcia

2nd Hautain (FR)   3yo c   55.5kg   **11/1**
by Sky High out of Haura (Rialto). Jean Stern / Max Bonaventure / Léon Flavien

3rd Point d'Amour III (FR)   3yo c   55.5kg   **30/1**
by Meridien out of Pointes des Landes (Quai d'Orsay). Marcel le Masson / Henri Gleizes / G Pézeril

Runners: 17 (FR 15, ITY 2). Distances: 3, 3. Going: heavy. Time: 2m 43.96s

Also ran: 4th **Esquimau** (FR) 3yo c, 5th **Santa Severa** (GB) 3yo f, 6th **Charlottesville** (GB) 3yo c, 7th **Clary** (FR) 3yo c, 8th **Flores** (FR) 3yo c, 9th **Sheshoon** (GB) 4yo c, 10th **Dalama** (FR) 3yo f. Unplaced: **Tiepoletto** (FR) 4yo c, **Rio Marin** (ITY) 4yo c, **Javelot** (FR) 4yo c, **Or du Rhin** (FR) 3yo c, **Timandra** (FR) 3yo f, **Wordpam** (GB) 3yo c, **Princillon** (FR) 4yo c.

1961
Molvedo too strong for Right Royal
Ribot's son the third winner for Camici

Background and fancied horses
The Étienne Pollet-trained Right Royal had only been beaten by one horse before lining up for the Arc, and that was on his debut when his stable companion was given too much rope.

Since then he'd gone from strength to strength, winning the Poule d'Essai des Poulains, the Prix Lupin, the Prix du Jockey Club, the King George VI and Queen Elizabeth Stakes – beating last year's Derby-winner St Paddy – and the Prix Henri Foy.

Right Royal could quite correctly be considered the best horse in Europe. Ridden by Roger Poincelet and coupled with pacemaker Le Tahitien, he was 1.5/1 to add to his spoils.

The most fancied of the three Italian challengers was Molvedo at 1.8/1. A son of Ribot, he'd missed the Italian Classics due to injury, although the collateral form of his win in the Premio d'Estate in July indicated that he was out of the top drawer. He confirmed that impression with a four-length success over some useful French types in the Grand Prix de Deauville.

Match was next in the betting at 9/1. He'd been second to Right Royal in the Prix Lupin and the Prix du Jockey Club, and after finishing second again, to Balto in the Grand Prix de Paris, had won the Prix Royal-Oak. It was then 12/1 about Grand Prix de Saint-Cloud-victor Dicta Drake, who'd been placed in the Derby and St Leger.

Last year's winner, Puissant Chef, had started the campaign by coming from a seemingly impossible position to win the Prix du Cadran. But he'd subsequently run down the field in the Ascot Gold Cup and Prix du Prince d'Orange and was a 16/1-chance.

Six runners trained outside France went to post. In addition to Molvedo, the two other challengers from Italy were the 1960 Oaks Italia-winner Caorlina and the returning Rio Marin, who'd won the Grosser Preis von Baden.

The other three hailed from England: the Great Voltigeur Stakes-winner Just Great, to be ridden by Lester Piggott; Tenacity, who'd come out on top in the Yorkshire Oaks and Princess Royal Stakes; and the front-running High Hat, owned by Winston Churchill.

The latter had notably taken the scalp of Petite Etoile in the Aly Khan International Memorial Gold Cup at Kempton in July. More recently, he'd been runner-up to St Paddy in the Jockey Club Stakes at Newmarket.

Betting

1.5/1 Right Royal & Le Tahitien (coupled), 1.8/1 Molvedo, 9/1 Match, 12/1 Dicta Drake, 16/1 Puissant Chef, 27/1 BAR.

Three-year-old form lines

Prix du Jockey Club: 1st **Right Royal**, 2nd **Match**, 3rd My Prince, 6th **Destral**, 0th **Devon**

Grand Prix de Paris: 1st **Balto**, 2nd **Match**, 3rd Granadero, 5th **Gisors**

Prix Royal-Oak: 1st **Match**, 2nd **Balto**, 3rd Sifair, 4th **Gisors**

Fillies only

Prix de Diane: 1st Hermières, 2nd Valadon, 3rd Carpe Diem

Prix Vermeille: DH1st Astola, DH1st Anne la Douce, 3rd La Bergerette

Older horses and inter-generational races

Grand Prix de Saint-Cloud: 1st **Dicta Drake**, 2nd Wordpam, 3rd **Destral**, 0th **Misti**,

La Coupe de Maisons-Laffitte: 1st Dalama, 2nd Bobar II, 3rd **Succès**

Grand Prix de Deauville: 1st **Molvedo**, 2nd **Misti**, 3rd Taine, 0th **Or du Rhin**

Prix du Prince d'Orange: 1st Wordpam, 2nd Le Français, 3rd **Okay II**, 0th **Puissant Chef**

Prix Henri Foy: 1st **Right Royal**, 2nd Carteret, 3rd (4th ptp) **Or du Rhin**, 4th (5th ptp) **Succès**, disq (3rd ptp) Javelot

Abroad

In England

Derby Stakes: 1st Psidium, 2nd **Dicta Drake**, 3rd Pardao, 4th Sovrango, 7th **Just Great**

Ascot Gold Cup: 1st Pandofell, 2nd Jet Stream, 3rd Prolific, 7th **Puissant Chef**

King George VI and Queen Elizabeth Stakes: 1st **Right Royal**, 2nd St Paddy, 3rd Rockavon

St Leger: 1st Aurelius, 2nd Bounteous, 3rd **Dicta Drake**

In Germany

Grosser Preis von Baden: 1st **Rio Marin**, 2nd Baalim, 3rd Kaiseradler

In Italy

Gran Premio di Milano: 1st Mexico, 2nd **Rio Marin**, 3rd Bazille

The race

After a false start, Le Tahitien led them away at the second time of asking from Match, Right Royal, Molvedo and High Hat. With 1,600 metres to travel, High Hat pushed on, opening up an advantage of two lengths.

Winston Churchill's charge still had the office turning in from Molvedo, on the rails, and Right Royal, as Match weakened and Misti made ground on the outer. Camici produced Molvedo as they approached the 200-metre pole and he mastered High Hat in a couple of strides.

Right Royal went off in pursuit but it turned out to be in vain; try as he might he was no match for Molvedo, who strode on to win by two lengths. There was a further half to Misti who deprived High Hat of third. Match was fifth with last year's winner, Puissant Chef, a never-nearer sixth.

Post-race

Trained by Arturo Maggi, Molvedo had, like his father Ribot, won the Arc, and for the same jockey. Enrico Camici had therefore taken his score to three and although he wouldn't stand on the top step of the podium again, another Camici would.

Molvedo was owned by shoe manufacturer Egidio Verga and his wife Bianca, who had purchased the bloodstock of Ortello's owner, Guiseppe del Montel, after his death in the mid-1940s.

Molvedo followed his Arc success with an easy win in the Gran Premio del Jockey Club, in a course-record time, before being retired to stud. His best progeny were the 1976 Derby Italiano-winner Red Arrow, and Gallio, who won the St Leger Italiano in the same season. Last year's Arc winner, Puissant Chef, was also retired but didn't produce any champions.

Result

1961 Prix de l'Arc de Triomphe
Longchamp. Sunday, 8 October 1961
Weights: 3yo c: 55.5kg, 3yo f: 54kg, 4yo+ c: 60kg, 4yo+ f: 58.5kg

1st Molvedo (ITY)   3yo c   55.5kg   **1.8/1**
by Ribot out of Maggiolina (Nakamuro). Egidio Verga / Arturo Maggi / Enrico Camici

2nd Right Royal (FR)   3yo c   55.5kg   **1.5/1 fav** (coupled with Le Tahitien)
by Owen Tudor out of Bastia (Victrix). Elisabeth Couturié / Étienne Pollet / Roger Poincelet

3rd Misti (FR)   3yo c   55.5kg   **28/1**
by Medium out of Mist (Tornado). Comte Guillaume d'Ornano / George Bridgland / Maurice Larraun

Runners: 19 (FR 13, ENG 3, ITY 3). Distances: 2, ½. Going: soft. Time: 2m 38.44s

Also ran: 4th **High Hat** (GB) 4yo c, 5th **Match** (FR) 3yo c, 6th **Puissant Chef** (FR) 4yo c, 7th **Succès** (FR) 4yo c, 8th **Destral** (FR) 3yo c, 9th **Devon** (FR) 3yo c, 10th **Just Great** (GB) 3yo c. Unplaced: **Or du Rhin** (FR) 4yo c, **Rio Marin** (ITY) 5yo h, **Caorlina** (ITY) 4yo f, **Okay II** (FR) 3yo c, **Le Tahitien** (FR) 3yo c, **Balto** (FR) 3yo c, **Dicta Drake** (FR) 3yo c, **Gisors** (FR) 3yo c, **Tenacity** (GB) 3yo f.

1962
Soltikoff atones for
Herbager disappointment
Carry Back takes the car park route

Background and fancied horses

François Dupré's Match, who'd finished fifth last year, had improved markedly for the application of a tongue-tie after a couple of dismal efforts early in the season. The new-improved Match had gone on to beat Exbury in the Grand Prix de Saint-Cloud before winning the King George VI and Queen Elizabeth Stakes. That form was good enough to see him top the Arc market at 3/1.

His jockey at Ascot had been Yves Saint-Martin. He was now on military service and was replaced by Jacques Fabre, who'd ridden him at Saint-Cloud. Guy de Rothschild's Exbury was second favourite at 5/1. After losing out to Match at Saint-Cloud he'd produced a stunning finish to land the Prix Henri Foy.

Next came the USA runner, Carry Back, who'd won the previous year's Kentucky Derby and Preakness Stakes. Unfortunately, he'd then picked up an injury and could only finish seventh in the Belmont Stakes. This term he'd added the Metropolitan Handicap, Monmouth Handicap and Whitney Stakes. Scobie Breasley had been engaged to ride him in the Arc and was given instructions to stay out of trouble.

England's best chance, the 1961 St Leger-hero Aurelius, who'd won this year's Hardwicke Stakes, was 6.5/1 with The Oaks and Prix Vermeille-winner Monade at 9.5/1.

Last year's third, Misti, had beaten the tongue-tieless Match in the Prix Ganay but had then finished behind him twice subsequently. Coupled with Picfort, the runner-up in the Prix du Jockey Club and Grand Prix de Paris, they were returned at 10/1.

The Prix du Jockey Club-winner, Val de Loir, failed at odds-on in the Grand Prix de Paris and had probably needed the run when third in the Prix du Prince d'Orange. The 12/1-shot would now be ridden by Jean-Pierre Boullenger as his usual pilot, Georges Chancelier, had tragically been killed in a car accident the week before the race. Among the longshots were Simone del Duca's pair, the veteran Etwild, runner-up in the Gran Premio di Milano, and Soltikoff, who had officially been a maiden until winning the Prix Henry Delamarre at the end of September. He'd run a few good races in defeat and had been first past the post in the Prix Edgard de la Charme at Saint-Cloud in May, only to be disqualified when it was found that he was not qualified to run in the race.

In addition to Carry Back and Aurelius, there were five more entrants from other countries. England also had Ormonde Stakes-winner Sovrango, while Ireland had Liberty Truck, the winner of the Prix Gontaut-Biron.

Italy was triple-handed with Surdi, the runner-up in both the Grand Prix de Deauville and Prix du Prince d'Orange, two-time winner of the Gran Premio di Milano, Mexico, and St Leger Italiano-victor Bragozzo.

Betting

3/1 Match, 5/1 Exbury, 5.5/1 Carry Back, 6.5/1 Aurelius, 9.5/1 Monade, 10/1 Misti & Picfort (coupled), 12/1 Val de Loir, 18/1 Surdi, 20/1 BAR.

Three-year-old form lines
Prix du Jockey Club: 1st **Val de Loir**, 2nd **Picfort**, 3rd **Exbury**, 4th Tambourine, 5th **Soltikoff**, 0th **Autre Prince**
Grand Prix de Paris: 1st Armistice, 2nd **Picfort**, 3rd Montfleur, 5th **Val de Loir**
Prix Royal-Oak: 1st Sicilian Prince, 2nd **Autre Prince**, 3rd **Picfort**, 4th **Trac**

Fillies only
Prix de Diane: 1st La Sega, 2nd Salinas, 3rd Ouananiche
Prix Vermeille: 1st **Monade**, 2nd Prima Donna, 3rd **Gaspesie**

Older horses and inter-generational races
Grand Prix de Saint-Cloud: 1st **Match**, 2nd **Exbury**, 3rd Empire, 4th **Misti**
Grand Prix de Deauville: 1st Bounteous, 2nd **Surdi**, 3rd **Misti**, 4th **Etwild**, 5th **Taine**, 8th **Liberty Truck**
Prix du Prince d'Orange: 1st Kistinie, 2nd **Surdi**, 3rd **Val de Loir**
Prix Henri Foy: 1st **Exbury**, 2nd Catilina, 3rd Carteret, 4th **Etwild**, 5th **Misti**, 0th **Taine**

Abroad
In England
Derby Stakes: 1st Larkspur, 2nd **Arcor**, 3rd Le Cantilien, 4th **Sovrango**
Oaks Stakes: 1st **Monade**, 2nd West Side Story, 3rd Tender Annie
King George VI and Queen Elizabeth Stakes: 1st **Match**, 2nd **Aurelius**, 3rd Arctic Storm, DH4th **Val de Loir**, DH4th **Sovrango**, 0th **Misti**

In Italy
Gran Premio di Milano: 1st **Mexico**, 2nd **Etwild**, 3rd **Surdi**

The race

Aurelius sweated in the preliminaries on what was an extremely hot day. Soltikoff ducked under the tapes at the start but lined up again quickly. Once away, the Neville Selwood-ridden Misti was first to show, closely followed by Taine, Surdi, Point d'Amour III, Monade and Match. Meanwhile Carry Back was running wide towards the rear.

Monade and Match challenged Misti, Taine and Surdi as they entered the straight, while at the back of the field Picfort came down. Monade took it up and pushed on, with the improving Soltikoff now leading the chasing bunch.

Soltikoff responded gamely to the urgings of Marcel Depalmas, catching and passing Monade in the final 100 metres before moving away stylishly to prevail by a length.

Val de Loir, finishing fast on the outside, was only a neck behind in third with a short head to Snob. He'd struggled to find a passage through the pack but had flown when eventually seeing daylight.

The favourite, Match, was fifth, a further neck back, followed by Exbury in sixth. The US-runner Carry Back was 10th, Scobie having taken a wide route the whole way as instructed.

Post-race

Simone del Duca, wife of the Italian-born newspaper magnate Cino del Duca, had tasted disappointment with favourite Herbager in 1959. But now she enjoyed emotions from the other end of the scale with a 40/1 outsider who'd been a maiden up until a week before the race.

Jockey Marcel Depalmas had come in for the ride on Soltikoff as Neville Sellwood was already booked for Misti before Soltikoff was confirmed as a runner. Tragically Sellwood, who was leading the jockeys' championship, died a month later in a fall at Maisons-Laffitte.

Trainer René Pelat added to his success with Nikellora in 1945. Soltikoff was roughed off for the season but would return.

Result

1962 Prix de l'Arc de Triomphe
Longchamp. Sunday, 7 October 1962
Weights: 3yo c: 55.5kg, 3yo f: 54kg, 4yo+ c: 60kg, 4yo+ f: 58.5kg

1st Soltikoff (FR)   3yo c   55.5kg   **40/1** (coupled with Picfort)
by Prince Chevalier out of Aglaé Grâce (Mousson). Simone del Duca / René Pelat / Marcel Depalmas

2nd Monade (FR)   3yo f   54kg   **9.5/1**
by Klairon out of Mormyre (Atys). George P. Goulandris / Joseph Lieux / Maurice Larraun

3rd Val de Loir (FR)   3yo c   55.5kg   **12/1**
by Vieux Manoir out of Vali (Sunny Boy). Madame la Marquise du Vivier / Max Bonaventure / Jean-Pierre Boullenger

Runners: 24 (FR 17, ITY 3, GB 2, IRE 1, USA 1). Distances: 1, nk. Going: good. Time: 2m 30.94s

Also ran: 4th **Snob** (FR) 3yo c, 5th **Match** (FR) 4yo c, 6th **Exbury** (FR) 3yo c, 7th **Misti** (FR) 4yo c, 8th **Taine** (FR) 5yo h, 9th **Etwild** (FR) 7yo h, 10th **Carry Back** (USA) 4yo c. Unplaced: **Bragozzo** (ITY) 3yo c, **Fatralo** (FR) 5yo h, **Trac** (FR) 3yo c, **Mexico** (ITY) 4yo c, **Aurelius** (GB) 4yo c, **Surdi** (ITY) 7yo h, **Sovrango** (GB) 4yo c, **Liberty Truck** (GB) 4yo c, **Point d'Amour III** (FR) 5yo h, **Autre Prince** (GB) 3yo c, **Gaspesie** (FR) 3yo f, **Pre Catelan** (FR) 5yo h, **Arcor** (FR) 3yo c, **Picfort** (FR) 3yo c (fell).

Exbury stays calm as favourite boils over

Rothschild dynasty continues in last Arc started by tape

Background and fancied horses

When Yves Saint-Martin steered François Dupré's Relko to a six-length success in the Derby, he almost single-handedly scared off all potential Arc runners from outside France.

Despite an ongoing enquiry into a potentially banned substance which limped on for several months – connections were eventually informed that there was no case to answer only three days before the Arc – no one could deny his authority over the opposition.

Trained by François Mathet, Relko had already won the Poule d'Essai des Poulains and was due a tilt at a third Classic, but he was found to be lame at the start of the Irish Derby and was withdrawn. However, after beating the Prix du Jockey Club-victor Sanctus on his return to the track in the Prix Royal-Oak, Relko was sent off at odds-on for the Arc, while Sanctus, who re-opposed, was 10/1.

There were three returnees including last year's winner Soltikoff. He'd been well-beaten in the Grand Prix de Saint-Cloud and King George VI and Queen Elizabeth Stakes, but had bounced back to form in the Prix du Prince d'Orange. Nonetheless, he was a 17/1 chance coupled with the only filly in the field, Royal Girl, who'd been third in the Prix de Diane.

Guy de Rothschild's Exbury, who'd finished sixth last year, was enjoying a stellar season and was second favourite after extending his unbeaten sequence to four when taking the Grand Prix de Saint-Cloud.

Misti, seventh home in 1962 and 13/1 this time, had finished second in the Ascot Gold Cup and arrived at Longchamp on the back of a win in the Prix Henri Foy. Last year's third, Val de Loir, was trained for the Arc but unfortunately his entry was lost in the post.

Other notable absentees included Ragusa who, after finishing third to Relko in the Derby, had won the Irish Derby, King George VI and Queen Elizabeth Stakes and St Leger. He would make his way to Longchamp the following year. The impressive Oaks-winner Noblesse had been retired to the paddocks after finishing lame in the Prix Vermeille.

One that did go was Étienne Pollet's Le Mesnil. He'd finished eighth after being sent off favourite in the Prix du Jockey Club, but had returned after a layoff to win the Prix de Chantilly – the forerunner of the race now run as the Prix Niel. Le Mesnil was fourth best in the market at 11/1.

Betting

0.9/1 Relko, 3.6/1 Exbury & Tang (coupled), 10/1 Sanctus, 11/1 Le Mesnil, 13/1 Misti, 17/1 Soltikoff & Royal Girl (coupled), 17/1 Blanc Bleu & Tournevent (coupled), 17/1 Déboulé, 24/1 BAR.

Three-year-old form lines
Prix du Jockey Club: 1st **Sanctus**, 2nd **Nyrcos**, 3rd Duc de Gueldre, 5th **Déboulé**, 8th **Le Mesnil**
Grand Prix de Paris: 1st **Sanctus**, 2nd Duc de Gueldre, 3rd Signor
Prix Royal-Oak: 1st **Relko**, 2nd **Déboulé**, 3rd **Nyrcos**, 4th **Sanctus**

Fillies only
Prix de Diane: 1st Belle Ferronniere, 2nd Cervinia, 3rd **Royal Girl**
Prix Vermeille: 1st Golden Girl, 2nd Chutney, 3rd Sweet Sue, 6th **Royal Girl**, 0th Noblesse

Older horses and inter-generational races
Grand Prix de Saint-Cloud: 1st **Exbury**, 2nd Val de Loir, 3rd Wild Hun, 6th **Soltikoff**, 0th **Misti**
La Coupe de Maisons-Laffitte: 1st Monade, 2nd **Relko**, 3rd Succès
Grand Prix de Deauville: 1st Val de Loir, 2nd **Boran**, 3rd Torero
Prix du Prince d'Orange: 1st **Soltikoff**, 2nd **Quiqui**, 3rd **Blanc Bleu**
Prix Henri Foy: 1st **Misti**, 2nd **Soltikoff**, 3rd _

Abroad
In England
Derby Stakes: 1st **Relko**, 2nd Merchant Venturer, 3rd Ragusa
Ascot Gold Cup: 1st Twilight Alley, 2nd **Misti**, 3rd Taine
King George VI and Queen Elizabeth Stakes: 1st Ragusa, 2nd Miralgo, 3rd Tarqogan, 6th **Nyrcos**, 7th **Soltikoff**

The race

As the tapes rose for the last time in an Arc – starting stalls would be used from 1964 – it was Relko who broke fastest. The favourite had sweated up in the humid conditions and was on his toes in the preliminaries. Now, with the race under way, Saint-Martin was having difficulty getting him to settle.

Exbury's pacemaker, Tang, had also been set alight and raced past Relko at breakneck speed to take it up. Prix Maurice de Nieuil-winner Tournevent and Le Mesnil were also prominent as they headed uphill with Saint-Martin still wrestling with the hard-pulling Relko.

Tang extended his advantage on the descent but tired on the turn for home, where Le Mesnil took up the running. He was followed through by Sanctus, Soltikoff and Misti, while Exbury was being angled out for a run.

Favourite backers were hugely disappointed when Relko found very little when let down, his early exertions seemingly having blunted his speed.

Exbury was still six or so lengths down, but unlike the others was closing. He moved into second with 100 metres to go and then, finding the proverbial extra gear, cut down Le Mesnil and zipped away to win by two lengths. Next came Misti, the fast-finishing Soltikoff and then Sanctus, with Relko only sixth.

Post-race

Owner Guy de Rothschild had previously been second with Alizier in 1950. But now, with Exbury going one place better, he'd emulated his father, Édouard, who'd scored with Exbury's grandsire, the great Brantôme, in 1934 and with Éclair au Chocolat four years later.

Trainer Geoff Watson was descended from one of the English families that had sent representatives to Chantilly in the 19th century. His uncle, James Cooper Watson, for example, had been trainer to Guy's father Édouard. However, his own father, John, had stayed in England to train Leopold de Rothschild's horses in Newmarket.

Geoff had been assistant to Frank Carter for five years before taking out his own licence in 1930. He trained many champions, including three winners of the Grand Prix de Paris and four of the Prix de Diane.

Jean Deforge rode his first winner in 1951 and went on to became Guy de Rothschild's retained rider. He was champion jockey twice in the late 1950s but this would be his only Arc win.

Exbury retired to stud at the family's famous Haras de Meautry near Deauville, producing many decent types, the best of which was probably St Leger-winner Crow, who finished runner-up in the Arc in 1976.

In 1969 the first Group race of the season, the Prix Boïard, which is run over 2,000 metres at Saint-Cloud in March, was renamed the Prix Exbury in his honour.

Brantôme 1931

|

Vieux Manoir 1947

|

Le Haar 1954

|

Exbury 1959

Result

1963 Prix de l'Arc de Triomphe
Longchamp. Sunday, 6 October 1963
Weights: 3yo c: 55.5kg, 3yo f: 54kg, 4yo+ c: 60kg, 4yo+ f: 58.5kg

1st Exbury (FR)   4yo c   60kg   **3.6/1** (coupled with Tang)
by Le Haar out of Greensward (Mossborough). Baron Guy de Rothschild / Geoff Watson / Jean Deforge

2nd Le Mesnil (FR)   3yo c   55.5kg   **11/1**
by Tyrone out of Flying Colours (Massine). Elisabeth Couturié / Étienne Pollet / Pat Glennon

3rd Misti (FR)   5yo c   60kg   **13/1**
by Médium out of Mist (Tornado). Le Comte Guillaume d'Ornano / George Bridgland / Maurice Larraun

Runners: 15 (FR 15). Distances: 2, nk. Going: soft. Time: 2m 34.98s

Also ran: 4th **Soltikoff** (FR) 4yo, 5th **Sanctus** (FR) 3yo c, 6th **Relko** (GB) 3yo c, 7th **Nyrcos** (FR) 3yo c, 8th **Boran** (GB) 3yo c, 9th **Blanc Bleu** (FR) 4yo c, 10th **Royal Girl** (FR) 3yo f. Unplaced: **Worcran** (FR) 5yo h, **Tang** (FR) 4yo c, **Tournevent** (FR) 3yo c, **Quiqui** (_) 3yo c, **Déboulé** (FR) 3yo c.

1964

Prince Royal prevails
in an incident-packed race

Starting stalls are used for the first time

Background and fancied horses

The winner's prize money had risen incrementally since the currency was revalued in 1960 and now reached the million-franc mark.

The home team's main chance seemed to lie with Le Fabuleux, who had notched up wins in the Prix Noailles, Prix Lupin and Prix du Jockey Club before taking a well-earned rest. On his return he was as good as ever, disposing of King George VI and Queen Elizabeth Stakes-winner Nasram by four lengths in the Prix du Prince d'Orange. Aided by pacemaker Mercure, he was supported into 1.5/1 for the Arc.

The second favourite was last year's Irish Derby and King George VI and Queen Elizabeth Stakes-winner Ragusa, who'd recovered from a pulled muscle to take this term's Eclipse Stakes.

Guy de Rothschild fielded four Runners: the filly La Bamba, who'd been third in The Oaks and Prix Vermeille; Grand Prix de Paris-winner White Label; the victor in the Prix Royal-Oak, Barbieri; and Free Ride, who'd been beset with health problems. The blanket price for the quartet was 9/1.

In addition to those four, Geoff Watson also trained the 10/1-shot Astaria, who'd been runner-up to Belle Sicambre in the Prix de Diane. She was followed in the betting by the formerly Italian-trained runner Prince Royal at 16/1.

He'd established his reputation when winning the Gran Premio di Milano. But, after following up with a 15-length success in the Premio Besana, Prince Royal had failed completely in the Prix Royal-Oak. Normally he liked to be prominent but on this occasion he was held up in a race that was run very slowly and which therefore culminated in a sprint finish.

The Aga Khan IV's Jour et Nuit III had only been beaten by one horse in seven runs, which included a dogged victory under a heavy burden in the Prix Eugène Adam. The 18/1-shot would be ridden by Scobie Breasley, who was taking over from Yves Saint-Martin. The latter was serving a suspension after being adjudged to have been responsible for a fall in the Prix Delamarre four days before. Lester Piggott had been knocked unconscious in that fall and as a result was also absent.

As well as Ragusa, Ireland was represented by Santa Claus – the winner of the English and Irish Derbys, who'd been beaten by Nasram when sent off at 1/6.5 in the King George VI and Queen Elizabeth Stakes – and Prix Kergorlay-winner Ashavan. Royal Avenue, who came home third behind Santa Claus at Ascot, was the sole challenger from England.

Unfortunately the 1962 Arc-winner Soltikoff was absent. He'd finished fourth in the Prix Ganay but soon afterwards fractured a leg in training and had to be put down.

Betting

1.5/1 Le Fabuleux & Mercure (coupled), 4.8/1 Ragusa, 9/1 La Bamba & White Label & Barbieri & Free Ride (all coupled), 10/1 Astaria, 16/1 Prince Royal, 18/1 Jour et Nuit III, 23/1 Santa Claus, 23/1 Frontin & Sigebert (coupled), 30/1 BAR.

Three-year-old form lines
Prix du Jockey Club: 1st **Le Fabuleux**, 2nd Trenel, 3rd Djel, 4th **Free Ride**, 6th **Barbieri**
Grand Prix de Paris: 1st **White Label**, 2nd Indiana, 3rd The Drake, 5th **Free Ride**
Prix Royal-Oak: 1st **Barbieri**, 2nd **Timmy Lad**, 3rd Trade Mark, last **Prince Royal**

Fillies only
Prix de Diane: 1st **Belle Sicambre**, 2nd **Astaria**, 3rd Vesperale
Prix Vermeille: 1st **Astaria**, 2nd Dreida, 3rd **La Bamba**, 4th **Belle Sicambre**, 5th **Carolle II**

Older horses and inter-generational races
Grand Prix de Saint-Cloud: 1st Relko, 2nd **Tournevent**, 3rd **Nasram**
Grand Prix de Deauville: 1st Sailor, 2nd **Timmy Lad**, 3rd Daoiz
Prix du Prince d'Orange: 1st **Le Fabuleux**, 2nd **Nasram**, 3rd **Mercure**

Abroad
In England
Derby Stakes: 1st **Santa Claus**, 2nd Indiana, 3rd Dilettante
Oaks Stakes: 1st Homeward Bound, 2nd Windmill Girl, 3rd **La Bamba**
King George VI and Queen Elizabeth Stakes: 1st **Nasram**, 2nd **Santa Claus**, 3rd **Royal Avenue**, 4th/last **Prima Donna**

In Ireland
Irish Derby: 1st **Santa Claus**, 2nd Lionhearted, 3rd Sunseeker

In Italy
Gran Premio di Milano: 1st **Prince Royal**, 2nd **Tournevent**, 3rd Crivelli

The race

On what was a pleasant autumn day, starting stalls were used for the first time to despatch the runners for the Arc. There was a delay before the loading commenced due to the need to fit in with television scheduling requirements. Favourite Le Fabuleux was in the first bunch to go in and had to wait several minutes in the superstructure before the off.

Mecure broke first, vying for the lead with Nasram who was galloping freely. Belle Sicambre and Soleil d'Or were next with Ragusa and Prince Royal. On the descent, Belle Sicambre took over as the pacesetters started to fade, and she led into the straight from Prince Royal and the under-pressure Le Fabuleux. Soleil d'Or, Sigebert and Santa Claus were all on the premises while La Bamba and Timmy Lad were making progress from the rear.

At the same time Ragusa took a bad step or hit some false ground – or both – which caused him to interfere with Mecure, who came crashing down. Santa Claus's progress was also halted when he was bumped by the favourite Le Fabuleux, who was dropping out of contention.

Inside the final 400 metres Prince Royal mastered Belle Sicambre. Back on an even keel, Santa Claus made rapid progress but could only get to within three parts of a length of Roger Poincelet's mount. La Bamba also finished off fast to grab third from Timmy Lad with the *longtemps animateur*, Belle Sicambre, having to settle for fifth place ahead of Frontin. The market leader, Le Fabuleux, finished nearer last than first.

Post-race

There were plenty of hard-luck stories, and afterwards Astaria was found to be injured which added to the list of woes. The stewards studied the film and found that Garnet Bougoure, Ragusa's Australian jockey, was at fault for Mecure's fall and he was banned for a month.

The crowd's wrath was reserved for Le Fabuleux, who was roundly booed by the part of the crowd who boo such things. His jockey put the poor run down to his long wait in the stalls.

Prince Royal, who'd benefited from a clean run, was a worthy winner for owner Rex Ellsworth. He'd purchased the son of Ribot before the Prix Royal-Oak but hadn't taken ownership until after the race. Ellsworth was a top owner/breeder who'd won the Kentucky Derby with Swaps in 1955, and the Preakness Stakes with Candy Spots in 1963, both ridden by the legendary jockey Bill Shoemaker.

The poor run in the Prix Royal-Oak proved to be pivotal with regard to the recruitment of Prince Royal's connections for the Arc. His intended new trainer Ernie Fellows refused to take him, thus George Bridgland, who did, was able to improve on his previous best – Misti's third places in 1961 and 1963. Likewise, Shoemaker wasn't keen to partner him and suggested Roger Poincelet, for whom it was a third victory after Coronation in 1949 and Nuccio three years later.

That performance in the Prix Royal-Oak came under further scrutiny as a rumour was spreading that it was part of a betting coup. The Société d'Encouragement looked into the matter and quickly found that there was no case to answer as it was self-evident that the different tactics utilised that day just didn't suit the horse.

Prince Royal, the second Arc winner for Ribot, retired to Ellsworth's stud in the USA. He wasn't a brilliant success but did sire the Californian Derby-winner Unconscious.

Result
1964 Prix de l'Arc de Triomphe
Longchamp. Sunday, 4 October 1964
Weights: 3yo c: 55.5kg, 3yo f: 54kg, 4yo+ c: 60kg, 4yo+ f: 58.5kg

1st Prince Royal (GB)   3yo c   55.5kg   **16/1**
by Ribot out of Pange (King's Bench). Rex Ellsworth / George Bridgland / Roger Poincelet

2nd Santa Claus (GB)   3yo c   55.5kg   **23/1**
by Chamossaire out of Aunt Clara (Arctic Prince). John Ismay / Mick Rogers / Jimmy Lindley

3rd La Bamba (FR)   3yo f   54kg   **9/1**
by Shantung out of Frontier Song (Dastur). Baron Guy de Rothschild / Geoff Watson / Jean-Claude Desaint

Runners: 22 (FR 18, IRE 3, GB 1). Distances: ¾, hd. Going: good. Time: 2m 35.50s

Also ran: 4th **Timmy Lad** (USA) 3yo c, 5th **Belle Sicambre** (FR) 3yo f, 6th **Frontin** (FR) 4yo c, 7th **Free Ride** (GB) 3yo c, 8th **Soleil d'Or** (FR) 3yo c, 9th **White Label** (FR) 3yo c, 10th **Ashavan** (GB) 4yo f. Unplaced: **Royal Avenue** (GB) 6yo h, **Nasram** (USA) 4yo c, **Ragusa** (IRE) 4yo c, **Tournevent** (FR) 4yo c, **Prima Donna** (FR) 5yo m, **Jour et Nuit III** (IRE) 3yo c, **Sigebert** (FR) 3yo c, **Le Fabuleux** (FR) 3yo c, **Barbieri** (GB) 3yo c, **Astaria** (FR) 3yo f, **Carolle II** (FR) 3yo f, **Mercure** (FR) 3yo c (fell).

Sea Bird flies into immortality

First Russian runner as Bing looks on

Background and fancied horses

Sea Bird and Reliance were both unbeaten in 1965 prior to the Arc. The former had sauntered home in both the Prix Greffulhe and Prix Lupin before putting in a scintillating performance in the Derby. He was head and shoulders better than the opposition and still had two lengths to spare over Meadow Court at the line, despite being heavily eased down.

Sea Bird put up a repeat performance in the Grand Prix de Saint-Cloud and in most years would have been odds-on for the Arc. Jean Ternynck's *crack* though was returned at 1.2/1, a reflection of the ability that had been shown by Reliance.

François Dupré's full brother of Match had won the Prix du Jockey Club on the bridle beating Diatome, before adding the Grand Prix de Paris with Diatome again taking second. After a rest, Reliance returned in the Prix Royal-Oak to claim his third Classic. He was 4.5/1 while Diatome, coupled with the returning Free Ride, was 7.5/1.

The Derby-second Meadow Court was a shade longer at 7.8/1. He'd gone on to win the Irish Derby where part-owner Bing Crosby treated the crowd around the winner's enclosure to an impromptu rendition of 'When Irish eyes are smiling'. Meadow Court had then won the King George VI and Queen Elizabeth Stakes before finishing second in the St Leger. He was accompanied to Longchamp by Irish St Leger-third Khalife, who would act as his pacemaker. Bing was also in attendance.

The USA-representative Tom Rolfe, at 8/1, had won the Preakness Stakes as well as being placed in the Kentucky Derby and Belmont Stakes. He'd also won four races in the autumn and would be having his 13th run of the season in the Arc, where he would be partnered by Bill Shoemaker, who this time made the long trip to France.

As well as Meadow Court and Khalife, Ireland had Great Voltigeur Stakes-winner Ragazzo, while England fielded Coronation Cup-winner Oncidium and Soderini, who'd obliged in the Hardwicke Stakes.

Gran Premio di Milano runner-up Marco Visconti represented Italy, and the total number of eight runners from outside France was completed by the 1964 Soviet Derby-winner Anilin. The first Russian horse to line up in the Arc, he had some reasonable collateral form but had suffered delays in transit.

Betting

1.2/1 Sea Bird, 4.5/1 Reliance, 7.5/1 Diatome & Free Ride (coupled), 7.8/1 Meadow Court & Khalife (coupled), 8/1 Tom Rolfe, 22/1 BAR.

Three-year-old form lines

Prix du Jockey Club: 1st **Reliance**, 2nd **Diatome**, 3rd **Carvin**

Grand Prix de Paris: 1st **Reliance**, 2nd **Diatome**, 3rd Vianen, 0th **Carvin**

Prix Royal-Oak: 1st **Reliance**, 2nd **Ragazzo**, 3rd **Carvin**

Fillies only

Prix de Diane: 1st **Blabla**, 2nd Cantilène, 3rd Yami

Prix Vermeille: 1st Aunt Edith, 2nd Dark Wave, 3rd Long Look, fell **Blabla**

Older horses and inter-generational races

Grand Prix de Saint-Cloud: 1st **Sea Bird**, 2nd Couroucou, 3rd **Francilus**, 5th **Free Ride**, 0th **Demi-Deuil**

Grand Prix de Deauville: 1st Sailor, 2nd **Timmy Lad**, 3rd Hammam

Prix du Prince d'Orange: 1st **Diatome**, 2nd Acer, 3rd Corfinio, 4th **Timmy Lad**, 0th **Marco Visconti**

Prix Henri Foy: 1st **Sigebert**, 2nd Corfinio, 3rd **Ardaban**

Abroad

In England

Derby Stakes: 1st **Sea Bird**, 2nd **Meadow Court**, 3rd I Say

King George VI and Queen Elizabeth Stakes: 1st **Meadow Court**, 2nd **Soderini**, 3rd **Oncidium**

St Leger: 1st Provoke, 2nd **Meadow Court**, 3rd Solstice

In Ireland

Irish Derby: 1st **Meadow Court**, 2nd Convamore, 3rd Wedding Present

Irish St Leger: 1st Craighouse, 2nd Alcalde, 3rd **Khalife**

In Germany

Grosser Preis von Baden: 1st **Demi-Deuil**, 2nd Prince Baladin, 3rd Kronzeuge

In Italy

Gran Premio di Milano: 1st Accrale, 2nd **Marco Visconti**, 3rd Fantomas

The race

In the preliminaries both Sea Bird and Reliance were in a lather on what was a warm sunny afternoon. The ground was riding on the dead side as the field set off, with Marco Visconti leading the way. Khalife, Meadow Court's pacemaker, missed the break.

The group behind Marco Visconti contained Blabla, Ardaban and Anilin, and they were quickly joined by Khalife who was being rushed up to try and get to the front. Tom Rolfe, Sea Bird and Reliance were settled in the midfield along with Meadow Court.

Anilin moved into second place as they reached the summit while Blabla and Khalife dropped back. On the approach to the straight, Sea Bird advanced into third on a tight rein.

Entering the *ligne d'arrivee*, Pat Glennon asked him to go and he swooped past Anilin and Marco Visconti. Only Reliance, ridden by Yves Saint-Martin, could go with him, although Diatome was passing some of the beaten horses.

Fleetingly the anticipated battle royal between Sea Bird and Reliance looked on the cards, before Sea Bird majestically started to draw away. Despite drifting off the rails, the gap kept opening and in the end he trounced Reliance by six lengths, with a further five back to Diatome, who finished alongside his stable companion Free Ride, with Anilin fifth and Tom Rolfe sixth.

Post-race

It was a staggering display by Sea Bird and is widely regarded as the best performance ever in the Arc. Sea Bird remains Timeform's top-rated horse over 2,400 metres (1m 4f). Only Frankel, who raced over shorter, has a higher rating. Sea Bird also became the first Derby winner to land the Arc.

Owner Jean Ternynck was the son of a cousin of Henri Ternynck who'd won with Massine in 1924. It was the second success for trainer Étienne Pollet, after his one-two with La Sorellina and Silnet, and he in turn was a cousin of the owner.

Jockey T. P. Glennon, better known as Pat, was formerly the stable jockey for Vincent O'Brien. He'd come to France in 1963 but eight days after his Arc success he returned to his native Australia for good.

Sea Bird also left France to stand in the USA, where he produced several horses that will feature in our story, including Allez France, Gyr and Arctic Tern. He is also the grandsire of Bering and Sea Pigeon. The latter was decent on the flat – winning the Ebor Handicap and two Chester Cups – but is best remembered for his two Champion Hurdle triumphs.

It was in the USA that the great horse became known as Sea Bird II, or sometimes Sea-Bird II. He is commemorated under his original name in several races in France, where versions of the Prix Sea Bird are, or have been, run at Le Lion d'Angers, Le Touquet, Argentan and Saint-Cloud.

Result
1965 Prix de l'Arc de Triomphe
Longchamp. Sunday, 3 October 1965
Weights: 3yo c: 55.5kg, 3yo f: 54kg, 4yo+ c: 60kg, 4yo+ f: 58.5kg

1st Sea Bird (FR)   3yo c   55.5kg **1.2/1 fav**
by Dan Cupid out of Sicalade (Sicambre). Jean Ternynck / Étienne Pollet / Pat Glennon

2nd Reliance (FR)   3yo c   55.5kg **4.5/1**
by Tantieme out of Relance (Relic). François Dupré / François Mathet / Yves Saint-Martin

3rd Diatome (GB)   3yo c   55.5kg **7.5/1** (coupled with Free Ride)
by Sicambre out of Dictaway (Honeyway). Baron Guy de Rothschild / Geoff Watson / Jean Deforge

Runners: 20 (FR 12, IRE 3, GB 2, ITY 1, RUS 1, USA 1). Distances: 6, 5. Going: good. Time: 2m 35.52s

Also ran: 4th **Free Ride** (GB) 4yo c, 5th **Anilin** (RUS) 4yo c, 6th **Tom Rolfe** (USA) 3yo c, 7th **Demi-Deuil** (FR) 4yo c, 8th **Carvin** (FR) 3yo c, 9th **Meadow Court** (IRE) 3yo c, 10th **Marco Visconti** (ITY) 3yo c. Unplaced: **Emerald** (FR) 4yo c, **Ardaban** (FR) 4yo c, **Soderini** (IRE) 4yo c, **Sigebert** (FR) 4yo c, **Francilius** (FR) 4yo c, **Oncidium** (GB) 4yo c, **Timmy Lad** (USA) 4yo c, **Khalife** (FR) 3yo c, **Ragazzo** (GB) 3yo c, **Blabla** (FR) 3yo f.

Freddy scores for grandfather on Bon Mot

Bonaventure pair take the places

Background and fancied horses

Longchamp underwent a facelift at the end of 1965, and by Arc day regular racegoers had become accustomed to the new grandstand, the new paddock situated directly behind it, and the new weighing room.

Less good news was that there had been an outbreak of swamp fever in France which meant no French horses could travel to Britain until mid-May. In the build-up to the Arc there were also several instances of coughing which resulted in some non-runners, including Prix du Jockey Club-winner Nelcius, and Hauban, who'd finished second in the Grand Prix de Paris.

In June, the day after his Danseur had beaten Hauban in the Grand Prix de Paris, François Dupré died. Dupré had owned many excellent horses including dual Arc-winner Tantième and last year's runner-up Reliance. Now running for his widow, Danseur was second favourite for the Arc at 5/1.

Representing the formidable team of Noel Murless and Lester Piggott, Aunt Edith at 3.75/1, was the first raider to head the market since Ribot. Last year's eight-length Prix Vermeille-winner had added to her haul this term in the Yorkshire Cup and the King George VI and Queen Elizabeth Stakes, but in between times had run inexplicably badly in the Hardwicke Stakes.

Third-favourite Bon Mot was to be the first Arc ride for Alec Head's 18-year-old son Frédéric Head – better known as Freddy – who on this occasion was riding for his grandfather. Bon Mot had been runner-up in the Prix du Jockey Club and Prix Royal-Oak and third in the Grand Prix de Paris, and the 5.3/1-shot would be suited by the soft underfoot conditions.

It was double figures bar, bringing in Prix de Diane-winner Fine Pearl, Prix du Jockey Club-third Behistoun, Grand Prix de Deauville-victor Lionel, and Prix Vermeille-fourth Si Sage.

Also in this price category was the best of the Italian runners Marco Visconti, who hadn't been seen since going one place better than last year in the Gran Premio di Milano.

Ciacolesso, down the field in the Grosser Preis von Baden, was also from Italy, while in addition to Aunt Edith, England was represented by Coronation

Cup-winner I Say, and Parthian Glance, who'd picked up the Ribblesdale Stakes, Yorkshire Oaks and Park Hill Stakes.

Hardwicke Stakes-winner Prominer was the sole Irish runner, although Valoris had been with Vincent O'Brien when winning The Oaks but was now trained in France by Ernie Fellows.

Betting

3.75/1 Aunt Edith, 5/1 Danseur, 5.3/1 Bon Mot, 11/1 Fine Pearl, 12/1 Behistoun, 13/1 Marco Visconti, 16/1 Lionel, 18/1 Si Sage, 20/1 BAR.

Three-year-old form lines

Prix du Jockey Club: 1st Nelcius, 2nd **Bon Mot**, 3rd **Behistoun**, 6th **Taneb**

Grand Prix de Paris: 1st **Danseur**, 2nd Hauban, 3rd **Bon Mot**, 5th **Taneb**, 0th **Vasco de Gama**, 0th **A Tempo**

Prix Royal-Oak: 1st **Vasco de Gama**, 2nd **Bon Mot**, 3rd Roi de Perse, 5th **A Tempo**

Fillies only

Prix de Diane: 1st **Fine Pearl**, 2nd Bergame, 3rd Sweet Sauce

Prix Vermeille: 1st Haltilala, 2nd Bubunia, 3rd **Fine Pearl**, 4th **Si Sage**, 0th **Valoris**, 0th **Fandine**

Older horses and inter-generational races

Grand Prix de Saint-Cloud: 1st Sea Hawk II, 2nd Diatome, 3rd **Behistoun**, 5th **Sigebert**

La Coupe de Maisons-Laffitte: DH1st **Red Vagabonde**, DH1st **Prominer**, 3rd Manderley, 0th **Corfinio**

Grand Prix de Deauville: 1st **Lionel**, 2nd Fantomas, 3rd **Corfinio**, 4th **Carvin**,

Prix du Prince d'Orange: 1st Pasquin, 2nd **Carvin**, 3rd _, 5th **Behistoun**

Abroad

In England

Derby Stakes: 1st Charlottown, 2nd Pretendre, 3rd Black Prince

Oaks Stakes: 1st **Valoris**, 2nd Berkeley Springs, 3rd Varinia

King George VI and Queen Elizabeth Stakes: 1st **Aunt Edith**, 2nd Sodium, 3rd **Prominer**

St Leger: 1st Sodium, 2nd Charlottown, 3rd David Jack

In Germany

Grosser Preis von Baden: 1st Atilla, 2nd Kronzeuge, 3rd Goldbube, 9th **Ciacolesso**

In Italy

Gran Premio di Milano: 1st **Marco Visconti**, 2nd Chio, 3rd Memling

The race

Like most of the preceding week, it was a wet and overcast day. Prominer was quick away but was soon passed by Marco Visconti, who'd made the pace last year.

At the summit of the climb, Ciacolesso and I Say were on terms with Marco Visconti, closely followed by a group containing Sigebert, A Tempo, Carvin and Aunt Edith. Bon Mot was not far behind in the next group.

Behistoun made ground on the downhill stretch and, rounding the home turn, Sigebert took over as Ciacolesso and I Say weakened. Only A Tempo and Bon Mot were able to respond, but favourite backers knew their fate as Aunt Edith couldn't accelerate with them.

At the 400-metre pole, Sigebert still had a bit of daylight over A Tempo, while on the outside Bon Mot closed in and moved into second with 200 metres to run. It took a moment for Bon Mot to attack Sigebert, whose supporters must have thought they were going to win. However, Freddy Head concentrated his mount and he wore Sigebert down stride by stride, finally poking his head into the lead in the final 50 metres to secure victory by half a length.

From a mile back Sigebert's stablemate, Lionel, who had been badly baulked early in the straight, ran on for third with A Tempo, Behistoun, and Carvin next. Favourite Aunt Edith came home a distant eighth.

Post-race

All of the first seven were trained in France, with the second and third hailing from the yard of Max Bonaventure. But it was Freddy Head who had scored on his first Arc ride, and for his grandfather Willie, who doubled his score, adding to Le Paillon in 1947.

Owner Walter Burmann bred pedigree cattle and had turned his attentions to horses a decade prior to winning the 1960 Irish Derby with Chamour. He'd also won the Irish Oaks four years later with Ancasta, and his current champion, Bon Mot, was to stay in training.

Result

1966 Prix de l'Arc de Triomphe

Longchamp. Sunday, 9 October 1966
Weights: 3yo c: 55.5kg, 3yo f: 54kg, 4yo+ c: 60kg, 4yo+ f: 58.5kg

1st Bon Mot (FR)　　　　3yo c　55.5kg　**5.3/1**
by Worden out of Djébel Idra (Phil Drake). Walter Burmann / Willie Head / Freddy Head

2nd Sigebert (FR)　　　　5yo h　60kg　**50/1**
by Alizier out of Senones (Prince Bio). Madame Jean Stern / Max Bonaventure / Léon Flavien

3rd Lionel (FR)　　　　3yo c　55.5kg　**16/1**
by Herbager out of La Strada (Fervent). Baron Guy de Rothschild / Max Bonaventure / Jean Deforge

Runners: 24 (FR 18, GB 3, ITY 2, IRE 1). Distances: ½, 2. Going: heavy.
Time: 2m 39.80s

Also ran: 4th **A Tempo** (FR) 3yo c, 5th **Behistoun** (FR) 3yo c, 6th **Carvin** (FR) 4yo c, 7th **Cherie Noire** (FR) 3yo f, 8th **Aunt Edith** (GB) 4yo f, 9th **I Say** (GB) 4yo c, 10th **Cadmus** (GB) 3yo c. Unplaced: **Red Vagabonde** (IRE) 5yo h, **Corfinio** (ITY) 4yo c **Prominer** (GB) 4yo c, **Marco Visconti** (ITY) 4yo c, **Eclat** (USA) 3yo c, **Danseur** (FR) 3yo c, **Vasco de Gama** (FR) 3yo c, **Ciacolesso** (ITY) 3yo c, **Taneb** (FR) 3yo c, **Valoris** (FR) 3yo f, **Si Sage** (GB) 3yo f, **Fandine** (FR) 3yo c, **Parthian Glance** (GB) 3yo f, **Fine Pearl** (FR) 3yo f.

Topyo wins in record 30-strong field

Jockey ends up in jail after steering outsider to victory

Background and fancied horses

The mounts of Yves Saint-Martin and Lester Piggott dominated the betting. Yves was riding the Étienne Pollet-trained Roi Dagobert, who'd made a big impact at the start of the season. After winning the Prix Greffulhe and Prix Noailles, he followed up with a battling success in the Prix Lupin. But then he suffered a setback in training and hadn't been seen for five months before lining up for the Arc, for which he was made the 3.5/1 favourite.

Piggott was aboard 5/1-shot Ribocco, who'd been a top two-year-old. The son of Ribot wasn't convincing at the start of this season but found his form when runner-up to Royal Palace in the Derby, before going one place better in the Irish version. A decent third in the King George VI and Queen Elizabeth Stakes followed before he won his second Classic with a superior performance in the St Leger.

It was 10/1 bar the pair, bringing in Grosser Preis von Baden-winner Salvo, who was one of the horses who'd finished ahead of Ribocco in the King George VI and Queen Elizabeth Stakes, and Guy de Rothschild's Frontal who was fourth in the Prix du Jockey Club.

The Russian-raider Anilin was having a second go and arrived at Longchamp on the back of a win over his stable companion Actash in a valuable race in Germany. They were coupled at 12/1.

Prix du Jockey Club-winner Astec, who'd found the extra trip too far in the Grand Prix de Paris, was two points longer with Étienne Pollet's other runner, the Prix de Diane-third Silver Cloud, the last horse under 20/1.

There were ten horses trained outside of France including two more from England: Dart Board, third in both the English and Irish Derbys, and last year's St Leger-winner Sodium, whose best effort this term was when runner-up to Salvo in the Hardwicke Stakes.

The Luigi Mantovani-trained Ciacolesso, who'd been fourth in the Prix du Prince d'Orange, was back for Italy, accompanied by his stablemate the 1966 Premio Roma-winner Astese. And the sole Irish runner was last year's Irish St Leger-winner White Gloves.

Also among the longshots was the erratic Topyo, who was running for Suzy Volterra. He'd taken the Prix La Force but was only ninth in the Prix du

Jockey Club. Later he won the Prix de la Côte Normande but again followed up with a poor run in the Prix de Chantilly, albeit having suffered some interference.

Last year's winner Bon Mot was not present. He'd won the Prix de Lutèce, and most recently been fourth home in the King George VI and Queen Elizabeth Stakes, but was retired soon after when he contracted a cough. His only top-class offspring was the 1973 Ascot Gold Cup and Prix Gladiateur-winner Lassalle.

Betting

3.5/1 Roi Dagobert, 5/1 Ribocco, 10/1 Salvo, 10/1 Frontal, 12/1 Anilin & Actash (coupled), 14/1 Astec, 19/1 Silver Cloud, 22/1 BAR.

Three-year-old form lines

Prix du Jockey Club: 1st **Astec**, 2nd Minamoto, 3rd **Taj Dewan**, 4th **Frontal**, 7th **Phaëton**, 8th **Pétrone**, 9th **Topyo**, 0th **Carmarthen**
Grand Prix de Paris: 1st **Phaëton**, 2nd **Pétrone**, 3rd **Astec**
Prix Royal-Oak: 1st Samos II, 2nd Rixtag, 3rd **Sucaryl**, 5th **Pétrone**, 6th **Phaëton**

Fillies only

Prix de Diane: 1st Gazala, 2nd Tidra, 3rd **Silver Cloud**
Prix Vermeille: 1st Casaque Grise, 2nd Percale, 3rd **Heath Rose**, 6th **Armoricana**

Older horses and inter-generational races

Grand Prix de Saint-Cloud: 1st **Taneb**, 2nd **Nelcius**, 3rd **Taj Dewan**, 6th Charlottown
La Coupe de Maisons-Laffitte: 1st **A Tempo**, 2nd **Nelcius**, 3rd Soleil d'Or
Grand Prix de Deauville: 1st **Lionel**, 2nd **A Tempo**, 3rd **Arjon**, 0th **Ciacolesso**, 0th **Astese**
Prix du Prince d'Orange: 1st **Carmarthen**, 2nd Fiasco, 3rd Fin Bon, 4th **Ciacolesso**
Prix Henri Foy: 1st Busted, 2nd Fiasco, 3rd **Carnaval**

Abroad

In England
Derby Stakes: 1st Royal Palace, 2nd **Ribocco**, 3rd **Dart Board**
King George VI and Queen Elizabeth Stakes: 1st Busted, 2nd **Salvo**, 3rd **Ribocco**, 4th Bon Mot, 0th **Sodium**, 0th **Nelcius**
St Leger: 1st **Ribocco**, 2nd Hopeful Venture, 3rd Ruysdael II, 4th **Dart Board**

In Ireland
Irish Derby: 1st **Ribocco**, 2nd **Sucaryl**, 3rd **Dart Board**

In Germany
Grosser Preis von Baden: 1st **Salvo**, 2nd Luciano, 3rd Goldbube

The race

The ground was heavy but the sun was out as Pot aux Roses was the first to show, Phaëton, though, was slow to stride. Heath Rose took over after about

400 metres with Sucaryl, Frontal and Nelcius all to the fore with Anilin and Topyo. Meanwhile Ribocco and Silver Cloud were at the back.

Going up the hill, Silver Cloud made a few places and Ribocco did the same on the downhill section. Entering the straight, Sucaryl moved into second but with 300 metres to go he faltered, and it was Topyo who emerged as the horse to challenge and then pass Heath Rose.

He was then faced by multiple challengers, headed by Silver Cloud and Roi Dagobert. Ribocco and Salvo were also closing in, but the latter was running in to a dead-end.

The lack of a recent race may have done for the favourite, as although Roi Dagobert took up second place for a moment, he couldn't find his trademark change of gear. Ribocco collared him only to be passed in turn by the flying Salvo, who finally found racing room as the tiring Heath Rose wandered off a straight line. But it was still Topyo who led.

Both Salvo and Ribocco dramatically reduced Topyo's advantage in the closing strides, but he still had a neck and a short head to spare at the line in what was a thrilling bunch finish.

Roi Dagobert and Heath Rose were only a further half a length and a neck back in fourth and fifth. Then there was a gap to Silver Cloud who was two lengths away in sixth place.

Post-race

It had definitely been a going day for the in-and-out performer Topyo, who was retired for the season. His trainer, the Chantilly-based Mick Bartholomew, had won with Puissant Chef in 1960. This time he'd saddled three outsiders and they had finished first, fifth and seventh at odds of 82/1, 80/1 and 130/1. The winner's return was a new record high, beating Oroso's previous mark by 30 points.

Owner Suzy Volterra, who'd been third with Amour Drake in 1949 and L'Amiral in 1950, had gone one place better than her late husband, Léon, who'd been runner-up with Casterari in Crapom's year.

It was also a great day for Topyo's jockey Bill Pyers; however, within a week, news of his success landed him in prison.

The 34-year-old Australian jockey was subject to an outstanding 12-month sentence, which had been passed in his absence, in relation to a car crash. The post-Arc publicity came to the attention of a lawyer involved in the case, and as a result Pyers spent several months in prison and also had his Arc prize money seized.

Result

1967 Prix de l'Arc de Triomphe
Longchamp. Sunday, 8 October 1967
Weights: 3yo c: 55.5kg, 3yo f: 54kg, 4yo+ c: 60kg, 4yo+ f: 58.5kg

1st Topyo (FR)　　　　　3yo c　55.5kg　**82/1**
by Fine Top out of Deliriosa (Delirium). Suzy Volterra / Mick Bartholomew / Bill Pyers

2nd Salvo (GB)　　　　　4yo c　60kg　**10/1**
by Right Royal out of Manera (Macherio). Gerry Oldham / Harry Wragg / Ron Hutchinson

3rd Ribocco (USA)　　　　3yo c　55.5kg　**5/1**
by Ribot out of Libra (Hyperion). Charles Engelhard / Fulke Johnson Houghton / Lester Piggott

Runners: 30 (FR 20, GB 5, ITY 2, RUS 2, IRE 1). Distances: nk, sh hd. Going: heavy. Time: 2m 38.20s

Also ran: 4th **Roi Dagobert** (FR) 3yo c, 5th **Heath Rose** (GB) 3yo f, 6th **Silver Cloud** (FR) 3yo f, 7th **Parthian Glance** (FR) 4yo f, 8th **Arjon** (GER) 4yo c, 9th **Sucaryl** (GB) 4yo c, 10th **Nelcius** (FR) 3yo c. Unplaced: **Anilin** (RUS) 6yo h, **Dédini** (USA) 3yo c, **Pot aux Roses** (FR) 6yo h, **Carnaval** (FR) 4yo c, **Ciacolesso** (ITY) 4yo c, **Astese** (ITY) 4yo c, **Taneb** (FR) 4yo c, **A Tempo** (FR) 4yo c, **White Gloves** (IRE) 4yo c, **Lionel** (FR) 4yo c, **Sodium** (GB) 4yo c, **Pétrone** (FR) 3yo c, **Taj Dewan** (FR) 3yo c, **Astec** (FR) 3yo c, **Frontal** (FR) 3yo c, **Dart Board** (GB) 3yo c, **Phaëton** (GB) 3yo c, **Carmarthen** (FR) 3yo c, **Actash** (RUS) 3yo c, **Armoricana** (FR) 3yo c.

1968

Vaguely Noble for Ireland, France and the USA

Pollet's charge comprehensively sees off Sir Ivor

Background and fancied horses

This was the year of the student riots in Paris which occurred in May and June. Although another French revolution was averted they did, in time, result in quite radical societal changes, albeit nothing that affected horse racing in the short term, where in the autumn, all eyes were still trained on the Arc.

The favourite was Vaguely Noble at 2.5/1. Bred in Ireland he'd ended his two-year-old campaign with an emphatic seven-length win in the Observer Gold Cup at Doncaster (now the Futurity Stakes). Inspired by that performance, Nelson Bunker Hunt bought a half-share at the Newmarket sales and Vaguely Noble decamped to France to join the yard of Étienne Pollet.

He proceeded to win the Prix de Guiche and Prix de Lys before seemingly being given too much to do when a fast-finishing third to Queen Elizabeth II's Hopeful Venture in the Grand Prix de Saint-Cloud. Jean Deforge was subsequently replaced by Bill Williamson when Vaguely Noble impressively won his prep race for the Arc.

Up against him were the pairing of Felicio and Pétrone. Owned by Daniel Wildenstein, the son of Georges Wildenstein and like him an art dealer, they were coupled on 5/1. The former had only been beaten by Royal Palace in the King George VI and Queen Elizabeth Stakes and had last year's winning jockey, the rehabilitated Bill Pyers, in the plate.

Pétrone was to be ridden by Yves Saint-Martin. He had some decent form, including winning the Prix Henri Foy. However, the restricted price of the Wildenstein duo was at least partly due to the popularity of the man in Pétrone's saddle.

Roselière, who was a point longer, could justifiably be regarded as the best filly in the field. Unbeaten as a three-year-old, she'd won the Prix de Diane and the Prix Vermeille, beating The Oaks-winner La Lagune both times.

Just a fraction longer than Roselière was Freddy Head's mount, Dhaudevi. He'd beaten the Prix du Jockey Club-winner Tapalqué in the Grand Prix de Paris and more recently had added the Prix Royal-Oak.

The best of the four raiders was the Vincent O'Brien-trained Sir Ivor. He'd won the 2000 Guineas and the Derby under Lester Piggott, before losing out to Ribero as an odds-on shot in the Irish Derby when ridden by Liam Ward.

A week later and with Piggott back in the plate he was runner-up again in the Eclipse Stakes and then, after a rest, also found one too good in the Prix Henry Delamarre when trying to give 4kg to the useful Prince Sao.

The German-trained Luciano, the winner of the 1967 Deutsches Derby and Deutsches St Leger, was unbeaten this term and had come out on top in the Grosser Preis von Baden.

Luthier at 11/1 was the last horse under 31/1. Owned by Guy de Rothschild, he'd been victorious in the Prix Noailles and Prix Lupin but couldn't go through with his effort when odds-on for the Prix du Jockey Club, where he finished sixth. Reverting to 1,600 metres he'd duly obliged in the Prix Jacques Le Marois.

As well as Ireland's Sir Ivor and Germany's Luciano, the other foreign challengers were the aforementioned Irish Derby and St Leger-winner Ribero for England, and Zbor, who'd won five times in Moscow, representing Russia.

Last year's winner, Topyo, ran his best race of the season when third in the King George VI and Queen Elizabeth Stakes, in what turned out to be his swansong. He was sold to Japan and produced a few winners but none at Group 1 level.

Betting
2.5/1 Vaguely Noble, 5/1 Felicio & Pétrone (coupled), 6/1 Roselière, 6.5/1 Dhaudevi, 6.5/1 Sir Ivor, 7.5/1 Luciano, 11/1 Luthier, 31/1 BAR.

Three-year-old form lines
Prix du Jockey Club: 1st Tapalqué, 2nd Timmy My Boy, 3rd Val d'Aoste, 4th **Soyeux**, 6th **Luthier**, 0th **Danoso**
Grand Prix de Paris: 1st **Dhaudevi**, 2nd Tapalqué, 3rd Aranas
Prix Royal-Oak: 1st **Dhaudevi**, 2nd Torpid, 3rd Levmoss, 4th **Soyeux**

Fillies only
Prix de Diane: 1st **Roselière**, 2nd Pola Bella, 3rd Terzina, 0th **La Lagune**
Prix Vermeille: 1st **Roselière**, 2nd Pola Bella, 3rd **La Lagune**

Older horses and inter-generational races
Grand Prix de Saint-Cloud: 1st Hopeful Venture, 2nd Minamoto, 3rd **Vaguely Noble**, 6th **Samos II**, 8th Topyo
Grand Prix de Deauville: 1st **Soyeux**, 2nd Blazer, 3rd **Pétrone**, 0th **Tit Bits**
Prix du Prince d'Orange: 1st **Pétrone**, 2nd Grandier, 3rd Bagdad
Prix Henri Foy: 1st **Pétrone**, 2nd Grandier, 3rd Adjader, 4th **Arjon**, 7th **Carmarthen**

Abroad

In England

Derby Stakes: 1st **Sir Ivor**, 2nd Connaught, 3rd Mount Athos, 4th Remand

Oaks Stakes: 1st **La Lagune**, 2nd Glad One, 3rd Pandora Bay

Ascot Gold Cup: 1st Pardallo, 2nd **Samos II**, 3rd **Pétrone**

King George VI and Queen Elizabeth Stakes: 1st Royal Palace, 2nd **Felicio**, 3rd Topyo, 4th **Ribero**

St Leger: 1st **Ribero**, 2nd Canterbury, 3rd Cold Storage

In Ireland

Irish Derby: 1st **Ribero**, 2nd **Sir Ivor**, 3rd Val d'Aoste

In Germany

Grosser Preis von Baden: 1st **Luciano**, 2nd Chicago, 3rd Birgitz

The race

The ground was holding as Luthier and Roselière broke quickly along with Pétrone and Zbor. Vaguely Noble was positioned in the following group with Sir Ivor to the rear, while Luciano, who'd played up in the preliminaries, was pulling hard.

Passing the Petit Bois, Sir Ivor moved a bit closer but the order remained pretty much the same until the descent, where Zbor and Soyeux faded. That left Luther and Roselière in front, followed by Vaguely Noble and Sir Ivor, as they turned into the straight.

When Bill Williamson asked Vaguely Noble to accelerate, he received an immediate response. In great style he quickly passed the leading pair and opened up daylight on the rest of the field.

Sir Ivor chased him through into a clear second place but was never going to get on terms with Vaguely Noble, who sauntered home by three lengths. There was a further four to the mudlark Carmarthen, then Roselière in fourth ahead of La Lagune and Dhaudevi.

Post-race

Vaguely Noble's comprehensive victory over a field that included seven winners of 11 Classics was a great success for joint USA owners Wilma Franklin, the wife of a Californian plastic surgeon, and the oil tycoon Nelson Bunker Hunt.

It was a third success for Étienne Pollet after La Sorellina and Sea Bird, and the first for Bill Williamson, who wouldn't have to wait long for another. Vaguely Noble retired and went to stud in the USA where he produced several notable horses, including Dahlia, Exceller, Mississippian, Empery, Nobiliary, Ace of Aces, and Inkerman.

Result

1968 Prix de l'Arc de Triomphe
Longchamp. Sunday, 6 October 1968
Weights: 3yo c: 55.5kg, 3yo f: 54kg, 4yo+ c: 60kg, 4yo+ f: 58.5kg

1st Vaguely Noble (IRE) 3yo c 55.5kg **2.5/1 fav**
by Vienna out of Noble Lassie (Nearco). Wilma Franklin & Nelson Bunker Hunt / Étienne Pollet / Bill Williamson

2nd Sir Ivor (USA) 3yo c 55.5kg **6.5/1**
by Sir Gaylord out of Attica (Mr Trouble). Raymond Guest / Vincent O'Brien / Lester Piggott

3rd Carmarthen (GB) 3yo c 60kg **90/1**
by Devon out of Kuwait (Persian Gulf). May Strassburger / George Bridgland / Jean-Luc Durry

Runners: 17 (FR 13, GB 1, IRE 1, GER 1, RUS 1). Distances: 3, 4. Going: holding. Time: 2m 35.20s

Also ran: 4th **Roselière** (FR) 3yo f, 5th **La Lagune** (FR) 3yo f, 6th **Dhaudevi** (FR) 3yo c, 7th **Felicio** (FR) 3yo c, 8th **Samos II** (IRE) 4yo c, 9th **Luthier** (FR) 3yo c, 10th **Soyeux** (FR) 3yo c. Unplaced: **Arjon** (GER) 5yo h, **Luciano** (GB) 4yo c, **Pétrone** (FR) 4yo c, **Danoso** (FR) 3yo c, **Ribero** (USA) 3yo c, **Tit Bits** (FR) 3yo c, **Zbor** (RUS) 3yo c.

Levmoss holds Park Top's late surge

Second Irish-trained winner is a grandson of the first

Background and fancied horses

Last year's winning-trainer, Étienne Pollet, was responsible for this season's market leader, Prince Regent, who was by Right Royal the favourite in 1961. He won the Prix Greffulhe but had been unlucky in the Derby, as after being hampered at Tattenham Corner, he ran on very strongly to finish third to Blakeney.

With Geoff Lewis in the plate at the Curragh, Prince Regent readily reversed the Epsom placings in the Irish Derby and was 2/1 for the Arc.

He was faced by the classy mare Park Top. She'd been in great form winning the Coronation Cup, Hardwicke Stakes, King George VI and Queen Elizabeth Stakes and the former Prix Henri Foy – which was run for the first time under its newly abbreviated title of the Prix Foy. Lester Piggott's mount was 4/1 and it was double figures bar.

Charles Engelhard's Roselière and Ribofilio were coupled at 11/1. The former had been fourth last year while the latter, after refusing to race in the 2000 Guineas, had finished runner-up in the Irish Derby and the St Leger, having been favourite for all three races.

Piggott had ridden Ribofilio and the Derby Italiano-winner Bonconte di Montefeltro but in the end rejected them for Park Top. Bonconte di Montefeltro was 12/1 along with Guy de Rothschild's Grand Prix de Deauville-winner Djakao, with the Prix Vermeille-heroine Saraca on 13/1.

They were followed by Chaparral, winner of the Grand Prix de Paris, and Belbury who had been successful in the Prix de Chantilly, the antecedent of the race now run as the Prix Niel.

There were nine challengers from countries outside of France. They included six from England: Park Top and Ribifilio; Remand, the winner of the Cumberland Lodge Stakes; the first two home in the Derby, Blakeney and Shoemaker; and Copsale, who'd won the Prix Maurice de Nieuil.

The previously mentioned Bonconte di Montefeltro represented Italy, Zbor was back for Russia, while Levmoss, who'd proved himself to be a very good stayer winning the Prix du Cadran and the Ascot Gold Cup, came over from Ireland.

The Japanese-bred Speed Symboli had won 18 times in his native land before coming to be trained in France in the summer. But after finishing fifth in the King George VI and Queen Elizabeth Stakes he'd trailed home in 10th place in the Grand Prix de Deauville.

Betting

2/1 Prince Regent, 4/1 Park Top, 11/1 Roselière & Ribofilio (coupled), 12/1 Bonconte di Montefeltro, 12/1 Djakao, 13/1 Saraca, 14/1 Chaparral, 19/1 Belbury, 24/1 BAR.

Three-year-old form lines

Prix du Jockey Club: 1st **Goodly**, 2nd **Beaugency**, 3rd **Djakao**

Grand Prix de Paris: 1st **Chaparral**, 2nd **Djakao**, 3rd **Durango**

Prix Royal-Oak: 1st Le Chouan, 2nd Honeyville, 3rd **Chaparral**, 4th **Bonconte di Montefeltro**

Fillies only

Prix de Diane: 1st **Crepellana**, 2nd **Saraca**, 3rd Glaneuse

Prix Vermeille: 1st **Saraca**, 2nd **Crepellana**, 3rd Riverside

Older horses and inter-generational races

Grand Prix de Saint-Cloud: 1st Felicio, 2nd **Goodly**, 3rd Soyeux

Grand Prix de Deauville: 1st **Djakao**, 2nd Arme d'Or, 3rd **Remand**, 10th **Speed Symboli**

Prix du Prince d'Orange: 1st **Goodly**, 2nd **Carmarthen**, 3rd **Candy Cane**

Prix Foy (Previously Prix Henri Foy) : 1st **Park Top**, 2nd Felicio, 3rd Pandora Bay

Abroad

In England

Derby Stakes: 1st **Blakeney**, 2nd **Shoemaker**, 3rd **Prince Regent**, 5th **Ribofilio**, 9th **Belbury**

Ascot Gold Cup: 1st **Levmoss**, 2nd Torpid, 3rd Fortissimo

King George VI and Queen Elizabeth Stakes: 1st **Park Top**, 2nd Crozier, 3rd Hogarth, 4th Felicio, 5th **Speed Symboli**

St Leger: 1st Intermezzo, 2nd **Ribofilio**, 3rd Prince Consort, 5th **Blakeney**, 8th **Shoemaker**

In Ireland

Irish Derby: 1st **Prince Regent**, 2nd **Ribofilio**, 4th **Blakeney**, 9th **Beaugency**

The race

Bonconte di Montefeltro and Blakeney broke fast with Levmoss running in third. Chaparral, Remand and Saraca followed, while Prince Regent was at the back with Park Top, on whom Piggott was exuding confidence after winning the first three races on the card.

Saraca lost her place at the top of the hill – she was later found to have pulled a tendon – as Shoemaker then Grandier made ground. Bonconte di Montefeltro still led on the final bend but drifted off the rail, allowing Bill Williamson to steer Levmoss through the gap and into the lead.

Prince Regent and Park Top started to pick their way through beaten horses. But the favourite soon ran out of resources and it was only Park Top who was able to mount a challenge.

Steering a wide course, she produced a tremendous burst of speed and made up ground rapidly. But the seven-length start she'd given him was too much, and Levmoss still had three parts of a length to spare at the line.

Three lengths behind, Grandier made the frame followed by Candy Cane, Prince Regent and Chaparral.

Post-race

Seen primarily as a stayer, Levmoss had largely been overlooked and was returned at the generous odds of 52/1. A grandson of the first Irish-trained Arc winner, Ballymoss, he was owned and trained by Seamus McGrath, the son of the legendary Joseph McGrath.

A prominent politician, businessman and racehorse owner, Joseph McGrath founded the Irish Hospitals' Sweepstake, which operated on races such as the Grand National and Derby and was for many years the sponsor of the Irish Derby.

He was commemorated in the title of the Joe McGrath Memorial Stakes, a race that became the Irish Champion Stakes in 1999. It is a great race in its own right but has also become a good pointer to the Arc.

Levmoss's jockey, Bill Williamson, became the first to win in consecutive years on different horses since Charles Semblat on Pearl Cap and Motrico in 1931 and 1932.

Levmoss retired to stud immediately, where his best offspring were the Irish St Leger and Grosser Preis von Baden-winner M'Loshan, and Shafaraz, who was successful in the Prix du Cadran. He was also the grandsire of Ardross, who will feature in our story in the early 1980s.

Mossborough 1947

|

Ballymoss 1954

|

Feemoss 1960

|

Levmoss 1965

|

Le Melody 1971

|

Ardross 1976

Result
1969 Prix de l'Arc de Triomphe
Longchamp. Sunday, 5 October 1969
Weights: 3yo c: 55.5kg, 3yo f: 54kg, 4yo+ c: 60kg, 4yo+ f: 58.5kg

1st Levmoss (IRE)　　　　3yo c　60kg　　**52/1**
by Le Levanstell out of Feemoss (Ballymoss). Seamus McGrath / Seamus McGrath / Bill Williamson

2nd Park Top (GB)　　　　5yo m　58.5kg　**4/1**
by Kalydon out of Nellie Park (Arctic Prince). Duke of Devonshire / Bernard van Cutsem / Lester Piggott

3rd Grandier (FR)　　　　5yo h　60kg　　**70/1**
by Tapioca out of Girga (Fine Top). Madame Pierre Ribes / John Cunnington jnr / Maurice Philipperon

Runners: 24 (FR 15, GB 6, IRE 1, ITY 1, RUS 1). Distances: ¾, 3. Going: good. Time: 2m 29.00s

Also ran: 4th **Candy Cane** (GB) 4yo c, 5th **Prince Regent** (FR) 3yo c, 6th **Chaparral** (FR) 3yo c, 7th **Remand** (GB) 4yo c, 8th **Belbury** (GB) 3yo c, 9th **Blakeney** (GB) 3yo c, 10th **Zbor** (RUS) 4yo c. Unplaced: **Fiasco** (IRE) 7yo h, **Copsale** (GB) 6yo h, **Speed Symboli** (JPN) 6yo h, **Carmarthen** (FR) 5yo h, **Roselière** (FR) 4yo f, **Ribofilio** (USA) 3yo c, **Shoemaker** (IRE) 3yo c, **Goodly** (FR) 3yo c, **Bonconte di Montefeltro** (ITY) 3yo c, **Djakao** (FR) 3yo c, **Beaugency** (FR) 3yo c, **Yelapa** (FR) 3yo c, **Crepellana** (FR) 3yo f, **Saraca** (GB) 3yo f.

Sassafras ends Nijinsky's unbeaten run

First Arc for Yves Saint-Martin

Background and fancied horses

In England it had been the year of Nijinsky. Vincent O'Brien's Canadian-bred had become the first winner of the colts' Triple Crown since Bahram in 1935.

Owned by Charles Engelhard, and named after the Russian ballet dancer Vaslav Nijinsky, the son of Northern Dancer had used his scintillating turn of speed to rack up a fabulous catalogue of successes. He won the Gladness Stakes, the 2000 Guineas, the Derby, the Irish Derby, and the King George VI and Queen Elizabeth Stakes, but then he had contracted ringworm.

It was quite a serious setback but, with Piggott nursing him home, Nijinsky completed the Triple Crown against a sub-standard field at Doncaster. The multitude of fans of the O'Brien/Piggott partnership thought Nijinsky was invincible and it was little wonder he started at 0.4/1 at Longchamp, where many in the huge crowd were expecting to see a lap of honour.

The second-favourite, Gyr, had won the Prix Daru and Prix Hocquart before finishing runner-up to Nijinsky in the Derby. Subsequently he won the Grand Prix de Saint-Cloud and, along with his pacemaker Golden Eagle, was returned at 7.5/1.

The Italian challengers Ortis – who'd won the Derby Italiano by five lengths – and his pacesetter Prix du Prince d'Orange-third Lar, were on 8.8/1. There was then a big gap to 19/1-chance Sassafras, the mount of Yves Saint-Martin.

Owned by Arpad Plesch, Sassafras had stepped-up on his two-year-old form when winning the Prix du Jockey Club. After being given a rest, Sassafras returned in the Prix Royal-Oak where he was badly hampered by Hallez when second past the post. It was no surprise that he was awarded the race in the Stewards' Room.

Three of the four runners from outside France have already been mentioned. The other was the returning 1969 Derby-winner Blakeney, who this year had been runner-up in the Ascot Gold Cup and King George VI and Queen Elizabeth Stakes.

Betting

0.4/1 Nijinsky, 7.5/1 Gyr & Golden Eagle (coupled), 8.8/1 Ortis & Lar (coupled), 19/1 Sassafras, 25/1 BAR.

Three-year-old form lines

Prix du Jockey Club: 1st **Sassafras**, 2nd Roll of Honour, 3rd Caro
Grand Prix de Paris: 1st Roll of Honour, 2nd Fontarabal, 3rd High Moon
Prix Royal-Oak: 1st (2nd ptp) **Sassafras**, 2nd (1st ptp) Hallez, 3rd High Moon

Fillies only

Prix de Diane: 1st Sweet Mimosa, 2nd Highest Hopes, 3rd Pampered Miss
Prix Vermeille: 1st Highest Hopes, 2nd **Miss Dan**, 3rd Parmelia, 0th Sweet Mimosa

Older horses and inter-generational races

Grand Prix de Saint-Cloud: 1st **Gyr**, 2nd **Grandier**, 3rd Hallez
Prix du Prince d'Orange: 1st **A Chara**, 2nd Tapalqué, 3rd **Lar**
Prix Foy: 1st Lorenzaccio, 2nd **Beaugency**, 3rd Schönbrunn

Abroad

In England
Derby Stakes: 1st **Nijinsky**, 2nd **Gyr**, 3rd **Stintino**
Ascot Gold Cup: 1st Precipice Wood, 2nd **Blakeney**, 3rd Clairon
King George VI and Queen Elizabeth Stakes: 1st **Nijinsky**, 2nd **Blakeney**, 3rd Crepellana
St Leger: 1st **Nijinsky**, 2nd Meadowville, 3rd Politico

In Ireland
Irish Derby: 1st **Nijinsky**, 2nd Meadowville, 3rd Master Guy

In Italy
Gran Premio di Milano: 1st **Beaugency**, 2nd Bacuco, 3rd Hogarth

The race

After some rain in the preceding days, the ground, which had been firm at the end of September, was now good. At the off Stintino was slow to stride while Lar and Golden Eagle fulfilled their roles as pacemakers by leading the field away.

Sassafras, Blakeney and Ortis came next. Piggott had Nijinsky further back in about 12th while Gyr wouldn't settle. Miss Dan joined the leading group at the summit and on the downhill stretch Nijinsky was starting to creep closer.

When the pacemakers folded, Miss Dan took over and led to the 400-metre pole, where she was mastered by Sassafras. Meanwhile Piggott switched Nijinsky off the rails.

The Triple Crown-winner engaged turbo and started to close the gap, eventually looking as though he had taken a narrow advantage. But he couldn't stretch away and Sassafras under Saint-Martin responded gamely, battling back to retake the lead in the last 25 metres to score by a head.

Miss Dan took third, a couple of lengths behind the epic dual, with Gyr, Blakeney and Beaugency coming home next. The 'unbeatable' had been beaten and the spoils went to Sassafras. The visitors were baffled, while the home team exulted in their champion.

Post-race

The Hungarian financier Arpad Plesch was delighted with what was the latest chapter in a *palmarès* that included: the 1959 Poule d'Essai des Poulains-winner Thymus; the 1961 Derby-victor Psidium; the hero of the 1968 Prix du Jockey Club Tapalqué; and the previous year's Prix Vermeille-heroine Saraca.

It was a third Arc for trainer François Mathet, after Tantième in 1950 and 1951, and he would still have a word or two more to say in Arc history. National hero, Yves Saint-Martin, went one place better than on Reliance in 1965, while his great rival Lester Piggott had finished second for the third year in a row.

Sassafras had no stamina doubts and had won on merit beating a great champion. But one who had been ill, and who, on a stiff course like Longchamp and with a testing gallop from the start, possibly didn't quite get the trip.

The first Prix du Jockey Club-winner to add the Arc since Ardan in 1944, Sassafras retired to stud. His best progeny was Henri Le Balafré, who won the 1975 Prix Royal-Oak. He could probably have done better given the chance, but life isn't fair and the bulletproof Sassafras rather got overlooked by breeders who opted more for the flashy acceleration of Nijinsky, who became the cornerstone of the Northern Dancer line.

Result

1970 Prix de l'Arc de Triomphe
Longchamp. Sunday, 4 October 1970
Weights: 3yo c: 55.5kg, 3yo f: 54kg, 4yo+ c: 60kg, 4yo+ f: 58.5kg

1st Sassafras (FR)   3yo c   55.5kg   **19/1**
by Sheshoon out of Ruta (Ratification). Arpad Plesch / François Mathet / Yves Saint-Martin

2nd Nijinsky (CAN)   3yo c   55.5kg   **0.4/1 fav**
by Northern Dancer out of Flaming Page (Bull Page). Charles Engelhard / Vincent O'Brien / Lester Piggott

3rd Miss Dan (FR)   3yo f   54kg   **38/1**
by Dan Cupid out of Miraloma (Clarion). Achille Fould / Philippe Lallie / Jean Tailard

Runners: 15 (FR 11, ITY 2, GB 1, IRE 1). Distances: hd, 2. Going: good. Time: 2m 29.70s

Also ran: 4th **Gyr** (USA) 3yo c, 5th **Blakeney** (GB) 4yo c, 6th **Beaugency** (FR) 4yo c, 7th **Soyeux** (FR) 5yo h, 8th **Quinquet** (FR) 4yo c, 9th **Grandier** (FR) 6yo h, 10th **A Chara** (IRE) 4yo c. Unplaced: **Golden Eagle** (FR) 5yo h, **La Bijute** (FR) 5yo m, **Stintino** (IRE) 3yo f, **Ortis** (ITY) 3yo f, **Lar** (GB) 3yo f.

Mill Reef cruises home in 50th Arc

Record time for first English-trained winner since 1948

Background and fancied horses

If it had all been about Nijinsky in England last year, this season it was all about Paul Mellon's Mill Reef. A brilliant two-year-old, he'd won the Greenham Stakes on his reappearance before splitting Brigadier Gerard and My Swallow in one of the most memorable renewals of the 2000 Guineas.

From then on Mill Reef dominated the middle distance races, scoring in style in the Derby, the Eclipse Stakes, and the King George VI and Queen Elizabeth Stakes, before being rested for the Arc.

Trained by Ian Balding at Kingsclere, he had a smooth flight over to Longchamp, departing from the nearby RAF base at Greenham Common – a venue that would become famous for other reasons in the 1980s. Could Mill Reef do what had eluded Nijinsky? Punters were confident enough and Geoff Lewis's mount was returned at 0.7/1.

The main defence from the home team was Alec Head's pair Pistol Packer and Bourbon, who were coupled at 4.3/1. The former had won the Prix de Diane and Prix Vermeille, each time beating Cambrizzia.

Bourbon, on the other hand, had started the season well, winning the Prix de Guiche and Prix Hocquart. But he'd then played up in the preliminaries for the Derby, breaking his bridle and later on unshipping Freddy Head.

Not surprisingly Bourbon finished out of the money on that occasion, but he'd redeemed himself when beating Oarsman in the Prix Royal-Oak. Freddy had chosen to ride Pistol Packer and Yves Saint-Martin was booked for Bourbon.

Next up were the trio trained by Geoff Watson, Ramsin and Ossian, owned by Thierry de Zuylen de Nyevelt, and Guy de Rothschild's Arlequino.

The last-named was only having his third career run when winning the Prix de Chantilly in September. Ramsin, on the other hand, as the winner of the Prix du Cadran and Grand Prix de Saint-Cloud, was thoroughly tried and tested. He would have the benefit of Ossian as a pacemaker, and together they were all grouped on 7/1.

As well as Mill Reef, Hardwicke Stakes-winner Ortis and Lady Beaverbrook's Royalty, who was unbeaten in four minor races, were also trained in England. One for All, who'd been victorious in some prestigious handicaps in North America, was the first challenger from the USA since Tom Rolfe in 1965.

Betting

0.7/1 Mill Reef, 4.3/1 Pistol Packer & Bourbon (coupled), 7/1 Arlequino & Ramsin & Ossian (all coupled), 21/1 BAR.

Three-year-old form lines
Prix du Jockey Club: 1st Rheffic, 2nd Nymbio, 3rd Tarbes
Grand Prix de Paris: 1st Rheffic, 2nd Point de Riz, 3rd Valdrague
Prix Royal-Oak: 1st **Bourbon**, 2nd **Oarsman**, 3rd Parnell

Fillies only
Prix de Diane: 1st **Pistol Packer**, 2nd **Cambrizzia**, 3rd Dixie
Prix Vermeille: 1st **Pistol Packer**, 2nd **Cambrizzia**, 3rd Pink Pearl

Older horses and inter-generational races
Grand Prix de Saint-Cloud: 1st **Ramsin**, 2nd Hokkaido, 3rd Tarbes, 5th **Hallez**, 7th **Bourbon**, 0th **Armos**
Grand Prix de Deauville: 1st **Miss Dan**, 2nd Valdrague, 3rd Crucible, 7th **Armos**
Prix du Prince d'Orange: 1st **Hallez**, 2nd _, 3rd _
Prix Foy: 1st Prominent, 2nd **Caro**, 3rd _, 4th **Mister Sic Top**

Abroad
In England
Derby Stakes: 1st **Mill Reef**, 2nd Linden Tree, 3rd **Irish Ball**, 0th **Bourbon**
King George VI and Queen Elizabeth Stakes: 1st **Mill Reef**, 2nd Ortis, 3rd Acclimatization, 5th **Irish Ball**

The race

One for All broke fast but it was Ossian who went on and dictated a fast pace. Mill Reef featured in fifth while Pistol Packer was at the back with Cambrizzia. Down the hill, Ossian still led from Ramsin and Hallez with Ortis and Sharapour just behind.

Caro and Pistol Packer started forward moves and, on the turn, Ossian finally capitulated, leaving Sharapour and Ortis in front. As they entered the straight, Piggott quickly took Hallez to the lead. But not far behind, Geoff Lewis steered Mill Reef off the rails to avoid the traffic and launched his charge, quickly passing the new leader on the inside before opening up a clear advantage.

Pistol Packer, Caro and Cambrizzia, who was coming from miles back, all made up ground in the straight. But the bird had flown.

Mill Reef, in his trademark sheepskin noseband, breezed home to record a three-length victory in the style of a true champion and in doing so broke the track record. Pistol Packer came through for second place followed by Cambrizzia, Caro, Hallez – Willie Head's last Arc runner – and Royalty.

Post-race

Mill Reef had done what Nijinsky hadn't been able to and received *l'acclamation célèbre*. In some quarters he was being compared with Sea Bird after becoming only the second winner of both the Derby and Prix de l'Arc de Triomphe.

Being by Never Bend, a son of Nasrullah, he was also the first of what would be many US-bred winners of the Arc. Nasrullah had been bred by the Aga Khan III in Europe but exported to America in 1950.

Businessman and art dealer Paul Mellon owned many decent horses but there is no doubt that Mill Reef was the best. His famous black and gold colours are still seen today on horses running under the Kingsclere banner.

The first English-trained winner since Migoli in 1948 was handled by Ian Balding, the younger brother of Toby, who won the Grand National with Highland Wedding and Little Polveir.

Ian had been assistant to Peter Hastings-Bass, and married his daughter, before taking over at Kingsclere. Mill Reef put him firmly on the map. It was also an iconic success for Geoff Lewis on his third try in the race.

Mill Reef was retired for the season but was kept in training.

Result
1971 Prix de l'Arc de Triomphe
Longchamp. Sunday, 3 October 1971
Weights: 3yo c: 55.5kg, 3yo f: 54kg, 4yo+ c: 60kg, 4yo+ f: 58.5kg

1st Mill Reef (USA)   3yo c   55.5kg   **0.7/1 fav**
by Never Bend out of Milan Mill (Princequillo). Paul Mellon / Ian Balding / Geoff Lewis

2nd Pistol Packer (USA)   3yo f   54kg   **4.3/1** (coupled with Bourbon)
by Gun Bow out of George's Girl (Ossian II [GB]). Ghislaine Head / Alec Head / Freddy Head

3rd Cambrizzia (FR)   3yo f   54kg   **39/1**
by Cambremont out of Aliziane (Alizier). Alex Weisweiller / D. Watson / Sandy Barclay

Runners: 18 (FR 14, GB 3, USA 1). Distances: 3, 1½. Going: firm. Time: 2m 28.30s

Also ran: 4th **Caro** (IRE) 4yo c, 5th **Hallez** (FR) 4yo c, 6th **Royalty** (GB) 3yo c, 7th **Bourbon** (FR) 3yo c, 8th **Arlequino** (FR) 3yo c, 9th **One for All** (USA) 5yo h, 10th **Irish Ball** (FR) 3yo c. Unplaced: **Mister Sic Top** (FR) 4yo c, **Armos** (IRE) 4yo c, **Ortis** (ITY) 3yo c, **Ramsin** (FR) 4yo c, **Ossian** (FR) 4yo c, **Miss Dan** (FR) 4yo f, **Sharapour** (FR) 3yo f, **Oarsman** (GB) 3yo f.

San San – first filly to win since La Sorellina

Freddy Head wins on spare ride

Background and fancied horses

The home team were behind the 1.25/1 favourite Hard To Beat, who'd been the top two-year-old of 1971. This term Angel Penna's charge had taken the Prix du Jockey Club by three lengths under Lester Piggott, but looked to be over the top when caught in the closing stages by Rheingold and Arlequino in the Grand Prix de Saint-Cloud.

Fully rested, Hard To Beat returned to action in the Prix Niel – formerly run as the Prix de Chantilly – beating Vincent O'Brien's Roberto, who Piggott had partnered to success in the Derby. The fact that Piggott had chosen Hard To Beat again in the Arc seemed to be a good indicator of their respective chances.

The Grand Prix de Paris and Prix Royal-Oak winner, Pleben, was one of two runners for Geoff Watson, the other being Rescousse, who had won the Prix de Diane but had disappointed for the first time when only fifth in the Prix Vermeille.

They were coupled at 4.5/1, the same price as the aforementioned Roberto who had been given the full Piggott treatment to outpoint Rheingold at Epsom. He'd failed miserably at the Curragh when trying to add the Irish version. But had shown his best when ending Brigadier Gerard's unbeaten run under an enterprising ride from Braulio Baeza in the inaugural running of the Benson & Hedges Gold Cup at York – now known as the Juddmonte International Stakes. Piggott, who this time had defected to Rheingold, finished fourth.

Parnell, who'd been second in both the Prix du Cadran and King George VI and Queen Elizabeth Stakes, was found to be lame ten days before the Arc and had missed some work. Nevertheless, he was still fancied to run a big race at 9.5/1.

In addition to Roberto, Vincent O'Brien also had the winner of the St Leger, Boucher, who, like the Aga Khan IV's Prix Dollar-winner Sharapour, was a 17/1-shot. The latter had been first past the post in the Prix du Prince d'Orange but was demoted to third by the stewards.

San San was a point and a half longer at 18.5/1. She'd dead-heated with Paysanne in the Prix Vermeille and would be ridden by Freddy Head, as her usual pilot Jean Cruguet had been injured in a recent fall.

There were six raiders in all: Roberto and Boucher for Ireland; the Gran Premio de Madrid-winner My Mourne, the first runner from Spain; and for England, in addition to Parnell, there was Erimo Hawk, who won the Ascot Gold Cup in the Stewards' Room, and the Irish Derby-winner Steel Pulse.

Unfortunately Mill Reef was not with them. Last year's winner had won the Prix Ganay and Coronation Cup but, after missing most of the summer with a virus, had broken his leg in a slow gallop when being prepared for the Arc.

He was fitted with a plaster cast – an image that made front-page news – and once recovered stood at the National Stud in Newmarket, producing horses of the calibre of Shirley Heights, Acamas, Fairy Footsteps, Doyoun, Glint of Gold, and Reference Point.

Betting

1.25/1 Hard To Beat, 4.5/1 Pleben & Rescousse (coupled), 4.5/1 Roberto, 9.5/1 Parnell, 17/1 Boucher, 17/1 Sharapour, 18.5/1 San San, 37/1 BAR.

Three-year-old form lines
Prix du Jockey Club: 1st **Hard To Beat**, 2nd **Sancy**, 3rd Flair Path, 7th **Pleben**
Grand Prix de Paris: 1st **Pleben**, 2nd Sukawa, 3rd Talleyrand
Prix Royal-Oak: 1st **Pleben**, 2nd Novius, 3rd Lassalle, 10th **Sancy**
Prix Niel (formerly the Prix de Chantilly): 1st **Hard To Beat**, 2nd **Roberto**, 3rd **Toujours Prêt**

Fillies only
Prix de Diane: 1st **Rescousse**, 2nd Prodice, 3rd Paysanne
Prix Vermeille: DH1st **San San**, DH1st Paysanne, 3rd Decigale, 4th Ginerva, 5th **Rescousse**, 0th **Regal Exception**

Older horses and inter-generational races
Grand Prix de Saint-Cloud: 1st Rheingold, 2nd Arlequino, 3rd **Hard To Beat**, last **Card King**
Prix du Prince d'Orange: 1st (2nd ptp) **Mister Sic Top**, 2nd (3rd ptp) Moulton, 3rd (1st ptp) **Sharapour**
Prix Foy: 1st **Snow Castle**, 2nd Crazy Rhythm, 3rd Pistol Packer

Abroad
In England
Derby Stakes: 1st **Roberto**, 2nd Rheingold, 3rd Pentland Firth, 4th Our Mirage, 8th **Steel Pulse**
Oaks Stakes: 1st Ginerva, 2nd **Regal Exception**, 3rd Arkadina

Ascot Gold Cup: 1st (2nd ptp) **Erimo Hawk**, 2nd (1st ptp) Rock Roi, 3rd Irvine

King George VI and Queen Elizabeth Stakes: 1st Brigadier Gerard, 2nd **Parnell**, 3rd Riverman, 4th **Steel Pulse**

St Leger: 1st **Boucher**, 2nd Our Mirage, 3rd Ginerva, last **Steel Pulse**

In Ireland
Irish Derby: 1st **Steel Pulse**, 2nd Scottish Rifle, 3rd Ballymore, 12th **Roberto**

In Italy
Gran Premio di Milano: 1st Beau Charmeur, 2nd **Card King**, 3rd Ami Allard

The race

On a lovely sunny afternoon, Roberto, who was sweating, sprinted from the stalls setting a frantic pace as he had at York, from Regal Exception, Snow Castle, Boucher, Sharapour, Parnell, and the favourite Hard To Beat.

Roberto still led down the hill, where Homeric made some ground to join the chasing group. The field trailed back to San San, Rescousse, and the Spanish challenger My Mourne.

Roberto couldn't shake off Regal Exception as they entered the *ligne d'arrivee*. However, Snow Castle was starting to crack. Boucher, Homeric and Sharapour were still on the premises with Hard To Beat, who was still travelling nicely, and San San, who'd made up lots of ground on the outside.

Entering the final 400 metres Regal Exception mastered Roberto, but was in turn quickly passed by Homeric followed by San San. Hard To Beat couldn't quicken and Boucher and Sharapour were also beaten.

San San relentlessly wore down Homeric inside the last 200 metres to take the lead, while on the wide outside Rescousse found another gear. The latter, who had been just about last entering the straight, closed in rapidly. However, San San still had one and a half lengths in hand at the line with another half to Homeric.

Regal Exception was fourth, followed by the fast-finishing Card King and Sharapour. Roberto in seventh was the first three-year-old colt to pass the post; favourite Hard To Beat came home eighth.

Post-race

Maurice Philipperon, the rider of Homeric who had finished lame, lodged an objection on the basis that San San had partially crossed him when taking the lead. The stewards overruled the objection and the result stood.

The fierce pace set by Roberto had helped San San equal Mill Reef's record time from the year before and she became the first filly to win since La Sorellina in 1953.

San San was owned by Comtesse Margit Batthyany, who had previously owned the top-class German horse Orsini. She'd also been fourth with Caro in last year's Arc and had won the Poule d'Essai des Pouliches this season with Mata Hari. The name of the latter seems a particularly bold choice taking into account her own wartime activities, the details of which didn't come to light until many years after her death.

San San's success capped a great first season in France for Angel Penna. He'd been champion trainer in his native Argentina, and in Venezuela, prior to his move to the USA in 1967, where he'd been successful with horses like Bold Reason and Czar Alexander.

It was a great spare ride for Freddy Head who added to his triumph in 1966 on Bon Mot – and in fact it was the only time he ever sat on San San's back. Both would be back next year but with different partners.

Result

1972 Prix de l'Arc de Triomphe
Longchamp. Sunday, 8 October 1972
Weights: 3yo c: 55.5kg, 3yo f: 54kg, 4yo+ c: 60kg, 4yo+ f: 58.5kg

1st San San (USA)   3yo f   54kg   **18.5/1**
by Bald Eagle out of Sail Navy (Princequillo). Comtesse Margit Batthyany / Angel Penna / Freddy Head

2nd Rescousse (FR)   3yo f   54kg   **4.5/1** (coupled with Pleben)
by Emerson out of Bella Mourne (Mourne). Baron de Redé / Geoff Watson / Yves Saint-Martin

3rd Homeric (GB)   4yo c   60kg   **39/1**
by Ragusa out of Darlene (Dante). Sir Michael Sobell / John Cunnington jnr / Maurice Philipperon

Runners: 19 (FR 13, GB 3, IRE 2, SPA 1). Distances: 1½, ½. Going: good to firm. Time: 2m 28.30s

Objection: the rider of the third objected to the winner for causing interference but was overruled

Also ran: 4th **Regal Exception** (USA) 3yo f, 5th **Card King** (USA) 4yo c, 6th **Sharapour** (FR) 4yo c, 7th **Roberto** (USA) 3yo c, 8th **Hard To Beat** (IRE) 3yo c, 9th **Parnell** (GB) 4yo c, 10th **Mister Sic Top** (FR) 5yo h. Unplaced: **Pleben** (GB) 3yo c, **Mejiro Musashi** (JPN) 5yo h, **Erimo Hawk** (IRE) 4yo c, **Snow Castle** (ARG) 3yo f, **My Mourne** (GB) 3yo c, **Sancy** (FR) 3yo c, **Toujours Prêt** (USA) 3yo c, **Boucher** (USA) 3yo c, **Steel Pulse** (GB) 3yo c.

Rheingold ends Piggott's drought

15th time lucky for The Long Fellow

Background and fancied horses

Five of last year's runners returned, headed by San San. The title holder had been largely disappointing, though, and was unconsidered at 74/1. Likewise, last year's favourite, Hard To Beat, had shown nothing in his only two appearances so far this term. However, he'd reportedly started to find some of his old sparkle at home in the build-up to the Arc, and as a result he was a 21/1-shot.

Daniel Wildenstein's Allez France topped the market after winning the Poule d'Essai des Pouliches, a strong running of the Prix de Diane and, on her return from a break, the Prix Vermeille. She had already taken on the mantle of 'superstar' with the home crowd and was sent off at 1.75/1.

Next came Tennyson, who had beaten Hard To Beat's half-brother, Authi, when taking the Grand Prix de Paris and had later been runner-up to Dahlia in the Prix Niel. Dahlia had subsequently finished lame in the Prix Vermeille, after slipping on the bend, and was only confirmed a definite runner four days before the Arc, for which she was now fourth favourite.

Third best in the betting was Rheingold, on whom Yves Saint-Martin had won the John Porter Stakes, Prix Ganay and Hardwicke Stakes before taking the Grand Prix de Saint-Cloud for the second year in a row.

He played up before the start of his next run, the King George VI and Queen Elizabeth Stakes, and was bumped in running but still managed to come home in second behind Dahlia.

Lester Piggott had been promised the ride on Rheingold in the Arc, as Saint-Martin was due to partner Allez France. So, when Piggott's intended mount in the Benson & Hedges Gold Cup, Roberto, was a late non-runner, Saint-Martin was unceremoniously jocked off and had to watch from the stands.

What he saw, though, was a lacklustre Rheingold trailing in third behind Moulton. Found to have been suffering from a blood disorder, Rheingold was rested and had gone well in his last piece of work before the Arc.

The only other horse less than 20/1 was Guy de Rothschild's Lady Berry. She'd only been beaten once – when sixth to Allez France in the Prix de

Diane – and arrived on the back of an impressive success in the Prix Royal-Oak, where Authi was second and Balompie third.

Betting
1.75/1 Allez France, 5.8/1 Tennyson, 7.7/1 Rheingold, 8/1 Dahlia, 8.8/1 Lady Berry, 17/1 Balompie & El Famoso (coupled), 21/1 Hard To Beat, 22/1 Attica Meli, 22/1 Authi, 22/1 Direct Flight, 29/1 Bonne Noël, 45/1 BAR.

Three-year-old form lines
Prix du Jockey Club: 1st Roi Lear, 2nd (3rd ptp) **Tennyson**, 3rd (2nd ptp) Gunter
Grand Prix de Paris: 1st **Tennyson**, 2nd **Authi**, 3rd Rasgavor
Prix Royal-Oak: 1st **Lady Berry**, 2nd **Authi**, 3rd **Balompie**
Prix Niel: 1st **Dahlia**, 2nd **Tennyson**, 3rd Dom Luc

Fillies only
Prix de Diane: 1st **Allez France**, 2nd **Dahlia**, 3rd Virunga, 6th **Lady Berry**
Prix Vermeille: 1st **Allez France**, 2nd **Hurry Harriet**, 3rd El Mina, 5th **Dahlia**

Older horses and inter-generational races
Grand Prix de Saint-Cloud: 1st **Rheingold**, 2nd **Direct Flight**, 3rd Roybet, 4th **Card King**, 0th **Parnell**
Grand Prix de Deauville: 1st **Card King**, 2nd **Balompie**, 3rd Authi, 4th **Primette**
Prix Foy: 1st **Direct Flight**, 2nd **Mister Sic Top**, 3rd **Sang Bleu**, 6th **Unicornus**

Abroad
In England
Derby Stakes: 1st Morston, 2nd Cavo Doro, 3rd Freefoot, 5th **Ragapan**, 10th **Balompie**
Ascot Gold Cup: 1st **Lassalle**, 2nd Celtic Cone, 3rd The Admiral
King George VI and Queen Elizabeth Stakes: 1st **Dahlia**, 2nd **Rheingold**, 3rd Our Mirage, 4th Weaver's Hall, 0th **Parnell**, 0th **Hard To Beat**, 0th **Card King**, 0th Roberto
St Leger: 1st Peleid, 2nd **Buoy**, 3rd Duke of Ragusa, 8th **Ragapan**

In Ireland
Irish Derby: 1st Weaver's Hall, 2nd **Ragapan**, 3rd **Buoy**, 7th **Star Appeal**
Irish St Leger: 1st Conor Pass, 2nd Sunyboy, 3rd **Star Appeal**

The race
On the way to the start, Hurry Harriet, under top US-jockey Angel Cordero jnr, bolted. She couldn't be pulled up until the Petit Bois, where she ignominiously deposited Cordero on the floor, leading to a 20-minute delay to the start.

Once finally underway Direct Flight was immediately prominent from Authi, Unicornus, Rheingold, Hard To Beat, Tennyson and Allez France, while Dahlia and last year's winner San San were nestled in rear.

Authi took over from Direct Flight on the downhill section, but the pace was not strong and they were closely grouped. As such, Tennyson suffered some interference and lost his pitch.

Rheingold was going extremely well and Piggott took a tug so as not to get there too early. Allez France also loomed up menacingly but Dahlia, who'd made some ground, was now starting to struggle. With 500 metres to go, Piggott let Rheingold go and he immediately responded, swooping through to lead with Allez France following in his wake. Hard To Beat also looked to have resources but was blocked in his run.

Entering the final 200 metres, Rheingold had two lengths to spare over Allez France who was closing, but she couldn't maintain her effort and Rheingold, under a hand ride, had an advantage of two and a half lengths at the wire.

Hard To Beat finally extricated himself to take third, four lengths behind Allez France, and was followed through by Card King, Lady Berry and Sang Bleu.

Post-race

At the 15th attempt Lester Piggott had finally won the Arc, having previously been in the frame four times – third on Ribocco in 1967, followed by second places on Sir Ivor, Park Top and Nijinsky.

It was also a first success for Barry Hills, who'd purchased South Bank stables from Keith Piggott – Lester's dad – with the proceeds of the coup he landed in the Lincoln Handicap with Frankincense in 1968.

Owner Henry Zeisal was a world-class violin player. The first piece he played when lead violinist for the Vienna Opera House Orchestra was Wagner's Das Rheingold, part of the Ring Cycle, hence the name of the horse.

Rheingold himself had maintained his unbeaten record in France, in the process taking the scalps of last year's victor and two future winners.

Unfortunately, he'd picked up a sprain in his near fore, so plans to compete in the Washington DC International – which went to Dahlia – were aborted and he retired to stud. His best offspring was Gildoran who won the Ascot Gold Cup in 1984 and 1985.

Result

1973 Prix de l'Arc de Triomphe

Longchamp. Sunday, 7 October 1973
Weights: 3yo c: 55.5kg, 3yo f: 54kg, 4yo+ c: 60kg, 4yo+ f: 58.5kg

1st Rheingold (IRE)   4yo c   60kg   **7.7/1**
by Fabergé II out of Athene (Supreme Court). Henry Zeisel / Barry Hills / Lester Piggott

2nd Allez France (USA)   3yo f   54kg   **1.75/1 fav**
by Sea Bird out of Priceless Gem (Hail to Reason). Daniel Wildenstein / Albert Klimscha / Yves Saint-Martin

3rd Hard To Beat (IRE)   4yo c   60kg   **21/1**
by Hardicanute out of Virtuous (Above Suspicion). Junzo Kashiyama / Richard Carver jnr / Gérard Thiboeuf

Runners: 27 (FR 17, GB 5, IRE 5). Distances: 2½, 4. Going: soft. Time: 2m 35.80s

Also ran: 4th **Card King** (USA) 5yo c, 5th **Lady Berry** (FR) 3yo f, 6th **Sang Bleu** (FR) 4yo c, 7th **Balompie** (GB) 3yo c, 8th **Buoy** (GB) 3yo c, 9th **Lassalle** (FR) 4yo c, 10th **Tennyson** (FR) 3yo c. Unplaced: **Mister Sic Top** (FR) 6yo c, **Parnell** (GB) 5yo c, **Direct Flight** (GB) 4yo c, **Unicornus** (ARG) 4yo c, **Novius** (FR) 4yo c, **Bonne Noël** (GB) 4yo c, **Firefright** (GB) 4yo c, **Attica Meli** (IRE) 4yo f, **Miss Therese** (GB) 4yo f, **Primette** (USA) 4yo f, **San San** (USA) 4yo f, **El Famoso** (GB) 3yo c, **Ragapan** (IRE) 3yo c, **Authi** (IRE) 3yo c, **Star Appeal** (IRE) 3yo c, **Dahlia** (USA) 3yo f, **Hurry Harriet** (IRE) 3yo f.

Out of control – Allez France and the crowd

Saint-Martin can't restrain his delight

Background and fancied horses

Last year's runner-up Allez France was now trained by Angel Penna, as Albert Klimscha had retired. She'd been in great heart, notching up successes in the Prix d'Harcourt, Prix Ganay and the Prix Foy. The doubts, as they were, surrounded the jockey, as Yves Saint-Martin had fractured a bone at the junction of his hip and thigh just ten days before the Arc. He was riding but was relying on painkillers.

Daniel Wildenstein was also represented by his useful three-year-old filly Paulista, who'd won the Prix Nonette and Prix Vermeille. Allez France and Paulista – who would be partnered by Freddy Head – were coupled at 0.5/1.

Nelson Bunker Hunt also ran two, Prix Niel-winner Mississipian and Busiris, who'd scored in the Prix Royal-Oak. Bunker Hunt's Dahlia, who like Mississipian was by the 1968 Arc-winner Vaguely Noble, had won the Grand Prix de Saint-Cloud and finished second in the King George VI and Queen Elizabeth Stakes, but would not be aimed at the Arc for another year. The pair that did line up were returned at 6.5/1.

Grand Prix de Paris-winner Sagaro and his pacemaker Valdo were next at 9.3/1, followed by the Aga Khan IV's Prix Royal-Oak runner-up Kamaraan at 14/1. Queen Elizabeth II had her first runner in the race with Prix de Diane-winner Highclere. At 15/1 she was the same price as last year's Grand Prix de Paris-victor Tennyson, who'd finished second to Allez France in the Prix Foy.

The three-strong overseas contingent all came from England. They were Highclere, Coup de Feu, who'd won the Eclipse Stakes as a 33/1-shot, and Proverb, the winner of the Goodwood Cup and Doncaster Cup..

Betting

0.5/1 Allez France & Paulista (coupled), 6.5/1 Mississipian & Busiris (coupled), 9.3/1 Sagaro & Valdo (coupled), 14/1 Kamaraan, 15/1 Highclere, 15/1 Tennyson, 29/1 BAR.

Three-year-old form lines

Prix du Jockey Club: 1st Caracolero, 2nd Dankaro, 3rd **Kamaraan**
Grand Prix de Paris: 1st **Sagaro**, 2nd Bustino, 3rd **Kamaraan**

Prix Royal-Oak: 1st **Busiris**, 2nd **Kamaraan**, 3rd Ashmore
Prix Niel: 1st **Mississipian**, 2nd Mount Hagen, 3rd **Sagaro**

Fillies only

Prix de Diane: 1st **Highclere**, 2nd **Comtesse de Loir**, 3rd Odisea
Prix Vermeille: 1st **Paulista**, 2nd **Comtesse de Loir**, 3rd Gaily

Older horses and inter-generational races

Grand Prix de Saint-Cloud: 1st Dahlia, 2nd **On My Way**, 3rd Direct Flight
Prix du Prince d'Orange: 1st **On My Way**, 2nd Toujours Prêt, 3rd Dahlia
Prix Foy: 1st **Allez France**, 2nd **Tennyson**, 3rd **Sang Bleu**

Abroad

In England

Derby Stakes: 1st Snow Knight, 2nd Imperial Prince, 3rd Giacometti
Ascot Gold Cup: 1st Ragstone, 2nd **Proverb**, 3rd Lassalle
King George VI and Queen Elizabeth Stakes: 1st Dahlia, 2nd **Highclere**, 3rd Dankaro

In Germany

Grosser Preis von Baden:
div 1: 1st Meautry, 2nd Bakuba, 3rd Récupéré
div 2: 1st Marduk, 2nd **Card King**, 3rd Athenagoras

In Italy

Gran Premio di Milano: 1st Orsa Maggiore, 2nd **Sang Bleu**, 3rd Veio

The race

It was a cold and overcast day as the crowd around the paddock were hushed to watch Yves Saint-Martin being legged-up on Allez France, in the knowledge that she could be fractious and he was injured. The manoeuvre went well and they reached the start without mishap. Soon they were off, with Valdo, Sagaro's pacemaker, leading from the get-go while Saint-Martin settled Allez France in rear.

At the Petit Bois, Paulista came across Highclere who shortly afterwards received a bump from Sang Bleu, which effectively ended the challenge of the Queen's representative. Down the hill Allez France made good ground on the outside, while up front Valdo weakened with Busiris taking it up. But not for long.

Allez France continued her run, sweeping past the rest of the field to reach the lead with 700 metres to go. With a clear advantage, it looked as though the only battle left was for second place. But then Comtesse de Loir appeared and along with Margouillat they started to close in on Allez France.

Entering the last 100 metres, Comtesse de Loir was less than a length down. Saint-Martin wanted to respond, but could only push with hands and heels due to his injury and the margin continued to close. As they crossed the line there wasn't much to choose between them and it went to a photo. The crowd erupted when Allez France was announced as the winner. She'd prevailed by a head with three parts back to Margouillat, who in turn was followed by Kamaraan, Paulista and Riboquill.

Post-race

Daniel Wildenstein had improved on his father Georges's record – he'd been second with Beau Prince II in 1955 and third with Balbo in 1957 – to secure a first victory for the Wildenstein family.

Daniel's horses had finished first and fifth but the irascible art dealer was not over the moon. He blamed himself for letting a not-fully fit Saint-Martin ride, which had led to Allez France having a harder race than necessary. He also blamed himself for running Paulista on the unsuitably soft ground.

Others were happier, including Angel Penna, who was recording his second Arc win after San San in 1972, as was a relieved Yves Saint-Martin, who, likewise, was doubling his score, adding to Sassafras in 1970.

Saint-Martin didn't ride again for several days, admitting that when Allez France was pushed wide she saw daylight and took off and there was nothing he could do about it in his injured state. Despite that, Allez France had won in game style and the daughter of Sea Bird, who'd become the fourth previous victor to sire a winner, was to be kept in training.

Result

1974 Prix de l'Arc de Triomphe
Longchamp. Sunday, 6 October 1974
Weights: 3yo c: 55.5kg, 3yo f: 54kg, 4yo+ c: 60kg, 4yo+ f: 58.5kg

1st Allez France (USA)   4yo f   58.5kg   **0.5/1 fav** (coupled with Paulista)
by Sea Bird out of Priceless Gem (Hail to Reason). Daniel Wildenstein / Angel Penna / Yves Saint-Martin

2nd Comtesse de Loir (FR)   3yo f   54kg   **53/1**
by Val de Loir out of Neriad (Princequillo). George Ohrstrom / John Cunnington jnr / Jean-Claude Desaint

3rd Margouillat (FR)   4yo c   60kg   **72/1**
by Diatome out of Tita (Tim Tam). Paul de Moussac / Robert de Mony-Pajol / Georges Doleuze

Runners: 20 (FR 17, GB 3). Distances: hd, ¾. Going: heavy. Time: 2m 36.90s

Also ran: 4th **Kamaraan** (FR) 3yo c, 5th **Paulista** (IRE) 3yo f, 6th **Riboquill** (USA) 3yo c, 7th **Card King** (USA) 4yo c, 8th **On My Way** (USA) 4yo c, 9th **Mississipian** (USA) 3yo c, 10th **Tennyson** (FR) 4yo c. Unplaced: **Sang Bleu** (FR) 4yo c, **Coup de Feu** (GB) 4yo c, **Proverb** (GB) 4yo c, **Récupéré** (GB) 4yo c, **Riot in Paris** (USA) 3yo c, **Busiris** (FR) 3yo c, **Un Kopeck** (FR) 3yo c, **Sagaro** (GB) 3yo c, **Valdo** (_) 3yo c, **Highclere** (GB) 3yo f.

1975

Star Appeal – the outsiders' outsider at 119/1

First German-trained winner

Background and fancied horses

Allez France was back to defend her title, and had enjoyed a good start to her summer campaign, taking the Prix Ganay and Prix Dollar before underperforming when only third to Ramirez in the Prix d'Ispahan. However, after a break she had shown all her old class when accounting for Duke of Marmalade in the Prix Foy, and was 1.75/1 for a repeat success.

Alec Head was able to field the winners of both the Poule d'Essai des Poulains and Poule d'Essai des Pouliches against the Wildenstein superstar, in the form of Green Dancer and Ivanjica, who were coupled at 4.3/1. The former had been favourite when finishing sixth in the Derby but had most recently been a good second in the Prix Niel.

The latter hadn't had the chance of adding the Prix de Diane to her *palmarès* as the race had been cancelled due to a stable staff strike. She had though, beaten Derby runner-up Nobiliary in the Prix Vermeille and was the choice of Freddy Head.

A fraction longer, at 4.5/1, came the best of the English-trained challengers, the St Leger-victor Bruni, who was followed by the Nelson Bunker Hunt duo of Dahlia and Nobiliary at 8.8/1.

The Prix de la Grotte and Prix Saint-Alary winner, Nobiliary, had been second to Grundy in the Derby and to Ivanjica in the Prix Vermeille. Her older stablemate, Dahlia, had watched on from third position as Grundy had just got the better of Bustino and his legion of pacemakers in the epic battle for the King George VI and Queen Elizabeth Stakes – a race that had been dubbed, possibly a touch hyperbolically, 'the Race of the Century'.

Lester Piggott was aboard 9.5/1-chance Duke of Marmalade, who had been disqualified after finishing first past the post in the Grand Prix de Deauville. Prior to that he was runner-up to Star Appeal in the Gran Premio di Milano and afterwards took the same position behind Allez France in the Prix Niel.

Last year's fourth, the Aga Khan IV's Kamaraan, had caught the eye on his return to action in a minor race at Evry and was a at 16/1 shot.

In addition to Bruni, Ryan Price ran the outsider Carolus. Intrepid Hero represented the USA, while Germany had the aforementioned Star Appeal, who'd won the Eclipse Stakes when a 20/1-shot.

Betting
1.75/1 Allez France, 4.3/1 Green Dancer & Ivanjica (coupled), 4.5/1 Bruni, 8.8/1 Dahlia & Nobiliary (coupled), 9.5/1 Duke of Marmalade, 16/1 Kamaraan, 21/1 BAR.

Three-year-old form lines
Prix du Jockey Club: 1st Val de l'Orne, 2nd Patch, 3rd Marracci, 8th **Citoyen**
Grand Prix de Paris: 1st Matahawk, 2nd **Citoyen**, 3rd Avance
Prix Royal-Oak: 1st **Henri Le Balafré**, 2nd **Citoyen**, 3rd **Olmeto**
Prix Niel: 1st Anne's Pretender, 2nd **Green Dancer**, 3rd Lioubov

Fillies only
Prix de Diane: no race (stable staff strike)
Prix Vermeille: 1st **Ivanjica**, 2nd **Nobiliary**, 3rd May Hill, 4th **Ambrellita**

Older horses and inter-generational races
Grand Prix de Saint-Cloud: 1st **Un Kopeck**, 2nd Ashmore, 3rd **On My Way**, 4th **Comtesse de Loir**, 5th **Dahlia**, 6th **Riboquill**, 8th **Card King**, 0th **Ambrellita**
Grand Prix de Deauville: 1st (2nd ptp) L'Ensorceleur, 2nd (3rd ptp) **Dahlia**, 3rd (4th ptp) **Riboquill**, 5th (1st ptp) **Duke of Marmalade**
Prix du Prince d'Orange: 1st **Kasteel**, 2nd Ramirez, 3rd **Dahlia**
Prix Foy: 1st **Allez France**, 2nd **Duke of Marmalade**, 3rd Rosy Ride

Abroad
In England
Derby Stakes: 1st Grundy, 2nd **Nobiliary**, 3rd Hunza Dancer, 6th **Green Dancer**, 14th **Bruni**, 0th **Carolus**
King George VI and Queen Elizabeth Stakes: 1st Grundy, 2nd Bustino, 3rd **Dahlia**, 4th **On My Way**, 5th **Card King**, 9th **Star Appeal**
St Leger: 1st **Bruni**, 2nd King Pellinore, 3rd Libra's Rib, 0th **Carolus**

In Germany
Grosser Preis von Baden: 1st Marduk, 2nd Lord Udo, 3rd **Card King**, 4th **Star Appeal**, 6th **Un Kopek**

In Italy
Gran Premio di Milano: 1st **Star Appeal**, 2nd **Duke of Marmalade**, 3rd Orange Bay

The race
With President Valéry Giscard d'Estaing, who had been elected in May, looking on, the 24-strong field, comprised of ten three-year-olds and 14 older horses, set off, with Citoyen setting a decent pace.

On the descent, Dahlia stumbled losing many places and all chance. Shortly afterwards Allez France was badly hampered, when Carolus pulled-up sharply after losing his action, and the favourite dropped to the rear of the field, triggering loud groans from the grandstands.

In the closing stages many still had chances including last year's runner-up Comtesse de Loir, and On My Way. Remarkably, Allez France, who'd fought back from a seemingly impossible position, was also in contention.

It was Star Appeal, though, who took off, producing a breathtaking turn of speed. The son of Appiani II steered a diagonal passage before blasting through the gap that opened up between Nobiliary and Un Kopek.

His impetus quickly carried him past Comtesse de Loir and on to a three-length victory over On My Way, who came through for second. Comtesse de Loir was third followed by Un Kopeck, Allez France – who couldn't quite work the miracle – and Nobiliary.

Post-race

Star Appeal was returned at 119/1, the longest price winner in the history of the Arc, beating Topyo who'd been 82/1 in 1967. However, the price wasn't a true reflection of his ability, more a great example of how the PMU can throw up freak dividends.

Punters were probably put off by the fact that no German-trained horse had previously won the Arc, and partly by how far back he'd finished in the King George VI and Queen Elizabeth Stakes.

In that race, though, he'd been rushed off his feet and his English pilot Greville Starkey had only ridden him hands and heels once his chance was gone, which meant he didn't have a hard race. His collateral form suggests that he should probably have been somewhere in the 25/1 to 33/1 bracket.

Owned by steel magnate Waldemar Zeitelhack and trained by Theo Grieper in Cologne, Star Appeal did indeed become the first German-trained winner of the Arc. He went on to finish fourth in the Champion Stakes and retired after finishing fifth to Nobiliary in the Washington DC International.

His best progeny was 1981 Prix de Diane-winner Madam Gay, who also finished runner-up in The Oaks, and to Shergar in the King George VI and Queen Elizabeth Stakes. He also sired the German 1000 Guineas-winner Walesiana.

Allez France had returned to unsaddle after the Arc with a shoe missing and a cut on her near hind. She gained revenge on Star Appeal in the Champion Stakes albeit they were both beaten by Rose Bowl.

She was retired, but didn't shine in the paddocks and her best offspring was Action Française who won the Prix de Sandringham in 1988.

Result

1975 Prix de l'Arc de Triomphe
Longchamp. Sunday, 5 October 1975
Weights: 3yo c: 55.5kg, 3yo f: 54kg, 4yo+ c: 60kg, 4yo+ f: 58.5kg

1st Star Appeal (IRE)   5yo h   60kg   119/1
by Appiani II out of Sterna (Neckar). Waldemar Zeitelhack / Theo Grieper / Greville Starkey

2nd On My Way (USA)   5yo h   60kg   79/1
by Laugh Aloud out of Gracious Me (Tulyar). Xavier Beau / Noël Pelat / Alfred Gibert

3rd Comtesse de Loir (FR)   4yo f   58.5kg   21/1
by Val de Loir out of Neriad (Princequillo). George Ohrstrom / John Cunnington jnr / Jean-Claude Desaint

Runners: 24 (FR 20, GB 2, GER 1, USA 1). Distances: 3, 2½. Going: soft. Time: 2m 33.60s

Also ran: 4th **Un Kopeck** (FR) 4yo c, 5th **Allez France** (USA) 5yo m, 6th **Nobiliary** (USA) 3yo f, 7th **Bruni** (IRE) 3yo c, 8th **Green Dancer** (USA) 3yo c, 9th **Kamaraan** (FR) 4yo c, 10th **Intrepid Hero** (USA) 3yo c. Unplaced: **Card King** (USA) 5yo h, **Duke of Marmalade** (USA) 4yo c, **Beau Buck** (USA) 4yo c, **Riboquill** (USA) 4yo, **Fabliau** (FR) 4yo c, **Dahlia** (USA) 5yo m, **Ambrellita** (FR) 4yo f, **Paddy's Princess** (GB) 4yo f, **Henri Le Balafré** (FR) 3yo c, **Olmeto** (IRE) 3yo c, **Citoyen** (GB) 3yo c, **Carolus** (GB) 3yo c, **Kasteel** (FR) 3yo c, **Ivanjica** (USA) 3yo f.

1976

Ivanjica's withering run seals it for Wertheimer

Post-race antics add to the drama

Background and fancied horses

The weights had been altered since last year, with the burden for the older horse being reduced from 60kg to 59, while the three-year-olds would have to carry half a kilogram more at 56kg. The fillies' and mares' allowance remained the same at 1.5kg.

Nelson Bunker Hunt was responsible for the favourites, Prix du Jockey Club-winner Youth and Exceller. Youth had prevailed by three lengths at Chantilly and a line through Malacate suggested he was better than Empery, who in the same ownership had won the Derby, in a year in which France won four of the English Classics.

Youth, though, had disappointed when running wide on the last bend in the King George VI and Queen Elizabeth Stakes, but was back on song in the Prix Niel. Joined by Exceller, who had put four lengths between himself and the runner-up in both the Grand Prix de Paris and Prix Royal-Oak, they were returned at 2/1.

Bruni at 2.5/1 was again the strongest candidate from England. But the grey had developed the tendency of being slow to stride, thereby forfeiting lots of ground at the start. Despite that, he'd still finished runner-up in the Hardwicke Stakes and in the King George VI and Queen Elizabeth Stakes, before winning the Cumberland Lodge Stakes.

Daniel Wildenstein's pair, Crow and Pawneese at 5.3/1, had both won Classics in England, the former the St Leger, the latter The Oaks. In addition, Pawneese had carried the *deux-ton bleu* silks to victory in the Prix de Diane and King George VI and Queen Elizabeth Stakes but had flopped in the Prix Vermeille.

The Alec Head-trained Riverqueen, who'd been second in the Prix de Diane and subsequently won the Grand Prix de Saint-Cloud, was coupled with Ivanjica at 7/1. Although she hadn't shown much in the early part of the year, Ivanjica returned after a mid-season break to win the Prix du Prince d'Orange in style.

Last year's runner-up, On My Way, at 14/1, hadn't been seen this term until finishing second in the Prix Foy in September.

François Boutin's 19/1-shot Trépan was first past the post in the Prince of Wales's Stakes at Royal Ascot and in the Eclipse Stakes, but was later disqualified from both after testing positive for theobromine after a medication mix-up at his stables.

Grand Prix de Deauville-third Duke of Marmalade was back but was now with Nick Vigors in England. Guy Reed's in-and-out performer Dakota, who'd won the 1975 Ebor, was also running for *les anglais*, while Norway was represented by dual Oslo Cup-winner Noble Dancer.

Betting
2/1 Youth & Exceller, 2.5/1 Bruni, 5.3/1 Crow & Pawneese (coupled), 7.1/1 Ivanjica & Riverqueen (coupled), 14/1 On My Way, 19/1 Trépan, 21/1 BAR.

Three-year-old form lines
NB Twig, Twig Moss and Tip Moss are three different horses
Prix du Jockey Club: 1st **Youth**, 2nd **Twig Moss**, 3rd Malacate, 0th **Arctic Tern**
Grand Prix de Paris: 1st **Exceller**, 2nd Secret Man, 3rd Caron
Prix Royal-Oak: 1st **Exceller**, 2nd Sir Montagu, 3rd Adam Van Vianen
Prix Niel: 1st **Youth**, 2nd **Arctic Tern**, 3rd Malacate

Fillies only
Prix de Diane: 1st **Pawneese**, 2nd **Riverqueen**, 3rd **Lagunette**
Prix Vermeille: 1st **Lagunette**, 2nd Sarah Siddons, 3rd **Floressa**, 7th **Pawneese**, 9th **Riverqueen**

Older horses and inter-generational races
Grand Prix de Saint-Cloud: 1st **Riverqueen**, 2nd Ashmore, 3rd Tip Moss, last **Beau Buck**
Grand Prix de Deauville: 1st Ashmore, 2nd Diagramatic, 3rd **Duke of Marmalade**
Prix du Prince d'Orange: 1st **Ivanjica**, 2nd Sea Sands, 3rd Twig, 4th **Trépan**, 5th **Infra Green**
Prix Foy: 1st **Kasteel**, 2nd **On My Way**, 3rd _, 4th **Beau Buck**

Abroad
In England
Derby Stakes: 1st Empery, 2nd Relkino, 3rd Oats
Oaks Stakes: 1st **Pawneese**, 2nd Roses For the Star, 3rd African Dancer
King George VI and Queen Elizabeth Stakes: 1st **Pawneese**, 2nd **Bruni**, 3rd Orange Bay, 4th **Dakota**, 9th **Youth**, last **Duke of Marmalade**
St Leger: 1st **Crow**, 2nd Secret Man, 3rd Scallywag

In Italy
Gran Premio di Milano: 1st Rouge Sang, 2nd Art Style, 3rd **Duke of Marmalade**

The race

The Norwegian-trained entry, Noble Dancer, was on his toes and unshipped Geoff Lewis in the paddock, while Dakota was reluctant to enter the stalls. But once they broke, English fans were pleased to see that Bruni had got away on level terms.

Kasteel led followed by Pawneese, and soon the pair built up a clear advantage. Meanwhile, Dakota and Ivanjica, who at the break had immediately switched from her wide draw to the inner, were right at the back.

At the top of the hill, Kasteel and Pawneese were six lengths up on the rest, and as they started the descent, Pawneese went on while Youth, Crow and Bruni took closer order.

Kasteel wasn't finished and although Pawneese was just in front entering the straight, Kasteel regained the lead momentarily only to be immediately overhauled by Youth followed by Crow and Bruni.

Meanwhile Ivanjica, who'd been on the rails among the backmarkers entering the home straight, had found racing room and was accelerating hard. With less than 300 metres to go, Crow collared Youth and crossed to the rails. Ivanjica was now in seventh and switched wide to avoid Noble Dancer who was blocked in by Youth.

Ivanjica continued her jinking run, zipping between Youth and Bruni. Then she accelerated past Crow to take the lead and won going away by two lengths. There was a further three to Youth then Noble Dancer – who made up late places once finding racing room – followed by Bruni and Beau Buck.

Post-race

For the second year in a row a horse had come from out of the clouds to mow down a wall of horses in spectacular style.

Freddy Head quite rightly wanted to celebrate, but as he paraded in front of the stands acknowledging the crowd Ivanjica suddenly ducked left and Freddy, unable to defy the force of gravity, ended up on the turf while Ivanjica galloped away, only to run into a rail.

Luckily when caught she had only suffered superficial wounds and after a delay was reunited with her jockey, who was able to weigh-in just before the 20-minute period laid down in the rules expired. Failure to do so would have meant automatic disqualification.

Safely weighed-in, Freddy's third win, after Bon Mot and San San, was confirmed. It was also a third for his father Alec, who'd previously scored with Nuccio and Saint Crespin.

It was a first Arc for Jacques Wertheimer and the Wertheimer family. Jacques was the son of Germaine Revel and businessman Pierre Wertheimer, who had co-founded the *Chanel* perfume business in 1924 and had owned many racehorses, including the excellent Epinard.

The association between the Head family and the Wertheimers will feature in our story on a regular basis, and still continues though horses like Goldikova and Solow, which became notable stars in the early part of the 21st century.

After finishing third to Youth in the Washington DC International, Ivanjica was retired. The following year she had her portrait painted by Andy Warhol, and at stud three of her five runners won races though none was a champion.

Result
1976 Prix de l'Arc de Triomphe
Longchamp. Sunday, 3 October 1976
Weights: 3yo c: 56kg, 3yo f: 54.5kg, 4yo+ c: 59kg, 4yo+ f: 57.5kg

1st Ivanjica (USA)   4yo f   57.5kg   **7.1/1** (coupled with Riverqueen)
by Sir Ivor out of Astuce (Vieux Manoir). Jacques Wertheimer / Alec Head / Freddy Head

2nd Crow (FR)   3yo c   56kg   **5.3/1** (coupled with Pawneese)
by Exbury out of Carmosina (Right of Way). Daniel Wildenstein / Angel Penna / Yves Saint-Martin

3rd Youth (USA)   3yo c   56kg   **2/1 fav** (coupled with Exceller)
by Ack Ack out of Gazala (Dark Star). Nelson Bunker Hunt / Maurice Zilber / Bill Pyers

Runners: 20 (FR 16, GB 3, NOR 1). Distances: 3, 2½. Going: soft. Time: 2m 39.40s

Also ran: 4th **Noble Dancer** (GB) 4yo c, 5th **Bruni** (IRE) 4yo c, 6th **Beau Buck** (USA) 5yo h, 7th **Infra Green** (GB) 4yo f, 8th **Java Rajah** (USA) 3yo c, 9th **On My Way** (USA) 6yo h, 10th **Kasteel** (FR) 4yo c. Unplaced: **Duke of Marmalade** (USA) 5yo h, **Dakota** (IRE) 5yo h, **Trépan** (FR) 4yo c, **Twig Moss** (FR) 3yo c, **Exceller** (USA) 3yo c, **Arctic Tern** (USA) 3yo c, **Pawneese** (IRE) 3yo f, **Lagunette** (FR) 3yo f, **Floressa** (FR) 3yo f, **Riverqueen** (FR) 3yo f.

1977

Alleged prevails in
a tactical masterclass

Piggott waits in front on Ireland's third winner

Background and fancied horses

This year the Prix Royal-Oak's place in the calendar was changed and it would now be run after the Prix de l'Arc de Triomphe. Thus, its additional role as a trial for the Arc ended being largely replaced by the Prix Niel.

Vincent O'Brien was enjoying a great year and his Alleged at 3.9/1 headed the market. Lester Piggott's mount had won the Great Voltigeur Stakes by seven lengths before being beaten by Dunfermline when favourite in the St Leger. However, punters thought that back in trip in the Arc he would reverse those placings.

Guy de Rothschild's Prix du Jockey Club-winner, Crystal Palace, was one of three horses at 8/1 along with Dunfermline and Orange Bay, who were both trained in England. Dunfermline was owned by Queen Elizabeth II – who was celebrating her Silver Jubilee – and had memorably won The Oaks prior to her success over Alleged. Orange Bay had been seen to best effect when second in the King George VI and Queen Elizabeth Stakes, a race in which Crystal Palace had finished fourth.

Last year's runner-up, Crow, was back but had yet to sparkle. However, loyal fans still lent him their support at 9.5/1. He was followed by Balmerino at 12/1. The New Zealand-bred had won 18 races in his native land but was now under the care of John Dunlop in England, and had produced an impressive turn of speed when a five-length winner of the Valdoe Stakes at Goodwood.

The 1976 Irish Derby-winner, Malacate, was the same price. He'd returned from stud to win the Prix Foy from On My Way, who was making his first appearance of 1977 and was 17/1 for the Arc. Between the pair were the first and third in the Prix Vermeille, Kamicia and Fabuleux Jane, who were both 14/1.

As well as Alleged, Ireland had last year's Prix Vermeille-second Sarah Siddons and the Blandford Stakes-winner Panamint. The USA was represented by Cunning Trick, who'd won some valuable handicaps. Germany had the moderate Vivi, and Argentina's Mia – who received a 2kg allowance for being six months younger than her Northern hemisphere rivals – had hosed up in the Gran Premio Seleccion before leaving for Europe.

Including the English trio – Dunfermline, Orange Bay and Balmerino – there were nine raiders in all. Derby-winner The Minstrel had been aimed at the Arc but left for the United States earlier than planned to avoid an import ban after an outbreak of metritis in Europe.

Betting
3.9/1 Alleged, 8/1 Crystal Palace, 8/1 Dunfermline, 8/1 Orange Bay, 9.5/1 Crow, 12/1 Balmerino, 12/1 Malacate, 14/1 Kamicia, 14/1 Fabuleux Jane, 17/1 On My Way, 20/1 BAR.

Three-year-old form lines
Prix du Jockey Club: 1st **Crystal Palace**, 2nd Artaius, 3rd Concertino, 0th **Carwhite**, 0th **Guadanini**
Grand Prix de Paris: 1st Funny Hobby, 2nd Valinsky, 3rd Midshipman, 5th **Guadanini**, 6th **Dom Alaric**
Prix Niel: 1st **Crystal Palace**, 2nd Paico, 3rd Vagaries, 5th **Amyntor**

Fillies only
Prix de Diane: 1st Madelia, 2nd Trillion, 3rd **Fabuleux Jane**
Prix Vermeille: 1st **Kamicia**, 2nd Royal Hive, 3rd **Fabuleux Jane**

Older horses and inter-generational races
Grand Prix de Saint-Cloud: 1st Exceller, 2nd Riboboy, 3rd **Iron Duke**, 4th **Crow**
Grand Prix de Deauville: 1st **Dom Alaric**, 2nd Midshipman, 3rd Vagaries
Prix du Prince d'Orange: 1st **Carwhite**, 2nd Gairloch, 3rd Waya, 0th **Montcontour**
Prix Foy: 1st **Malacate**, 2nd **On My Way**, 3rd Ranimer, 4th **Arctic Tern**, 6th/last **Shafaraz**

Abroad
In England
Derby Stakes: 1st The Minstrel, 2nd Hot Grove, 3rd Blushing Groom, 4th **Monseigneur**
Oaks Stakes: 1st **Dunfermline**, 2nd Freeze the Secret, 3rd Vaguely Deb, 6th **Fabuleux Jane**
King George VI and Queen Elizabeth Stakes: 1st The Minstrel, 2nd **Orange Bay**, 3rd Exceller, 4th **Crystal Palace**, 9th **Crow**
St Leger: 1st **Dunfermline**, 2nd **Alleged**, 3rd Classic Example

The race
Yelpana led early with Alleged slotting into second place. No one was keen to go on and it was at an unusually leisurely pace that they made their way to the Petis Bois, where Alleged took over with Piggott content to wait in front.

At the top of the hill, Crystal Palace was second followed by Crow, Yelpana and Orange Bay then Dunfermline. On the descent, Crow moved into second and Balmerino started to make some progress.

On the turn into the straight, Piggott increased the tempo, opening up a four-length margin over Crytsal Palace and Crow. Meanwhile, Dunfermline's way was obstructed on the inner by the fading Yelpana. Balmerino was still getting closer, moving past Crystal Palace into second. He closed the gap but never looked like troubling Alleged, who won by one and a half lengths.

Crystal Palace took the lowest step on the podium from the fast-finishing Dunfermline, who was later found to have lost a shoe. *La pouliche de la reine* was followed by Crow and Monseigneur.

Post-race

A vintage Piggott masterclass had secured The Long Fellow's second Arc after his success with Rheingold in 1973. Vincent O'Brien had waited longer for his second win, 19 years to be precise since Ballymoss in 1958.

O'Brien had bought Alleged as a two-year-old with Mrs Shirley Taylor and Robert Fluor. Later on, Fluor's share was purchased by Robert Sangster in whose colours Alleged ran at Longchamp.

Sangster, the son of Vernon Sangster of Vernons Football Pools fame, went on with O'Brien and John Magnier – collectively dubbed 'the Brethren' – to develop the Ballydoyle/Coolmore racing operation and breeding empire into one of the world's dominant teams. Alleged called stumps for the season but was kept in training.

Result

1977 Prix de l'Arc de Triomphe
Longchamp. Sunday, 2 October 1977
Weights: 3yo c: 56kg, 3yo f: 54.5kg, 4yo+ c: 59kg, 4yo+ f: 57.5kg

1st Alleged (USA)　　　3yo c　56kg　**3.9/1 fav**
by Hoist the Flag out of Princess Pout (Prince John). Robert Sangster / Vincent O'Brien / Lester Piggott

2nd Balmerino (NZ)　　5yo h　59kg　**12/1**
by Trictrac out of Dulcie (Duccio). Ralph Stuart / John Dunlop / Ron Hutchinson

3rd Crystal Palace (FR)　3yo c　56kg　**8/1**
by Caro out of Hermières (Sicambre). Nelson Bunker Hunt / Maurice Zilber / Alain Badel

Runners: 26 (FR 17, ENG 3 IRE 3, ARG 1, GER 1, USA 1). Distances: 1½, 2. Going: good/good to soft. Time: 2m 30.60s

Also ran: 4th **Dunfermline** (GB) 3yo c, 5th **Crow** (FR) 4yo c, 6th **Monseigneur** (USA) 3yo c, 7th **Infra Green** (GB) 5yo m, 8th **Malacate** (USA) 4yo c, 9th **Yelpana** (FR) 3yo c, 10th **Guadanini** (FR) 3yo c. Unplaced: **On My Way** (USA) 7yo h, **Orange Bay** (GB) 5yo h, **Arctic Tern** (USA) 4yo c, **Shafaraz** (FR) 4yo c, **Cunning Trick** (USA) 4yo c, **Iron Duke** (FR) 4yo c, **Vivi** (GER) 5yo m, **Sarah Siddons** (FR) 4yo f, **Amyntor** (FR) 3yo c, **Panamint** (IRE) 3yo c, **Montcontour** (FR) 3yo c, **Dom Alaric** (FR) 3yo c, **Carwhite** (IRE) 3yo c, **Kamicia** (FR) 3yo f, **Fabuleux Jane** (USA) 3yo f, **Mia** (ARG) 3yo f.

Alleged again
O'Brien's charge recovers from virus to retain crown

Background and fancied horses
Alleged had started 1978 by winning the Royal Whip at the Curragh but was then laid low by a virus. Vincent O'Brien gave his charge plenty of time to recover and Alleged missed several engagements before returning in the Prix du Prince d'Orange, which he won with aplomb.

On the evidence of that performance the reigning champion was backed into 1.4/1 for the Arc repeat, despite the ground being on the soft side of good which he hadn't encountered before.

The second favourite, Acamas at 3.8/1, had become the 12th winner of the Prix du Jockey Club in Marcel Boussac's colours. Unfortunately, though, the veteran-owner's textile business was now in the hands of the receiver, and in due course all his bloodstock was put up for sale and purchased by the Aga Khan IV. Acamas went on to Ascot where he finished second in the King George VI and Queen Elizabeth Stakes but was later disqualified after testing positive for a banned substance.

Jacques Wertheimer was doubly represented by Poule d'Essai des Pouliches-winner Dancing Maid, who'd finished runner-up in The Oaks and would be ridden by Freddy Head, and Gay Mécène the winner of the Prix Eugène Adam and Prix Niel. Together they were coupled at 4/1.

After a ten-point gap came Frère Basile, who'd been second in the Prix du Jockey Club and third in the Prix Niel, followed by Prix Prix Foy-winner Trillion and Julio Mariner the 28/1-winner of the St Leger.

Exdirectory, like Alleged, represented Ireland and had been second to Derby-winner Shirley Heights in the Irish version of the Epsom Classic. The German-trained Lido and the previously mentioned Julio Mariner, representing England, made up the quartet of horses from outside of France.

Betting
1.4/1 Alleged, 3.8/1 Acamas, 4/1 Dancing Maid & Gay Mécène (coupled), 14/1 Frère Basile, 16/1 Trillion, 17/1 Julio Mariner, 24/1 BAR.

> **Three-year-old form lines**
> Prix du Jockey Club: 1st **Acamas**, 2nd **Frère Basile**, 3rd **Turville**, 4th **Noir et Or**, 6th **Dancing Master**
> Grand Prix de Paris: 1st **Galiani**, 2nd Roi de Mai, 3rd Whitstead

Prix Niel: 1st **Gay Mécène**, 2nd **Noir et Or**, 3rd **Frère Basile**, 4th **Dancing Master**, 7th **Turville**

Fillies only

Prix de Diane: 1st Reine de Saba, 2nd Cistus, 3rd Calderina

Prix Vermeille: 1st **Dancing Maid**, 2nd Relfo, 3rd Amazer, 5th Fair Salinia

Older horses and inter-generational races

Grand Prix de Saint-Cloud: 1st **Guadanini**, 2nd **Trillion**, 3rd **Noir et Or**, 4th **Dom Alaric**, 7th **Montcontour**

Prix du Prince d'Orange: 1st **Alleged**, 2nd Louksor, 3rd Pevero

Prix Foy: 1st **Trillion**, 2nd **Monseigneur**, 3rd **Dom Alaric**, 4th **Guadanini**

Abroad

In England

Derby Stakes: 1st Shirley Heights, 2nd Hawaiian Sound, 3rd Remainder Man, 6th **Julio Mariner**, 13th **Exdirectory**

Oaks Stakes: 1st Fair Salinia, 2nd **Dancing Maid**, 3rd Suni

King George VI and Queen Elizabeth Stakes: 1st Ile De Bourbon, 2nd Hawaiian Sound, 3rd **Montcontour**, 6th **Exdirectory**, 7th **Guadanini**, 12th **Trillion**, disq (2nd ptp tested positive for prohibited substance salicylic acid) **Acamas**

St Leger: 1st **Julio Mariner**, 2nd Le Moss, 3rd M-Lolshan, 5th **Galiani**

In Ireland

Irish Derby: 1st Shirley Heights, 2nd **Exdirectory**, 3rd Hawaiian Sound

In Germany

Grosser Preis von Baden: 1st Valour, 2nd Tip Moss, 3rd Märzvogel, 4th **Montcontour**, 6th **Lido**

The race

It was cold and windy and, although the rain had stopped, the ground had eased and it was now good to soft. Acamas played up before the start, but once despatched it was Trillion who led for the first 400 metres before Dom Alaric took over as Trillion was steadied back by Bill Shoemaker.

Dom Alaric, racing at a steady pace, led them all the way to the final *ligne droite*, where he was followed in by Frère Basile, Alleged, Trillion, and Dancing Maid.

Alleged was travelling sweetly. With just under 400 metres remaining Piggott let him go and he readily accelerated away, opening up daylight to the others.

It was all over, and Alleged glided home, winning comfortably by two lengths to Trillion with the same to Dancing Maid followed by Frère Basile, and the fast-finishing Guadanini and Montcontour.

Post-race

Horse and rider were mobbed on the course by members of the media and other hangers-on. One miscreant, who got too close, was contemptuously swatted away by the famously mercurial Piggott.

It was an excellent performance by Alleged, who had recovered from illness to become the first double winner since Ribot 22 years before. He'd never run on a surface described with the word 'soft' in it previously, but had handled the ground well to take Vincent O'Brien's and Lester Piggott's Arc tallies to three. Sangster had doubled his score and would catch O'Brien and Piggott up in a couple of years.

There was talk of Alleged going to the Champion Stakes but eventually that was shelved and he was retired. Syndicated for 16 million US dollars he stood in the USA at Lexington, siring a whole host of top horses including Irish Derby-winner Law Society, Champion Stakes-winner Legal Case, Oaks-winner Midway Lady, Breeders' Cup Turf-winner Miss Alleged and Grand Prix de Deauville-winner Strategic Choice, who will feature in the Arc story.

Result

1978 Prix de l'Arc de Triomphe
Longchamp. Sunday, 1 October 1978
Weights: 3yo c: 56kg, 3yo f: 54.5kg, 4yo+ c: 59kg, 4yo+ f: 57.5kg

1st Alleged (USA)   4yo c   59kg   **1.4/1 fav**
by Hoist the Flag out of Princess Pout (Prince John). Robert Sangster / Vincent O'Brien / Lester Piggott

2nd Trillion (USA)   4yo f   57.5kg   **16/1**
by Hail to Reason out of Margarethen (Tulyar). Edward Stephenson / Maurice Zilber / Bill Shoemaker

3rd Dancing Maid (FR)   3yo f   54.5kg   **4/1** (coupled with Gay Mécène)
by Lyphard out of Morana (Val de Loir). Jacques Wertheimer / Alec Head / Freddy Head

Runners: 18 (FR 14, IRE 2, GB 1. GER 1). Distances: 2, 2. Going: good to soft. Time: 2m 36.50s

Also ran: 4th **Frère Basile** (FR) 3yo c, 5th **Guadanini** (FR) 4yo c, 6th **Montcontour** (FR) 4yo c, 7th **Noir et Or** (GB) 3yo c, 8th **Gay Mécène** (USA) 3yo c, 9th **Dancing Master** (FR) 3yo c, 10th **Lido** (GER) 5yo h. Unplaced: **Shafaraz** (FR) 5yo h, **Dom Alaric** (FR) 4yo c, **Monseigneur** (USA) 4yo c, **Acamas** (GB) 3yo c, **Galiani** (IRE) 3yo c, **Turville** (FR) 3yo c, **Julio Mariner** (GB) 3yo c, **Exdirectory** (GB) 3yo c.

Three Troïkas triumphs for four Heads

Criquette the first female trainer to score

Background and fancied horses

In England, Troy, owned by Sir Michael Sobell and Lord Arnold Weinstock, had been a runaway winner in the Derby and had then added the Irish version in facile style. Next up he took a below-standard King George VI and Queen Elizabeth Stakes, before having to work hard to reel in the opposition in the Benson & Hedges Gold Cup. After a seven-week break and with two pacemakers, Rivadon and the French-trained Player, he lined up as favourite for the Arc at 0.8/1.

After that trio were the Aga Khan IV's pair at 5.8/1 headed by Top Ville, who'd won the Prix du Jockey Club in record time. He hadn't been suited by the soft surface when fourth in the Prix Niel, which was ominous as the ground at Longchamp was good to soft. His pacemaker, Kamaridaan, though, had shown a liking for ground with some give in it when beating the future St Leger-winner Son of Love at Maisons-Laffitte in the spring.

Prix du Jockey Club runner-up Le Marmot, who'd won the Prix Niel, traded at 7.3/1, followed by Three Troïkas and Fabulous Dancer coupled at 8.8/1.

Owned by Alec Head's wife, trained by his daughter and ridden by his son, Three Troïkas had obliged in the Poule d'Essai des Pouliches and Prix Saint-Alary before finishing second in the Prix de Diane, which was run in heavy rain and where she finished with a bruised foot.

Recovered, and after having the benefit of a mid-season break, she won the Prix Vermeille without being extended. She was accompanied to post by Fabulous Dancer, who'd run no sort of race in the Irish Derby but had shown his true ability when runner-up in the Prix Niel.

The 1978 King George VI and Queen Elizabeth Stakes-winner Ile De Bourbon was next at 9/1. He was owned by Sir Philip Oppenheimer, whose son would taste Arc glory.

The Lester Piggott-ridden Trillion, who'd been runner-up last year and filled the same berth in the Prix Foy this term, traded at 16/1 with Telescopico a point longer. The latter was a top performer in Argentina who'd come to France in the summer. He'd then had a trip across *la Manche* when fifth in the King George VI and Queen Elizabeth Stakes, and a week before the Arc had won the Prix Saint-Laurent at Maisons-Laffitte.

England's raiding party numbered seven: Troy, Rivadon and Ile De Bourbon; plus Prince of Wales's Stakes-winner Crimson Beau; Noble Saint, who'd won the Great Voltigeur Stakes; Joe McGrath Memorial Stakes-runner-up Two of Diamonds; and Valour. That septet were joined by the formerly Norwegian-trained Noble Dancer, who was now based in the USA, and the German-trained, but Polish-bred, Pawiment.

Betting

0.8/1 Troy & Player & Rivadon (all coupled), 5.8/1 Kamaridaan & Top Ville (coupled), 7.3/1 Le Marmot, 8.8/1 Three Troïkas & Fabulous Dancer (coupled), 9/1 Ile De Bourbon, 16/1 Trillion, 17/1 Telescopico, 35/1 BAR

Three-year-old form lines
Prix du Jockey Club: 1st **Top Ville**, 2nd **Le Marmot**, 3rd Sharpman
Grand Prix de Paris: 1st Soleil Noir, 2nd Son of Love, 3rd Stout Fellow
Prix Niel: 1st **Le Marmot**, 2nd **Fabulous Dancer**, 3rd **Kamaridaan**, 4th **Top Ville**

Fillies only
Prix de Diane: 1st Dunette, 2nd **Three Troïkas**, 3rd Producer, 4th **Pitasia**
Prix Vermeille: 1st **Three Troïkas**, 2nd Salpinx, 3rd **Pitasia**

Older horses and inter-generational races
Grand Prix de Saint-Cloud: 1st Gay Mécène, 2nd Ela-Mana-Mou, 3rd Gain, 8th **Valour**, 0th **Trillion**
Grand Prix de Deauville: 1st First Prayer, 2nd **Jeune Loup**, 3rd African Hope
Prix Foy: 1st **Pevero**, 2nd **Trillion**, 3rd Gay Mécène
Prix du Prince d'Orange: 1st Rusticaro, 2nd **Trillion**, 3rd **Northern Baby**

Abroad
In England
Derby Stakes: 1st **Troy**, 2nd Dickens Hill, 3rd **Northern Baby**, 14th **Two of Diamonds**
King George VI and Queen Elizabeth Stakes: 1st **Troy**, 2nd Gay Mécène, 3rd Ela-Mana-Mou, 5th **Telescopico**

In Ireland
Irish Derby: 1st **Troy**, 2nd Dickens Hill, 3rd Bohemian Grove, 9th **Fabulous Dancer**
Joe McGrath Memorial Stakes (inaugurated 1976): 1st Fordham, 2nd **Two of Diamonds**, 3rd Bold Theme

The race

On a sunny day, racing had been held up by several hundred motorbikes and scooters on the road parallel to the back straight, whose riders were protesting about a new tax that had been imposed on their vehicles. When the action got underway, Rivadon and Player were fast to stride while Pevero, who'd had to be led to the start, was slow away. Troy settled at the back along with Three Troïkas, who had tacked over to the inside from a wide draw.

By the top of the hill, Crimson Beau had gone on, quickly opening up a gap of five lengths to the others. Northern Baby was now in second followed by a group containing Le Marmot. Meanwhile, Three Troïkas started to make progress after being switched wide, and Troy also gained a few places joining Ile De Bourbon in midfield.

Crimson Beau managed to hold the lead until the straight but was then quickly overhauled by Northern Baby, who in turn was passed by Le Marmot. Not far behind, Three Troïkas and Trillion were moving into challenging positions.

Troy still had plenty of ground to make up from seventh place, but was starting to reduce the deficit as Three Troïkas, in the centre of the track, mastered Le Marmot with 200 metres to go and drew clear.

Three Troïkas wasn't stopping and at the line she had three lengths to spare over Le Marmot, with Troy, who'd made up a lot of ground, a length further back in third. Pevero also finished fast for fourth and was followed home by Trillion and Northern Baby.

Post-race

The connections of Three Troïkas included three members of the Head family, owner Ghislaine, trainer Christiane and jockey Freddy – and all masterminded by the owner's husband, who was also the trainer's and jockey's *papa*, Alec.

Christiane, who is better known by her nickname Criquette, became the first woman to train an Arc winner, and Freddy equalled Jacques Doyasbère's record of four winners. Doyasbère had won on Djébel in 1942, Ardan in 1944, and Tantième in 1950 and 1951, while Freddy's previous winners were Bon Mot in 1966, San San in 1972, and Ivanjica in 1976.

Three Troïkas was retired for the year but was kept in training.

Result

1979 Prix de l'Arc de Triomphe
Longchamp. Sunday, 7 October 1979
Weights: 3yo c: 56kg, 3yo f: 54.5kg, 4yo+ c: 59kg, 4yo+ f: 57.5kg

1st Three Troïkas (FR) 3yo f 54.5kg 8.8/1
by Lyphard out of Three Roses (Dual). Ghislaine Head / Christiane Head / Freddy Head

2nd Le Marmot (FR) 3yo c 56kg 7.3/1
by Amarko out of Molinka (Molvedo). Rudolph Schäfer / François Boutin / Philippe Paquet

3rd Troy (GB) 3yo c 56kg 0.8/1 fav
by Petingo out of La Milo (Hornbeam). Sir Michael Sobell & Lord Weinstock / Dick Hern / Willie Carson

Runners: 22 (FR 13, ENG 7, GER 1, USA 1). Distances: 3, 1. Going: good to soft. Time: 2m 28.90s

Also ran: 4th **Pevero** (IRE) 4yo c, 5th **Trillion** (USA) 5yo m, 6th **Northern Baby** (CAN) 3yo c, 7th **Jeune Loup** (FR) 4yo c, 8th **Noble Saint** (USA) 3yo c, 9th **Pawiment** (POL) 5yo h, 10th **Crimson Beau** (GB) 4yo c. Unplaced: **Noble Dancer** (GB) 7yo h, **Ile De Bourbon** (USA) 4yo c, **Valour** (USA) 4yo c, **Telescopico** (ARG) 4yo c, **Kamaridaan** (GB) 3yo c, **Top Ville** (IRE) 3yo c, **Fabulous Dancer** (USA) 3yo c, **Two of Diamonds** (GB) 3yo c, **Player** (FR) 3yo c, **Rivadon** (USA) 3yo c, **Pitasia** (IRE) 3yo f, **Princess Redowa** (GB) 3yo f.

1946: Caracalla is superbly turned out prior to winning a fifth Arc for Marcel Boussac.
Charlie Elliott wears the famous orange with a grey cap, plus a sash to distinguish him from last
year's winner Ardan who also ran

1950: Tantième (above right) records his first win, from Alizier (centre) and L'Amiral (rail)

1963: Exbury with jockey Jean Deforge and owners Baron Guy de Rothschild and wife Marie-Hélène

Left: Corrida and Charlie Elliott, winners in 1936 and 1937. Right: 1934-victor Brantôme, Charles Bouillon up

The brilliant Ribot, under Enrico Camici, doubles his Arc tally in 1956

1958: Ballymoss beats Fric to become the first Irish-trained Arc winner

1967: Topyo's owner Suzy Volterra looks on as jockey Bill Pyers is all smiles – for now

1965: Owner Jean Ternynck leads in Sea Bird after his breath-taking victory

1976: Freddy Head tries to catch Ivanjica after being deposited on the ground during the victory celebrations

Left: Mill Reef, Geoff Lewis up, becomes the first English-trained Arc winner since 1948 when scooting home in 1971. Right: the scintillating winner in 1986, Dancing Brave, the middle leg of Pat Eddery's Arc hat-trick

1968: Vaguely Noble, Bill Williamson up, is all class as he leaves Sir Ivor trailing in his wake

Lester Piggott steers Alleged to success in 1977, Balmerino is second

Allez France, Yves Saint-Martin up, overcomes adversity to score in 1974, the first of four Arc winners for Daniel Wildenstein (pictured right)

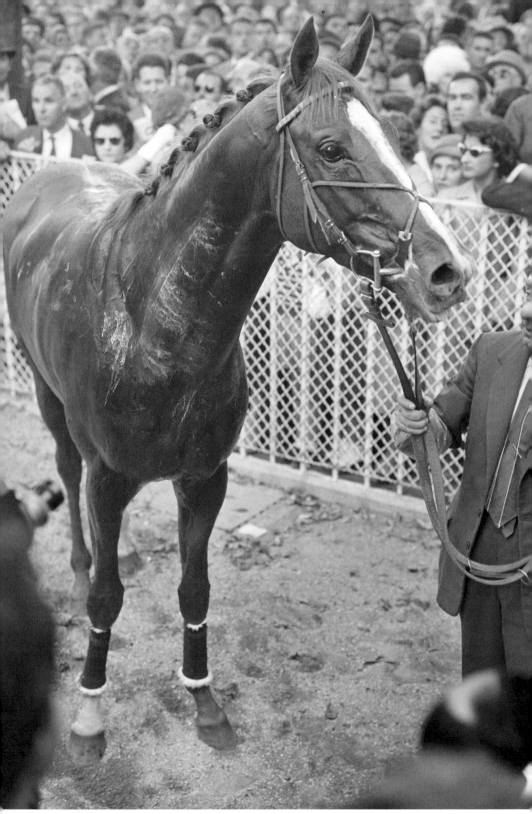

1959: The Aly Khan's Saint Crespin, who won half the race on the track and the other half in the Stewards' Room

Detroit battles it out under Eddery

Sangster's third win in four years

Background and fancied horses

The Dick Hern-trained Ela-Mana-Mou had been most impressive during the summer in England, winning the Prince of Wales's Stakes, the Eclipse Stakes, and the King George VI and Queen Elizabeth Stakes. He was then rested before Longchamp and was 2/1 coupled with last year's runner-up Le Marmot, as Captain Tim Rogers of Airlie Stud had an interest in both horses.

Le Marmot won the Prix Ganay and was sent off favourite for the King George VI and Queen Elizabeth Stakes. However, he'd picked up a knock on the way over to Ascot and ran below par. Returning from a break he'd struggled to win the Prix Foy.

Last year's winner, Three Troïkas, had damaged a bone in her off-fore leg in the Prix Dollar at the beginning of June. She wasn't seen again until the Prix du Prince d'Orange, in which she finished a creditable second to Dunette, only being beaten by half a length, and as such was supported into 4/1 at Longchamp.

Robert Sangster's Detroit was proving to be a useful filly after winning the Prix Chloë and the Prix de la Nonette. She was ridden by Pat Eddery for the first time in the Prix Vermeille. Eddery was to be Sangster's retained jockey from 1981, replacing Lester Piggott. It would be a successful partnership but didn't start perfectly as Detroit found herself boxed-in, eventually running on strongly to take third once finding some room. At 6.7/1 Detroit was just a fraction shorter than the German challenger Nebos. He'd only been beaten by three horses in his 13-race career, and had accounted for two who would re-oppose in the Arc when winning the Grosser Preis von Baden.

Lester Piggott's ride, the Grand Prix de Deauville-winner Glenorum, was the first of three horses on the 12/1 mark, along with Mrs Penny and Policeman. Mrs Penny had won the Prix de Diane and Prix Vermeille, as well as finishing runner-up to Ela-Mana-Mou in the King George VI and Queen Elizabeth Stakes, while Policeman had caused a shock in the Prix du Jockey Club when winning at 54/1. He would have the benefit of a pacemaker in the Arc in the form of Iseo.

Dunette, at 15/1, had dead-heated in the Grand Prix de Saint-Cloud and would have won outright if jockey Georges Doleuze hadn't celebrated too soon. Dunette was withdrawn from the Prix Foy due to colic but recovered in time to win the Prix du Prince d'Orange.

Apart from Ela-Mana-Mou and Mrs Penny, the English challengers were: Irish St Leger-winner Niniski and his pacemaker Lindoro, who were both owned by Lady Beaverbrook; the returning Noble Saint, who'd won the Yorkshire Cup; and the victor in the Princess of Wales's Stakes and Geoffrey Freer Stakes, Nicholas Bill.

Little Bonny, who'd finished second in the Cheshire Oaks, Irish Oaks and Prix Vermeille, represented Ireland, and with Nebos running for Germany, there were eight foreign challengers against the home team's dozen. Yves Saint-Martin was left without a ride after Aryenne was withdrawn with a mouth abscess on the morning of the race.

Betting

2/1 Ela-Mana-Mou & Le Marmot (coupled), 4/1 Three Troïkas, 6.7/1 Detroit, 7/1 Nebos, 12/1 Glenorum, 12/1 Mrs Penny, 12/1 Policeman & Iseo (coupled), 15/1 Dunette, 21/1 BAR.

Three-year-old form lines
Prix du Jockey Club: 1st **Policeman**, 2nd Shakapour, 3rd **Providential**, 0th **Argument**
Grand Prix de Paris: 1st Valiant Heart, 2nd What a Joy, 3rd Water Mill
Prix Niel: 1st Prince Bee, 2nd **Satilla**, 3rd **Ruscelli**, last **Policeman**

Fillies only
Prix de Diane: 1st **Mrs Penny**, 2nd Aryenne, 3rd Paranète
Prix Vermeille: 1st **Mrs Penny**, 2nd **Little Bonny**, 3rd **Detroit**, 4th **Gold River**

Older horses and inter-generational races
Grand Prix de Saint-Cloud: DH1st **Dunette**, DH1st Shakapour, 3rd **Policeman**, 5th **Noble Saint**
Grand Prix de Deauville: 1st **Glenorum**, 2nd Perrault, 3rd Vincent
Prix du Prince d'Orange: 1st **Dunette**, 2nd **Three Troïkas**, 3rd Northern Baby, 5th **Providential**, 6th **Moulouki**
Prix Foy: 1st **Le Marmot**, 2nd Anifa, 3rd Gain

Abroad
In England
Derby Stakes: 1st Henbit, 2nd Master Willie, 3rd Rankin
King George VI and Queen Elizabeth Stakes: 1st **Ela-Mana-Mou**, 2nd **Mrs Penny**, 3rd Gregorian, 4th **Dunette**, 5th **Le Marmot**, 0th Tyrnavos

In Germany
Grosser Preis von Baden: 1st **Nebos**, 2nd Cherubin, 3rd Marracci, 4th **Nicholas Bill**, 5th **Argument**

The race

The pacemakers Lindoro and Iseo led the field away and although Nicholas Bill was slow to stride, he was on their heels by the top of the hill. As was Policeman who took it up when the pacemakers faded, with Ela-Mana-Mou following him through into second place.

The German-raider Nebos, under Lutz Maeder, made some eye-catching progress, but it didn't last long as his impetus was stopped when he came into contact with Niniski.

Turning in to the *dernier ligne droite*, Policeman still led but was overtaken by Ela-Mana-Mou inside the last 400 metres. Three Troïkas took closer order, while back in ninth position Eddery switched Detroit out wide and, after a few strides, she started to make impressive headway.

Nebos was starting a second run and Argument was also making rapid headway. At the 200-metre pole Ela-Mana-Mou's advantage had been whittled down to half a length by Three Troïkas, while Detroit continued to fly home out wide. Three Troïkas couldn't get past Ela-Mana-Mou, but Detroit could.

However, it wasn't over as outsider Argument closed in rapidly on her inside. In a thrilling finish Detroit passed the post just in front, winning by a diminishing half a length from Argument, who deprived Ela-Mana-Mou of second by a short head. Three Troïkas was just a neck further back followed by Nebos and Nicholas Bill.

Post-race

In a course-record time Detroit had given Robert Sangster a third Arc victory just two years after Alleged's second success. While Trainer Olivier Douieb and jockey Pat Eddery opened their accounts.

Both had solid credentials as Douieb was the son-in-law of Pierre Pelat, trainer of the 1954 Arc-winner Sica Boy, whose father had won with Nikellora in 1945 and Soltikoff in 1962. Eddery's father, Jimmy, was also no slouch, having won the 1955 Irish Derby on Panaslipper.

Detroit was retired for the season but would be back at Longchamp to defend her crown.

Result

1980 Prix de l'Arc de Triomphe

Longchamp. Sunday, 5 October 1980
Weights: 3yo c: 56kg, 3yo f: 54.5kg, 4yo+ c: 59kg, 4yo+ f: 57.5kg

1st Detroit (FR)   3yo f   54.5kg   **6.7/1**
by Riverman out of Derna (Sunny Boy). Robert Sangster / Olivier Douieb / Pat Eddery

2nd Argument (FR)   3yo c   56kg   **74/1**
by Kautokeino out of Arantelle (Tapioca). Pierre Ribes / John Cunnington jnr / Jean-Claude Desaint

3rd Ela-Mana-Mou (IRE)   4yo c   59kg   **2/1 fav** (coupled with Le Marmot)
by Petingo out of La Milo (Hornbeam). Sir Michael Sobell / Dick Hern / Willie Carson

Runners: 20 (FR 12, GB 6, GER 1, IRE 1). Distances: ½, sh hd. Going: firm. Time: 2m 28.00s

Also ran: 4th **Three Troïkas** (FR) 4yo f, 5th **Nebos** (GER) 4yo c, 6th **Nicholas Bill** (GB) 5yo h, 7th **Dunette** (FR) 4yo f, 8th **Le Marmot** (FR) 4yo c, 9th **Ruscelli** (FR) 3yo c, 10th **Satilla** (FR) 3yo f. Unplaced: **Lindoro** (FR) 4yo c, **Niniski** (USA) 4yo c, **Noble Saint** (USA) 4yo c **Iseo** (FR) 5yo h, **Providential** (IRE) 3yo c, **Moulouki** (IRE) 3yo c, **Glenorum** (CAN) 3yo c, **Policeman** (FR) 3yo c, **Mrs Penny** (USA) 3yo f, **Little Bonny** (IRE) 3yo f.

1981

Gold River suited by track and pace

Gary Moore emulates father who won on Saint Crespin

Background and fancied horses

The prize money for the winner, which had stood at 1.2 million francs since 1970, was raised to two million francs. But, with the currency devalued in line with the European Monetary System agreement in Brussels, it wasn't actually worth quite as much in that overused phrase 'real terms'.

The Aga Khan IV's Akarad had been given plenty to do off the final turn in the Prix du Jockey Club, and despite making up lots of ground had to be content with finishing second to Patrick Biancone's Bikala. He reversed the placings in the Grand Prix de Saint-Cloud, and, after a good win in the Prix Niel, was sent off 2/1 favourite for the Arc.

Up until the St Leger it had seemed as though the Aga's strongest hope would be the ultra-impressive Derby-winner Shergar. But he flopped at Doncaster which led to his withdrawal from the Arc.

Robert Sangster had full or part ownership in three horses who were bundled together at 3.5/1. Last year's winner, Detroit, had again come good in late summer winning three times, culminating in the Prix Foy.

Freddy Head, who had been riding her this season, was released from his retainer with Jacques Wertheimer so he could maintain the partnership with Detroit. Otherwise he would have had to ride another filly, the 53/1-shot Gold River. The winner of the 1980 Prix Royal-Oak had disappointed in this term's Grand Prix de Saint-Cloud before finishing third in the Prix Foy, three and a half lengths behind Detroit.

Snow Day, the second Sangster horse, had won the Prix de Royaumont and Prix Fille de l'Air, but had finished fifth when her saddle had slipped in the Prix Vermeille. The trio was completed by the Pat Eddery-ridden King's Lake, who'd been reinstated as the winner of the Irish 2000 Guineas after being disqualified on the day when first past the post. He later won the Sussex Stakes and the Joe McGrath Memorial Stakes, but had never raced as far as 2,400 metres.

The Ascot Gold Cup-winner Ardross, with Lester Piggott up, was 5.5/1, followed by the Prix Vermeille-heroine April Run and Blue Wind, who'd won the English and Irish Oaks. They were both owned by Diana Firestone and coupled at 6.5/1.

Beldale Flutter, who'd come out on top in the Benson & Hedges Gold Cup, was next at 12/1. Then came the previously mentioned Bikala, who'd finished his Arc preparation with second place to the Aga Khan-owned Vayrann in the Prix du Prince d'Orange.

At 14/1 Bikala was on the same mark as Michael Sobell's 1980 Prix Niel-victor Prince Bee, who'd won this season's Valdoe Stakes at Goodwood, and Lancastrian, who was third home in the Grand Prix de Saint-Cloud.

The English runners, in addition to Ardross, Beldale Flutter and Prince Bee, were: John Dunlop's Prix du Jockey Club-third Gap of Dunloe, who was to be the first Arc ride for Walter Swinburn; Cut Above, the 28/1 winner of the St Leger; and the Grosser Preis von Baden-winner Pèlerin.

Ireland had Yorkshire Oaks-winner Condessa, as well as King's Lake and Blue Wind. Action Man was there for Denmark and not surprisingly the New Zealand Derby-winner Ring the Bell was representing New Zealand. Which made a total of 11 runners trained outside *l'hexagone*.

The action was going ahead after a 12-hour meeting two days before, when the threat of industrial action specifically targeting the race was averted.

Betting

2/1 Akarad, 3.5/1 Snow Day & Detroit & King's Lake (all coupled), 5.5/1 Ardross, 6.5/1 April Run & Blue Wind (coupled), 12/1 Beldale Flutter, 14/1 Bikala, 14/1 Prince Bee & Lancastrian (coupled), 25/1 BAR.

Three-year-old form lines
Prix du Jockey Club: 1st **Bikala**, 2nd **Akarad**, 3rd **Gap of Dunloe**, 4th **Rahotep**
Grand Prix de Paris: 1st Glint of Gold, 2nd Tipperary Fixer, 3rd Vayrann
Prix Niel: 1st **Akarad**, 2nd **Rahotep**, 3rd Lydian

Fillies only
Prix de Diane: 1st Madam Gay, 2nd Val d'Erica, 3rd **April Run**, 5th **Tootens**
Prix Vermeille: 1st **April Run**, 2nd **Léandra**, 3rd Madam Gay, 5th **Snow Day**, 7th **Tootens**

Older horses and inter-generational races
Grand Prix de Saint-Cloud: 1st **Akarad**, 2nd **Bikala**, 3rd **Lancastrian**, 4th **April Run**, 5th **Gold River**, 6th **Prince Bee**, 7th **Argument**
Grand Prix de Deauville: 1st **Perrault**, 2nd Castle Keep, 3rd Glenorum
Prix du Prince d'Orange: 1st Vayrann, 2nd **Bikala**, 3rd Diamond Prospect, 6th **Ring the Bell**
Prix Foy: 1st **Detroit**, 2nd **Lancastrian**, 3rd **Gold River**

Abroad
In England
Derby Stakes: 1st Shergar, 2nd Glint of Gold, 3rd Scintillating Air

Oaks Stakes: 1st **Blue Wind**, 2nd Madam Gay, 3rd Leap Lively
Ascot Gold Cup: 1st **Ardross**, 2nd Shoot A Line, 3rd Ayyabaan
King George VI and Queen Elizabeth Stakes: 1st Shergar, 2nd Madam Gay, 3rd
Fingal's Cave, 5th **Pèlerin**
St Leger: 1st **Cut Above**, 2nd Glint of Gold, 3rd Bustomi, 4th Shergar

In Ireland
Irish Derby: 1st Shergar, 2nd **Cut Above**, 3rd Dance Bid, 6th **Gap of Dunloe**
Joe McGrath Memorial Stakes: 1st **King's Lake**, 2nd Erins Isle, 3rd Kind of Hush,
4th **Blue Wind**

In Germany
Grosser Preis von Baden: 1st **Pèlerin**, 2nd Hohritt, 3rd Maivogel

The race

On a windy, cloudy, cold day, Ring the Bell was lightning quick out of the
stalls but it was Bikala who led on the inside after 100 metres. Ardross, who
had been drawn widest of all, was prominent on the outer, while Condessa
was slow away and was in rear with the Gary Moore-ridden Gold River.

Bikala lengthened his advantage at the Petit Bois, going on from Ardross,
Detroit, Beldale Flutter and the favourite Akarad, who pulled hard when
they made the descent. Entering the straight, Detroit and Akarad were the
first to crack followed by Ardross. Gold River, though, was making ground
as Perrault moved into second behind Bikala.

Gold River kept coming, finding plenty in lane four. She wore down
Perrault and then Bikala and went on stylishly to secure a cosy victory by
three parts of a length.

April Run, who had been held up for a moment by the tiring Akarad, tried
to follow Gold River through, but Bikala just held her off, albeit by a rapidly
diminishing neck for second with daylight to the fading Perrault followed
by Ardross and Argument.

Post-race

The reception for Gold River was slightly muted, as many in the crowd had
backed Freddy Head's chosen mount Detroit, with only a few siding with the
53/1-winner. Freddy had missed out but his dad hadn't and Alec added to his
official wins with Nuccio, Saint Crespin, and Ivanjica to equal the record of
Charles Semblat. Alec had of course also played a major part in the success
of Three Troïkas.

The slow pace in both the Grand Prix de Saint-Cloud and Prix Foy hadn't
suited Gold River. However, the strong gallop in the Arc had certainly brought
out the best in the daughter of Riverman. It was now two Arcs in a row for
Riverman, who was also the sire of Detroit.

Owner Jacques Wertheimer had seen his colours carried to a second Arc after Ivanjica, and Freddy's substitute, Gary Moore, had played his part with aplomb. The son of George Moore, who'd won on Saint Crespin in 1959, was paying a fleeting visit to France. He'd ridden a winner in Hong Kong the day before, Saturday, and was back in Hong Kong by Tuesday.

This Gary Moore should not be confused with the former jump jockey from England who now trains in Sussex. That Gary Moore is the father of Ryan who will figure in our story in a couple of decades.

At stud, Gold River produced a few decent sorts, with the best being Prix Saint-Alary winner Rivière d'Or, who was runner-up to Resless Kara in the 1988 Prix de Diane. Detroit also went to the covering sheds and produced a handful of winners of which the standout was the 1994 Arc-winner Carnégie.

Riverman 1969

Detroit 1977	*Gold River* 1977	*Dockage* 1984	Bahri 1992
Carnégie 1991		*Docklands* 1989	Sakhee 1997
		Rail Link 2003	

Result
1981 Prix de l'Arc de Triomphe
Longchamp. Sunday, 4 October 1981
Weights: 3yo c: 56kg, 3yo f: 54.5kg, 4yo+ c: 59kg, 4yo+ f: 57.5kg

1st Gold River (FR)   4yo f   57.5kg   **53/1**
by Riverman out of Glaneuse (Snob). Jacques Wertheimer / Alec Head/ Gary W. Moore

2nd Bikala (IRE)   3yo c   56kg   **14/1**
by Kalamoun out of Irish Bird (Sea Bird). Jules Ouaki / Patrick Biancone / Serge Gorli

3rd April Run (IRE)   3yo f   54.5kg   **6.5/1**
by Run the Gantlet out of April Fancy (No Argument). Diana Firestone / François Boutin / Philippe Paquet

Runners: Runners: 24 (FR 13, GB 6, IRE 3, DEN 1, NZ 1). Distances: ¾, nk. Going: good to soft. Time: 2m 35.20s

Also ran: 4th **Perrault** (GB) 4yo c, 5th **Ardross** (IRE) 5yo h, 6th **Argument** (FR) 4yo c, 7th **Akarad** (FR) 3yo c, 8th **Tootens** (IRE) 3yo f, 9th **Léandra** (FR) 3yo f, 10th **Snow Day** (FR) 3yo f. Unplaced: **Action Man** (DEN) 6yo h, **Pèlerin** (FR) 4yo c, **Lancastrian** (IRE) 4yo c, **Prince Bee** (GB) 4yo c, **Ring the Bell** (NZ) 4yo f, **Gilded Vanity** (IRE) 4yo f, **Detroit** (FR) 4yo f, **Cut Above** (GB) 3yo c, **King's Lake** (USA) 3yo c, **Gap of Dunloe** (FR) 3yo c, **Beldale Flutter** (USA) 3yo c, **Rahotep** (FR) 3yo c, **Blue Wind** (IRE) 3yo f, **Condessa** (IRE) 3yo f.

Akiyda leads home the A-team

Aga Khan IV's first Arc winner

Background and fancied horses

This was the last year that the Loterie Nationale used the Arc for its sweepstake and the first time that the race was sponsored. The international hotel chain Trusthouse Forte, which was London-based but which had two prestige hotels in Paris, had signed up to a four-year deal.

However, the first Trusthouse Forte Prix de l'Arc de Triomphe was put in jeopardy by yet another strike, this time by track workers. An agreement was achieved shortly before the first race on the card, which meant that the fresh ground dolled off on the inside of the track would be in use for the Arc. Some trainers had threatened to withdraw their horses if they'd been forced to run on the old churned up part of the track.

Robert Sangster's Assert, a half-brother of Bikala, had won both the Prix du Jockey Club and Irish Derby before having to play second fiddle to Kalaglow in the King George VI and Queen Elizabeth Stakes. Trained by Vincent O'Brien's son David, he was back to winning form in the Benson & Hedges Gold Cup and Joe McGrath Memorial Stakes. All of Assert's wins had come on good or firmer and the 2.5/1 Arc favourite would run on soft, albeit virgin soft ground, for the first time at Longchamp.

Second favourite Bon Sang, at 5.5/1, had been a decent two-year-old but was not seen until July due to Mahmoud Foustok's yard being out of sorts after all the horses had been given too much anti-worm vaccine. After a couple of near misses, Bon Sang opened his 1982 account in the Prix Niel.

The Henry Cecil-trained Ardross, who'd won the Ascot Gold Cup for the second time, was back and a 6.3/1-chance, the same price as Freddy Head's mount the Prix de Diane-winner Harbour.

Last year's runner-up Bikala, who'd been second in the Prix du Prince d'Orange, was a fraction longer, followed by the first horse in double figures Akiyda. The 11/1-chance was a full sister to last year's favourite Akarad, and had found one too good in both the Prix de Diane and Prix Vermeille, but on the plus side had a predilection for a soft surface.

The Prix Foy-winner, April Run, and Akarad's conqueror in the Prix Vermeille, All Along, were 15/1 and 17/1 respectively.

In addition to the Irish-trained favourite Assert, and Ardross from England, there were four other *étrangers*; the Ukrainian-bred Kastet, representing the Soviet Union, and three more from England: Musidora Stakes-winner Last Feather; Critique, who'd won the 1981 Cumberland Lodge Stakes; and the first horse to wear Sheikh Mohammed Al Maktoum's maroon and white colours in the Arc, the Yorkshire Oaks-winner Awaasif.

Betting
2.5/1 Assert, 5.5/1 Bon Sang, 6.3/1 Ardross, 6.3/1 Harbour, 6.5/1 Bikala, 11/1 Akiyda, 15/1 April Run, 17/1 All Along, 22/1 BAR.

Three-year-old form lines
Prix du Jockey Club: 1st **Assert**, 2nd **Real Shadaï**, 3rd Bois de Grâce, 4th Alfred's Choice, 8th **Cadoudal**, 10th **Newjdar**
Grand Prix de Paris: 1st Le Nain Jaune, 2nd Chem, 3rd Rhoecus, 4th Alfred's Choice
Prix Niel: 1st **Bon Sang**, 2nd Alfred's Choice, 3rd Bakst, 6th **Cadoudal**

Fillies only
Prix de Diane: 1st **Harbour**, 2nd **Akiyda**, 3rd Paradise, 5th **All Along**
Prix Vermeille: 1st **All Along**, 2nd **Akiyda** 3rd Grease, 4th **Harbour**, 7th **Awaasif**

Older horses and inter-generational races
Grand Prix de Saint-Cloud: 1st Glint of Gold, 2nd Lancastrian, 3rd **Real Shadaï**
Grand Prix de Deauville: 1st **Real Shadai**, 2nd **No Attention**, 3rd Oak Dancer
Prix du Prince d'Orange: 1st General Holme, 2nd **Bikala**, 3rd Commodore Blake
Prix Foy: 1st **April Run**, 2nd **No Attention**, 3rd **Mariacho**

Abroad
In England
Derby Stakes: 1st Golden Fleece, 2nd Touching Wood, 3rd Silver Hawk
Oaks Stakes: 1st Time Charter, 2nd Slightly Dangerous, 3rd **Last Feather**, 4th **Awaasif**, 6th **All Along**
Ascot Gold Cup: 1st **Ardross**, 2nd Tipperary Fixer, 3rd El Badr
King George VI and Queen Elizabeth Stakes: 1st Kalaglow, 2nd **Assert**, 3rd Glint of Gold, 4th **Critique**, 5th **Bikala**

In Ireland
Irish Derby: 1st **Assert**, 2nd Silver Hawk, 3rd Patcher
Joe McGrath Memorial Stakes: 1st **Assert**, 2nd Kind of Hush, 3rd Punctilio

The race
April Run, Last feather, Bon Sang and Akiyda were all prominent early on, until Bikala, out wide, hit the front. Approaching the summit, Bon Sang took over and was still in front entering the straight.

Yves Saint-Martin enterprisingly steered Akiyda between the pacemakers to take the lead with 400 metres to run. On the outside, Awaasif moved in to second position. Harbour and Assert were back-pedalling but April Run and Ardross still had cards to play.

Inside the final 200 metres Akiyda had a length advantage from Awaasif, who was gradually being caught by Ardross on her inside. Piggott kept asking his mount for more and gamely Ardross gave more, pushing his nose in front of Awaasif and then aiming for Akiyda.

What followed was a battle royal between Yves Saint-Martin and Lester Piggott, both geniuses in the saddle, both respected in each other's countries. Piggott was the English Saint-Martin and Saint-Martin was the French Piggott.

Ardross cut the margin to Akiyda from a length, to a half, to a neck, to a head and on the line it was a photo. However a head was as close as Ardross got to Akiyda who was called the winner.

Awaasif also ran with great credit, finishing half a length behind Ardross, with April Run only a further head behind in what had also been a great scrap for third. The first four had drawn four lengths clear of Real Shadaï and No Attention in fifth and sixth.

Post-race

Four of the six horses in the race whose names began with the letter A – Akiyda, Ardross, Awaasif, and April Run – had all brought their A-games to the Arc and produced a thrilling race.

Akiyda was the first Arc winner for the Aga Khan IV, whose father had won with Saint Crespin in 1959, and whose grandfather had scored with Migoli and Nuccio. Yves Saint-Martin was recording his third win after Sassafras and Allez France.

It was a fourth success for 74-year-old François Mathet, who'd previously triumphed with Tantième in 1950 and 1951, and Sassafras in 1970, and who now equalled the record of Charles Semblat and Alec Head. Unfortunately, le sphinx de Gouvieux never had a chance to better his score as he died three months later.

Between 1961 and 1982 Mathet had been champion trainer by number of winners 27 times in a row and 14 times based on the amount of prize money won. A listed race at Saint-Cloud in late March, the Prix François Mathet, honours his memory.

It was the last race for both of the principals. Akiyda only produced one foal, Akishka, who in turn produced a few winners, the best of whom was the 2002 Henry II Stakes-winner Akbar. Ardross was more successful, siring the useful Karinga Bay and several decent jumpers, notably champion hurdler Alderbrook.

Result

1982 Trusthouse Forte Prix de l'Arc de Triomphe
Longchamp. Sunday, 3 October 1982
Weights: 3yo c: 56kg, 3yo f: 54.5kg, 4yo+ c: 59kg, 4yo+ f: 57.5kg

1st Akiyda (GB)   3yo f   54.5kg   **11/1**
by Labus out of Licata (Abdos). HH Aga Khan IV / François Mathet / Yves Saint-Martin

2nd Ardross (IRE)   6yo h   59kg   **6.3/1**
by Run the Gantlet out of Le Melody (Levmoss). Charles St George / Henry Cecil / Lester Piggott

3rd Awaasif (CAN)   3yo f   54.5kg   **90/1**
by Snow Knight out of Royal Statute (Northern Dancer). Sheikh Mohammed Al Maktoum / John Dunlop / Willie Carson

Runners: 17 (FR 11, GB 4, IRE 1, Soviet Union 1). Distances: hd, ½. Going: soft. Time: 2m 37.00s

Also ran: 4th **April Run** (IRE) 4yo f, 5th **Real Shadai** (USA) 3yo c, 6th **No Attention** (FR) 4yo c, 7th **Cadoudal** (FR) 3yo c, 8th **Critique** (USA) 4yo c, 9th **Harbour** (FR) 3yo f, 10th **Newjdar** (FR) 3yo c. Unplaced: **Assert** (IRE) 3yo c, **Bikala** (IRE) 4yo c, **Bon Sang** (FR) 3yo c, **Last Feather** (USA) 3yo f, **All Along** (FR) 3yo f, **Mariacho** (IRE) 4yo c, **Kastet** (UKR) 3yo c.

Dream passage for All Along

Fillies to the 'four' as Wildenstein doubles his tally

Background and fancied horses

The eight-strong challenge from England was dominated by two fillies, with Sun Princess, from the yard of Dick Hern, heading the Classic generation after winning The Oaks and St Leger.

In between those triumphs, though, she was beaten by the previous year's Oaks and Champion Stakes-winner, Time Charter, in the King George VI and Queen Elizabeth Stakes.

Henry Candy's charge also won the Prix Foy and was the subject of late money at Longchamp, in the end being sent off favourite at 3.3/1. The Michael Sobell-owned trio featuring the aforementioned Sun Princess together with Grand Prix de Saint-Cloud runner-up Lancastrian and Sailor's Dance were coupled at just over twice that price.

Another English-trained candidate, Paul Mellon's Diamond Shoal, who'd beaten Lancastrian at Saint-Cloud and also taken the Grosser Preis von Baden, was 7.3/1.

Ireland was doubly represented with the Joe McGrath Memorial-winner Stanerra at 7.8/1 being more fancied than Robert Sangster's Salmon Leap, who was a 15/1 shot.

The first of the home team in the betting was the Aga Khan IV's Prix Vermeille-winner Sharaya, trained by Alain de Royer-Dupré and ridden by Yves Saint-Martin, on 9/1.

Last year's third, Awaasif – the chosen mount of Lester Piggott – was on the 13/1 mark. And the other horses under 20/1 included André Fabre's Zalataia, Luth Enchantée, who'd won the Prix Jacques le Marois and the Prix du Moulin, and the Prix de Diane-heroine Escaline.

The horse that Piggott rejected, the Patrick Biancone-trained All Along, had won last year's Prix Vermeille on fast ground before being well-beaten in the Arc on soft. She was back on song after finishing second to Time Charter in the Prix Foy, and would be partnered by 'The Choirboy' Walter Swinburn, who wore the first colours of Daniel Wildenstein, while Alfred Gibert on his other runner Sagace, would wear a distinguishing light blue sash.

The German challenger Orofino, Denmark's Dalby Jaguar and the Robert Collet threesome – Dom Pasquini, Marie de Litz and Welsh Term – were all among the long shots. Prix du Jockey Club-winner Caerleon was absent after disappointing in the King George VI and Queen Elizabeth Stakes.

Betting

3.3/1 Time Charter, 6.8/1 Sun Princess & Sailor's Dance & Lancastrian (all coupled), 7.3/1 Diamond Shoal, 7.8/1 Stanerra, 9/1 Sharaya, 13/1 Awaasif, 15/1 Salmon Leap, 16/1 Zalataia, 17/1 All Along & Sagace (coupled), 17/1 Luth Enchantee, 18/1 Escaline, 21/1 BAR.

Three-year-old form lines
Prix du Jockey Club: 1st Caerleon, 2nd L'Emigrant, 3rd Esprit du Nord
Grand Prix de Paris: 1st Yawa, 2nd Fubymam du Tenu, 3rd Jasper
Prix Niel: 1st **Sagace**, 2nd Mourjane, 3rd Full of Stars

Fillies only
Prix de Diane: 1st **Escaline**, 2nd Smuggly, 3rd Air Distingué
Prix Vermeille: 1st **Sharaya**, 2nd Estrapade, 3rd Vosges

Older horses and inter-generational races
Grand Prix de Saint-Cloud: 1st **Diamond Shoal**, 2nd **Lancastrian**, 3rd **Zalataïa**
Grand Prix de Deauville: 1st **Zalataïa**, 2nd **Dom Pasquini**, 3rd **Orofino**
Prix du Prince d'Orange: 1st **Lovely Dancer**, 2nd Darly, 3rd Cost Control
Prix Foy: 1st **Time Charter**, 2nd **All Along**, 3rd Great Substence

Abroad
In England
Derby Stakes: 1st Teenoso, 2nd Carlingford Castle, 3rd Shearwalk
Oaks Stakes: 1st **Sun Princess**, 2nd Acclimatise, 3rd New Coins
King George VI and Queen Elizabeth Stakes: 1st **Time Charter**, 2nd **Diamond Shoal**, 3rd **Sun Princess**, 4th **Awaasif**, 5th **Lancastrian**, last Caerleon
St Leger: 1st **Sun Princess**, 2nd Esprit du Nord, 3rd Carlingford Castle

In Ireland
Joe McGrath Memorial Stakes: 1st **Stanerra**, 2nd Wassl, 3rd **General Holme**

In Germany
Grosser Preis von Baden: 1st **Diamond Shoal**, 2nd Abary, 3rd **Prima Voce**

The race

Dalby Jaguar broke fast but was soon overhauled by Sailor's Dance, who quickly opened up a clear lead on the outside. He led them a merry dance until capitulating on the approach to the turn-in, leaving Sun Princess in front from Diamond Shoal and, out wide, Time Charter.

Stanerra was also in the mix looking dangerous and, at the same time on the outside, Maurice Philipperon on Luth Enchantée was coming with a run.

Plenty had chances, but then the action changed dramatically as a path opened up for All Along on the inside – like the parting of the Red Sea – and she blitzed through in spectacular style making ground hand over fist.

After slipping through between Sun Princess and Stanerra, she took the lead and then extended the advantage to a decisive length in the final ten strides. The gallant Sun Princess just held off Luth Enchantée for second by a short neck, with Time Charter and Salmon Leap next, followed by the weakening Stanerra in sixth.

Post-race

Fillies filled the first four places and the winner wasn't done for the season. All Along crossed the Atlantic to win the Washington DC International, Canadian International, and Turf Classic, and in doing so picked up a huge bonus and the horse of the year title in France and the United States.

It was a first Arc for trainer Patrick Biancone, who'd been second with Bikala in 1981, and also for jockey Walter Swinburn, who'd come to fame when partnering Shergar to his scintillating Derby success two years before.

For Daniel Wildenstein it was a second Arc, nine years after the legendary Allez France in 1974. Wildenstein and Biancone wouldn't have to wait long to add to their scores.

Result

1983 Trusthouse Forte Prix de l'Arc de Triomphe
Longchamp. Sunday, 2 October 1983
Weights: 3yo c: 56kg, 3yo f: 54.5kg, 4yo+ c: 59kg, 4yo+ f: 57.5kg

1st All Along (FR)   4yo f 57.5kg **17/1**
by Targowice out of Agujita (Vieux Manoir). Daniel Wildenstein / Patrick Biancone / Walter Swinburn

2nd Sun Princess (IRE)   3yo f 54.5kg **6.8/1** (coupled with Lancastrian & Sailor's Dance)
by English Prince out of Sunny Valley (Val de Loir). Sir Michael Sobell / Dick Hern / Willie Carson

3rd Luth Enchantée (FR) 3yo f 54.5kg **17/1**
by Be My Guest out of Viole d'Amour (Luthier). Paul de Moussac / John Cunnington jnr / Maurice Philipperon

Runners: 26 (FR 14, GB 8, IRE 2, DEN 1, GER 1). Distances: 1, sh nk. Going: firm. Time: 2m 28.10s

Also ran: 4th **Time Charter** (IRE) 4yo f, 5th **Salmon Leap** (USA) 3yo c, 6th **Stanerra** (IRE) 5yo m, 7th **Lovely Dancer** (IRE) 3yo c, 8th **Zalataïa** (FR) 4yo f, 9th **Lancastrian** (IRE) 6yo h, 10th **Marie de Litz** (FR) 3yo f, 11th **Sagace** (FR) 3yo c, 12th **Diamond Shoal** (GB) 4yo c, 13th **Awaasif** (CAN) 4yo f, 14th **Seymour Hicks** (FR) 3yo c, 15th **Orofino** (GER) 5yo h, 16th **Prima Voce** (USA) 4yo c, 17th **General Holme** (USA) 4yo c, 18th **Guns of Navarone** (IRE) 3yo c, 19th **Escaline** (FR) 3yo f, 20th **Dalby Jaguar** (GB) 5yo h, 21st **Sharaya** (USA) 3yo f, 22nd **Welsh Term** (IRE) 4yo c, 23rd **Dom Pasquini** (FR) 3yo c, 24th **Acamas** (GB) 8yo h, 25th **Dzudo** (POL) 6yo h, 26th **Sailor's Dance** (GB) 3yo c.

Wildenstein again with Sagace

Deux-ton bleu first and third

Background and fancied horses

Northern Trick, sporting the colours of Stavros Niarchos, had established her reputation when coming with a great late run to win the Prix de Diane. After a break, she added the Prix de la Nonette and then took the scalp of Oaks-winner Circus Plume in the Prix Vermeille. Trained by François Boutin and ridden by the former Brian Asmussen, who had legally changed his forename to Cash, she headed the market at 2/1.

Robert Sangster's Sadler's Wells was 12/1 in some of the English books, but was coupled with Northern Trick on the PMU as Sangster and Niarchos had interests in both horses. That association has been renewed through their heirs – Coolmore and Flaxman Stables – with their joint interest in 2019 St James's Palace Stakes and Prix du Moulin de Longchamp-winner Circus Maximus.

Sadler's Wells had won the Irish 2000 Guineas before finishing second to Darshaan in the Prix du Jockey Club. He reverted to winning ways when taking the Eclipse Stakes and the Phoenix Champion Stakes, the latter being the new title for the race previously run as the Joe McGrath Memorial Stakes.

The main danger to Northern Trick appeared to be the three-strong Wildenstein battalion led by the title holder, All Along. After her successful campaign in North America the previous autumn, she had understandably been rested, and the Arc would be only her second appearance of the year and her first in Europe.

Sagace, who had been overwhelmed in last year's Arc, had started the new campaign with second place in the Prix Ganay before winning the Prix Foy. Castle Guard was being run to ensure a good gallop and together the threesome were grouped at 2.9/1.

Andre Fabre's Cariellor, the winner of the Prix Noailles, Prix Eugène Adam and Prix Niel, was next at 6.8/1, coupled with Fly Me and Garde Royale.

The English contingent consisted of the previous year's fourth and second, the old adversaries Time Charter and Sun Princess, alongside Rainbow Quest and his pacemaker Donzel.

Time Charter had recovered from a hip injury to convincingly beat Sun Princess in the Coronation Cup. However, they were both well-beaten in the King George VI and Queen Elizabeth Stakes.

Rainbow Quest, who had been third in the Prix du Jockey Club and second in the Irish Derby, arrived on the back of a good win in the Great Voltigeur Stakes, and in England he was the favourite for the Arc.

Germany had Abary, while Strawberry Road represented Australia. The trio from Ireland were the previously mentioned Sadler's Wells, Irish Oaks-winner Princess Pati, and Arctic Lord, who'd won the Blandford Stakes.

Betting
2/1 Northern Trick & Sadler's Wells (coupled), 2.9/1 All Along & Sagace & Castle Guard (all coupled), 6.8/1 Cariellor & Fly Me & Garde Royale (all coupled), 9/1 Time Charter, 11/1 Strawberry Road, 12/1 Rainbow Quest & Donzel (coupled), 15/1 Sun Princess, 17/1 Lovely Dancer, 25/1 BAR.

Three-year-old form lines
Prix du Jockey Club: 1st Darshaan, 2nd **Sadler's Wells**, 3rd **Rainbow Quest**
Grand Prix de Paris: 1st At Talaq, 2nd Woolskin, 3rd Spicy Story
Prix Niel: 1st **Cariellor**, 2nd **Long Mick**, 3rd Darshaan

Fillies only
Prix de Diane: 1st **Northern Trick**, 2nd Grise Mine, 3rd Pampa Bella
Prix Vermeille: 1st **Northern Trick**, 2nd Circus Plume, 3rd Treizième

Older horses and inter-generational races
Grand Prix de Saint-Cloud: 1st Teenoso, 2nd **Fly Me**, 3rd **Esprit du Nord**
La Coupe de Maisons-Laffitte: 1st **Estrapade**, 2nd Palace Music, 3rd Bob Back
Grand Prix de Deauville: 1st Ti King, 2nd **Margello**, 3rd Jupiter Island
Prix du Prince d'Orange: 1st **Lovely Dancer**, 2nd **Fly Me**, 3rd Darly
Prix Foy: 1st **Sagace**, 2nd **Castle Guard**, 3rd **Garde Royale**

Abroad
In England
Derby Stakes: 1st Secreto, 2nd El Gran Senor, 3rd Mighty Flutter
King George VI and Queen Elizabeth Stakes: 1st Teenoso, 2nd **Sadler's Wells**, 3rd Tolomeo, 4th **Time Charter**, 5th **Sun Princess**

In Ireland
Irish Derby: 1st El Gran Senor, 2nd **Rainbow Quest**, 3rd Dahar
Phoenix Champion Stakes (previously the Joe McGrath Memorial Stakes) 1st **Sadler's Wells**, 2nd Seattle Song, 3rd **Princess Pati**

In Germany
Grosser Preis von Baden: 1st **Strawberry Road**, 2nd **Esprit du Nord**, 3rd **Abary**

The race

Donzel was soon in the lead, cutting out the pace for Rainbow Quest. Castle Guard and Princess Pati were in close attendance, and the trio were three lengths clear as they started the descent.

The pacemakers came back to the pack on the *faux ligne droite* and Strawberry Road emerged as the new leader from Esprit du Nord, Sagace and Sadler's Wells. Sun Princess and Time Charter were mounting challenges on the outside while favourite Northern Trick was weaving through beaten horses.

Racing up the middle of the track, Sagace dominated Strawberry Road, and pulled clear, but Northern Trick was still coming and got to within a length and a quarter in the closing stages.

However, Sagace still had plenty in the locker and extended the advantage to two lengths at the line. The pair had opened up a massive six-length gap to last year's winner All Along, who, with the staying-on Esprit du Nord, engulfed Strawberry Road in the closing stages, all of them finishing in a bunch with sixth-placed Cariellor.

Post-race

Daniel Wildenstein had won in consecutive years and owned the third-placed horse as well. It was his third win in all after Allez France in 1974 and All Along last year, and a second for trainer Patrick Biancone.

For Yves Saint-Martin it was a fourth and record-equalling success as he drew level with Jacques Doyasbère and Freddy Head. He'd ridden all three of Wildenstein's winners as well as Sassafras in 1970, and nine years later would have the joy of seeing his son ride in the race.

Sagace would be back, but All Along wouldn't. She went to stud after finishing second in the Breeders' Cup Turf, the forerunner of which, the Washington DC International, she'd won the year before.

All Along didn't produce anything great at stud. However, the imaginatively named Along All did finish second in the Grand Critérium at Longchamp in 1988, before winning the Prix Greffulhe the following year.

Sadler's Wells, who'd finished eighth, did excel himself at stud, going on to become one of the most influential sires of the modern era.

Result

1984 Trusthouse Forte Prix de l'Arc de Triomphe
Longchamp. Sunday, 7 October 1984
Weights: 3yo c: 56kg, 3yo f: 54.5kg, 4yo+ c: 59kg, 4yo+ f: 57.5kg

1st Sagace (FR)   4yo c 59kg   **2.9/1** (coupled with All Along & Castle Guard)
by Luthier out of Seneca (Chaparral). Daniel Wildenstein / Patrick Biancone / Yves Saint-Martin

2nd Northern Trick (USA) 3yo f 54.5kg **2/1 fav** (coupled with Sadler's Wells)
by Northern Dancer out of Trick Chick (Prince John). Stavros Niarchos / François Boutin / Cash Asmussen

3rd All Along (FR)   5yo f 57.5kg **2.9/1** (coupled with Sagace & Castle Guard)
by Targowice out of Agujita (Vieux Manoir). Daniel Wildenstein / Patrick Biancone / Walter Swinburn

Runners: 22 (FR 13, GB 4, IRE 3, AUS 1, GER 1). Distances: 2, 6. Going: heavy. Time: 2m 39.10s

Also ran: 4th **Esprit du Nord** (USA) 4yo c, 5th **Strawberry Road** (AUS) 5yo h, 6th **Cariellor** (FR) 3yo c, 7th **Long Mick** (FR) 3yo c, 8th **Sadler's Wells** (USA) 3yo c, 9th **Sun Princess** (IRE) 4yo f, 10th **Lovely Dancer** (IRE) 4yo c, 11th **Time Charter** (IRE) 4yo f, 12th **Margello** (IRE) 6yo m, 13th **Garde Royale** (IRE) 4yo c, 14th **Princess Pati** (IRE) 3yo f, 15th **Estrapade** (USA) 4yo f, 16th **Arctic Lord** (IRE) 4yo c, 17th **Abary** (GER) 4yo c, 18th **Rainbow Quest** (USA) 3yo c, 19th **Balkan Prince** (FR) 3yo c, 20th **Fly Me** (FR) 4yo f, 21st **Castle Guard** (IRE) 4yo c, 22nd **Donzel** (USA) 3yo c.

Rainbow Quest wins it in the Stewards' Room

Last year's winner demoted

Background and fancied horses

Sagace was back and topped the market in his bid to join the ranks of the dual winners. In the early part of the year he'd won the Prix Ganay for Yves Saint-Martin and the Prix d'Ispahan for his replacement Eric Legrix. After a rest, he added the Prix Foy in preparation for the double bid. At 0.6/1 he was a warm order and went to post with Daniel Wildenstein's other two runners, the good stayer Balitou, and Heraldiste.

Up against the Wildenstein trio were three owned by the Aga Khan IV, Kozana, Sumayr and Shernazar. Kozana was the champion three-year-old filly in France, having won the Prix de Sandringham and Prix de Malleret. Most recently she'd finished second to Rousillon in the Prix du Moulin de Longchamp. She was joined by the Grand Prix de Paris-winner Sumayr, the mount of Saint-Martin, and Shernazar a half-brother to Shergar.

Shernazar, who was unbeaten as a four-year-old, which included accounting for the Derby-winner Slip Anchor in the September Stakes, was trained by Michael Stoute. There were three other English-trained runners: Sheikh Mohammed's Oaks-fourth Kiliniski; the dual Hardwicke Stakes-winner Jupiter Island; and the returning Rainbow Quest.

This year Rainbow Quest had won the Coronation Cup before finishing second to Pebbles in the Eclipse Stakes. He was then third home in the King George VI and Queen Elizabeth Stakes.

The last raider was Italy's Don Orazio, who'd won the Derby Italiano. Others to consider included Sheikh Maktoum Al Maktoum's Prix de Diane and Prix Vermeille runner-up Fitnah, and the Lester Piggott-ridden Galla Placidia, who'd been third in the Prix Vermeille.

Betting

0.6/1 Sagace & Balitou & Heraldiste (all coupled), 2.8/1 Kozana & Sumayr & Shernazar (all coupled), 7.1/1 Rainbow Quest, 12/1 Fitnah, 19/1 Galla Placidia, 32/1 BAR.

Three-year-old form lines
Prix du Jockey Club: 1st Mouktar, 2nd Air de Cour, 3rd Premier Rôle

Grand Prix de Paris: 1st **Sumayr**, 2nd Exactly Right, 3rd Montécito
Prix Niel: 1st Mouktar, 2nd Saint Estèphe, 3rd Premier Rôle

Fillies only
Prix de Diane: 1st Lypharita, 2nd **Fitnah**, 3rd Persona
Prix Vermeille: 1st Walensee, 2nd **Fitnah**, 3rd **Galla Placidia**

Older horses and inter-generational races
La Coupe de Maisons-Laffitte: 1st Palace Music, 2nd **Iades**, 3rd Devalois
Prix Foy: 1st **Sagace**, 2nd **Complice**, 3rd Castle Guard

Abroad
In England
Derby Stakes: 1st Slip Anchor, 2nd Law Society, 3rd Damister
Oaks Stakes: 1st Oh So Sharp, 2nd Triptych, 3rd Dubian, 4th **Kiliniski**
King George VI and Queen Elizabeth Stakes: 1st Petoski, 2nd Oh So Sharp, 3rd **Rainbow Quest**

The race

Heraldiste was fast away, leading Sagace, and they were followed by Iades and the grey Sumayr. The quartet remained prominent until the bottom of the hill, where Rainbow Quest made some ground on the outside.

On the false straight, Heraldiste moved off the rail to allow Sagace through on the inside. But in doing so set in motion a domino effect that resulted in a shortage of room for Rainbow Quest, Kozana and Don Orazio in particular.

The outcome was that Sagace led by two lengths entering the *dernière ligne droite*, with Rainbow Quest, who was back on an even keel, racing four wide and moving into second but simultaneously drifting in towards the rails.

The pair drew clear of the rest as Rainbow Quest tried to chase down Sagace. Pat Eddery drove Rainbow Quest closer and got to within a short neck but couldn't get by. Sagace was resolute and eventually prevailed by a full neck.

Two lengths back there was a similar battle royal for third, with Kozana just beating stable companion Sumayr, with Fitnah fifth and another Wildenstein inmate, Balitou, sixth.

The three Wildenstein horses paraded together in front of the stands receiving the plaudits of the crowd. But then, after a while the siren sounded as a stewards' inquiry was called.

The replays showed that Sagace had come off the rails, veering left as Legrix applied the whip with his right hand, making contact twice with Rainbow Quest who was alongside after himself drifting right. Pat Eddery never stopped riding and it looked as though the best horse had won.

The rules in force now would probably have resulted in the placings remaining unaltered. But the more stringent rules of the time led to Sagace being demoted in what looks now to be a relatively soft reversal.

Post-race

The Wildenstein hat-trick had been foiled in what is still one of the most discussed finishes to the Arc. Although no one knew at the time, it was the start of a hat-trick that would be completed. The bottom line, though, was that Rainbow Quest had become the first English-trained winner since Rheingold in 1973.

It was the first Arc success for Khalid Abdullah and it wouldn't be his last. Trainer Jeremy Tree added the greatest race in Europe to his four English Classics, and for Pat Eddery it was a second victory after Detroit in 1980.

The winner and second were both retired and were successful at stud. Rainbow Quest produced horses like Saumarez, who we shall meet soon, as well as Derby-winner Quest for Fame, Spectrum, Croco Rouge, Nedawi, and Millenary.

Sagace also sired plenty of winners, including the 1993 Prix d'Ispahan and Breeders' Cup Classic-winner Arcangues. He was also responsible for the useful filly Saganeca, who ran in the Arc but didn't do as well as her son, Sagamix.

It also turned out to be the last Arc ride for Lester Piggott, who trained for a while before spending a brief stay in one of the Queen's less salubrious properties for tax evasion. Putting that behind him, he came out of retirement to ride Royal Academy to a famous victory in the 1990 Breeders' Cup Mile.

Royal Academy was trained by his old boss Vincent O'Brien for whom he'd ridden Alleged to win the Arc in 1977 and 1978, adding to Rheingold's win in 1973.

Result

1985 Trusthouse Forte Prix de l'Arc de Triomphe
Longchamp. Sunday, 6 October 1985
Weights: 3yo c: 56kg, 3yo f: 54.5kg, 4yo+ c: 59kg, 4yo+ f: 57.5kg

1st Rainbow Quest (USA) 4yo c 59k 7.1/1
by Blushing Groom out of I Will Follow (Herbager). Khalid Abdullah / Jeremy Tree / Pat Eddery

2nd Sagace (FR) 5yo h 59k 0.6/1 fav (coupled with Balitou & Heraldiste)
by Luthier out of Seneca (Chaparral). Daniel Wildenstein / Patrick Biancone / Eric Legrix

3rd Kozana (GB) 3yo f 54.5k 2.8/1 (coupled with Sumayr & Shernazar)
by Kris out of Koblenza (Hugh Lupus). HH Aga Khan IV / Alain de Royer-Dupré / Alain Lequeux

Runners: 15 (FR 10, GB 4, ITY 1). Distances: nk, 2. Going: Good to firm.
Time: 2m 29.50s

Stewards' Inquiry: Sagace finished first but was disqualified and placed second after being adjudged to have caused interference to Rainbow Quest

Also ran: 4th **Sumayr** (IRE) 3yo c, 5th **Fitnah** (GB) 3yo f, 6th **Balitou** (FR) 6yo h, 7th **Don Orazio** (GB) 3yo c, 8th **Jupiter Island** (GB) 6yo c, 9th **Galla Placidia** (FR) 3yo f, 10th **Iades** (FR) 3yo c, 11th **Kiliniski** (GB) 3yo f, 12th **Badinage** (FR) 5yo m, 13th **Shernazar** (IRE) 4yo c, 14th **Complice** (FR) 4yo c, 15th **Heraldiste** (USA) 3yo c.

1986
Dancing Brave – high, wide and handsome

Eddery again as Derby-second produces
a tremendous finishing burst

Background and fancied horses

Last year's winning owner and jockey had, if anything, a better candidate this time. Dancing Brave had won the 2000 Guineas in brilliant style but then suffered a famous defeat in the Derby. Finding himself out of position coming down the hill, he almost achieved the impossible when coming from miles back in the straight to nearly, but not quite, catch the Aga Khan IV's Shahrastani.

There was plenty of discussion on the ride Greville Starkey had given him, but next time at Sandown the pair gained some recompense when winning the Eclipse Stakes with consummate ease. Starkey, though, was injured for Dancing Brave's next appointment, the King George VI and Queen Elizabeth Stakes, and Pat Eddery took over on top.

At Ascot, Dancing Brave gained revenge on Shahrastani – who in the interim had won the Irish Derby – beating him into fifth place with another Aga Khan horse, Shardari, giving him most to do in the end. After a break and a win in the Select Stakes, with Eddery now confirmed as his regular partner, Dancing Brave was 1.1/1 to add the Arc.

The home team's leading candidate was Bering at 2.8/1. Criquette Head's son of Arctic Tern was sent off at odds-on when running out an impressive winner of the Prix du Jockey Club. He'd also had a mid-season break before winning the Prix Niel in facile fashion.

Last year's Deutsches Derby-winner, Acatenango, was the most fancied older horse after taking the Grand Prix de Saint-Cloud and Grosser Preis von Baden. The 3.8/1-shot was followed in the betting by a quartet of horses representing the Aga Khan on 4.5/1. They were the aforementioned Shahrastani and Shardari, along with Prix Vermeille-winner Darara and Dihistan, who'd won the Hardwicke Stakes and September Stakes.

The only other horse under 20/1 was André Fabre's Coronation Cup-winner Saint Estèphe, who'd finished runner-up in both the Grand Prix de Saint-Cloud and Prix du Prince d'Orange. Daniel Wildenstein's Mersey, the winner of the Prix Royal-Oak last year and of the Prix Foy this, was 21/1 and it was 64/1 bar.

In addition to Germany's Acatenango and England's Dancing Brave, Shahrastani, Shardari, and Dihistan, the remainder of the raiders were last year's St Leger-fourth, Nemain, who'd won two runnings of the Blandford Stakes, representing Ireland, and Chile's Maria Fumata. The latter had won the 1985 Chilean version of The Oaks as well as finishing second in the equivalents of the 1000 Guineas and Derby.

Betting

1.1/1 Dancing Brave, 2.8/1 Bering, 3.8/1 Acatenango, 4.5/1 Shahrastani & Shardari & Darara & Dihistan (all coupled), 16/1 Saint Estèphe, 21/1 Mersey, 64/1 BAR.

Three-year-old form lines
Prix du Jockey Club: 1st **Bering**, 2nd Altayan, 3rd Bakharoff
Grand Prix de Paris: 1st Swink, 2nd War Hero, 3rd Silver Word
Prix Niel: 1st **Bering**, 2nd Malakim, 3rd Arctic Blast

Fillies only
Prix de Diane: 1st Lacovia, 2nd Secret Form, 3rd Galunpe
Prix Vermeille: 1st **Darara**, 2nd Reloy, 3rd Lacovia

Older horses and inter-generational races
Grand Prix de Saint-Cloud: 1st **Acatenango**, 2nd **Saint Estèphe**, 3rd Noble Fighter
Grand Prix de Deauville: 1st **Baby Turk**, 2nd Faburola, 3rd Night Line
Prix du Prince d'Orange: 1st Fitnah, 2nd **Saint Estèphe**, 3rd Fast Topaze
Prix Foy: 1st **Mersey**, 2nd **Sirius Symboli**, 3rd Antheus

Abroad
In England
Derby Stakes: 1st **Shahrastani**, 2nd **Dancing Brave**, 3rd Mashkour
King George VI and Queen Elizabeth Stakes: 1st **Dancing Brave**, 2nd **Shardari**, 3rd **Triptych**, 4th **Shahrastani**, 5th **Dihistan**

In Ireland
Irish Derby: 1st **Shahrastani**, 2nd Bonhomie, 3rd Bakharoff
Phoenix Champion Stakes: 1st Park Express, 2nd Double Bed, 3rd **Triptych**

In Germany
Grosser Preis von Baden: 1st **Acatenango**, 2nd St Hilarion, 3rd Daun

The race

Darara and Acatenango took turns in the lead on the back straight, before Baby Turk took over going down the hill. As the field fanned out into the straight he still just led from Nemain and Acatenango on the inside, with the Aga Khan quartet mid-track, and Bering widest of all being slipstreamed by Dancing Brave.

With 400 metres to run, the front rank was eight-strong with Shahrastani and Bering seemingly just going the best as they closed in on the leaders. That was until Dancing Brave from 12th place took off, producing an extended finishing burst in the centre of the track that carried him firstly past Shadari, who had led fleetingly at the 300-metre mark.

Dancing Brave then overtook Shahrastani, carrying on to master Bering and secure a memorable victory by one and a half lengths. At the line he was still going away, despite Eddery having stopped riding.

Bering was an honourable second with a further length to the 1985 Irish 2000 Guineas-winner Triptych, who'd been sent off at a long price. She'd been blocked several times but, like the winner, had made up a tremendous amount of late ground to take a step on the podium. They were followed by three of the Aga Khan's battalion, namely Shahrastani, Shardari and Darara.

Post-race

The favourite had done it in style, breaking the course record in the process, to become a second winner in a row for Khalid Abdullah and Pat Eddery, with Eddery taking his tally to three in all. Sussex-trainer Guy Harwood, who'd been third with Ela-Mana-Mou in 1980, added the Arc to his illustrious *palmarès*.

Dancing Brave ran one more time when fourth to Manila in the Breeders' Cup Turf. He didn't produce his trademark finishing burst, perhaps due to the eye injury he received mid-race when hit by a clod of mud thrown up by one of the other runners.

At stud he produced several talented individuals including Derby-winner Commander in Chief and White Muzzle, who will feature later in our story.

Timeform rated Dancing Brave as the fourth best Arc winner after Sea Bird, Ribot, and Mill Reef, and he remains equal fourth best at the time of writing.

Result

1986 Trusthouse Forte Prix de l'Arc de Triomphe

Longchamp. Sunday, 5 October 1986
Weights: 3yo c: 56kg, 3yo f: 54.5kg, 4yo+ c: 59kg, 4yo+ f: 57.5kg

1st Dancing Brave (USA)   3yo c   56kg   **1.1/1 fav**
by Lyphard out of Navajo Princess (Drone). Khalid Abdullah / Guy Harwood / Pat Eddery

2nd Bering (GB)   3yo c   56kg   **2.8/1**
by Arctic Tern out of Beaune (Lyphard). Ghislaine Head / Christiane Head / Gary W. Moore

3rd Triptych (USA)   4yo f   57.5kg   **64/1**
by Riverman out of Trillion (Hail to Reason). Alan Clore / Patrick Biancone / Angel Cordero jnr

Runners: 15 (FR 8, GB 4, CHI 1, GER 1, IRE 1). Distances: 1½, 1. Going: firm. Time: 2m 27.70s

Also ran: 4th **Shahrastani** (USA) 3yo c, 5th **Shardari** (IRE) 4yo c, 6th **Darara** (GB) 3yo f, 7th **Acatenango** (GER) 4yo c, 8th **Mersey** (GB) 4yo f, 9th **Saint Estèphe** (FR) 4yo c, 10th **Dihistan** (IRE) 4yo c, 11th **Iades** (FR) 4yo c, 12th **Baby Turk** (IRE) 4yo c, 13th **Nemain** (USA) 4yo c, 14th **Sirius Symboli** (JPN) 4yo c, 15th **Maria Fumata** (CHI) 4yo f.

1987
Trempolino leads home three Ts
Eddery completes hat-trick

Background and fancied horses

The Henry Cecil-trained Reference Point had been the season's headline act in England. He missed the 2000 Guineas with a sinus problem but was installed as favourite for the Derby after winning the Dante Stakes.

At Epsom he carried the yellow with black spots of Louis Freedman to an impressive victory and in a lightning-quick time. Reference Point then came off second best to the four-year-old Mtoto in a tremendous duel for the Eclipse Stakes, before winning the King George VI and Queen Elizabeth Stakes.

Back against his own generation, he added the Great Voltigeur Stakes – despite pulling a muscle on the falsely soft surface – and the St Leger. Reference Point was having a fantastically successful, albeit long season, and was odds-on to win the Arc.

The best of the home team appeared to be last year's flying-third Triptych, who had gone on to take the Champion Stakes. This term the 4.8/1-chance had won the Prix Ganay, the Coronation Cup, the International Stakes (formerly the Benson & Hedges Gold Cup) and the Phoenix Champion Stakes. But she had been beaten by Reference Point in the Eclipse Stakes and King George VI and Queen Elizabeth Stakes.

The Aga Khan IV had three runners, all trained by Alain de Royer-Dupré. Yves Saint-Martin was aboard Natroun, who'd got up in the last strides to beat Trempolino in the Prix du Jockey Club. After a break, the latter took revenge on the son of Akarad in the Prix Niel which turned into a sprint after a slow early pace. Joined by Tabayaan, who'd won La Coupe de Maisons-Laffitte, and Grand Prix d'Évry-winner Sharaniya, who was to act as pacemaker, the Aga Khan trio were grouped together on 5.3/1.

The previously mentioned Eclipse Stakes-victor Mtoto, who'd also won the Prince of Wales's Stakes at Royal Ascot, was next at 6.3/1. Then came the Tony Clout-trained Groom Dancer at 10/1. He'd won the Prix Lupin and Prix de Guiche in May but could only manage seventh in the Derby. However, he'd been back in winning form since, including taking the Prix du Prince d'Orange.

Pat Eddery's mount, Trempolino, had finished second in the Prix Lupin before being touched off in the Prix du Jockey Club. Afterwards he came third in the Grand Prix de Paris – which was run over 2,000 metres instead of 3,000 metres for the first time. As mentioned above, Trempolino had most recently outpointed his rivals in the Prix Niel when producing the best acceleration off a slow pace.

The challengers from outside of France were Reference Point, Mtoto, and Hardwicke Stakes-winner Orban for England, and Italy's Grosser Preis von Baden-winner Tony Bin.

Betting
0.7/1 Reference Point, 4.8/1 Triptych, 5.3/1 Tabayaan & Natroun & Sharaniya (all coupled), 6.3/1 Mtoto, 10/1 Groom Dancer, 20/1 Trempolino, 25/1 BAR.

Three-year-old form lines
Prix du Jockey Club: 1st **Natroun**, 2nd **Trempolino**, 3rd Naheez
Grand Prix de Paris: 1st Risk Me, 2nd Seattle Dancer, 3rd **Trempolino**
Prix Niel: 1st **Trempolino**, 2nd Video Rock, 3rd Saint Andrews, DH4th **Natroun**, DH4th Boyatino

Fillies only
Prix de Diane: 1st Indian Skimmer, 2nd Miesque, 3rd Masmouda
Prix Vermeille: 1st Bint Pasha, 2nd Three Tails, 3rd Something True

Older horses and inter-generational races
Grand Prix de Saint-Cloud: 1st Moon Madness, 2nd **Tony Bin**, 3rd Grand Pavois
La Coupe de Maisons-Laffitte: 1st **Tabayaan**, 2nd Trokhos, 3rd Mill Native
Prix du Prince d'Orange: 1st **Groom Dancer**, 2nd Sadjiyd, 3rd Luth Dancer

Abroad
In England
Derby Stakes: 1st **Reference Point**, 2nd Most Welcome, 3rd Bellotto, 7th **Groom Dancer**
King George VI and Queen Elizabeth Stakes: 1st **Reference Point**, 2nd Celestial Storm, 3rd **Triptych**, 5th **Tony Bin**, 6th **Acatenango**
St Leger: 1st **Reference Point**, 2nd Mountain Kingdom, 3rd Dry Dock

In Ireland
Phoenix Champion Stakes: 1st **Triptych**, 2nd Entitled, 3rd Cockney Lass

In Germany
Grosser Preis von Baden: 1st **Acatenango**, 2nd Moon Madness, 3rd Winwood

In Italy
Grosser Preis von Baden: 1st **Tony Bin**, 2nd Our Eliaso, 3rd Jung

The race
Reference Point broke sharply but was harried by Sharaniya all the way up the back straight. Down the hill, the pair were two to three lengths clear of

Orban and Natroun, with the field stretching back to Trempolino and Tony Bin, in last and last but one respectively.

Entering the home run, a multitude of challengers were ranged across the track ready to tackle Reference Point, from Triptych on the inside to Mtoto on the wide outside.

In a replica of last year's running, it was Pat Eddery who coaxed the best turn of speed from his mount. Trempolino simply took off, slicing through the field to open up daylight between himself and the other runners.

The flashy chestnut with a white face and four white legs, kept pouring on the speed while Tony Bin, who'd also been to the rear, followed him through to take a clear second. Tony Bin closed the gap marginally but was never going to get on terms with Trempolino, who stormed home by two lengths with three to Triptych who was third for the second year in a row.

She was just a head to the good over Mtoto, with Tabayaan and Orban three lengths and two and a half further back. The favourite, Reference Point, who finished back in eighth, was later found to have an abscess on one of his feet. However, he'd been taken on all the way, which may have been more of a factor.

Post-race

Trempolino in the easily recognisable bumble bee colours of Paul de Moussac, who had been third with Luth Enchantée in 1983, had destroyed the opposition and led home a one-two-three of horses whose names all began with the letter 'T'.

During the build-up to the Arc, de Moussac had sold half a share in the horse to the American businessman and owner of the Los Angeles Kings ice hockey team, Bruce McNall, of whom we shall hear more.

Pat Eddery equalled the record of four winners held by Jacques Doyasbère, Freddy Head and Yves Saint-Martin, but became the first to complete a hat-trick after Rainbow Quest and Dancing Brave in the preceding years. For Saint-Martin himself, it was his last ride in the Arc but he would be back in another capacity in 1993.

It was the first win for trainer André Fabre. He'd been a top jump jockey and won the Grand Steeple-Chase de Paris on Corps à Corps in 1977. Soon after he started training and in his new capacity won the same race four times in a row between 1980 and 1983. Having turned his attention to the flat, he was about to become champion trainer – a title he would hold for the next 21 years.

Trempolino ran once more, when second to Theatrical in the Breeders' Cup Turf, before going to stud. His best progeny include 1994 Champion

Stakes-winner Dernier Empereur and Valixir, who won the Prix d'Ispahan and Queen Anne Stakes in 2005.

Result
1987 Trusthouse Forte Prix de l'Arc de Triomphe
Longchamp. Sunday, 4 October 1987
Weights: 3yo c: 56kg, 3yo f: 54.5kg, 4yo+ c: 59kg, 4yo+ f: 57.5kg

1st Trempolino (USA)　　3yo c　56kg　**20/1**
by Sharpen Up out of Trephine (Viceregal). Paul de Moussac & Bruce McNall / André Fabre / Pat Eddery

2nd Tony Bin (GB)　　4yo c　59kg　**29/1**
by Kampala out of Severn Bridge (Hornbeam). Veronica del Bono Caucci / Luigi Camici / Cash Asmussen

3rd Triptych (USA)　　5yo f　57.5kg　**4.8/1**
by Riverman out of Trillion (Hail to Reason). Alan Clore / Patrick Biancone / Tony Cruz

Runners: 11 (FR 7, GB 3, ITY 1). Distances: 2, 3. Going: firm. Time: 2m 26.30s

Also ran: 4th **Mtoto** (GB) 4yo c, 5th **Tabayaan** (FR) 3yo c, 6th **Orban** (USA) 4yo c, 7th **Teresa** (SPA) 3yo f, 8th **Reference Point** (GB) 3yo c, 9th **Natroun** (FR) 3yo c, 10th **Sharaniya** (USA) 4yo f, 11th **Groom Dancer** (USA) 3yo c.

Tony Bin goes one place better

First Italian-trained winner since 1961

Background and fancied horses

If last year's fourth, Mtoto, was good in 1987, he was brilliant in 1988. The son of Busted, who was now five, won the Prince of Wales's Stakes and Eclipse Stakes, both for the second time, and then added the King George VI and Queen Elizabeth Stakes beating Unfuwain and Tony Bin.

After a break, Sheikh Ahmed Al Maktoum's charge returned in the Select Stakes at Goodwood, where he accelerated when asked to land the odds as a 1/4-shot should. He was odds against in the more exalted company he faced in the Arc, but still a warm order at 1.5/1.

The Aga Khan IV's desire to win as many runnings of the Prix de l'Arc de Triomphe as possible was well known. As a major shareholder of the new sponsor of the race, the Italian Ciga Hotels group, that aspiration was further strengthened.

His team of three was spearheaded by Kahyasi, who'd accounted for Glacial Storm and Unfuwain in the Derby. He doubled up in the Irish version, where Patrick Biancone's Prix du Jockey Club-winner, Hours After, came home ninth after being hampered.

On his return from a break, Kahyasi met with defeat, going down by a neck to the Grand Prix de Paris-winner Fijar Tango in a bunch finish for the Prix Niel. With Roushayd and Taboushkan in attendance to ensure a decent gallop, the trio were grouped on 3.8/1.

After finishing third in the 1000 Guineas, the Henry Cecil-trained Diminuendo showed that middle distances were her forte by racking up successes in three versions of the Oaks – the original, the Irish and the Yorkshire. In her last outing before the Arc she finished runner-up to the durable Minster Son in the St Leger.

Sheikh Mohammed also ran Sarhoob, who was under the care of André Fabre. She'd won the Prix Eugène Adam and last time out was involved in the finish of the Prix Niel. The fillies in maroon and white were coupled at 7.3/1.

Indian Rose, who'd finished fourth in The Oaks and won the Prix Vermeille, was 8/1 with Pat Eddery in the plate looking for a four-timer. The previously mentioned Fijar Tango, trained by Georges Mikhalidès, was next at 14/1 along with last year's runner-up Tony Bin.

The latter had won two Group 1s in Italy this season under Pat Eddery; the Premio Presidente della Republica and the Gran Premio di Milano. On his only trip to England he was a respectable third in the King George VI and Queen Elizabeth Stakes. Most recently, he'd won the Premio Federico Tesio back in his native land with John Reid taking over on top for the first time.

The other horses under 20/1 were: Hamdan Al Maktoum's Princess of Wales's Stakes-winner Unfuwain and his pacemaker Polemos; Stavros Niarchos's Dark Lomond coupled with Robert Sangster's Glacial Storm, who'd made the frame in both the English and Irish Derbys.

Triptych, who'd been third for the last two years, had won the Coronation Cup and Prix du Prince d'Orange this season and was 21/1, the same price as the Grand Prix de Saint-Cloud victor Village Star, and it was 50/1 bar.

In addition to the seven English-trained horses mentioned above, there was also the Prix du Jockey Club-third, Emmson. The Irish St Leger-winner Dark Lomond represented the emerald isle, and of course Tony Bin was back again for Italy.

Betting
1.5/1 Mtoto, 3.8/1 Kahyasi & Roushayd & Taboushkan (all coupled), 7.3/1 Diminuendo & Sarhoob (coupled), 8/1 Indian Rose, 14/1 Fijar Tango, 14/1 Tony Bin, 17/1 Unfuwain & Polemos (coupled), 18/1 Dark Lomond & Glacial Storm (coupled), 21/1 Triptych, 21/1 Village Star, 50/1 BAR.

Three-year-old form lines
Prix du Jockey Club: 1st **Hours After**, 2nd Ghost Buster's, 3rd **Emmson**, 6th **Waki River**, 9th **Soft Machine**
Grand Prix de Paris: 1st **Fijar Tango**, 2nd Pasakos, 3rd Welkin, 7th **Soft Machine**
Prix Niel: 1st **Fijar Tango**, 2nd **Kahyasi**, 3rd **Sarhoob**, 5th **Waki River**, 10th **Hours After**, 12th **Soft Machine**

Fillies only
Prix de Diane: 1st Resless Kara, 2nd Rivière d'Or, 3rd Raintree Renegade, 5th **Light the Lights**
Prix Vermeille: 1st **Indian Rose**, 2nd Sudden Love, 3rd **Light the Lights**

Older horses and inter-generational races
Grand Prix de Saint-Cloud: 1st **Village Star**, 2nd Saint Andrews, 3rd Frankly Perfect 5th **Boyatino**
Grand Prix de Deauville: 1st Ibn Bey, 2nd Sudden Victory, 3rd **Luth Dancer**
Prix du Prince d'Orange: 1st **Triptych**, 2nd Masmouda, 3rd Splendid Day
Prix Foy: 1st Beeshi, 2nd **Luth Dance**, 3rd **Village Star**, 5th Saint Andrews

Abroad

In England

Derby Stakes: 1st **Kahyasi**, 2nd **Glacial Storm**, 3rd Doyoun, 7th **Unfuwain**

Oaks Stakes: 1st **Diminuendo**, 2nd Sudden Love, 3rd Animatrice, 4th **Indian Rose**

King George VI and Queen Elizabeth Stakes: 1st **Mtoto**, 2nd **Unfuwain**, 3rd **Tony Bin**, 7th **Soft Machine**, 8th **Glacial Storm**

St Leger: 1st Minster Son, 2nd **Diminuendo**, 3rd Sheriff's Star

In Ireland

Irish Derby: 1st **Kahyasi**, 2nd Insan, 3rd **Glacial Storm**, 9th **Hours After**

Phoenix Champion Stakes: 1st Indian Skimmer, 2nd Shady Heights, 3rd **Triptych**

In Germany

Grosser Preis von Baden: 1st Carroll House, 2nd Helikon, 3rd **Boyatino**

In Italy

Gran Premio di Milano: 1st **Tony Bin**, 2nd Tisserand, 3rd Duca Di Busted

The race

Taboushkan set a fast early pace before Polemos took over on the downhill section. Approaching the straight, Tony Ives kicked Emmson to the lead and was followed through by Frankly Perfect and Boyatino.

The three outsiders were just ahead of the pack in which Diminuendo and Unfuwain were to the fore. Behind them, Tony Bin was looking for racing room a length ahead of Mtoto.

Boyatino was finishing to some effect, and at the 200-metre pole he ranged alongside Emmson with Unfuwain now moving into third. However, on the outside Tony Bin was now free and in full flight.

John Reid's mount went from fifth to first in eight strides, but behind him Mtoto and Village Star were finishing even faster. In the closing stages, Mtoto cut the deficit between himself and the leader from three lengths to a long neck, but Tony Bin had just done enough to hold on and win the crown.

There was a further length back to Boyatino, who just got the better of Unfuwain and Village Star in a three-way photo for third. Just behind them Kahyasi was sixth. Further back, Triptych came home in 13th, ten places further down the field than in the previous two years.

Post-race

Tony Bin had run a tremendous race to become the first Italian-trained winner since Molvedo in 1961, and the sixth in all after Ortello, Crapom and Ribot twice.

Molvedo and Ribot had both been ridden by Enrico Camici, and now Tony Bin had won for his cousin, the trainer Luigi. Tony Bin ran in the name of Veronica del Bono Caucci, the wife of the entrepreneur Luciano Caucci, who, when president of the Perugia football team, had been very successful but extremely controversial.

This would be the only Arc win for jockey John Reid, although he would be placed twice more, and many of his best career successes were still to come, including victories in four English Classics.

Tony Bin ran twice more, firstly in the Gran Premio Del Jockey Club, where he finished second when ridden by Gianfranco Dettori – Frankie's father – and then in the Japan Cup, where he was fifth to Pay The Butler.

Purchased by Zenya Yoshida, he stood in Japan and produced several champions, including Winning Ticket and Jungle Pocket, who both won the Tokyo Yushun (Japanese Derby). Jungle Pocket also won the Japan Cup.

In addition, Tony Bin produced the Japanese Oaks winners Vega and Air Groove, and was the grandsire on the dam's side of Heart's Cry, the first horse to beat Deep Impact. The last-named will feature in our narrative in due course.

Result

1988 Ciga Prix de l'Arc de Triomphe
Longchamp. Sunday, 2 October 1988
Weights: 3yo c: 56kg, 3yo f: 54.5kg, 4yo+ c: 59kg, 4yo+ f: 57.5kg

1st Tony Bin (IRE)   5yo h   59kg   **14/1**
by Kampala out of Severn Bridge (Hornbeam). Veronica del Bono Caucci / Luigi Camici / John Reid

2nd Mtoto (GB)   5yo h   59kg   **1.5/1 fav**
by Busted out of Amazer (Mincio). Sheikh Ahmed Al Maktoum / Alec Stewart / Michael Roberts

3rd Boyatino (FR)   4yo c   57.5kg   **138/1**
by Concertino out of Boyarina (Beaugency). Georges Blizniansky / Jean Lesbordes / Maurice Philipperon

Runners: 24 (FR 14, GB 8, IRE 1, ITY 1). Distances: nk, 1. Going: firm. Time: 2m 27.30s

Also ran: 4th **Unfuwain** (USA) 3yo c, 5th **Village Star** (FR) 5yo h, 6th **Kahyasi** (IRE) 3yo c, 7th **Fijar Tango** (FR) 3yo c, 8th **Emmson** (IRE) 3yo c, 9th **Light the Lights** (FR) 3yo f, 10th **Diminuendo** (USA) 3yo f, 11th **Dark Lomond** (IRE) 3yo f, 12th **Sarhoob** (USA) 3yo c, 13th **Triptych** (USA) 6yo m, 14th **Frankly Perfect** (USA) 3yo c, 15th **Glacial Storm** (USA) 3yo c, 16th **Hours After** (USA) 3yo c, 17th **Indian Rose** (FR) 3yo f, 18th **Waki River** (FR) 3yo c, 19th **Luth Dancer** (USA) 4yo c, 20th **Roushayd** (IRE) 4yo c, 21st **Lesotho** (USA) 5yo c, 22nd **Soft Machine** (USA) 3yo c, 23rd **Polemos** (IRE) 4yo c, 24th **Taboushkan** (IRE) 4yo c.

Carroll House collects
for Jarvis and Balzarini

First winner for Mick Kinane

Background and fancied horses

The lightly raced In The Wings headed the market, on what was to be only the fourth career outing for the three-year-old. Sheikh Ahmed Al Maktoum's son of Sadler's Wells had won over six and then seven furlongs in June and August 1988, but then wasn't seen again for 13 months.

However, his performance when returning to action in the Prix du Prince d'Orange, where he beat the useful yardstick Mansonnien and last year's Prix de l'Opera-winner Athyka, was loaded with potential and caught the imagination of punters who backed him into 3.8/1.

Saint Andrews, who himself beat Mansonnien when winning the Prix Ganay for the second time, was running for Suzy Volterra who'd won with Topyo in 1967. He had some good form in the book but had virtually refused to race in the Prix Foy, being pulled up after only 200 metres. Trained by Jean-Marie Béguigné he was coupled at 5/1 with the trainer's own Young Mother who had won the Prix Vermeille.

Cacoethes, at 5/1, was the shortest of the six English-trained runners. After finishing third in the Derby he'd won the King Edward VII Stakes at Royal Ascot. He was then beaten again by Nashwan in the King George VI and Queen Elizabeth Stakes and was also second, this time to Ile De Chypre in the Juddmonte International Stakes before taking a break.

The Aga Khan IV ran two high-class fillies in the form of Aliysa and Behera. The former won The Oaks – although later she tested positive for a metabolite of the banned substance camphor – before finishing runner-up to Alydaress in the Irish version when odds-on. She then enjoyed a spell of downtime, unaware of the controversy surrounding her, before lining up at Longchamp.

Behera had won the Group 1 Prix Saint-Alary on her second appearance in May, and after a break was third to Sierra Roberta in the Prix de la Nonette at the start of September. Together the talented fillies were available at 6/1.

Daniel Wildenstein's Prix Foy-winner, Star Lift, was half a point longer, followed by Golden Pheasant at 10/1, who had finished ahead of Star Lift in the Grand Prix de Saint-Cloud. He'd then produced a power-packed finish in the Prix Niel to beat French Glory and the Derby-winner Nashwan.

The Prix de la Nonette-winner and Prix Vermeille-second, Sierra Roberta, was one of two entrants running for Paul de Moussac who were coupled at 15/1. The other was Harvest Time, who had won his first two outings, including beating Golden Pheasant and French Glory in the Prix du Lys. However, since then he'd finished last in the Prix Maurice de Nieuil in July. Khalid Abdullah's French Glory, who has already been mentioned, was a point longer at 16/1.

Luca Cumani's Legal Case, who'd only been beaten by one horse in his four runs, which included a four-length win in the Select Stakes at Goodwood, was 19/1. Also 19/1 was last year's Grosser Preis von Baden-winner, Carroll House, who'd been fifth to Nashwan in the King George VI and Queen Elizabeth Stakes and was arriving on the back of a win in the Phoenix Champion Stakes.

As well as Cacoethes, Aliysa, Carroll House, and Legal Case, England also had Clive Brittain's King George VI and Queen Elizabeth Stakes-third, Top Class, and the winner of La Coupe de Maisons-Laffitte, Petrullo, who'd finished third in the Phoenix Champion Stakes. Ironically, the filly called Britannia was running for Germany; she'd won the 1988 Deutsches St Leger and had come home fourth in this year's Grosser Preis von Baden.

Betting
3.8/1 In The Wings, 5/1 Saint Andrews & Young Mother (coupled), 5/1 Cacoethes, 6/1 Aliysa & Behera (coupled), 6.5/1 Star Lift, 10/1 Golden Pheasant, 15/1 Sierra Roberta & Harvest Time (coupled), 16/1 French Glory, 19/1 Carroll House, 19/1 Legal Case, 24/1 BAR.

Three-year-old form lines
Prix du Jockey Club: 1st Old Vic, 2nd Dancehall, 3rd Galetto, 4th **Norberto**
Grand Prix de Paris: 1st Dancehall, 2nd **Norberto**, 3rd Creator
Prix Niel: 1st **Golden Pheasant**, 2nd **French Glory**, 3rd Nashwan

Fillies only
Prix de Diane: 1st Lady in Silver, 2nd Louveterie, 3rd Premier Amour
Prix Vermeille: 1st **Young Mother**, 2nd **Sierra Roberta**, 3rd Colorado Dancer

Older horses and inter-generational races
Grand Prix de Saint-Cloud: 1st Sheriff's Star, 2nd **Golden Pheasant**, 3rd Boyatino, 4th **Star Lift**
La Coupe de Maisons-Laffitte: 1st **Petrullo**, 2nd Silver Lane, 3rd Hello Calder
Grand Prix de Deauville: 1st Borromini, 2nd **Norberto**, 3rd Apache
Prix du Prince d'Orange: 1st **In The Wings**, 2nd **Mansonnien**, 3rd Athyka
Prix Foy: 1st **Star Lift**, 2nd **Robore**, 3rd Apache, PU **Saint Andrews**

Abroad

In England

Derby Stakes: 1st Nashwan, 2nd Terimon, 3rd **Cacoethes**

Oaks Stakes: 1st Snow Bride, 2nd Roseate Tern, 3rd Mamaluna, disq **Aliysa** (1st ptp subsequently disqualified after testing positive for banned substance)

King George VI and Queen Elizabeth Stakes: 1st Nashwan, 2nd **Cacoethes**, 3rd **Top Class**, 5th **Carroll House**

In Ireland

Phoenix Champion Stakes: 1st **Carroll House**, 2nd Citidancer, 3rd **Petrullo**

In Germany

Grosser Preis von Baden: 1st Mondrian, 2nd Per Quod, 3rd Summer Trip, 4th **Britannia**

The race

Henri-Alex Pantall's Harvest Time was the first to show from Star Lift, Behera, and Saint Andrews, with the favourite In The Wings in rear. Saint Andrews moved into second on the descent and passed Harvest Time approaching the straight, while on the outside Carroll House made several places.

At the start of the *dernière ligne droite* Saint Andrews opened up a two-length advantage over Behera, who'd moved into second. But Carroll House was still coming and after passing Behera at the 400-metre pole, he drifted towards the inner while gradually wearing down Saint Andrews, who was on the rail.

As a result, Behera had nowhere to go, but once Carroll House passed Saint Andrews the course opened up again for Behera who started to close again. At the line Carroll House prevailed by one and a half lengths, with Behera getting up for second by a short head from Saint Andrews. Young Mother made good late ground for fourth, followed by Sierra Roberta and Robore. The favourite, In The Wings, was always in rear and only managed 11th place.

Not surprisingly the stewards called an inquiry, but after their deliberations the placings remained unchanged.

Post-race

This was another major win for the businessman Antonio Balzarini, who'd won the Derby Italiano with Prorutori earlier in the year. He'd also had some notable successes with Bob Back, and in years to come would win several more Classics in Italy, as well as some big races in England, France and the USA.

Michael Jarvis, who trained Prorutori as well as Carroll House, would win the Prix du Jockey Club with Holding Court as well as enjoying many successes with the enigmatic Rakti.

It was the first Arc triumph for Mick Kinane who was destined to visit the top step of the podium twice more on a couple of class acts. Carroll House was sold after the Arc to Zenya Yoshida and ran once more in 1989, finishing last in the Japan Cup, before being retired for the season.

Meanwhile the Aliysa affair kept rolling on. She was eventually disqualified but various court cases and appeals continued for over five years, and the Aga Khan, who was unhappy with the testing regime, which he saw as flawed, removed his horses from England.

Result

1989 Ciga Prix de l'Arc de Triomphe

Longchamp. Sunday, 8 October 1989
Weights: 3yo c: 56kg, 3yo f: 54.5kg, 4yo+ c: 59kg, 4yo+ f: 57.5kg

1st Carroll House (IRE)   4yo c   59kg   **19/1**
by Lord Gayle out of Tuna (Silver Shark). Antonio Balzarini / Michael Jarvis / Mick Kinane

2nd Behera (GB)   3yo f   54.5kg   **6/1** (coupled with Aliysa)
by Mill Reef out of Borushka (Bustino). HH Aga Khan IV / Alain de Royer-Dupré / Alain Lequeux

3rd Saint Andrews (USA) 5yo h   59kg   **5/1** (coupled with Young Mother)
by Kenmare out of Hardiona (Hard To Beat). Frank Stonach / Jean-Marie Béguigné / Eric Legrix

Runners: 19 (FR 12, GB 6, GER 1). Distances: 1½, sh hd. Going: good to soft. Time: 2m 30.80s

Also ran: 4th **Young Mother** (FR) 3yo f, 5th **Sierra Roberta** (FR) 3yo f, 6th **Robore** (FR) 4yo c, 7th **Norberto** (USA) 3yo c, 8th **Legal Case** (IRE) 3yo c, 9th **Britannia** (GER) 4yo f, 10th **Aliysa** (IRE) 3yo f, 11th **In The Wings** (GB) 3yo c, 12th **Top Class** (GB) 3yo c, 13th **Mansonnien** (FR) 5yo h, 14th **Golden Pheasant** (USA) 3yo c, 15th **Harvest Time** (FR) 3yo c, 16th **Cacoethes** (USA) 3yo c, 17th **Petrullo** (GB) 4yo c, 18th **French Glory** (IRE) 3yo c, 19th **Star Lift** (GB) 5yo h.

1990

Saumarez for l'homme
aux gants blancs

Rainbow Quest becomes fifth previous victor to sire a winner

Background and fanced horses

Eleven of the 20 runners were trained in England, including the favourite Salsabil, who was in the care of John Dunlop. She'd ended her two-year-old career by winning the Prix Marcel Boussac and this term had become the star of the summer in England.

After recording successes in the Fred Darling Stakes, the 1000 Guineas, The Oaks, and the Irish Derby – she was the first filly to win that race since Gallinaria in 1900 – she had a well-earned break before returning to Paris to take the Prix Vermeille. With Grand Prix de Deauville-fourth Albadr to make the pace, Hamdan Al Maktoum's filly was 1.5/1 to win again in the Bois de Boulogne.

Last year's market leader, In The Wings, who was now racing in Sheikh Mohammed's maroon and white, had won the Coronation Cup and the Grand Prix de Saint-Cloud prior to coming fifth when favourite in the King George VI and Queen Elizabeth Stakes. The first and second that day, Belmez and Old Vic, were also both owned by Sheikh Mohammed.

After a rest, André Fabre brought In The Wings back to win the Prix Foy. Belmez also lined up in the Arc. Before his win at Ascot he'd beaten the future Derby-winner Quest for Fame in the Chester Vase, and finished third to Salsabil in the Irish Derby. After Ascot he added the Great Voltigeur Stakes, prevailing by a head over Snurge.

The third member of the Sheikh Mohammed trio, who were grouped at 3.5/1, was the Prix Guillaume d'Ornano-winner Antisaar, who'd been runner-up to Epervier Bleu in the Prix Niel.

Daniel Wildenstein's Epervier Bleu had won the Prix Greffulhe and the Prix Lupin before finding Sanglamore too good in the Prix du Jockey Club. As already stated, Dominique Boeuf's mount returned after a mid-season hiatus to score in the Prix Niel and was 5/1 for the Arc.

The St Leger-winner Snurge was next at 7.5/1, with the filly he beat at Doncaster, Hellenic, who'd won the Yorkshire Oaks, on 14/1. Juddmonte International Stakes-winner and Prix Vermeille-third, In The Groove, was a point shorter while Saumarez was a point longer.

Saumarez was initially owned by Charles St George, of Ardross fame, and was trained by Henry Cecil at Newmarket. After finishing second to the future Derby runner-up Blue Stag in the Dee Stakes, he was transferred to Nicolas Clément in Chantilly.

From there he won the Grand Prix de Paris, before finishing seventh to Elmaamul in the Phoenix Champion Stakes for new owners Bruce McNall and the legendary ice hockey-player Wayne Gretzky. Back in France, Saumarez won the Prix du Prince d'Orange. The only other horses under 30/1 were the Prix du Jockey Club-third Erdelistan and his pacemaker Abyad. The Aga Khan IV's pair were coupled at 17/1.

The rest of the raiders were: the Hardwicke Stakes-winner Assatis; the returning Legal Case, who'd won the Champion Stakes after last year's Arc but who had disappointed in the King George VI and Queen Elizabeth Stakes this term; Premio Ribot-winner Sikeston in the Tony Bin colours; Cumberland Lodge Stakes-winner Ile de Nisky; and Charmer, who'd won the Geoffrey Freer Stakes at Newbury.

Last year's winner, Carroll House, had dropped back to last place after being prominent on his reappearance in the Hardwicke Stakes, before finishing fourth in Grand Prix de Saint-Cloud. But he picked up an injury in doing so and was retired. At stud he produced plenty of winners, especially over jumps, but no champions.

Betting

1.5/1 Salsabil & Albadr (coupled), 3.5/1 In The Wings & Belmez & Antisaar (all coupled), 5/1 Epervier Bleu, 7.5/1 Snurge, 13/1 In The Groove, 14/1 Hellenic, 15/1 Saumarez, 17/1 Erdelistan & Abyad (coupled), 30/1 BAR.

Three-year-old form lines
Prix du Jockey Club: 1st Sanglamore, 2nd **Epervier Bleu**, 3rd **Erdelistan**
Grand Prix de Paris: 1st **Saumarez**, 2nd Priolo, 3rd Tirol
Prix Niel: 1st **Epervier Bleu**, 2nd **Antisaar**, 3rd Passing Sale

Fillies only
Prix de Diane: 1st Rafha, 2nd Moon Cactus, 3rd Air de Rien, 6th **Guiza**
Prix Vermeille: 1st **Salsabil**, 2nd Miss Alleged, 3rd **In The Groove**

Older horses and inter-generational races
Grand Prix de Saint-Cloud: 1st **In The Wings**, 2nd Ode, 3rd **Zartota**, 4th Carroll House
Grand Prix de Deauville: 1st Robertet, 2nd Theatre Critic, 3rd French Glory, 4th **Albadr**
Prix du Prince d'Orange: 1st **Saumarez**, 2nd **Mister Riv**, 3rd Creator
Prix Foy: 1st **In The Wings**, 2nd **Zartota**, 3rd Robertet, 5th/last **Robore**

Abroad

In England

Derby Stakes: 1st Quest for Fame, 2nd Blue Stag, 3rd Elmaamul

Oaks Stakes: 1st **Salsabil**, 2nd Game Plan, 3rd Knight's Baroness, 4th **In The Groove**

King George VI and Queen Elizabeth Stakes: 1st **Belmez**, 2nd Old Vic, 3rd **Assatis**, 5th **In The Wings**, 7th **Charmer**, 10th **Legal Case**

St Leger: 1st **Snurge**, 2nd **Hellenic**, 3rd River God

In Ireland

Irish Derby: 1st **Salsabil**, 2nd Deploy, 3rd **Belmez**

Phoenix Champion Stakes: 1st Elmaamul, 2nd **Sikeston**, 3rd Kostroma, 7th **Saumarez**

The race

Abyad broke well and led on the inside before being overtaken by Albadr. Saumarez was third with Belmez in fourth. Meanwhile favourite Salasabil slotted in towards the rear of the midfield.

The pacemakers continued to cut it out, up and down the hill and along the false straight, with Saumarez always going well cruising in behind. On the home bend, Gérald Mossé, in his trademark white gloves, let Saumarez go and they quickly moved two lengths clear of Belmez, Sikeston and Erdelistan. That advantage became four lengths by the 200-metre pole, although Snurge, Epervier Bleu and In The Wings were now accelerating.

Suddenly what had been a commanding advantage was now rapidly diminishing. Saumarez, though, kept galloping and although Epervier Bleu did eventually get to within three parts of length at the line, he never quite looked like overhauling Saumarez.

Snurge was another half a length back with the Sheikh Mohammed pair, In The Wings and Belmez, fourth and fifth, followed by Legal Case. The market leader, Salasabil, who was one-paced after finding her way temporarily blocked at the head of the straight, came in 10th.

Post-race

After purchasing half of Trempolino before the 1987 Arc, Bruce McNall had made another canny purchase in Saumarez. And this time he shared the triumph with ice hockey superstar Wayne Gretzky, who he'd signed for his Los Angeles Kings in 1988. They also bought an interest in Golden Pheasant – who'd been unplaced in last year's Arc – before he won the Japan Cup in 1991.

It was a notable milestone in the burgeoning career of Chantilly-based trainer Nicolas Clément. The son of Miguel Clément, who won the 1966 Prix du Jockey Club with Nelcius, Nicolas had spells with John Gosden, Vincent O'Brien and François Boutin before taking out his own licence in 1988.

It was an enterprising ride by top jockey Gérald Mossé, the man famous for always wearing white gloves. *L'homme aux gants blancs* – as he is known in France – knew Saumarez wanted to go and Mossé used all his experience to let him go rather than disappoint him, which would probably have resulted in Saumarez wasting vital energy fighting against being restrained.

Saumarez raced once more, finishing fifth to In The Wings in the Breeders' Cup Turf, before going to stud. He produced plenty of winners but nothing special. However, via his daughter Funsie he is a grandsire of the 2007 Derby-winner Authorized. Being by Rainbow Quest, Saumarez enabled the 1985 Arc winner to become the fifth previous victor to sire a winner.

Result
1990 Ciga Prix de l'Arc de Triomphe
Longchamp. Sunday, 7 October 1990
Weights: 3yo c: 56kg, 3yo f: 54.5kg, 4yo+ c: 59kg, 4yo+ f: 57.5kg

1st Saumarez (GB)   3yo c   56kg   **15/1**
by Rainbow Quest out of Fiesta Fun (Welsh Pageant). Bruce McNall & Wayne Gretzky / Nicolas Clément / Gérald Mossé

2nd Epervier Bleu (GB)   3yo c   56kg   **5/1**
by Saint Cyrien out of Equadif (Abdos). Daniel Wildenstein / Élie Lellouche /
Dominique Boeuf

3rd Snurge (GB)   3yo c   56kg   **7.5/1**
by Ela-Mana-Mou out of Finlandia (Faraway Son). Sir Martyn Arbib / Paul Cole / Richard Quinn

Runners: 21 (FR 10, GB 11). Distances: ¾, ½. Going: good/good to soft. Time: 2m 29.80s

Also ran: 4th **In The Wings** (GB) 4yo c, 5th **Belmez** (USA) 3yo c, 6th **Legal Case** (IRE) 4yo c, 7th **Erdelistan** (GB) 3yo c, 8th **Hellenic** (IRE) 3yo f, 9th **In The Groove** (GB) 3yo f, 10th **Salsabil** (IRE) 3yo f, 11th **Antisaar** (USA) 3yo c, 12th **Assatis** (USA) 5yo h, 13th **Robore** (FR) 5yo h, 14th **Charmer** (IRE) 5yo h, 15th **Mister Riv** (FR) 5yo h, 16th **Zartota** (USA) 4yo f, 17th **Guiza** (USA) 3yo f, 18th **Sikeston** (USA) 4yo c, 19th **Ile de Nisky** (GB) 4yo c, 20th **Albadr** (USA) 5yo h, 21st **Abyad** (GB) 3yo c.

Suave Dancer is sublime

Cash steers Prix du Jockey Club-winner to victory

Background and fancied horses

The surprise 50/1 winner of the 1990 Dewhurst Stakes, Generous, had animated the season in England, notching up successes in the Derby and the King George VI and Queen Elizabeth Stakes under Alan Munro. In between, the flashy chestnut had beaten the Prix du Jockey Club-winner Suave Dancer in the Irish Derby.

The latter had gone on to take the Irish Champion Stakes, which was run at Leopardstown for the first time. Punters, though, were convinced that Generous would confirm the Curragh placings in the Arc, and he was 0.9/1 while John Hammond's charge was 3.7/1.

The winner of the Prix Noialles and Prix Hocquart, Pistolet Bleu, who finished second to Subotica in the Prix Niel, was Daniel Wildenstein's first string. With Art Bleu accompanying him to make the pace, he was returned at 6.8/1.

Last year's St Leger-winner and Arc-third, Snurge, was priced at 8/1. He'd added the Grand Prix de Deauville and Gran Premio di Milano to his *palmarès* this term. This year's St Leger-winner Toulon was 10/1 coupled with 1990 Derby-victor Quest for Fame. Prix Vermeille-heroine Magic Night, trained by Philippe Demercastel, was the same price and it was 26/1 bar.

In addition to Generous, Quest for Fame and Snurge, England also had the returning In The Groove, who'd won the Coronation Cup, and Shamshir. The last-named had been second in The Oaks to the longshot Jet Ski Lady, who also lined up at Longchamp as Ireland's sole representative.

The final raider was El Senor for the USA. The seven-year-old had won some valuable handicaps and had been third to In The Wings in the most recent renewal of the Breeders' Cup Turf.

Betting

0.9/1 Generous, 3.7/1 Suave Dancer, 6.8/1 Pistolet Bleu & Art Bleu (coupled), 8/1 Snurge, 10/1 Toulon & Quest for Fame (coupled), 10/1 Magic Night, 26/1 BAR.

Three-year-old form lines

Prix du Jockey Club: 1st **Suave Dancer**, 2nd Subotica, 3rd Cudas

Grand Prix de Paris: 1st Subotica, 2nd Sillery, 3rd Kotashaan

Prix Niel: 1st Subotica, 2nd **Pistolet Bleu**, 3rd Arcangues

Fillies only

Prix de Diane: 1st Caerlina, 2nd **Magic Night**, 3rd Louve Romaine

Prix Vermeille: 1st **Magic Night**, 2nd Pink Turtle, 3rd Crnagora, 10th **Shamshir**

Older horses and inter-generational races

Grand Prix de Saint-Cloud: 1st Epervier Bleu, 2nd Rock Hopper, 3rd Passing Sale, 4th **Miss Alleged**

Grand Prix de Deauville: 1st **Snurge**, 2nd Crnagora, 3rd **Pigeon Voyageur**

Prix du Prince d'Orange: 1st Passing Sale, 2nd **Miss Alleged**, 3rd Glity

Prix Foy: 1st Splash of Colour, 2nd Panoramic, 3rd Echoes, 5th **Art Bleu**

Abroad

In England

Derby Stakes: 1st **Generous**, 2nd Marju, 3rd Star of Gdansk, 9th **Toulon**

Oaks Stakes: 1st **Jet Ski Lady**, 2nd **Shamshir**, 3rd Shadayid

King George VI and Queen Elizabeth Stakes: 1st **Generous**, 2nd Sanglamore, 3rd Rock Hopper

St Leger: 1st **Toulon**, 2nd Saddlers' Hall, 3rd Micheletti

In Ireland

Irish Derby: 1st **Generous**, 2nd **Suave Dancer**, 3rd Star of Gdansk

Irish Champion Stakes (previously the Phoenix Champion Stakes) 1st **Suave Dancer**, 2nd Environment Friend, 3rd Stagecraft

In Italy

Gran Premio di Milano: 1st **Snurge**, 2nd Erdelistan, 3rd Bateau Rouge

The race

Pacemaker Art Bleu was first to show from stablemate Pistolet Bleu, who was on the inner, and Quest for Fame racing three wide. Jet Ski Lady had to be pushed along to go into fourth and Generous slotted in behind. Suave Dancer was held up in rear while El Senor, who was very slow away, was not keen to race and was tailing off.

On the descent, Jet Ski Lady dropped back but, apart from that, the order of the leaders remained just about the same. Rounding the final bend, predictably Art Bleu moved off the rail allowing Pistolet Bleu a clear passage through on his inner. Quest for Fame and Generous were both starting their efforts, followed by In The Groove, Suave Dancer and Toulon.

Pistolet Bleu, under champion jockey-elect Dominique Boeuf, readily took over with 450 metres to travel, followed through on the inner by Magic Night. Generous and Miss Alleged started to back pedal. However, Quest for

Fame was still there and In The Groove and Suave Dancer were motoring on the outer.

At the 300-metre pole Cash Asmussen pressed the button on Suave Dancer and he immediately accelerated, swamping his rivals in the style of a class horse. Pushed out hands and heels in the closing stages, he had two lengths to spare at the wire over Magic Night, who just got the better of Pistolet Bleu for second, with a massive gap to Toulon, Pigeon Voyageur and In The Groove.

A stewards' inquiry was called to look into possible interference by the winner. Suave Dancer had moved off a straight line but it hadn't affected the outcome and the result stood.

Post-race

After finishing second twice, on Northern Trick and Tony Bin, jockey Cash Asmussen registered his first success wearing the white, blue hollow box, hooped sleeves and cap of Henri Chalhoub, who plied his trade in the insurance game. It was a particularly sweet success for Cash, as he had originally purchased the horse for the owner.

It was also a first win for the English-born John Hammond who trained at Chantilly, and he would be back with another superstar in 1999. Suave Dancer, the first Prix du Jockey Club-winner to add the Arc since 1970, was seen once more on a racetrack when finishing third to Subotica in the following year's Prix Ganay.

Shortly afterwards, he picked up an injury and was retired. He stood at the National Stud in Newmarket for a few seasons, and then shuttled between Europe and Australia before meeting an untimely end, being struck by lightning while in the southern hemisphere. His best progeny were Prix Ganay-winner Execute, Compton Admiral, who won the Eclipse Stakes, and Prix Vermeille-winner Volvoreta, who will feature in our story.

Result

1991 Ciga Prix de l'Arc de Triomphe
Longchamp. Sunday, 6 October 1991
Weights: 3yo c: 56kg, 3yo f: 54.5kg, 4yo+ c: 59kg, 4yo+ f: 57.5kg

1st Suave Dancer (USA)   3yo c   56kg   **3.7/1**
by Green Dancer out of Suavite (Alleged). Henri Chalhoub / John Hammond / Cash Asmussen

2nd Magic Night (FR)   3yo f   54.5kg   **10/1**
by Le Nain Jaune out of Pin Up Babe (Prominer). H. Yokoyama / Philippe Demercastel / Alain Badel

3rd Pistolet Bleu (IRE)   3yo c   56kg   **6.8/1**
by Top Ville out of Pampa Bella (Armos). Daniel Wildenstein / Élie Lellouche / Dominique Boeuf

Runners: 14 (FR 7, GB 5, IRE 1, USA 1). Distances: 2, 1. Going: good to soft. Time: 2m 31.40s

Stewards' Inquiry: result stands after an inquiry into whether the winner caused interference

Also ran: 4th **Toulon** (GB) 3yo c, 5th **Pigeon Voyageur** (IRE) 3yo c, 6th **In The Groove** (GB) 4yo f, 7th **Quest for Fame** (GB) 4yo c, 8th **Generous** (IRE) 3yo c, 9th **El Senor** (USA) 7yo h, 10th **Shamshir** (GB) 3yo f, 11th **Miss Alleged** (USA) 4yo f, 12th **Art Bleu** (GB) 4yo c, 13th **Jet Ski Lady** (USA) 3yo f, 14th **Snurge** (GB) 4yo c.

Subotica slugs it out
for Fabre and Jarnet

Favourite just loses out after running too free

Background and fancied horses

The Clive Brittain-trained User Friendly was the standout filly of the season in England. She'd won the Lingfield Oaks Trial on her second outing, before taking The Oaks itself, followed by the Irish and Yorkshire versions. Facing colts for the first time, she showed her mettle when winning the St Leger by three and a half lengths, and she topped the Arc market at 3.3/1.

Last year's runner-up, Magic Night, had gone on to finish second to Golden Pheasant in the Japan Cup, and this season had filled the same berth in the Grand Prix de Saint-Cloud before winning the Prix Foy. Philippe Demercastel's daughter of Le Nain Jaune was second best in the market at 4.5/1.

The best three-year-old filly in France was Jolypha at 5.5/1. One of three representatives from the André Fabre yard, she'd won both the Prix de Diane and Prix Vermeille.

The first colts in the market were St Jovite and Dr Devious at 6.5/1 and 7/1 respectively. Jim Bolger's St Jovite has been beaten by Dr Devious, trained by Peter Chapple-Hyam, in the Derby but had gained revenge at the Curragh. St Jovite then added the King George VI and Queen Elizabeth Stakes before going down to Dr Devious again in the Irish Champion Stakes.

Fabre's 1991 Grand Prix de Paris and Prix Niel-winner Subotica, who'd been third in the Grand Prix de Saint-Cloud, was next at 8.8/1, followed by the Wildenstein pair, Verveine and Arcangues.

Verveine hadn't won in 1992 but had been involved in the finish of all the top fillies' races as well as the Grand Prix de Paris. Last year's winner of the Prix Eugène Adam, Arcangues, was arriving on the back of success in the Prix du Prince d'Orange.

The connections of the previous year's winner Suave Dancer were represented by Arlington Million-winner Dear Doctor at 16/1.

Also running for England, in addition to User Friendly and Dr Devious, were: Princess of Wales's Stakes-winner Saddlers' Hall; Mashaallah, who'd won the Gran Premio di Milano and Grosser Preis von Baden; the 1991

Racing Post Trophy-winner Seattle Rhyme; and Sapience, who'd been third to Mashaallah in Germany.

Irish Oaks-second Market Booster as well as St Jovite were representing Ireland, bringing the total number of raiders to eight.

Betting
3.3/1 User Friendly, 4.5/1 Magic Night, 5.5/1 Jolypha, 6.5/1 St Jovite, 7/1 Dr Devious, 8.8/1 Subotica, 12/1 Verveine & Arcangues (coupled), 16/1 Dear Doctor, 21/1 BAR.

Three-year-old form lines
Prix du Jockey Club: 1st **Polytain**, 2nd Marignan, 3rd Contested Bid
Grand Prix de Paris: 1st Homme de Loi, 2nd Kitwood, 3rd Guislaine, 5th **Verveine**
Prix Niel: 1st Songlines, 2nd **Petit Loup**, 3rd Apple Tree, 8th/last **Polytain**

Fillies only
Prix de Diane: 1st **Jolypha**, 2nd Sheba Dancer, 3rd **Verveine**
Prix Vermeille: 1st **Jolypha**, 2nd Cunning, 3rd Urban Sea, 4th **Verveine**, 5th **Market Booster**

Older horses and inter-generational races
Grand Prix de Saint-Cloud: 1st Pistolet Bleu, 2nd **Magic Night**, 3rd **Subotica**, 4th **Saganeca**
Prix du Prince d'Orange: 1st **Arcangues**, 2nd Prince Polino, 3rd Arazi
Prix Foy: 1st **Magic Night**, 2nd **Subotica**, 3rd Tel Quel, 4th/last **Saganeca**

Abroad
In England
Derby Stakes: 1st **Dr Devious**, 2nd **St Jovite**, 3rd Silver Wisp
Oaks Stakes: 1st **User Friendly**, 2nd All At Sea, 3rd Pearl Angel
King George VI and Queen Elizabeth Stakes: 1st **St Jovite**, 2nd **Saddlers' Hall**, 3rd Opera House, 4th **Sapience**
St Leger: 1st **User Friendly**, 2nd Sonus, 3rd Bonny Scot

In Ireland
Irish Derby: 1st **St Jovite**, 2nd **Dr Devious**, 3rd Contested Bid
Irish Champion Stakes: 1st **Dr Devious**, 2nd **St Jovite**, 3rd Alflora

In Germany
Grosser Preis von Baden: 1st **Mashaallah**, 2nd Platini, 3rd **Sapience**

In Italy
Gran Premio di Milano: 1st **Mashaallah**, 2nd Saganeca, 3rd Lara's Idea

The race
Saddlers' Hall, Mashaallah and User Friendly were all prominent early on, galloping at a breakneck speed. Behind the Petit Bois the pace settled a little and soon after Sapience took over, with St Jovite moving into second.

Meanwhile, Subotica, who'd been last away, was now in the mid-division, but User Friendly was still running too free.

Sapience and St Jovite still held sway on the turn-in with Saddlers' Hall, Petit Loup and User Friendly in the second rank. They were followed by Magic Night, on the inner of Mashaallah, with Dr Devious and Seattle Rhyme on the outer and Subotica just behind.

In the straight, St Jovite quickly despatched Sapience, but immediately faced the challenge of User Friendly, who still had reserves despite her earlier exertions. However, the big white face of Subotica was also looming large as he burst free of the pack into third.

User Friendly took a neck advantage over St Jovite passing the 300-metre marker, but Subotica was still coming and the two joined battle, slugging it out, with Subotica just prevailing by a neck at the post. The pair were two lengths clear of Vert Amande, who finished fastest of all, followed by St Jovite, Saganeca and Dr Devious.

Post-race

Owner Olivier Lecerf, the chairman and CEO of a large building materials company, had enjoyed the pleasure of seeing his black colours with a blue cap come from last to first. It was a second Arc for trainer André Fabre, after Trempolino in 1987; the master of his trade had been champion trainer since then and would remain so until 2007.

Jockey Thierry Jarnet, who went on to became Champion jockey – and would hold the title for four years – was breaking his Arc duck. Both he and Fabre will appear many more times in our story. Subotica had one more race, finishing fifth to Fraise in the Breeders' Cup Turf, before going to stud where he produced many winners, including some decent sorts over jumps.

Result

1992 Ciga Prix de l'Arc de Triomphe
Longchamp. Sunday, 4 October 1992
Weights: 3yo c: 56kg, 3yo f: 54.5kg, 4yo+ c: 59kg, 4yo+ f: 57.5kg

1st Subotica (FR)　　　　4yo c　59kg　**8.8/1**
by Pampabird out of Terre de Feu (Busted). Olivier Lecerf / André Fabre / Thierry Jarnet

2nd User Friendly (GB)　　3yo f　54.5kg　**3.3/1 fav**
by Slip Anchor out of Rostova (Blakeney). Bill Gredley / Clive Brittain / George Duffield

3rd Vert Amande (FR)　　4yo c　59kg　**75/1**
by Kenmare out of Lady Berry (Violon d'Ingres). Enrique Sarasola / Élie Lellouche / Eric Legrix

Runners: 18 (FR 10, GB 6, IRE 2). Distances: nk, 2. Going: soft. Time: 2m 39.00s

Also ran: 4th **St Jovite** (USA) 3yo c, 5th **Saganeca** (USA) 4yo f, 6th **Dr Devious** (IRE) 3yo c, 7th **Arcangues** (USA) 4yo c, 8th **Jolypha** (USA) 3yo f, 9th **Verveine** (USA) 3yo c, 10th **Dear Doctor** (FR) 5yo h, 11th **Mashaallah** (USA) 4yo c, 12th **Petit Loup** (USA) 3yo c, 13th **Magic Night** (FR) 4yo f, 14th **Sapience** (GB) 6yo h, 15th **Saddlers' Hall** (IRE) 4yo c, 16th **Market Booster** (USA) 3yo f, 17th **Seattle Rhyme** (USA) 3yo c, 18th **Polytain** (FR) 3yo c.

Urban Sea for Saint-Martin junior

Outsider wins on merit and becomes a most influential dam

Background and fancied horses

Hernando dominated the summer in France, beating Armiger in the Prix Lupin, before being sent off favourite when winning the Prix du Jockey Club by two and a half lengths from Dernier Empereur.

Stavros Niarchos's charge wasn't disgraced when going down by three parts of a length to Epsom Derby-winner Commander in Chief in the Irish Derby, before resuming winning ways in the Prix Niel on his first run back from a break. Not surprisingly, Hernando was the Arc favourite at 3.8/1.

The strongest candidate from the nine-strong party from England looked to be the Sheikh Mohammed-owned Opera House. The winner of the Coronation Cup, Eclipse Stakes and King George VI and Queen Elizabeth Stakes was coupled at 4/1 with the best of the quartet trained by André Fabre, namely Intrepidity who'd taken The Oaks and Prix Vermeille.

The Aga Khan IV's Prix de Diane-winner, Shemaka, was 7.8/1 with the Italian representative Misil at 9/1. He'd finished runner-up in the Eclipse Stakes and arrived on the back of a win in the Premio Federico Tesio. Earlier in his career Misil had been ridden on half a dozen occasions by Gianfranco Dettori, while in the Arc it would be his son's ninth time aboard the horse.

Last year's runner-up User Friendly, who'd won the Grand Prix de Saint-Cloud, was 12/1. Other English-trained runners with chances included the first and second in the St Leger, Bob's Return at 13/1 and the aforementioned Armiger.

Armiger himself was on 4/1 coupled with Fabre's Irish Oaks-winner Wemyss Bight, as they were both running in the silks of Khalid Abdullah – the former wearing the English colours incorporating a sash and the latter sporting the French version with epaulettes.

Only Royale at 19/1 and Vert Amande, a point longer, had finished first and third in the Prix Foy, and it was 25/1 bar.

Germany was represented by Platini, and Ireland's only runner was Market Booster. Yves-Saint-Martin's son Eric got the leg up on Urban Sea, who'd been third in the previous year's Prix Vermeille and had won the Group 3 Prix Gontaut-Biron last time out.

Also among the longshots was White Muzzle, who'd won the Derby Italiano for Peter Chapple-Hyam, before finishing second to Opera House in the King George VI and Queen Elizabeth Stakes.

Betting

3.8/1 Hernando, 4/1 Opera House & Intrepidity (coupled), 4/1 Wemyss Bight & Armiger (coupled), 7.8/1 Shemaka, 9/1 Misil, 12/1 User Friendly, 13/1 Bob's Return, 19/1 Only Royale, 20/1 Vert Amande, 25/1 BAR.

Three-year-old form lines

Prix du Jockey Club: 1st **Hernando**, 2nd Dernier Empereur, 3rd Hunting Hawk, 6th **Badolato**

Grand Prix de Paris: 1st Fort Wood, 2nd Bigstone, 3rd Siam

Prix Niel: 1st **Hernando**, 2nd Dernier Empereur, 3rd **Dancienne**

Fillies only

Prix de Diane: 1st **Shemaka**, 2nd Baya, 3rd **Dancienne**, 5th **Bright Moon**

Prix Vermeille: 1st **Intrepidity**, 2nd **Wemyss Bight**, 3rd **Bright Moon**

Older horses and inter-generational races

Grand Prix de Saint-Cloud: 1st **User Friendly**, 2nd Apple Tree, 3rd Modhish, 6th **Vert Amande**

Prix Foy: 1st **Only Royale**, 2nd Modhish, 3rd **Vert Amande**

Abroad

In England

Derby Stakes: 1st Commander in Chief, 2nd Blue Judge, 3rd Blues Traveller, 6th **Bob's Return**

Oaks Stakes: 1st **Intrepidity**, 2nd Royal Ballerina, 3rd Oakmead, 5th **Wemyss Bight**

King George VI and Queen Elizabeth Stakes: 1st **Opera House**, 2nd **White Muzzle**, 3rd Commander in Chief, 4th **User Friendly**, 10th/last **Platini**

St Leger: 1st **Bob's Return**, 2nd **Armiger**, 3rd Edbaysaan

In Ireland

Irish Derby: 1st Commander in Chief, 2nd **Hernando**, 3rd Foresee

Irish Champion Stakes: 1st Muhtarram, 2nd **Opera House**, 3rd Lord of the Field, 4th **Market Booster**

In Germany

Grosser Preis von Baden: 1st Lando, 2nd **Platini**, 3rd George Augustus

The race

Armiger and User Friendly, who was lit up like last year, led them away before Dariyoun came through to take it up, followed by Shemaka. In doing so, they tightened up the original leaders, with User Friendly faring worst, losing several places.

At the Petit Bois, Always Friendly rushed around the pack moving from last place to take up second position alongside Shemaka. They were followed by Armiger, Bob's Return and Urban Sea. Meanwhile market-leader Hernando was content to wait in rear.

Rounding the final bend, Dariyoun on the rail was challenged by a rank of four consisting of Bob's Return, Opera House, Market Booster and Talloires, with just behind them White Muzzle starting to get into the picture. Urban Sea had lost a few places and had to be switched off the inside to find racing room.

Talloires, in the de Moussac colours, looked dangerous on the outer in a closing fourth. But then he ducked sharply to the left. After Olivier Peslier corrected him, the son of Trempolino showed his versatility by repeating the manoeuvre, this time, though, jinking to the right which cost him any chance he had left.

At the same time Bob's Return overtook Dariyoun only to be challenged immediately by Opera House. On the inner, Urban Sea followed Bob's Return through, squeezing into the gap between Mark Tompkins's horse and the fading Dariyoun.

The moment Opera House made it to the front dangers appeared on both sides – White Muzzle on the outer and Urban Sea on his inside. The three-way war for victory was won by Urban Sea, who opened up a length gap at the 100-metre marker, before White Muzzle closed the advantage to a neck in the last couple of strides, in what was a mesmerising finish.

Opera House was only half a length back in third for Sheikh Mohammed, with his other runner, Intrepidity, finishing like a whirlwind to claim fourth ahead of Only Royale and Bob's Return. Hernando, who'd been a few lengths off the pace turning in, hadn't been able to change gear and was eased down once his chance was gone.

Post-race

Urban Sea was a popular winner despite being an outsider – 37/1 on the PMU but 66/1 for those who'd had a wager *outre-Manche* – it wasn't because many had backed her but because of who was on top.

It was Eric Saint-Martin the son of the legendary Yves, who had won the Arc on Sassafras, Allez France, Akiyda and Sagace. It was also a great day for trainer Jean Lesbordes, whose previous best in the race had been to prepare Boyatino to finish third in 1989.

Saint-Martin starred in all the headlines. However, as one son emulated his father, another father was about to start his own dynasty. That man was the owner of Urban Sea, Hong Kong businessman David Tsui.

Urban Sea was a great-great-granddaughter of dual Arc-winner Tantième and went on to win the Prix d'Harcourt the following April. Unfortunately, her career ended a couple of months later when she picked up a fetlock injury during the Coronation Cup, in which she finished fourth.

Excellent on the track, Urban Sea was a revelation off it. One of her first offspring was Galileo who won the English and Irish Derbys and King George VI and Queen Elizabeth Stakes in 2001.

Galileo has subsequently become the most influential sire in modern times and has made a big mark on the Arc. He was responsible for the first three home in 2016, as well as winning with Waldgeist in 2019, and, via his son Nathaniel, is the grandsire of dual Arc-winner Enable.

To produce one great champion is a tremendous feat, to then add another is remarkable. But that's exactly what Urban Sea did in the form of Sea The Stars, who ran in the colours of Tsui's son Christopher, a variation of his father's yellow and purple silks.

The 2009 essay in this book will cover Sea The Stars in more detail. Suffice to say that his nine-race unbeaten career culminated in a superlative performance at Longchamp in the October of that year.

Sea The Stars in turn fathered Sea Of Class, the runner-up to Enable in the 2018 Arc. Owned by the Tsui family's breeding company Sunderland Holding Inc, Sea Of Class sported another version of the yellow and purple-themed silks. Incidentally, Sea The Stars was also responsible for the third home that day, Cloth Of Stars, who'd been second the year before.

Urban Sea by dint of her deeds, on and off the course, is one of the most influential mares of modern times.

Tantième 1947
|
Agio 1955
|
Lombard 1967
|
Allegretta 1978
|
Urban Sea 1989
|
Sea The Stars 2006

Result

1993 Ciga Prix de l'Arc de Triomphe
Longchamp. Sunday, 3 October 1993
Weights: 3yo c: 56kg, 3yo f: 54.5kg, 4yo+ c: 59kg, 4yo+ f: 57.5kg

1st Urban Sea (USA)   4yo f   57.5kg   **37/1**
by Miswaki out of Allegretta (Lombard). David Tsui / Jean Lesbordes /
Eric Saint-Martin

2nd White Muzzle (GB)   3yo c   56kg   **54/1**
by Dancing Brave out of Fair of the Furze (Ela-Mana-Mou). Exors of Zenya Yoshida / Peter Chapple-Hyam /
John Reid

3rd Opera House (GB)   5yo h   59kg   **4/1** (coupled with Intrepidity)
by Sadler's Wells out of Colorspin (High Top). Sheikh Mohammed / Sir Michael Stoute / Michael Roberts

Runners: 23 (FR 11, GB 9, GER 1, IRE 1, ITY 1). Distances: nk, ½. Going: heavy. Time: 2m 37.90s

Also ran: 4th **Intrepidity** (GB) 3yo f, 5th **Only Royale** (IRE) 4yo f, 6th **Bob's Return** (IRE) 3yo c, 7th **Misil** (USA) 5yo h, 8th **Talloires** (USA) 3yo c, 9th **Vert Amande** (FR) 5yo h, 10th **Market Booster** (USA) 4yo f, 11th **Dariyoun** (USA) 5yo h, 12th **Dancienne** (FR) 3yo f, 13th **Platini** (GER) 4yo c, 14th **Badolato** (USA) 3yo c, 15th **Armiger** (GB) 3yo c, 16th **Hernando** (FR) 3yo c, 17th **Ezzoud** (IRE) 4yo c, 18th **Bright Moon** (USA) 3yo f, 19th **Garden Of Heaven** (USA) 4yo c, 20th **Always Friendly** (GB) 5yo m, 21st **Wemyss Bight** (GB) 3yo f, 22nd **User Friendly** (GB) 4yo f, 23rd **Shemaka** (IRE) 3yo f.

1994

Like mother like son as Carnégie emulates Detroit

André Fabre first, third and fifth

Background and fancied horses

Sheikh Mohammed was mob-handed with four runners, headed by the Henry Cecil-trained King's Theatre, who'd been runner-up in the English and Irish derbys before winning the King George VI and Queen Elizabeth Stakes. Most recently he'd finished third to Ezzoud in the Juddmonte International Stakes in mid-August before having a break.

The other three were 60 per cent of a quintet trained by André Fabre, namely the winner of the Prix Eugène Adam and Prix Niel, Carnégie, and the four-year-olds Richard Of York and Intrepidity, who'd finished first and second in the Prix Foy. Grouped together, Sheikh Mohammed's foursome were returned at 3/1.

Last year's second, White Muzzle, was next at 3.5/1. Runner-up to King's Theatre in the King George VI and Queen Elizabeth Stakes, he'd subsequently won the Grand Prix de Deauville, beating Bright Moon – another Fabre-trained Arc runner who was priced at 24/1.

After White Muzzle came Jean-Claude Rouget's Millkom, at 5/1, who was unbeaten in four outings including the Grand Prix de Paris and Prix du Prince d'Orange.

Only Royale, at 6.5/1, who'd taken the Yorkshire Oaks for the second time was next, followed by last year's favourite Hernando, who was 6.8/1. This season he'd won the Prix Gontaut-Biron on his reappearance in August, but was a distant fourth in the Prix Foy when sent off at odds-on.

The Prix du Jockey Club-winner Celtic Arms and Sierra Madre, the Prix Vermeille-heroine, both hailed from the yard of Pascal Bary. They would be ridden by Gérald Mossé and Freddy Head respectively, and were priced at 9/1.

André Fabre's fifth runner, the Grand Prix de Saint-Cloud-winner Apple Tree, was coupled at 14/1 with the recently purchased St Leger-second Broadway Flyer.

The previously mentioned Ezzoud was 19/1. He'd won the Eclipse Stakes in addition to the Juddmonte International Stakes, but had unshipped his pilot coming out of the stalls in the King George VI and Queen Elizabeth Stakes.

The five English challengers – King's Theatre, White Muzzle, Only Royale, Broadway Flyer and Ezzoud – have all been mentioned; they were joined by the dual Grosser Preis von Baden-winner Lando for Germany, Italy's Big Tobin, and Much Better, who won two Group 1 races in Brazil before heading to Europe.

On the sponsorship front, the deal with Ciga, which had lasted six years, was over and Trusthouse Forte were back at the helm under their shortened rebranded title of 'Forte'.

Betting

3/1 King's Theatre & Carnégie & Intrepidity & Richard Of York (all coupled), 3.5/1 White Muzzle, 5/1 Millkom, 6.5/1 Only Royale, 6.8/1 Hernando, 9/1 Celtic Arms & Sierra Madre (coupled), 14/1 Apple Tree & Broadway Flyer (coupled), 19/1 Ezzoud, 23/1 BAR.

Three-year-old form lines

Prix du Jockey Club: 1st **Celtic Arms**, 2nd Solid Illusion 3rd Alriffa
Grand Prix de Paris: 1st **Millkom**, 2nd Solid Illusion, 3rd **Celtic Arms**
Prix Niel: 1st **Carnégie**, 2nd Northern Spur, 3rd Sunshack, 4th **Celtic Arms**

Fillies only

Prix de Diane: 1st East of the Moon, 2nd Her Ladyship, 3rd Agathe, 5th **Sierra Madre**
Prix Vermeille: 1st **Sierra Madre**, 2nd Yenda, 3rd State Crystal

Older horses and inter-generational races

Grand Prix de Saint-Cloud: 1st **Apple Tree**, 2nd Muhtarram, 3rd Zimzalabim, 4th **Bright Moon**
Grand Prix de Deauville: 1st **White Muzzle**, 2nd **Bright Moon**, 3rd Jackdidi, 5th **Big Tobin**
Prix du Prince d'Orange: 1st **Millkom**, 2nd Volochine, 3rd Sand Reef
Prix Foy: 1st **Richard of York**, 2nd **Intrepidity**, 3rd **Apple Tree**, 4th **Hernando**

Abroad

In England
Derby Stakes: 1st Erhaab, 2nd **King's Theatre**, 3rd Colonel Collins
King George VI and Queen Elizabeth Stakes: 1st **King's Theatre**, 2nd **White Muzzle**, 3rd Wagon Master, 4th **Apple Tree**, UR **Ezzoud**
St Leger: 1st Moonax, 2nd **Broadway Flyer**, 3rd Double Trigger

In Ireland
Irish Derby: 1st Balanchine, 2nd **King's Theatre**, 3rd Colonel Collins

In Germany
Grosser Preis von Baden: 1st **Lando**, 2nd Monsun, 3rd Kornado 5th **Vert Amande**

In Italy
Gran Premio Di Milano: 1st Petit Loup, 2nd Snurge, 3rd Vert Amande, 4th **Big Tobin**

The race

Dancienne was slow to stride and flashed her tail as Broadway Flyer led them away. Sierra Madre, who'd been drawn wide, came across to join the pack, slotting into second place, and was followed by the Sheikh Mohammed quartet.

Running downhill, Broadway Flyer opened up a six-length gap to the rest of the field, with King's Theatre now in second and Intrepidity third. The leader came under pressure entering the straight and the advantage was already down to four lengths.

At the 300-metre pole, Broadway Flyer was engulfed by the pack, led by King's Theatre, and over half the field were within a length of the lead.

Carnégie, from the second rank, immediately pounced on King's Theatre to take the lead, followed by Hernando and Bright Moon. Meanwhile, Apple Tree and Ezzoud were flying home on the inside, but it was Hernando – who'd had to side-step an opponent before finding racing room – who was gaining quickest on Carnégie.

The pair battled for superiority in the last 75 metres with the game Carnégie finding more to just hold Hernando by a short neck on the line. Three quarters of a length behind, Apple Tree just got the better of Ezzoud and Bright Moon, with all five covered by just over a length. Last year's runner-up, White Muzzle, who came from way back, flashed home in sixth.

Post-race

Sheikh Mohammed bin Rashid Al Maktoum had improved on his third with Opera House in 1993, to post his first Arc win. In the future he would have more success under the Godolphin banner and, indeed, his nephew would win in just 12 months' time.

It was the third win for André Fabre, after Trempolino and Subotica, and three of his five runners had been there at the death, finishing first, third and fifth. Thierry Jarnet, who'd ridden Subotica, doubled his score and like Sheikh Mohammed and Fabre would be back for more.

Carnégie, whose dam Detroit became the first female Arc winner to produce another, was kept in training and would also return'.

Result

1994 Forte Prix de l'Arc de Triomphe

Longchamp. Sunday, 2 October 1994
Weights: 3yo c: 56kg, 3yo f: 54.5kg, 4yo+ c: 59kg, 4yo+ f: 57.5kg

1st Carnégie (IRE)   3yo c   56kg   **3/1 fav** (coupled*)
by Sadler's Wells out at Detroit (Riverman). Sheikh Mohammed / André Fabre / Thierry Jarnet

2nd Hernando (FR)   4yo c   59kg   **6.8/1**
by Niniski out of Whakilyric (Miswaki). Stavros Niarchos / François Boutin / Cash Asmussen

3rd Apple Tree (FR)   5yo h   59kg   **14/1**
by Bikala out of Pomme Rose (Carvin). Sultan Al Kabeer / André Fabre / John Reid
*with King's Theatre, Intrepidity & Richard Of York

Runners: 20 (FR 12, GB 5, BRZ 1, GER 1, ITY 1). Distances: sh nk, ¾. Going: good to soft. Time: 2m 31.10s

Also ran: 4th **Ezzoud** (IRE) 3yo f, 5th **Bright Moon** (USA) 4yo f, 6th **White Muzzle** (GB) 4yo c, 7th **Only Royale** (IRE) 5yo m, 8th **Lando** (GER) 4yo c, 9th **Millkom** (GB) 3yo c, 10th **King's Theatre** (IRE) 3yo c, 11th **Celtic Arms** (FR) 3yo c, 12th **Richard Of York** (GB) 4yo c, 13th **Intrepidity** (GB) 4yo f, 14th **Much Better** (BRZ) 5yo h, 15th **Broadway Flyer** (USA) 3yo c, 16th **Sierra Madre** (FR) 3yo f, 17th **Big Tobin** (ITY) 5yo h, 18th **Truly A Dream** (IRE) 3yo f, 19th **Vert Amande** (FR) 6yo h, 20th **Dancienne** (FR) 4yo f.

1995

Lammtarra wins it all in less than ten minutes

First triumph for Frankie Dettori

Background and fancied horses

The favourite for the Arc was Lammtarra at 2.1/1. As a two-year-old he'd been trained by Alex Scott. Sporting the light green with a white chevron and striped sleeved colours of Sheikh Saeed Maktoum Al Maktoum, he won the Washington Singer Stakes at Newbury in August on debut,

Tragically, though, Scott was shot dead by a disconsolate stable lad the following month, and as a mark of respect, Lammtarra didn't run again in 1994. He was sent to Dubai in November, as part of the Godolphin experiment in which horses were sent to warmer climes to avoid the harsh temperatures of the northern European winter. The theory was that with the sun on their back, horses would develop quicker and have an edge over those who'd stayed in Europe.

In Dubai however, Lammtarra suffered initially from a serious lung infection, but by the time he was due to return was fully recovered. Back in Newmarket, under the aegis of Saeed bin Suroor, he was trained for the Derby.

Sent off at 14/1 and ridden by Walter Swinburn, Lammtarra met with some interference early on, losing several places, and only had three behind him at the top of the hill. He started to make ground but still had eight lengths to find with 600 metres to travel. But running down the centre of the track, he made up the ground in dazzling style to win in course record time.

A month later, and with the retained Godolphin jockey Frankie Dettori now in the plate, Lammtarra showed great resolution to gamely win the King George VI and Queen Elizabeth Stakes from Pentire, before being given a break. The Arc would be his fourth career appearance.

Sheikh Saeed Maktoum Al Maktoum faced some stern opposition from his uncle, Sheikh Mohammed, who had an embarrassment of riches headed by Swain. He'd completed a four-timer when winning the Grand Prix de Deauville, and was joined by last year's Arc-victor Carnégie, who'd won the Grand Prix de Saint-Cloud and Prix Foy. In between, though, he'd failed in the King George VI and Queen Elizabeth Stakes, when a one-paced sixth of seven.

Sheikh Mohammed's trio, priced at 2.3/1, was completed by Balanchine. She'd been the flagbearer for Godolphin in 1994, having wintered in Dubai before winning The Oaks and Irish Derby, but her season had been ended by a severe bout of colic. After a year off she failed to fire on her comeback, but showed signs of a return to form next time out when second to Carnégie in the Prix Foy.

The best filly in France had been Carling, who'd added the Prix Vermeille to her Prix de Diane victory. Corine Barande Barbe's daughter of Garde Royale was a 5.5/1-chance, a point shorter than Daniel Wildenstein's pairing of Irish Champion Stakes runner-up Freedom Cry, trained by André Fabre, and Gunboat Diplomacy, the winner of La Coupe de Maisons-Laffitte. He was in the care of Élie Lellouche, who also trained the 67/1-shot Partipral.

As well as Lammtarra, Balanchine and Pure Grain, England was represented by the Derby Italiano-winner Luso, and Strategic Choice, who'd obliged in the Irish St Leger. Lando, who'd won the Gran Premio di Milano, returned for Germany while Argentina's El Sembrador was supplemented and received the southern hemisphere weight allowance. The Gran Premio Brasil-winner was a great-great-grandson of the 1958 Arc-winner Ballymoss.

Betting
2.1/1 Lammtarra, 2.3/1 Swain & Carnégie & Balanchine (all coupled), 5.5/1 Carling, 6.5/1 Freedom Cry & Gunboat Diplomacy (coupled), 8.8/1 Pure Grain, 21/1 BAR.

Three-year-old form lines
Prix du Jockey Club: 1st Celtic Swing, 2nd Poliglote, 3rd Winged Love
Grand Prix de Paris: 1st Valanour, 2nd Singspiel, 3rd Diamond Mix, 7th **Tot Ou Tard**, 9th **Carling**
Prix Niel: 1st Housamix, 2nd Poliglote, 3rd Winged Love

Fillies only
Prix de Diane: 1st **Carling**, 2nd Matiara, 3rd Tryphosa
Prix Vermeille: 1st **Carling**, 2nd Valley of Gold, 3rd Larrocha

Older horses and inter-generational races
Grand Prix de Saint-Cloud: 1st **Carnégie**, 2nd **Luso**, 3rd Only Royale, 7th **Tot Ou Tard**
La Coupe de Maisons-Laffitte: 1st **Gunboat Diplomacy**, 2nd Dernier Empereur, 3rd Northern Spy
Grand Prix de Deauville: 1st **Swain**, 2nd Zilzal Zamaan, 3rd **Sunrise Song**
Prix Foy: 1st **Carnégie**, 2nd **Balanchine**, 3rd **Tot Ou Tard**

Abroad

In England

Derby Stakes: 1st **Lammtarra**, 2nd Tamure, 3rd Presenting

Oaks Stakes: 1st Moonshell, 2nd Dance A Dream, 3rd **Pure Grain**

King George VI and Queen Elizabeth Stakes: 1st **Lammtarra**, 2nd Pentire, 3rd **Strategic Choice**, 6th **Carnégie**

St Leger: 1st Classic Cliché, 2nd Minds Music, 3rd Istidaad, 8th **Luso**

In Ireland

Irish Champion Stakes: 1st Pentire, 2nd **Freedom Cry**, 3rd Flagbird

In Germany

Grosser Preis von Baden: 1st Germany, 2nd Lecroix, 3rd Right Win, 7th **Lando**, 9th **Strategic Choice**

Gran Premio di Milano: 1st **Lando**, 2nd Broadway Flyer, 3rd **Strategic Choice**

The race

As they sorted themselves out, it was Luso who came through to lead in the early stages with Carling in second. Strategic Choice and Lammtarra then made ground on the inner to take up second and third at the Petit Bois, with Carling demoted to fourth.

Lammtarra moved into second on the downhill section, and with 1,000 metres to go it was Luso by three lengths to Lammtarra, then one and a half lengths to Strategic Choice, Carling and last year's winner Carnégie, who raced just ahead of Pure Grain.

Lammtarra closed the gap and then passed Luso approaching the straight. Pure Grain, Carnégie and Swain set off in pursuit, along with Freedom Cry on the outer. And it was the last-named who became the biggest danger, but try as he might Freedom Cry couldn't quite get there as Lammtarra kept gamely pulling out a bit more.

At the line he still had three parts to spare and his unbeaten record remained intact.

It was two lengths further back to Swain, with the fast-finishing Lando next, ahead of Pure Grain and then Carnégie, in sixth.

Post-race

Owned by Saeed Maktoum Al Maktoum, and bred by his father Maktoum Al Maktoum, Lammtarra was another Arc winner for the embryonic Darley/Godolphin operation, who were to be the main rivals to the Ballydoyle/Coolmore concern over the following decades.

Despite owning the third-placed horse, Sheikh Mohammed was understandably in the winner's enclosure to share the family triumph, in his twin roles as uncle to the owner and as the mastermind behind the whole operation.

Lammtarra was the first Arc winner for the former policeman turned trainer, Saeed bin Suroor, who would add to his tally in the early part of the next century. It was also the first for Lanfranco Dettori, universally known as Frankie.

Lammtarra was only the third horse to win both the Derby and the Arc, and emulated Mill Reef's feat of winning the King George VI and Queen Elizabeth Stakes in between. His stellar career was sweet but short; he retired having raced for a mere nine minutes and 3.38 seconds in total.

At stud he started and finished at Sheikh Mohammed's Dalham Hall Stud in Newmarket, but spent most of his time in Japan where he produced many winners including some at Grade 3 level.

Result

1995 Forte Prix de l'Arc de Triomphe
Longchamp. Sunday, 1 October 1995
Weights: 3yo c: 56kg, 3yo f: 54.5kg, 4yo+ c: 59.5kg, 4yo+ f: 58kg

1st Lammtarra (USA)　　3yo c　56kg　**2.1/1 fav**
by Nijinsky out of Snow Bride (Blushing Groom). Sheikh Saeed Maktoum Al Maktoum / Saeed bin Suroor / Frankie Dettori

2nd Freedom Cry (GB)　4yo c　59.5kg　**6.5/1**
by Soviet Star out of Falling Star (Mount Hagen). Daniel Wildenstein / André Fabre / Olivier Peslier

3rd Swain (IRE)　　　　3yo c　56kg　　**2.3/1** (coupled with Carnégie & Balanchine)
by Nashwan out of Love Smitten (Key To the Mint). Sheikh Mohammed / André Fabre / Mick Kinane

Runners: 16 (FR 9, GB 5, ARG 1, GER 1). Distances: ¾, 2. Going: very soft. Time: 2m 31.80s

Also ran: 4th **Lando** (GER) 5yo c, 5th **Pure Grain** (GB) 3yo f, 6th **Carnégie** (IRE) 4yo c, 7th **Partipral** (USA) 6yo h, 8th **Gunboat Diplomacy** (FR) 4yo c, 9th **Carling** (FR) 3yo f, 10th **Balanchine** (USA) 4yo f, 11th **El Tenor** (FR) 3yo c, 12th **Tot Ou Tard** (IRE) 5yo h, 13th **Luso** (GB) 3yo c, 14th **Strategic Choice** (USA) 4yo c, 15th **El Sembrador** (ARG) 4yo c, 16th **Sunrise Song** (FR) 4yo f.

Hélissio clearly the best in 75th Arc

*Peslier loses his cap but not his head
as he dictates from the front*

Background and fancied horses

Enrique Sarasola's Hélissio had only lost one of his six races prior to the Arc, which had included wins in the Prix Lupin, the Grand Prix de Saint-Cloud and the Prix Niel. The failure came in the Prix du Jockey Club, where he was sent off favourite but pulled very hard and didn't get a clear run. That blip apart, he was the clear form choice and was returned as the 1.8/1 favourite.

Next best in the market was a trio comprised of two owned outright by Sheikh Mohammed, Swain and Tamure, and Classic Cliché representing the bourgeoning Godolphin project, in what was to become their trademark royal blue colours. Together they were priced at 2.5/1.

Third last year, Swain had been runner-up to Hélissio in the Grand Prix de Saint-Cloud this season before winning the Prix Foy.

Tamure had finished second to Lammtarra in last year's Derby, and ended that campaign with fourth places in the Champion Stakes and Breeders' Cup Turf, but he hadn't been seen for 12 months.

The 1995 St Leger-hero, Classic Cliché, landed the Ascot Gold Cup before returning to Berkshire when second to Pentire in the King George VI and Queen Elizabeth Stakes.

Zagreb, one of two Irish-trained runners, won the Irish Derby on his third career outing and this would be the 6.5/1-chance's fourth run. His more experienced compatriot, Oscar Schindler at 15/1, had bagged the Hardwicke Stakes and the Irish St Leger.

In between the pair were Pentire at 7.3/1 and Darazari at 8/1. The former started the year with fourth place behind Cigar in the inaugural Dubai World Cup, before winning the King George VI and Queen Elizabeth Stakes, and most recently he'd finished second to Swain in the Prix Foy.

The Aga Khan IV-owned Darazari had won the Prix Maurice de Nieuil prior to finishing second best behind Hélissio in the Prix Niel.

Derby-winner Shaamit, Grosser Preis von Baden-winner Pilsudski, and Polaris Flight, runner-up in the Prix du Jockey Club and Irish Derby, along with Tamure, Classic Cliché and Pentire were the six English runners. Together with the two Irish representatives, Zagreb and Oscar

Schindler, there were eight raiders in total matched against the home team's own octet.

Forte sponsored again but, with a new acquisition under its belt, this year using the brand name Forte Méridien.

Betting
1.8/1 Hélissio, 2.5/1 Swain & Tamure & Classic Cliché (all coupled), 6.5/1 Zagreb, 7.3/1 Pentire, 8/1 Darazari, 15/1 Oscar Schindler, 22/1 BAR.

Three-year-old form lines
Prix du Jockey Club: 1st Ragmar, 2nd **Polaris Flight**, 3rd **Le Destin**, 5th **Hélissio**, 0th **Radevore**
Grand Prix de Paris: 1st Grape Tree Road, 2nd Glory of Dancer, 3rd Android
Prix Niel: 1st **Hélissio**, 2nd **Darazari**, 3rd **Radevore**, 8th **Le Destin**, 9th **Polaris Flight**

Fillies only
Prix de Diane: 1st Sil Sila, 2nd Miss Tahiti, 3rd Matiya, 7th **Luna Wells**
Prix Vermeille: 1st My Emma, 2nd Papering, 3rd Miss Tahiti, 4th **Leonila**

Older horses and inter-generational races
Grand Prix de Saint-Cloud: 1st **Hélissio**, 2nd **Swain**, 3rd Poliglote
Prix Foy: 1st **Swain**, 2nd **Pentire**, 3rd **Leeds**

Abroad
In England
Derby Stakes: 1st **Shaamit**, 2nd Dushyantor, 3rd Shantou
King George VI and Queen Elizabeth Stakes: 1st **Pentire**, 2nd **Classic Cliché**, 3rd **Shaamit**, 4th **Oscar Schindler**

In Ireland
Irish Derby: 1st **Zagreb**, 2nd **Polaris Flight**, 3rd His Excellence
Irish Champion Stakes: 1st Timarida, 2nd Dance Design, 3rd Glory of Dancer, 4th **Shaamit**

In Germany
Grosser Preis von Baden: 1st **Pilsudski**, 2nd Germany, 3rd Sunshack

The race
Zagreb broke fast on the rail along with Classic Cliché on the wide outside. Between them Hélissio was also on the premises but Pentire and Le Destin were slow to stride.

Hélissio soon came through to lead with Pilsudski, Shaamit, Classic Cliché and Zagreb in his wake. Olivier Peslier then moved the favourite to the rail and dictated a decent but sensible gallop.

Still going comfortably, he entered the straight with a length advantage over Pilsudski, and just before the 400-metre pole Peslier let Hélissio go, and he simply slipped the field going further and further clear.

Approaching the post, Peslier looked round to see that he was well clear – at which time he lost his yellow cap – and had plenty of time to salute the crowd and his mount before crossing the line five lengths clear.

Pilsudski, the winner of the Breeders' Cup Turf three weeks later, just held on for second from the fast-finishing Oscar Schindler, followed by Swain, Luna Wells and Le Destin.

Post-race

Spanish businessman and politician, Enrique Sarasola, went two places better than his third with Vert Amande in 1992. It was also a first Arc for the Tunisian-born trainer Élie Lellouche, who'd previously been placed with Epervier Bleu, Pistolet Bleu and Vert Amande.

Jockey Olivier Peslier, runner-up the year before on Freedom Cry, was just about to become champion jockey for the first time. His waiting-in-front ride on Hélissio was comparable with Lester Piggott on Alleged in 1977. Hélissio was kept in training and he and Peslier would be back in 12 months – but not together.

Result

1996 Forte Méridien Prix de l'Arc de Triomphe
Longchamp. Sunday, 6 October 1996
Weights: 3yo c: 56kg, 3yo f: 54.5kg, 4yo+ c: 59.5kg, 4yo+ f: 58kg

1st Hélissio (FR)   3yo c   56kg   **1.8/1 fav**
by Fairy King out of Helice (Slewpy). Enrique Sarasola / Élie Lellouche / Olivier Peslier

2nd Pilsudski (IRE)   4yo c   59.5kg   **22/1**
by Polish Precedent out of Cocotte (Troy). Exors of Simon Weinstock / Sir Michael Stoute / Walter Swinburn

3rd Oscar Schindler (IRE) 4yo c   59.5kg   **15/1**
by Royal Academy out of Saraday (Northfields). Oliver Lehane / Kevin Prendergast / Cash Asmussen

Runners: 16 (FR 8, GB 6, IRE 2). Distances: 5, sh nk. Going: good to soft. Time: 2m 29.90s

Also ran: 4th **Swain** (IRE) 4yo c, 5th **Luna Wells** (IRE) 3yo f, 6th **Le Destin** (FR) 3yo c, 7th **Shaamit** (IRE) 3yo c. 8th **Leeds** (IRE) 4yo c, 9th **Leonila** (IRE) 3yo f, 10th **Pentire** (GB) 4yo c, 11th **Darazari** (IRE) 3yo c, 12th **Radevore** (GB) 3yo c, 13th **Zagreb** (USA) 3yo c, 14th **Tamure** (IRE) 4yo c, 15th **Classic Cliché** (IRE) 4yo c, fell **Polaris Flight** (USA) 3yo c.

1997

Peintre Célèbre is picture perfect

Course record by 3.4 seconds
for only three-year-old colt in the field

Background and fancied horses

Daniel Wildenstein's Peintre Célèbre had been the standout colt of the summer in France, winning the Prix Greffulhe on his seasonal bow before adding the Prix du Jockey Club and Grand Prix de Paris.

However, after nearly three months off, he returned to action only to be beaten by a neck by Rajpoute when 1/10 favourite in the Prix Niel – but there were excuses. Hopelessly boxed-in for most of the straight, he'd sprinted home when finally finding racing room and made up nearly four lengths in the final 100 metres. Olivier Peslier had ridden him in all his races and Peintre Célèbre was 2.2/1 to get there on time in the Arc.

Not much longer at 2.5/1 was the previous year's winner for Peslier, Hélissio, who would be ridden by Dominique Boeuf this time. Cash Asmussen, though, was on board when he won the Grand Prix de Saint-Cloud and when he finished third in the King George VI and Queen Elizabeth Stakes.

Last year's runner-up Pilsudski had gone on to win the Breeders' Cup Turf and was enjoying another excellent season. The 3.8/1 shot for the Arc had won the Eclipse Stakes and the Irish Champion Stakes, in between times finishing second to Swain in the King George VI and Queen Elizabeth Stakes.

Swain himself was 9.5/1 coupled with Predappio. Now racing in Godolphin blue after moving from André Fabre to Saeed bin Suroor in May, Swain had won the King George VI and Queen Elizabeth Stakes in style, before being beaten by two short heads in the Arc Trial at Newbury. Hardwicke Stakes-winner Predappio had formerly been with John Oxx in Ireland.

The winner of the Irish St Leger for the second time, Oscar Schindler, was still trained in Ireland. The 12/1-shot was followed by two horses at 16/1: the 1996 Prix Vermeille-winner My Emma; and Germany's Borgia, the Deutsches Derby and Grosser Preis von Baden-hero, who was to be the first Arc ride for Kieren Fallon.

England sent over the Newbury Arc Trial-winner Posidonas and the Barry Hills-trained Busy Flight as well as Swain, Predappio, and My Emma. Germany had the Preis der Diana-heroine Que Belle in addition to Borgia, while Ireland was represented by Oscar Schindler and – bringing the number of raiders to ten – the Aga Khan IV's Ebadiyla, winner of the Irish Oaks and the Prix Royal-Oak.

The arrangement with Forte Méridien had ended and the race was run without a sponsor for the first time since 1981.

Betting
2.2/1 Peintre Célèbre, 2.5/1 Hélissio, 3.8/1 Pilsudski, 9.5/1 Swain & Predappio (coupled), 12/1 Oscar Schindler, 16/1 Borgia, 16.1/1 My Emma, 31/1 BAR.

Three-year-old form lines
Prix du Jockey Club: 1st **Peintre Célèbre**, 2nd Oscar, 3rd Astarabad, 4th Fragrant Mix
Grand Prix de Paris: 1st **Peintre Célèbre**, 2nd Ithaki, 3rd Shaka
Prix Niel: 1st Rajpoute, 2nd **Peintre Célèbre**, 3rd Ivan Luis

Fillies only
Prix de Diane: 1st Vereva, 2nd Mousse Glacée, 3rd Brilliance, 9th **Queen Maud**
Prix Vermeille: 1st **Queen Maud**, 2nd **Gazelle Royale**, 3rd Brilliance

Older horses and inter-generational races
Grand Prix de Saint-Cloud: 1st **Hélissio**, 2nd Magellano, 3rd Riyadian
Prix Foy: 1st Yokohama, 2nd **Nothin' Leica Dane**, 3rd **Le Destin**

Abroad
In England
Derby Stakes: 1st Benny the Dip, 2nd Silver Patriarch, 3rd Romanov
Oaks Stakes: 1st Reams of Verse, 2nd **Gazelle Royale**, 3rd Crown of Light, 5th **Ebadiyla**
King George VI and Queen Elizabeth Stakes: 1st **Swain**, 2nd **Pilsudski**, 3rd **Hélissio**, 7th **Predappio**

In Ireland
Irish Champion Stakes: 1st **Pilsudski**, 2nd Desert King, 3rd Alhaarth

In Germany
Grosser Preis von Baden: 1st **Borgia**, 2nd Luso, 3rd **Predappio**

The race
Busy Flight made the early pace, while on the inner Olivier Peslier on Peintre Célèbre was trying to move up a rank. However, as John Reid manoeuvred Predappio to the rail it became very congested and Gazelle Royale had to put the brakes on, which in turn caused interference to Peintre Célèbre, who was knocked back several places.

At the top of the hill, Hélissio took over in front relegating Busy Flight to second with the Godolphin duo, Predappio and Swain, sharing third just ahead of Posidonas.

Hélissio, trying to repeat last year's tactics, still held sway on the final turn. Meanwhile Peintre Célèbre in 10th place, switched off the rail and quickly started to make rapid progress into the front six. A length and a half behind him, Pilsudski was also starting his run.

But Peintre Célèbre had been launched and, answering Peslier's urgings, he moved through the field to strike the front with 200 metres to go. Pilsudski followed him through but once in front Peintre Célèbre seemingly engaged the turbo, as he accelerated again to pull five lengths clear of Pilsudski, who finished runner-up for the second year in a row.

Two and a half lengths further back, Borgia claimed third in a bunch finish for the minor honours, just ahead of Oscar Schindler, Predappio, and last year's winner Hélissio. This time Peslier left his exuberant celebrations until he'd passed the line and once pulling-up received a hug from his friend Franke Dettori, who'd ridden Swain.

Post-race

It was a fantastic performance, which was confirmed by the new record time that smashed the old mark by a staggering 3.4 seconds. For veteran owner Daniel Wildenstein it was a fourth Arc after Allez France, All Along and Sagace.

André Fabre also moved on to four adding to his previous successes with Trempolino, Subotica and Carnégie, and thus equalled the records of Charles Semblat, Alec Head and François Mathet.

Olivier Peslier – resplendent in his trademark *papillon* brooch – had won in consecutive years after Hélissio last year, and was about to be crowned champion jockey for the second time – although there is no crown, but instead a rather splendid golden whip or *cravache d'or*.

Peintre Célèbre, the eighth Prix du Jockey Club-winner to secure the Arc, was kept in training but didn't race again as he injured a tendon before the new season. At stud he produced plenty of winners, including Prince of Wales's Stakes-winner Byword and the very useful Pride, who we will encounter later.

Result

1997 Prix de l'Arc de Triomphe
Longchamp. Sunday, 5 October 1997
Weights: 3yo c: 56kg, 3yo f: 54.5kg, 4yo+ c: 59.5kg, 4yo+ f: 58kg

1st Peintre Célèbre (USA) 3yo c   56kg   **2.2/1 fav**
by Nureyev out of Peinture Bleue (Alydar). Daniel Wildenstein / André Fabre / Olivier Peslier

2nd Pilsudski (IRE)   5yo c   59.5kg   **3.8/1**
by Polish Precedent out of Cocotte (Troy). Lord Weinstock / Sir Michael Stoute / Mick Kinane

3rd Borgia (GER)   3yo f   54.5kg   **16/1**
by Acatenango out of Britannia (Tarim). Gestüt Ammerland / Bruno Schütz / Kieren Fallon

Runners: 18 (FR 8, GB 6, GER 2, IRE 2). Distances: 5, 2½. Going: good/good to soft. Time: 2m 24.60s

Also ran: 4th **Oscar Schindler** (IRE) 5yo h, 5th **Predappio** (GB) 4yo c, 6th **Hélissio** (FR) 4yo c, 7th **Swain** (IRE) 5yo h, 8th **Que Belle** (CAN) 3yo f, 9th **Posidonas** (GB) 5yo h, 10th **Busy Flight** (GB) 4yo c, 11th **My Emma** (GB) 4yo f, 12th **Ebadiyla** (IRE) 3yo f, 13th **Gazelle Royale** (FR) 3yo f, 14th **Steward** (FR) 4yo c, 15th **Queen Maud** (IRE) 3yo f, 16th **Le Destin** (FR) 4yo c, 17th **Nothin' Leica Dane** (AUS) 4yo h, 18th **Yokohama** (USA) 6yo h.

1998
Sagamix battles home for Lagardère
Shades of Eddery as Peslier completes hat-trick

Background and fancied horses

Jean-Luc Lagardère's Sagamix didn't race at two, but after winning a couple of times in the spring he erupted on to the big stage when, on his third outing, he took the Prix Niel beating the first and second in the Prix du Jockey Club.

All three of his races had been on soft or heavy ground, and with similar conditions for the Arc he topped the market at 2.5/1 coupled with Fragrant Mix, both being trained by André Fabre, who had three runners in all.

Fourth to Peintre Célèbre in the previous season's Prix du Jockey Club, Fragrant Mix – who like Sagamix was a son of Linamix – had won twice this term including the Grand Prix de Saint-Cloud. Most recently, he'd been second to Limnos in the Prix Foy. With Peslier aboard Sagamix, he was to be ridden by Alain Junk.

Next in the betting was the Godolphin/Sheikh Mohammed trio of Sea Wave, Happy Valentine and Limpid, at 3.8/1. The first two were trained by Saeed bin Suroor, the latter by Fabre.

Sea Wave had hosed up in the Great Voltigeur Stakes but had then unshipped Frankie Dettori exiting the stalls in the Prix Niel. Happy Valentine was also in the royal blue colours, and was there to ensure a good gallop, while Grand Prix de Paris-winner Limpid was sporting the maroon and white.

Derby-winner High-Rise was 4/1, followed by Prix du Jockey Club-victor Dream Well at 5.3/1, and the horse he beat, Croco Rouge, at 7.8/1. The best of the German-trained duo was Georg von Ullmann's Tiger Hill at 9.5/1. He'd won the German 2000 Guineas and the Grosser Preis von Baden.

The second home in the latter race, Caitano, was also in the Arc field, while the winners of the Prix de Diane and Prix Vermeille, Zainta and Leggera, were 15/1 and 16/1 respectively.

In addition to the German duo, England had half a dozen entrants. They were the previously mentioned Sea Wave, Happy Valentine, High-Rise and Leggera, and the Paul Cole-trained pairing of the returning Posidonas, who'd added this season's Hardwicke Stakes to his tally, and the Sandown Classic Trial-winner Courteous. Like last year there was no Arc sponsor.

Betting

2.5/1 Sagamix & Fragrant Mix (coupled), 3.8/1 Sea Wave & Happy Valentine & Limpid (all coupled), 4/1 High-Rise, 5.3/1 Dream Well, 7.8/1 Croco Rouge, 9.5/1 Tiger Hill, 15/1 Zainta, 16/1 Leggera, 33/1 BAR.

Three-year-old form lines

Prix du Jockey Club: 1st **Dream Well**, 2nd **Croco Rouge**, 3rd Sestino
Grand Prix de Paris: 1st **Limpid**, 2nd Almutawakel, 3rd **Croco Rouge**
Prix Niel: 1st **Sagamix**, 2nd **Croco Rouge**, 3rd **Dream Well**, UR **Sea Wave**

Fillies only

Prix de Diane: 1st **Zainta**, 2nd Abbatiale, 3rd Insight
Prix Vermeille: 1st **Leggera**, 2nd Cloud Castle, 3rd **Zainta**

Older horses and inter-generational races

Grand Prix de Saint-Cloud: 1st **Fragrant Mix**, 2nd Romanov, 3rd Gazelle Royale
Prix Foy: 1st Limnos, 2nd **Fragrant Mix**, 3rd Oa Baldixe

Abroad

In England
Derby Stakes: 1st **High-Rise**, 2nd City Honours, 3rd Border Arrow, 5th Greek Dance, 12th **Courteous**
King George VI and Queen Elizabeth Stakes: 1st Swain, 2nd **High-Rise**, 3rd Royal Anthem, 4th Daylami, 7th **Happy Valentine**

In Ireland
Irish Derby: 1st **Dream Well**, 2nd City Honours, 3rd Desert Fox
Irish Champion Stakes: 1st Swain, 2nd Alborada, 3rd Xaar, 7th **Happy Valentine**

In Germany
Grosser Preis von Baden: 1st **Tiger Hill**, 2nd **Caitano**, 3rd Public Purse

In Italy
Gran Premio di Milano: 1st Ungaro, 2nd Santillana, 3rd March Groom, 9th **Caitano**

The race

Zainta and Caitano were slow away, leaving Fragrant Mix, Leggera and Posidonas to the fore, until the Godolphin-pacemaker Happy Valentine came through to take it up.

At the Petit Bois, Happy Valentine had a three-length advantage which, turning downhill, he quickly extended to 12 lengths. He still led into the straight but now only by four lengths, and was being reeled in by Leggera, who led the chasing group.

On the outside Sea Wave looked dangerous for a few strides, but it was Sagamix, despite having come under pressure on the false straight, who began to close in. With 250 metres to run, Leggera finally caught Happy Valentine but was instantly challenged on her inner by Tiger Hill, and on the outer by Sagamix.

Olivier Peslier's mount found most, digging deep to take Leggera's measure in the final three or four strides to win by a neck on the line, and complete a hat-trick in the race for Peslier. There was three parts of a length back to Tiger Hill, followed by Croco Rouge, Caitano and the winner's stable companion Fragrant Mix in sixth.

Post-race

It was the third time that the famous colours of grey with a pink cap had come out on top in the Arc. The silks had previously been used by François Dupré, who won with Tantième in 1950 and 1951.

Now they were registered to Jean-Luc Lagardère, the current owner of Dupré's Haras d'Ouilly in Normandy. The CEO of the eponymous Lagardère Group was a major owner/breeder and the first president of France Galop when it was formed to unify the four existing racing authorities in 1995. Lagardère was given a fitting memorial when the Grand Critérium, which was inaugurated in 1853, was retitled the Prix Jean-Luc Lagardère after his death in 2003.

But back to Sagamix, who for trainer André Fabre was a fifth Arc winner after Trempolino, Subotica, Carnégie and Peintre Célèbre, which made him the outright winning-most Arc trainer. It was also, of course, the final leg of a hat-trick for Olivier Peslier, equalling Pat Eddery's feat in the 1980s.

Sagamix was kept in training until 2000 but didn't win again. He ran five times in that period but never on his favoured soft ground. He has produced many winners, the best of which on the flat was Siljan's Saga, as well as plenty over jumps, albeit nothing of superstar status.

Result

1998 Prix de l'Arc de Triomphe

Longchamp. Sunday, 4 October 1998
Weights: 3yo c: 56kg, 3yo f: 54.5kg, 4yo+ c: 59.5kg, 4yo+ f: 58kg

1st Sagamix (FR)   3yo c   56kg   **2.5/1 fav** (coupled with Fragrant Mix)
by Linamix out of Saganeca (Sagace). Jean-Luc Lagardère / André Fabre / Olivier Peslier

2nd Leggera (IRE)   3yo f   54.5kg   **16/1**
by Sadler's Wells out of Lady Ambassador (General Assembly). Hildegard Focke / John Dunlop / Richard Quinn

3rd Tiger Hill (IRE)   3yo c   56kg   **9.5/1**
by Danehill out of The Filly (Appiani II). Georg von Ullmann / Peter Schiergen / Andreas Suborics

Runners: 14 (FR 6, GB 6, GER 2). Distances: nk, ¾. Going: soft. Time: 2m 34.50s

Also ran: 4th **Croco Rouge** (IRE) 3yo f, 5th **Caitano** (GB) 4yo c, 6th **Fragrant Mix** (IRE) 4yo c, 7th **High-Rise** (IRE) 3yo c, 8th **Dream Well** (FR) 3yo c, 9th **Sea Wave** (IRE) 3yo c, 10th **Happy Valentine** (GB) 4yo c, 11th **Courteous** (GB) 3yo c, 12th **Limpid** (GB) 3yo c, 13th **Zainta** (IRE) 3yo f, 14th **Posidonas** (GB) 4yo c.

1999

Magnificent Montjeu
sprints to glory

First winner for Michael Tabor

Background and fancied horses

Michael Tabor's Montjeu had put up two of the most eye-catching performances of the year when coming from off the pace to storm clear in the Prix du Jockey Club by four lengths, and then in the Irish Derby, this time by five lengths. Returning from a break, he got up on the line to take the Prix Niel, and primed for the Arc was sent off favourite at 1.5/1, coupled with his pacemaker Genghis Khan.

Second favourite El Condor Pasa, at 3.5/1, was the latest high-profile runner from Japan. He'd won the Japan Cup last year and was runner-up in the Prix d'Ispahan on his first run in France in May. After that he won the Grand Prix de Saint-Cloud in good style and then the Prix Foy, battling back after being headed.

The grey Daylami at 4/1, who'd won the 1997 Poule d'Essai des Poulains for the Aga Khan IV, was now with Godolphin and had won this season's King George VI and Queen Elizabeth Stakes and the Irish Champion Stakes.

Daryaba, who was still with the Aga Khan, had led from flag fall to win the Prix de Diane before coming late to land the Prix Vermeille. She was priced at 7.5/1 and it was nearly double those odds to last year's fourth, Croco Rouge, who'd beaten El Condor Pasa in the Prix d'Ispahan, but was then beaten by that horse in the Prix Foy.

Tiger Hill, who'd finished in front of Croco Rouge last year, was 15/1 and had won the Grosser Preis von Baden for the second year running, in the process beating the other German-runner in the Arc, Flamingo Road.

With El Condor Pasa for Japan, the Norwegian-trained Albaran and a quartet from England – the aforementioned Daylami, the returning Leggera, the Newbury Arc Trial-winner Fantastic Light and Greek Dance, who'd been fifth in last year's Derby – there were nine foreign runners.

The Arc had a new sponsor in the form of the hotel and casino group Lucien Barrière.

Betting

1.5/1 Montjeu & Genghis Khan (coupled), 3.5/1 El Condor Pasa, 4/1 Daylami, 7.5/1 Daryaba, 14/1 Borgia, 14/1 Croco Rouge, 15/1 Tiger Hill, 21/1 Leggera, 33/1 BAR.

Three-year-old form lines

Prix du Jockey Club: 1st **Montjeu**, 2nd Nowhere to Exit, 3rd Rhagaas
Grand Prix de Paris: 1st Slickly, 2nd Indian Danehill, 3rd Sardaukar
Prix Niel: 1st **Montjeu**, 2nd Bienamado, 3rd First Magnitude

Fillies only

Prix de Diane: 1st **Daryaba**, 2nd Star of Akkar, 3rd Visionnaire, 11th **Cerulean Sky**
Prix Vermeille: 1st **Daryaba**, 2nd Etizaaz, 3rd **Cerulean Sky**

Older horses and inter-generational races

Grand Prix de Saint-Cloud: 1st **El Condor Pasa**, 2nd **Tiger Hill**, 3rd Dream Well, 4th Sagamix, 5th **Borgia**, 9th **Greek Dance**
Prix Foy: 1st **El Condor Pasa**, 2nd **Borgia**, 3rd/last **Croco Rouge**

Abroad

In England
Derby Stakes: 1st Oath, 2nd Daliapour, 3rd Beat All
King George VI and Queen Elizabeth Stakes: 1st **Daylami**, 2nd Nedawi, 3rd Fruits of Love

In Ireland
Irish Derby: 1st **Montjeu**, 2nd Daliapour, 3rd Tchaikovsky, 9th **Genghis Khan**
Irish Champion Stakes: 1st **Daylami**, 2nd Dazzling Park, 3rd Dream Well

In Germany
Grosser Preis von Baden: 1st **Tiger Hill**, 2nd **Flamingo Road**, 3rd Belenus

The race

On a sunny day, El Condor Pasa broke quickest and led on the inner. Montjeu's pacemaker Genghis Khan, in the dark blue Magnier colours, was being scrubbed along in order to try and pass him, but had to be content to slot into second. Montjeu himself was on the rail in the third rank.

El Condor Pasa stretched the advantage over Genghis Khan to three lengths at the Petit Bois, with Greek Dance now in a share of third with Tiger Hill and Leggera. Going down the hill, Greek Dance and Tiger Hill passed Genghis Khan, one on each side, followed by Montjeu who moved into fourth on the rail.

Into the straight, El Condor Pasa's lead had been reduced to one and a half lengths by the chasing group, who were being joined by Croco Rouge and Daylami.

Entering the final 400 metres, Mick Kinane angled Montjeu out from the rail to find racing room. Once in a clear lane, he unleashed a devastating turn of foot to come between Tiger Hill and Leggera, cutting the deficit with El Condor Pasa, who'd gone four lengths clear again, by half that at the 200-metre mark.

On terms at the 100-metre pole, he forged on to secure a notable triumph by half a length, with six lengths to Croco Rouge, who had run on best of the rest, in splendid isolation as there was another five lengths to Leggera, Tiger Hill and Greek Dance.

Post-race

This was the first Arc winner for former bookmaker and professional punter Michael Tabor in his blue and orange colours. Together with John Magnier, his wife Sue – the daughter of Vincent O'Brien – and others including Derrick Smith, they would continue the work of Robert Sangster and Vincent O'Brien in promoting Coolmore to become one of the two global racing powerhouses.

After Suave Dancer in 1991, it was the second time in the Arc winner's enclosure for John Hammond, who trained at Chantilly until his retirement at the end of 2019. It was also a second Arc for Mick Kinane the rider of Carroll House ten years before. Montjeu, the ninth Prix du Jockey Club-winner to land the Arc, had put up a spectacular performance and would be back to defend the title.

Result

1999 Prix de l'Arc de Triomphe Lucien Barrière
Longchamp. Sunday, 3 October 1999
Weights: 3yo c: 56kg, 3yo f: 54.5kg, 4yo+ c: 59.5kg, 4yo+ f: 58kg

1st Montjeu (IRE)　　　3yo c　56kg　**1.5/1 fav** (coupled with Genghis Khan)
by Sadler's Wells out of Floripedes (Top Ville). Michael Tabor / John Hammond / Mick Kinane

2nd El Condor Pasa (USA) 4yo f　59.5kg　**3.5/1**
by Kingmambo out of Saddlers Gal (Sadler's Wells). Takao Watanabe / Yoshitaka Ninomiya / Masayoshi Ebina

3rd Croco Rouge (IRE)　4yo c　59.5kg　**14/1**
by Rainbow Quest out of Alligatrix (Alleged). Wafic Saïd / Pascal Bary / Thierry Jarnet

Runners: 14 (FR 5, GB 4, GER 2, IRE 1, JPN 1 NOR 1). Distances: ½, 6. Going: heavy. Time: 2m 38.50s

Also ran: 4th **Leggera** (IRE) 4yo f, 5th **Tiger Hill** (IRE) 4yo c, 6th **Greek Dance** (IRE) 4yo c, 7th **Borgia** (GER) 5yo m, 8th **Cerulean Sky** (IRE) 3yo f, 9th **Daylami** (IRE) 5yo h, 10th **Flamingo Road** (GER) 3yo f, 11th **Fantastic Light** (USA) 3yo c, 12th **Albaran** (GER) 6yo h, 13th **Daryaba** (IRE) 3yo f, 14th **Genghis Khan** (IRE) 3yo c.

Sinndar is superlative

First Irish-winner since Alleged

Background and fancied horses

After last year's win Montjeu had gone on to finish fourth in the Japan Cup. He'd been back in winning form with a vengeance this term taking the Grand Prix de Saint-Cloud, King George VI and Queen Elizabeth Stakes, and the Prix Foy. Odds-on to win a second Arc, he was in great form, but would face a very strong younger challenger from Ireland.

The John Oxx-trained runner, Sinndar, had gone from strength to strength, and had only been beaten by one horse in seven outings, picking up the English and Irish Derbys and the Prix Niel along the way – the last two by nine and eight lengths respectively. Accompanied by his stablemate and pacemaker Raypour, the Aga Khan IV's duo were 1.5/1.

Germany's Deutsches Derby and Grosser Preis von Baden-winner Samum, at 7.5/1, completed the three-strong party of foreign runners in the field of ten, which was the smallest since 1964.

With the Carlos Lerner-trained Volvoreta, who'd been second to Egyptband in the Prix Diane before winning the Prix Vermeille, at 8.5/1, it was 25/1 bar. The outsiders included Grand Prix de Deauville first and second, Russian Hope and Daring Miss, and Hightori, who'd won the Prix du Prince d'Orange.

Betting

0.8/1 Montjeu, 1.5/1 Sinndar & Raypour (coupled), 7.5/1 Samum, 8.5/1 Volvoreta, 25/1 Egyptband, 46/1 BAR.

Three-year-old form lines

Prix du Jockey Club: 1st Holding Court, 2nd Lord Flasheart, 3rd Circus Dance, 10th **Hesiode**

Grand Prix de Paris: 1st Beat Hollow, 2nd Premier Pas, 3rd Rhenium

Prix Niel: 1st **Sinndar**, 2nd Crimson Quest, 3rd Sobieski, 6th/last **Raypour**

Fillies only

Prix de Diane: 1st **Egyptband**, 2nd **Volvoreta**, 3rd Goldamix

Prix Vermeille: 1st **Volvoreta**, 2nd Rêve d'Oscar, 3rd **Egyptband**

Older horses and inter-generational races

Grand Prix de Saint-Cloud: 1st **Montjeu**, 2nd **Daring Miss**, 3rd Sagamix

Grand Prix de Deauville: 1st **Russian Hope**, 2nd **Daring Miss**, 3rd Mont Rocher

Prix du Prince d'Orange: 1st **Hightori**, 2nd Bleu D'Altair, 3rd Rhenium

Prix Foy: 1st **Montjeu**, 2nd Crillon, 3rd Commander Collins

Abroad

In England

Derby Stakes: 1st **Sinndar**, 2nd Sakhee, 3rd Beat Hollow

King George VI and Queen Elizabeth Stakes: 1st **Montjeu**, 2nd Fantastic Light, 3rd Daliapour, 6th **Raypour**

In Ireland

Irish Derby: 1st **Sinndar**, 2nd Glyndebourne, 3rd Ciro, 4th **Raypour**, 6th Holding Court

In Germany

Grosser Preis von Baden: 1st **Samum**, 2nd Boréal, 3rd Fruits of Love, 5th Holding Court

The race

Sinndar flew out of the stalls, leaving Johnny Murtagh looking round to see where his pacemaker, Raypour, was. It took quite a while before Niall McCullagh could force Raypour to the front. There was then a gap of three lengths, after the Aga Khan pair, to Russian Hope in third. Meanwhile Montjeu and Egyptband were in rear, about seven lengths off the pace.

On the turn-in, Raypour, in the distinguishing red cap, capitulated leaving Sinndar in front from a menacing-looking Volvoreta, with Hightori wide, followed by Egyptband and Montjeu, who had made ground on the descent.

Audaciously, Peslier switched Volvoreta to the inside of Sinndar while Montjeu now had racing room. Volvoreta got to within a neck of Sinndar but then started to drop back, while on the outside Egyptband started to flash home.

Sinndar, though, had plenty in reserve and held off the challenge of Egyptband by one and a half lengths, with three back to Volvoreta then Montjeu – who didn't find much off the bridle – in fourth. Hightori and Samum completed the first six.

Post-race

Sinndar – in the green, red epaulettes, and a green cap – doubled the Aga Khan's Arc tally, adding to Akiyda in 1982, and was the first Irish-trained winner since Alleged in 1978.

He was the first Arc winner for John Oxx, who'd trained future Arc-winner Star Appeal when he was unplaced in 1973. Oxx would be back with another superstar at the end of the decade.

Johnny Murtagh, who would go on to be Coolmore's retained jockey, was also opening his Arc account. Sinndar was retired and sired many winners including Prix Vermeille-heroine Shawanda. He was also responsible for a couple that were famous for finishing second, Youmzain and Shareta, who will both figure in our narrative.

After Sea Bird, Mill Reef and Lammtarra, Sinndar was the fourth Derby winner to take the Arc.

Result
2000 Prix de l'Arc de Triomphe Lucien Barrière
Longchamp. Sunday, 1 October 2000
Weights: 3yo c: 56kg, 3yo f: 54.5kg, 4yo+ c: 59.5kg, 4yo+ f: 58kg

1st Sinndar (IRE) 3yo c 56kg **1.5/1** (coupled with Raypour)
by Grand Lodge out of Sinntara (Lashkari). HH Aga Khan IV / John Oxx / Johnny Murtagh

2nd Egyptband (USA) 3yo f 54.5kg **25/1**
by Dixieland Band out of Egyptown (Top Ville). Wertheimer & Frere / Christiane Head-Maarek / Olivier Doleuze

3rd Volvoreta (GB) 4yo f 54.5kg **8.5/1**
by Suave Dancer out of Robertiya (Don Roberto). Maria-Soledad Vidal & Enrique Sarasola / Carlos Lerner / Olivier Peslier

Runners: 10 (FR 7, IRE 2, GER 1). Distances: 1½, 3. Going: good. Time: 2m 25.80s

Also ran: 4th **Montjeu** (IRE) 4yo c, 5th **Hightori** (FR) 3yo c, 6th **Samum** (GER) 3yo c, 7th **Daring Miss** (GB) 4yo f, 8th **Russian Hope** (IRE) 5yo h, 9th **Hesiode** (FR) 3yo c, 10th **Raypour** (IRE) 3yo c.

Sakhee supreme and six million francs richer

Godolphin's charge equals longest winning margin

Background and fancied horses

The market leader at 2.2/1 was Godolphin's Sakhee. Runner-up to Sinndar in last year's Derby before being injured in the Eclipse Stakes, he'd returned after a year on the sidelines to win the Steventon Stakes at Newbury. He'd then added the Juddmonte International Stakes by an eased-down seven lengths.

Daniel Wildenstein's Aquarelliste, who'd won the Prix de Diane and Prix Vermeille, was co-second best at 4.8/1, along with the Magnier/Tabor pairing of Milan and Saddler's Creek. Milan had improved through the year and arrived on the back of a five-length success in the St Leger. Saddler's Creek was in attendance to ensure a strong gallop.

Michael Stoute's Golan, at 7.5/1, had won the 2000 Guineas before finishing second in the Derby, and was then third in the Irish Derby. He was back to winning form in the Prix Niel, where he beat the Prix du Jockey Club-winner Anabaa Blue, who was 11/1 for the Arc.

Between the pair, on 9.5/1, was last year's fifth, Hightori, who'd been a creditable third in the King George VI and Queen Elizabeth Stakes.

Jean-Luc Lagardère's representatives, Prix du Prince d'Orange-second Sagacity and Diamilina, runner-up in the Prix Vermeille, were 15/1. The returning Egyptband, who wasn't disgraced when third in the Grand Prix de Saint-Cloud, was a 17/1-shot. Last year's Prix du Jockey Club-winner Holding Court was on 22/1, and it was 39/1 bar.

In addition to Sakhee, Golan, and Holding Court, England had Ebor Handicap-second Foreign Affairs, and Prix Foy-fourth Little Rock. Ireland had Milan, Saddler's Creek, and rank outsider Chimes at Midnight, while Germany was represented by Anzillero, who'd won a Group 1 at Dusseldorf.

It was to be the last time that the prize money was to be paid in francs – six million to the winner on this occasion – before that currency was replaced by the euro.

Betting

2.2/1 Sakhee, 4.8/1 Aquarelliste, 4.8/1 Milan & Saddler's Creek (coupled), 7.5/1 Golan, 9.5/1 Hightori, 11/1 Anabaa Blue, 15/1 Diamilina & Sagacity (coupled), 17/1 Egyptband, 22/1 Holding Court, 39/1 BAR.

Three-year-old form lines

Prix du Jockey Club: 1st **Anabaa Blue**, 2nd Chichicastenango, 3rd Grandera, 5th **Milan**, 9th **Sagacity**

Grand Prix de Paris: 1st Chichicastenango, 2nd Mizzen Mast, 3rd Bonnard

Prix Niel: 1st **Golan**, 2nd **Anabaa Blue**, 3rd Chichicastenango

Fillies only

Prix de Diane: 1st **Aquarelliste**, 2nd Nadia, 3rd Time Away

Prix Vermeille: 1st **Aquarelliste**, 2nd **Diamilina**, 3rd Mare Nostrum

Older horses and inter-generational races

Grand Prix de Saint-Cloud: 1st Mirio, 2nd Perfect Sunday, 3rd **Egyptband**

Grand Prix de Deauville: 1st **Holding Court**, 2nd Marienbard, 3rd **Idaho Quest**

Prix du Prince d'Orange: 1st Equerry, 2nd **Sagacity**, 3rd Poussin

Prix Foy: 1st **Hightori**, 2nd **Idaho Quest**, 3rd Slew the Red, 4th **Little Rock**

Abroad

In England

Derby Stakes: 1st Galileo, 2nd **Golan**, 3rd Tobougg

King George VI and Queen Elizabeth Stakes: 1st Galileo, 2nd Fantastic Light, 3rd **Hightori**, 7th **Anabaa Blue**, 10th **Chimes At Midnight**

St Leger: 1st **Milan**, 2nd Demophilos, 3rd Mr Combustible, 9th **Chimes At Midnight**

In Ireland

Irish Derby: 1st Galileo, 2nd Morshdi, 3rd **Golan**

Irish Champion Stakes: 1st Fantastic Light, 2nd Galileo, 3rd Bach, 7th/last **Chimes At Midnight**

The race

Chimes At Midnight was slow to stride while Saddler's Creek and Anzillero were the first to show from Anabaa Blue, Golan and Sakhee. By the Petit Bois, Saddler's Creek had moved across from the outside to lane two and was the overall leader.

Going downhill Anzillero took over and still led on the false straight from Anabaa Blue and Sakhee. Many still had chances and only Chimes At Midnight was already beaten. Approaching the entrance to the straight, Sakhee cruised alongside Anzillero to take it up. At the same time, Soumillon pushed Anabaa Blue up on the inside of the fading former leader.

With 450 metres to run, Dettori asked Sakhee to extend and from there on in it became a procession, with the favourite drawing six lengths clear to win easily and become the tenth British-trained winner.

Golan set off in vain pursuit and was clear in second place until running out of petrol with 150 metres remaining. He was then overhauled by the Dominique Boeuf-ridden Aquarelliste and Sagacity. Milan ran through in fifth with Little Rock sixth.

Post-race

Sahkee was *suprême*, and his fabulous performance equalled the record for the widest winning margin of six lengths, which was set by Ribot in 1956 and first equalled by Sea Bird in 1965. Elite company indeed.

It was a first win for the royal blue colours of Godolphin. Sheikh Mohammed, though, had won with Carnégie in 1994 in his own maroon and white silks, and had been heavily involved with Lammtarra in 1995.

Saeed bin Suroor and Frankie Dettori, who had trained and ridden Lammtarra, moved their scores on to two, and the whole team wouldn't be away from the winner's enclosure for long.

Sakhee went on to America, where he finished just a nose behind Tiznow in the Breeders' Cup Classic before drawing stumps for the season.

Result

2001 Prix de l'Arc de Triomphe Lucien Barrière
Longchamp. Sunday, 7 October 2001
Weights: 3yo c: 56kg, 3yo f: 54.5kg, 4yo+ c: 59.5kg, 4yo+ f: 58kg

1st Sakhee (USA)   4yo c   59.5kg   **2.2/1 fav**
by Bahri out of Thawakib (Sadler's Wells). Godolphin / Saeed bin Suroor / Frankie Dettori

2nd Aquarelliste (FR)   3yo f   54.5kg   **4.8/1**
by Danehill out of Agathe (Manila). Daniel Wildenstein / Élie Lellouche / Dominique Boeuf

3rd Sagacity (FR)   3yo c   56kg   **15/1** (coupled with Diamilina)
by Suave Dancer out of Robertiya (Don Roberto). Jean-Luc Lagardère / André Fabre / Yutaka Take

Runners: 17 (FR 8, GB 5, IRE 3, GER 1). Distances: 6, 1. Going: holding. Time: 2m 36.10s

Also ran: 4th **Golan** (IRE) 3yo c, 5th **Milan** (GB) 3yo c, 6th **Little Rock** (GB) 5yo h, 7th **Hightori** (FR) 4yo c, 8th **Egyptband** (USA) 4yo f, 9th **Anabaa Blue** (GB) 3yo c, 10th **Foreign Affairs** (GB) 3yo c, 11th **Diamilina** (FR) 3yo f, 12th **Honorifique** (FR) 4yo f, 13th **Anzillero** (GER) 4yo c, 14th **Idaho Quest** (GB) 4yo c, 15th **Holding Court** (GB) 4yo c, 16th **Saddler's Creek** (USA) 3yo c, 17th **Chimes At Midnight** (USA) 4yo c.

Marvellous Marienbard takes home the euros

Last year's winning team do it again

Background and fancied horses

The Irish-trained High Chaparral, who'd won the Epsom Derby beating stable companion Hawk Wing, had been the horse of the year outside of France, and Aidan O'Brien's charge had only been beaten by one horse in seven races.

Most recently, he'd been seen sauntering home at the head of another one-two-three for O'Brien in the Irish Derby. With the benefit of a three-month break, but no prep race, High Chaparral was a short order for the Arc, coupled with his pacemaker Black Sam Bellamy.

The last-named had been a distant fifth of 15 to the Niarchos family's Sulamani in the Prix du Jockey Club, where the son of Hernando had taken the scalp of the previously unbeaten odds-on favourite Act One, with the pair pulling five lengths clear of the rest. Sulamani had added the Prix Niel on his reappearance after a break.

Daniel Wildenstein had died in late October 2001, at the age of 84, and so 4/1-chance Aquarelliste, who was second last year and had won the Prix Ganay and Prix Foy this term, was now running in the ownership of Ecurie Wildenstein – stable Wildenstein. Anabaa Blue, who came second in the Prix Foy, was also back but not fancied at 22/1.

The 2002 Japanese St Leger-winner, Manhattan Café, had many supporters while the Italians were represented by Gran Premio di Milano-winner Falbrav.

Lord Weinstock's Yorkshire Oaks-winner, Islington, was the shortest of the English trio which included Godolphin's Marienbard, who'd scored in good style in the Grosser Preis von Baden the previous month. And they were all racing for a winning purse of 1.6 million of the new-fangled euros.

Les Visiteurs: Islington, Marienbard, and September Stakes-winner Asian Heights for England; Ireland's High Chaparral and Black Sam Bellamy; Manhattan Café for Japan; Italy's Falbrav; and Coronation Cup-winner Boréal representing Germany.

Betting

2/1 High Chaparral & Black Sam Bellamy (coupled), 4/1 Sulamani & Sensible (coupled), 4/1 Aquarelliste, 7/1 Islington, 8/1 Manhattan Café, 15/1 Falbrav, 16/1 Marienbard, 22/1 Anabaa Blue, 33/1 BAR.

Three-year-old form lines
Prix du Jockey Club: 1st **Sulamani**, 2nd Act One, 3rd Simeon, 5th **Black Sam Bellamy**
Grand Prix de Paris: 1st Khalkevi, 2nd Shaanmer, 3rd Without Connexion
Prix Niel: 1st **Sulamani**, 2nd Gulf News, 3rd/last Morozov

Fillies only
Prix de Diane: 1st Bright Sky, 2nd Dance Routine, 3rd **Ana Marie**
Prix Vermeille: 1st Pearly Shells, 2nd **Ana Marie**, 3rd Bright Sky

Older horses and inter-generational races
Grand Prix de Saint-Cloud: 1st Ange Gabriel, 2nd Polish Summer, 3rd **Aquarelliste**, 4th **Califet**, 5th **Anabaa Blue**
La Coupe de Maisons-Laffitte: 1st **Fair Mix**, 2nd Jim And Tonic, 3rd Cherbon
Grand Prix de Deauville: 1st Polish Summer, 2nd **Califet**, 3rd **Fair Mix**
Prix Foy: 1st **Aquarelliste**, 2nd **Anabaa Blue**, 3rd **Falbrav**

Abroad
In England
Derby Stakes: 1st **High Chaparral**, 2nd Hawk Wing, 3rd Moon Ballad
Oaks Stakes: 1st Kazzia, 2nd Quarter Moon, 3rd Shadow Dancing, 8th **Islington**
King George VI and Queen Elizabeth Stakes: 1st Golan, 2nd Nayef, 3rd Zindabad, 4th **Aquarelliste**, 7th **Boréal**

In Ireland

Irish Derby: 1st **High Chaparral**, 2nd Sholokhov, 3rd Ballingarry

In Germany
Grosser Preis von Baden: 1st **Marienbard**, 2nd Salve Regina, 3rd Noroit, 4th **Califet**, 6th **Boréal**

In Italy
Gran Premio di Milano: 1st **Falbrav**, 2nd Narrative, 3rd Hawkeye

The race
High Chaparral's pacemaker, Black Sam Bellamy, made it to the front after about 50 metres, pushing on by two lengths to Islington on the rail. The lead was extended to three down the hill and Black Sam Bellamy still led entering the *dernier ligne droite*.

Then Islington took over in front from Califet and High Chaparral with 400 metres to travel. In the centre of the track, Aquarelliste and Marienbard still had chances, as did Anabaa Blue and Sulamani on the wide outside.

Anabaa Blue cracked first, which – with 150 metres to go – left six horses ranged across the track. Marienbard drifted right, joining battle with Islington, Califet and High Chaparral on the rails. He mastered all three, but then had to contend with Sulamani, who had also wandered off a straight line, and was now only three wide of Frankie's charge and making ground fast.

But Marienbard was resolute and Sulamani couldn't close in any further, and at the line was officially three parts behind Marienbard – although it looked more like a length and a bit. High Chaparral finished half a length back in third followed by Califet, Islington and Aquarelliste.

Post-race

After Sakhee last year, it was successive wins in Godolphin blue and a fourth for Sheikh Mohammed's family, adding to his Carnégie in 1994 and his nephew's Lammtarra the following year.

It was Arc number three for Saeed bin Suroor and Frankie Dettori, who'd trained and ridden respectively Lammtarra in 1995 and Sakhee last year.

Marienbard retired to stud standing first in Japan – where he sired a few decent winners of which Tosen Luce won the most prize money – before moving to Ireland in 2009.

Runner-up Sulamani embarked on a successful international career that would culminate with victory in the Canadian International in 2004. While third-placed High Chaparral went on to win the Breeders' Cup Turf 20 days after the Arc, and would be back at Longchamp in 12 months' time.

Result

2002 Prix de l'Arc de Triomphe Lucien Barrière
Longchamp. Sunday, 6 October 2002
Weights: 3yo c: 56kg, 3yo f: 54.5kg, 4yo+ c: 59.5kg, 4yo+ f: 58kg

1st Marienbard (IRE)   5yo h   59.5kg   **16/1**
by Caerleon out of Marienbad (Darshaan). Godolphin / Saeed bin Suroor / Frankie Dettori

2nd Sulamani (IRE)   3yo c   56kg   **4/1** (coupled with Sensible)
by Hernando out of Soul Dream (Alleged). Famille Niarchos / Pascal Bary / Thierry Thulliez

3rd High Chaparral (IRE) 3yo c   56kg   **2/1 fav** (coupled with Black Sam Bellamy)
by Sadler's Wells out of Kasora (Darshaan). Michael Tabor / Aidan O'Brien / Mick Kinane

Runners: 16 (FR 8, GB 3, IRE 2, GER 1, ITY 1, JPN 1). Distances: ¾, ½. Going: good. Time: 2m 26.70s

Also ran: 4th **Califet** (FR) 4yo c, 5th **Islington** (IRE) 3yo f, 6th **Aquarelliste** (FR) 4yo f, 7th **Anabaa Blue** (GB) 4yo c, 8th **Fair Mix** (IRE) 4yo c, 9th **Falbrav** (IRE) 4yo c, 10th **Black Sam Bellamy** (IRE) 3yo c, 11th **Ana Marie** (FR) 3yo f, 12th **Foundation Spirit** (FR) 4yo c, 13th **Manhattan Café** (JPN) 4yo c, 14th **Asian Heights** (GB) 4yo c, 15th **Boréal** (GER) 4yo c, 16th **Sensible** (FR) 4yo c.

2003

Dalakhani destroys the opposition

*Aga Khan IV equals his father and
grandfather's combined score*

Background and fancied horses

English bookmakers had for a long time been subject to mixed feelings about
the PMU returns. Like all pool betting it is a popularity contest, and therefore
the dividend returned doesn't always reflect the actual probability of that
horse's winning chance. The prime example of a horse at too long a price was
Star Appeal in 1975, while at the other end of the scale the horse best known
for being too short was only three years away.

In pool betting all dividends are covered by, and inextricably linked to, the
money staked, while in bookmaking huge liabilities can occur if the wrong
prices are laid to big sums of money.

This could cause problems and as a result many English bookmaking firms
offered their own individual odds. At around this time a conglomeration of
those prices labelled as the 'industry prices' became available.

The PMU favourite this year was the Aga Khan IV's Dalakhani, who'd
been unbeaten in three races as a two-year-old, and had extended that
sequence to six in the Prix du Jockey Club, where the steel grey showed an
exhilarating turn of speed.

In the Irish Derby, though, he was beaten by the John Oxx-trained
Alamshar – also owned by the Aga Khan, but running in his late father's
hooped colours – who went on to win the King George VI and Queen
Elizabeth Stakes. Back in France, Dalakhani accounted for Doyen and the
Derby-winner Kris Kin in the Prix Niel. On the PMU he topped the market
at 1.5/1.

Last year's third, the dual Derby and Breeders' Cup Turf-winner High
Chaparral, was second favourite at 2.8/1 to go two places better this time.
After a long rest he won the Royal Whip at the Curragh on his reappearance
in August, before beating the useful Falbrav in the Irish Champion Stakes,
and on the British Industry Prices he was the market leader.

The front two were followed by Ange Gabriel at 7/1; he'd won the Grand
Prix de Saint-Cloud last year and again this term. The previously mentioned
André Fabre-trained Doyen was 7.3/1. Owned by Sheikh Mohammed it was
only his fifth run when he spilt Dalakhani and Kris Kin.

Deutsches Derby-winner Dai Jin traded at 12/1, with the Derby-winner Kris Kin three points longer. Kris Kin finished third in the King George VI and Queen Elizabeth Stakes before taking the same berth in the Prix Niel.

Dual Irish St Leger-winner Vinnie Roe, at 16/1, was the last horse under 33/1 in a field of 13 comprised entirely of male horses.

Les Visiteurs: The English quartet were: Kris Kin; Mubtaker, who'd won his last four outings including two runnings of the Geoffrey Freer Stakes; 2002 St Leger-winner Bollin Eric; and First Charter, who was running in the same colours as Kris Kin. Ireland had three Runners: High Chaparral; Vinnie Roe; and the returning Black Sam Bellamy, who'd been runner-up in the Grosser Preis von Baden. Germany had the Deutsches Derby-winner Dai Jin.

Betting
1.5/1 Dalakhani & Diyapour (coupled), 2.8/1 High Chaparral & Black Sam Bellamy (coupled), 7/1 Ange Gabriel, 7.3/1 Doyen, 12/1 Dai Jin, 15/1 Kris Kin & First Charter (coupled), 16/1 Vinnie Roe, 33/1 BAR

British Industry Prices
1.63/1 High Chaparral, 2.25/1 Dalakhani, 5.5/1 Doyen, 9/1 Ange Gabriel, 11/1 Vinnie Roe, 11/1 Kris Kin, 16/1 Dai Jin, 25/1 BAR.

Three-year-old form lines
Prix du Jockey Club: 1st **Dalakhani**, 2nd Super Célèbre, 3rd Coroner, 7th/last **Diyapour**
Grand Prix de Paris: 1st Vespone, 2nd Magistretti, 3rd Look Honey
Prix Niel: 1st **Dalakhani**, 2nd **Doyen**, 3rd **Kris Kin**, 7th/last **Diyapour**

Fillies only
Prix de Diane: 1st Nebraska Tornado, 2nd Time Ahead, 3rd Musical Chimes
Prix Vermeille: 1st Mezzo Soprano, 2nd Yesterday, 3rd Fidélité, 4th Vallée Enchantée

Older horses and inter-generational races
Grand Prix de Saint-Cloud: 1st **Ange Gabriel**, 2nd Polish Summer, 3rd Loxias
Grand Prix de Deauville: 1st **Policy Maker**, 2nd Polish Summer, 3rd Craig's Falcon
Prix Foy: 1st **Ange Gabriel**, 2nd Martaline, 3rd Imperial Dancer

Abroad
In England
Derby Stakes: 1st **Kris Kin**, 2nd The Great Gatsby, 3rd Alamshar
King George VI and Queen Elizabeth Stakes: 1st Alamshar, 2nd Sulamani, 3rd **Kris Kin**, 4th **Bollin Eric**

In Ireland
Irish Derby: 1st Alamshar, 2nd **Dalakhani**, 3rd Roosevelt

Irish Champion Stakes: 1st **High Chaparral**, 2nd Falbrav, 3rd Islington, 4th Alamshar

In Germany

Grosser Preis von Baden: 1st Mamool, 2nd **Black Sam Bellamy**, 3rd Dano-Mast

The race

Dalakhani's perennial pacemaker, Diyapour, went straight to the front and led by three lengths at the Petit Bois, where First Charter and Black Sam Bellamy had moved into second and third followed by Mubtaker.

Running downhill, Black Sam Bellamy came through on the inner to take it up, and he was joined by Mubtaker on the false straight. High Chaparral moved closer, taking a share of third with Bollin Eric and Vinnie Roe, as Diyapour and First Charter dropped away. Further back Dalakhani, who'd been in rear, was starting to make ground into sixth.

At the 400-metre pole, Mubtaker overtook Black Sam Bellamy and moved on by a length. Vinnie Roe was now in third, as four wide Dalakhani unleashed his effort. The steel grey son of Darshaan smoothly made up the ground on Mubtaker and then accelerated past him at the 200-metre marker.

Ridden hands and heels only, Dalakhani maintained a three-quarters-of-a-length margin to the line, to win with something in hand. There was fully five lengths back to High Chaparral – who took the bottom step on the podium for the second year – followed by Doyen, Vinnie Roe and Black Sam Bellamy.

Post-race

The Aga Khan III had won with Migoli in 1948 and Nuccio in 1952, while Prince Aly Khan had triumphed with Saint Crespin in 1959. Now the grandson of the former and son of the latter had equalled their combined score with Dalakhani, adding to the triumphs of Akiyda in 1982 and Sinndar in 2000.

It was a first Arc for Alain de Royer-Dupré, who had been third with Kozana in Rainbow Quest's year and second with Behera behind Carroll House. Champion jockey-elect Christophe Soumillon was also scoring for the first time.

Dalakhani, the tenth winner of the Prix du Jockey Club to win the Arc, retired having only been beaten by one horse in nine races. At stud he produced many winners of which arguably the three best – Conduit, Reliable Man and Defoe – will all feature later.

Result

2003 Prix de l'Arc de Triomphe Lucien Barrière
Longchamp. Sunday, 5 October 2003
Weights: 3yo c: 56kg, 3yo f: 54.5kg, 4yo+ c: 59.5kg, 4yo+ f: 58kg

1st Dalakhani (IRE)   3yo c   56kg   **1.5/1 fav** (coupled with Diyapour)
by Darshaan out of Daltawa (Miswaki). HH Aga Khan IV / Alain de Royer-Dupré / Christophe Soumillon

2nd Mubtaker (USA)   6yo h   59.5kg   **33/1**
by Silver Hawk out of Gazayil (Irish River). Hamdan Al Maktoum / Marcus Tregoning / Richard Hills

3rd High Chaparral (IRE)   4yo c   59.5kg   **2.8/1** (coupled with Black Sam Bellamy)
by Sadler's Wells out of Kasora (Darshaan). Michael Tabor / Aidan O'Brien / Mick Kinane

Runners: 13 (FR 5, GB 4, IRE 3, GER 1). Distances: ¾, 5. Going: holding.
Time: 2m 32.30s

Also ran: 4th **Doyen** (IRE) 3yo c, 5th **Vinnie Roe** (IRE) 5yo h, 6th **Black Sam Bellamy** (IRE) 4yo c, 7th **Dai Jin** (GB) 3yo c, 8th **Bollin Eric** (GB) 4yo c, 9th **Ange Gabriel** (FR) 5yo h, 10th **Policy Maker** (IRE) 3yo c, 11th **Kris Kin** (USA) 3yo c, 12th **First Charter** (GB) 4yo c, 13th **Diyapour** (FR) 3yo c.

2004
Bago bags it for Niarchos heirs

Gillet conjures stunning run from son of Nashwan

Background and fancied horses

In an open renewal Prospect Park was eventually sent off favourite at 5/1. Running in the familiar Wertheimer colours, he'd only gone down to Blue Canari in the final stride in the Prix du Jockey Club. He'd then won the Prix du Lys before again being touched off close home, this time by Valixir, in the Prix Niel with Blue Canari back in fifth.

The English Derby-winner North Light was next at 5.5/1. Sir Michael Stoute's charge had come to prominence when winning the Dante Stakes, and had followed up at Epsom in style, kicking on entering the last 400 metres to record a clear victory.

North Light was odds-on to double up at the Curragh, but was caught in the closing stages by Dermot Weld's Grey Swallow. North Light wasn't seen again until Longchamp, however Grey Swallow subsequently finished fourth in the Irish Champion Stakes and was a 7/1-shot.

Next on 7.7/1 was Bago, who'd been an exciting two-year-old, winning all four of his races. This term he'd triumphed in the Prix Jean Prat and Grand Prix de Paris, before tasting defeat in the Juddmonte International Stakes.

In that race, Bago was beaten three parts and the same by Sulamani and Norse Dancer, with a further five lengths back to the fourth. Most recently the son of Nashwan hadn't been able to get on terms with the front two, when third again, this time in the Prix Niel.

The English and Irish Oaks-winner Ouija Board was 9/1, followed by the 2003 Japan Cup-winner Tap Dance City. He'd won the Group 1 Takarazuka Kinen in June before making his way to France.

Warrsan, at 12/1, had taken the Coronation Cup for the second time and had also won the Grosser Preis von Baden. The 2003 winner of that race, Mamool at 13/1, represented Godolphin and had won this season's September Stakes.

Valixir carried the famous grey with a pink cap which was now registered under Famille Lagardère, after Jean-Luc's death at age 75 in the March of the year before. By Trempolino out of a Linamix mare, Valixir had won the Prix Eugène Adam and the Prix Niel, in the latter beating three who were lining up again. Famille Lagardère were also represented by Grand Prix de Deauville-winner Cherry Mix, wearing a distinguishing pink sash, and together they were 14/1.

Policy Maker, who was tenth last year, was back and had just won the Prix Foy. He was 22/1 coupled with last year's Prix du Conseil de Paris and Hong Kong Vase-winner Vallée Enchantée, who was also owned by Ecurie Wildenstein. The already-mentioned Blue Canari was 29/1, and it was 35/1 bar.

Les Visiteurs: Newbury Arc Trial-second, Imperial Dancer, joined North Light, Ouija Board, Warrsan, and Mamool in the five-strong English team. The pairing of Grey Swallow and the Tabor/Magnier-hope Acropolis, who'd won a Listed race at Leopardstown, represented Ireland, and Tap Dance City was the latest Japanese hope.

Betting
5/1 Prospect Park, 5.5/1 North Light, 7/1 Grey Swallow, 7.7/1 Bago, 9/1 Ouija Board, 11/1 Tap Dance City, 12/1 Warrsan, 13/1 Mamool, 14/1 Valixir & Cherry Mix (coupled), 22/1 Policy Maker & Vallée Enchantée (coupled), 29/1 Blue Canari, 35/1 BAR

British Industry Prices
4.5/1 North Light, 5/1 Grey Swallow, 7/1 Ouija Board, 9/1 Warrsan, 9/1 Valixir, 10/1Bago, 10/1 Prospect Park, 10/1 Tap Dance City, 11/1 Mamool, 13.1/1 Policy Maker, 14/1 Vallée Enchantée, 28/1 BAR.

Three-year-old form lines
Prix du Jockey Club: 1st **Blue Canari**, 2nd **Prospect Park**, 3rd **Valixir**
Grand Prix de Paris: 1st **Bago**, 2nd Cacique, 3rd Alnitak
Prix Niel: 1st **Valixir**, 2nd **Prospect Park**, 3rd **Bago**, 5th **Blue Canari**

Fillies only
Prix de Diane: 1st **Latice**, 2nd Millionaia, 3rd Grey Lilas
Prix Vermeille: 1st Sweet Stream, 2nd Royal Fantasy, 3rd **Pride**, 6th **Silverskaya**, 8th **Latice**

Older horses and inter-generational races
Grand Prix de Saint-Cloud: 1st Gamut, 2nd **Policy Maker**, 3rd Visorama, 5th **Pride**
Grand Prix de Deauville: 1st **Cherry Mix**, 2nd Martaline, 3rd Bailador
Prix Foy: 1st **Policy Maker**, 2nd Short Pause, 3rd Nysaean

Abroad
In England
Derby Stakes: 1st **North Light**, 2nd Rule of Law, 3rd Let the Lion Roar
Oaks Stakes: 1st **Ouija Board**, 2nd All Too Beautiful, 3rd Punctilious
King George VI and Queen Elizabeth Stakes: 1st Doyen, 2nd Hard Buck, 3rd Sulamani, 5th **Vallée Enchantée**, 9th **Warrsan**

In Ireland

Irish Derby: 1st **Grey Swallow**, 2nd **North Light**, 3rd Tycoon

Irish Champion Stakes: 1st Azamour, 2nd Norse Dancer, 3rd Powerscourt, 4th **Grey Swallow**, 6th **Imperial Dancer**

In Germany

Grosser Preis von Baden: 1st **Warrsan**, 2nd Egerton, 3rd Shirocco

The race

Policy Maker was quickly into the lead from Prospect Park and Bago, before North Light came through to lead at the Petit Bois. Running downhill, Tap Dance City took over from North Light and they moved on by three lengths.

The battle up front continued into the straight with North Light winning, but in reality he and Tap Dance City had cut each other's throats. Cherry Mix ridden by Christophe Soumillon, who was seeking successive victories, overhauled both of them with 350 metres to travel, and was followed through by Bago and Mamool.

Cherry Mix was two lengths clear entering the last 200 metres. However, Thierry Gillet was conjuring a fantastic finish out of Bago while, on the inner, Acropolis was also having a dream run through, passing several beaten horses. On the outside, Ouija Board, and further back, Vallée Enchantée, had also made up lots of places.

But there was no stopping Bago, who cut down Cherry Mix inside the last 40 metres, scoring by half a length, with Ouija Board getting to within a length of the first two, followed by Acropolis, North Light and Vallée Enchantée.

Post-race

Famille Niarchos had gone one place better than their patriarch Stavros, who'd been second with Northern Trick in 1984 and with Hernando a decade later – two years before his death at age 86. Trainer Jonathan Pease and jockey Thierry Gillet were also recording their first wins.

English-born Pease had learnt his trade with Toby Balding and Clive Brittain, before serving spells in America and Australia. He then moved to France where he worked for François Mathet – who'd won the Arc with Tantième, Sassafras and Akiyda – before striking out on his own.

For Gillet, who wore the dark blue with light blue cross belts and striped sleeves with a white cap, it would be his only Arc win. He would make the frame again before retiring in 2009 having ridden over 900 winners. But that was a long way off and in the meantime Gillet and Bago would return to Longchamp the following year.

Result

2004 Prix de l'Arc de Triomphe Lucien Barrière

Longchamp. Sunday, 3 October 2004
Weights: 3yo c: 56kg, 3yo f: 54.5kg, 4yo+ c: 59.5kg, 4yo+ f: 58kg

1st Bago (FR)   3yo c   56kg   **7.7/1**
by Nashwan out of Moonlight's Box (Nureyev). Famille Niarchos / Jonathan Pease / Thierry Gillet

2nd Cherry Mix (FR)   3yo c   56kg   **14/1** (coupled with Valixir)
by Linamix out of Cherry Moon (Quiet American). Famille Lagardère / André Fabre / Christophe Soumillon

3rd Ouija Board (GB)   3yo f   54.5kg   **9/1**
by Cape Cross out of Selection Board (Welsh Pageant). Lord Derby / Ed Dunlop / Johnny Murtagh

Runners: 19 (FR 11, GB 5, IRE 2, JPN 1). Distances: ½, 1. Going: good. Time: 2m 25.00s

Also ran: 4th **Acropolis** (IRE) 3yo f, 5th **North Light** (IRE) 3yo c, 6th **Vallée Enchantée** (IRE) 4yo f, 7th **Latice** (IRE) 3yo f, 8th **Silverskaya** (USA) 3yo f, 9th **Warrsan** (IRE) 6yo h, 10th **Valixir** (IRE) 3yo c, 11th **Execute** (FR) 7yo h, 12th **Blue Canari** (FR) 3yo c, 13th **Pride** (FR) 4yo f, 14th **Imperial Dancer** (GB) 6yo h, 15th **Mamool** (IRE) 5yo h, 16th **Prospect Park** (GB) 3yo c, 17th **Tap Dance City** (USA) 7yo h, 18th **Grey Swallow** (IRE) 3yo c, 19th **Policy Maker** (IRE) 4yo c.

2005
Hurricane Run like a whirlwind
Son of Montjeu is Fabre's sixth Arc winner

Background and fancied horses

In Paris the favourite was the Aga Khan IV's Shawanda. After finishing second on debut, she won her next five starts, incorporating the Irish Oaks and, most recently, a comfortable success in the Prix Vermeille.

Punters *outre-Manche,* on the other hand, liked the Derby-winner Motivator. Owned by the Royal Ascot Racing Club, he'd won the Racing Post Trophy at two and then the Dante Stakes this year before storming home at Epsom. Since then, though, he'd been beaten by Aidan O'Brien's Oratorio in both the Eclipse Stakes and Irish Champion Stakes.

Both markets had the André Fabre-trained Hurricane Run as second favourite. The runner-up in the Prix du Jockey Club had won the Irish Derby for Gestüt Ammerland before being purchased by Michael Tabor. He then strolled home by three lengths in the Prix Niel, and in the Arc was coupled with the other Coolmore horse, Sue Magnier's Scorpion, who'd been ridden by Godolphin's retained rider Frankie Dettori when winning the St Leger.

Dettori was back in royal blue for the Arc on board Cherry Mix, who Godolphin had purchased from Famille Lagardère. More fancied, though, was the returning Bago, who'd been third in both the Grand Prix de Saint-Cloud and King George VI and Queen Elizabeth Stakes.

As well as Shawanda, Alain de Royer-Dupré also ran Prix Jean Romanet and Prix Foy-winner Pride. Fabre's second string was 2004 Deutsches Derby-winner Shirocco. While Wildenstein interests lay with Westerner, who'd won the Ascot Gold Cup, and his pacemaker Voltmeter. They were all competing for a winning purse that had risen to €1.8m.

Les Visiteurs: England's handful of runners were: Motivator and Cherry Mix; Mubtaker, who was back and had won this term's Cumberland Lodge Stakes; Warrsan, winner of the Grosser Preis von Baden; and King George VI and Queen Elizabeth Stakes-second Norse Dancer. While Ireland was represented by Scorpion.

Betting

2.1/1 Shawanda & Windya (coupled), 2.9/1 Hurricane Run & Scorpion (coupled), 3.8/1 Motivator, 12/1 Bago, 18/1 Cherry Mix, 18/1 Pride, 18/1 Westerner & Voltmeter (coupled), 25/1 Shirocco, 55/1 BAR

British Industry Prices

2.5/1 Motivator, 2.75/1 Hurricane Run, 3/1 Shawanda, 8/1 Bago, 10/1 Scorpion, 16/1 Pride, 16/1 Westerner, 25/1 Shirocco, 28/1 Cherry Mix, 40/1 BAR.

Three-year-old form lines

Prix du Jockey Club: 1st Shamardal, 2nd **Hurricane Run**, 3rd Rocamadour, 16th **Scorpion**

Grand Prix de Paris: 1st **Scorpion**, 2nd Desideratum, 3rd Orion Star

Prix Niel: 1st **Hurricane Run**, 2nd Runaway, 3rd Perfect Hedge

Fillies only

Prix de Diane: 1st Divine Proportions, 2nd Argentina, 3rd Paita

Prix Vermeille: 1st **Shawanda**, 2nd Royal Highness, 3rd Paita

Older horses and inter-generational races

Grand Prix de Saint-Cloud: 1st Alkaased, 2nd Policy Maker, 3rd **Bago**

Prix Foy: 1st **Pride**, 2nd Alkaased, 3rd **Shirocco**

Abroad

In England

Derby Stakes: 1st **Motivator**, 2nd Walk in the Park, 3rd Dubawi

King George VI and Queen Elizabeth Stakes: 1st Azamour, 2nd **Norse Dancer**, 3rd **Bago**, 4th **Warrsan**, 11th **Mubtaker**

St Leger: 1st **Scorpion**, 2nd The Geezer, 3rd Tawqeet

In Ireland

Irish Derby: 1st **Hurricane Run**, 2nd **Scorpion**, 3rd Shalapour

Irish Champion Stakes: 1st Oratorio, 2nd **Motivator**, 3rd Alexander Goldrun, 8th **Norse Dancer**

In Germany

Grosser Preis von Baden: 1st **Warrsan**, 2nd Gonbarda, 3rd **Westerner**, 4th **Samando**, 5th **Cherry Mix**

The race

Windya won the early skirmishes in the rain and was three lengths to the good over Voltmeter and Westerner at the Petit Bois. Voltmeter dropped back on the false straight and it was Shawanda who moved through on the inside of Windya to lead rounding the home run.

Cherry Mix and Scorpion were prominent with Motivator coming through on the rail. Further back, racing room was tight on the inside, Pride was impeded while Hurricane Run was pushed sideways into Samando, who momentarily touched the rails.

Early in the straight, Motivator challenged Shawanda on her inner, with Westerner, Shirocco, Scorpion and Bago all coming into the picture on the outside. Hurricane Run made some rapid headway against the rail. But then Fallon had to wait patiently until Motivator, who was ahead of him and hanging to the left, had completed his manoeuvre, before being able to take the gap that was presented to him.

He duly whizzed through, hitting the front in the final 100 metres to dominate his rivals in dazzling style and grab the spoils by two and a half lengths. Westerner was a clear second with last year's winner, Bago, scorching past the remainder to take third followed by Shirocco, Motivator and Shawanda.

Post-race

Hurricane Run had overcome his bad luck – the bump on the home turn – and made the most of his good luck – the gap opening on the rails – to become the second Arc winner for Michael Tabor.

The first had been Montjeu in 1999, the father of Hurricane Run, who was now the seventh former winner to become a parent of another victor. Hurricane Run was the sixth to triumph for André Fabre, who extended his record as the winning-most trainer in Arc history.

It was the first success for jockey Kieren Fallon, who'd been third on Borgia in 1997. Both Hurricane Run and Borgia were bred by Gestüt Ammerland, who were to have more Arc success in the future.

Hurricane Run was kept in training and would be back. Bago, though, was retired after finishing down the field in the Japan Cup, where he lost a shoe and sustained a serious cut. Standing in Japan, he hasn't been overly successful, although his Big Week did win the Japanese St Leger in 2010.

Result
2005 Prix de l'Arc de Triomphe Lucien Barrière
Longchamp. Sunday, 2 October 2005
Weights: 3yo c: 56kg, 3yo f: 54.5kg, 4yo+ c: 59.5kg, 4yo+ f: 58kg

1st Hurricane Run (IRE)   3yo c   56kg   **2.9/1** (coupled with Scorpion)
by Montjeu out of Hold On (Surumu). Michael Tabor / André Fabre / Kieren Fallon

2nd Westerner (GB)   6yo h   59.5kg   **18/1** (coupled with Voltmeter)
by Danehill out of Walensee (Troy). Ecurie Wildenstein / Élie Lellouche / Olivier Peslier

3rd Bago (FR)   4yo c   59.5kg   **12/1**
by Nashwan out of Moonlight's Box (Nureyev). Famille Niarchos / Jonathan Pease / Thierry Gillet

Runners: 15 (FR 9, GB 5, IRE 1). Distances: 2, 1½. Going: good to soft. Time: 2m 27.40s

Also ran: 4th **Shirocco** (GER) 4yo c, 5th **Motivator** (GB) 3yo c, 6th **Shawanda** (IRE) 3yo f, 7th **Pride** (FR) 5yo m, 8th **Warrsan** (IRE) 7yo h, 9th **Mubtaker** (USA) 8yo h, 10th **Scorpion** (IRE) 3yo c, 11th **Norse Dancer** (IRE) 5yo h, 12th **Cherry Mix** (FR) 4yo c, 13th **Samando** (FR) 5yo m, 14th **Windya** (FR) 3yo f, 15th **Voltmeter** (IRE) 3yo c.

Rail Link makes all the right connections

PMU prices skewed as Japanese punters make a Deep Impact

Background and fancied horses

Just eight went to post, the smallest field since 1941, but it was all quality and included last year's winner Hurricane Run, who was back to defend his crown. He'd won the King George VI and Queen Elizabeth Stakes at Ascot in June, before engaging in a couple of tussles with Pride. In the Grand Prix de Saint-Cloud the mare had won, but Hurricane Run took revenge in the Prix Foy, where they were both beaten by another Fabre inmate, Shirocco.

The last-named, who was owned by Baron von Ullmann, had been fourth in last year's Arc, and had ended the year on a high when securing the Breeders' Cup Turf at Belmont Park. This term he'd taken the Coronation Cup at Epsom prior to his win in the Prix Foy.

As such, Shirocco was the most fancied of the six-strong French team, of which Fabre fielded three, his other being the three-year-old colt Rail Link, who'd won the Grand Prix de Paris and the Prix Niel.

However, all the buzz surrounded the Japanese superstar Deep Impact. The son of Sunday Silence had only been beaten by one horse – Heart's Cry – in 11 races, which included five Group 1s.

The Japanese contingent at the course backed the four-year-old as though defeat was totally out of the question, and the opening price indication for Deep Impact was 0.1/1, and at one time it was 23/1 bar one.

Eventually, with late money coming for other horses, the dividend for Deep Impact was finalised at 0.5/1 compared with 2.25/1 in the industry prices across the water – that's 1/2 and 9/4 in old money.

The other two French-trained runners were Prix du Jockey Club-second Best Name and Grand Prix de Deauville-winner Irish Wells. In addition to Deep Impact, the only other *visiteur* was the English-trained St Leger-winner Sixties Icon. Meanwhile the prize money on offer to the winner had climbed to €2m.

Betting

0.5/1 Deep Impact, 4/1 Hurricane Run, 4/1 Shirocco, 17/1 Sixties Icon, 22/1 Pride, 24/1 Rail Link, 92/1 Irish Wells, 99/1 Best Name

British Industry Prices
2.25/1 Deep Impact, 2.5/1 Hurricane Run, 2.75/1 Shirocco, 8/1 Rail Link, 10/1 Sixties Icon, 11/1 Pride, 100/1 BAR.

Three-year-old form lines
Prix du Jockey Club: 1st Darsi, 2nd **Best Name**, 3rd Arras, 5th **Irish Wells**
Grand Prix de Paris: 1st **Rail Link**, 2nd Red Rocks, 3rd Sudan
Prix Niel: 1st **Rail Link**, 2nd Youmzain, 3rd Sudan

Fillies only
Prix de Diane: 1st Confidential Lady, 2nd Germance, 3rd Queen Cleopatra
Prix Vermeille: 1st Mandesha, 2nd Montare, 3rd Royal Highness

Older horses and inter-generational races
Grand Prix de Saint-Cloud: 1st **Pride**, 2nd **Hurricane Run**, 3rd Laverock
Grand Prix de Deauville: 1st **Irish Wells**, 2nd Groom Tesse, 3rd Marend
Prix du Prince d'Orange: 1st **Best Name**, 2nd Champs-Élysées, 3rd Daramsar
Prix Foy: 1st **Shirocco**, 2nd **Hurricane Run**, 3rd **Pride**

Abroad
In England
Derby Stakes: 1st Sir Percy, 2nd Dragon Dancer, 3rd Dylan Thomas, 7th **Sixties Icon**
King George VI and Queen Elizabeth Stakes: 1st **Hurricane Run**, 2nd Electrocutionist, 3rd Heart's Cry
St Leger: 1st **Sixties Icon**, 2nd The Last Drop, 3rd Red Rocks

In Ireland
Irish Derby: 1st Dylan Thomas, 2nd Gentlewave, 3rd Best Alibi, 8th **Best Name**

The race
Irish Wells went straight into the lead with Deep Impact not far behind, while Shirocco pulled his way into third to race more prominently than usual. Rail Link, who'd broken well, was taken back to the third rank with Hurricane Run, while Pride was held up in last place.

Entering the home straight, Irish Wells was joined by Shirocco, who was still running freely, and Deep Impact. Hurricane Run, though, was boxed-in on the inside with Best Name. Rail Link was starting to make progress just ahead of Pride, who was also starting her run.

Deep Impact took a narrow advantage with 300 metres to run, but was joined immediately by Rail Link. They battled it out to the last 50 metres where Rail Link prevailed. However, he was then faced by another challenger in the shape of Pride. She closed all the way to the line but in the end was a neck shy of success, with Deep Impact just half a length further away.

The unlucky Hurricane Run – who was blocked at the crucial moment – was two and half lengths back in fourth, while Shirocco faded back to last. It was a thrilling finish with the gamble being thwarted.

Post-race

Yutaka Take received some criticism in the press for his ride on Deep Impact. That Shirocco was pulling hard near him didn't help with settling Deep Impact, but overall he didn't do much wrong. Afterwards Take, whose status in Japan is akin to that of Lennon or McCartney during Beatlemania, confirmed on numerous occasions that he is a jockey of great ability.

Two weeks later, following a stewards' inquiry, Deep Impact was disqualified from third place after testing positive for the banned substance Ipratropium, which had shown up in his sample. This was related to a treatment for bronchitis, combined with ignorance of how long the medication would stay in the horse's system.

The PMU dividend for Rail Link was 24/1, while in England the returned starting price was 8/1. This meant that any English bookmakers who were still offering PMU odds could have been liable to large losses paying out at the vastly inflated odds.

The betting controversy aside, Rail Link was a worthy winner and Khalid Abdullah's charge became the first horse to win in his pink, green, and white colours – albeit in the French configuration with epaulettes instead of a sash – since Dancing Brave 20 years ago, and the third in all.

André Fabre, already the winning-most trainer in Arc history, extended his tally to seven to equal Charles Semblat's achievement of three wins as a jockey and four as a trainer. Jockey Stéphane Pasquier, who'd been fourth on Shirocco last year, broke his duck.

He'd just returned to action after sustaining an injured hand when, in the heat of the moment, he'd crushed a drinking glass after David Trezeguet missed the penalty for France that led to *Les Bleus* losing out to Italy in the 2006 World Cup Final.

Rail Link was kept in training initially, but retired to stud after injuring a tendon during the winter. He sired a host of winners, a couple of the best being Australian Cup-winner Spillway and Trip To Rhodos, who won the St Leger Italiano.

Result

2006 Prix de l'Arc de Triomphe Lucien Barrière
Longchamp. Sunday, 1 October 2006
Weights: 3yo c: 56kg, 3yo f: 54.5kg, 4yo+ c: 59.5kg, 4yo+ f: 58kg

1st Rail Link (GB)   3yo c   56kg   **24/1**
by Dansili out of Docklands (Theatrical). Khalid Abdullah / André Fabre / Stéphane Pasquier

2nd Pride (FR)   6yo m   58kg   **22/1**
by Peintre Célèbre out of Specificity (Alleged). N P Bloodstock / Alain de Royer-Dupré / Christophe Patrice Lemaire

3rd Hurricane Run (IRE)   4yo c   59.5kg   **4/1**
by Montjeu out of Hold On (Surumu). Michael Tabor / André Fabre / Kieren Fallon

Runners: 8 (FR 6, GB 1, JPN 1). Distances: nk, ½. Going: good. Time: 2m 26.30s

Stewards' Inquiry: Deep Impact finished third but was subsequently disqualified and placed last after testing positive for the banned substance Ipratropium

Also ran: 4th **Best Name** (GB) 3yo c, 5th **Irish Wells** (FR) 3yo c, 6th **Sixties Icon** (GB) 3yo c, 7th **Shirocco** (GER) 5yo h, disq (3td ptp) **Deep Impact** (JPN) 4yo h.

Dylan Thomas is poetry in motion

First Arc for Aidan O'Brien, albeit with a few bumps

Background and fancied horses

Frankie Dettori, who'd been trying for a while, finally won the Derby when Authorized sauntered home five lengths clear of Eagle Mountain at Epsom. Authorized then led home the group on the inside rail in the Eclipse Stakes, but was outfoxed by Ryan Moore, who had steered Notnowcato wide under the stand's rail, in what was an inspired tactical move.

Peter Chapple-Hyam's son of Montjeu reversed the placing with Notnowcato in the Juddmonte International Stakes, when they were first and third with Dylan Thomas taking second. Understandably, Authorized was the punters' number one choice on both sides of *la Manche*.

Dylan Thomas, one of Aidan O'Brien's four runners, had won the Irish Derby and Irish Champion Stakes as a three-year-old. This year he'd taken the King George VI and Queen Elizabeth Stakes before his defeat at York, and afterwards had retained his Irish Champion Stakes crown.

Punters across the water preferred his stablemate, Soldier Of Fortune, who'd won this season's Irish Derby and most recently the Prix Niel. In that race he'd accounted for Pascal Bary's Grand Prix de Paris-winner Zambezi Sun, who finished third.

Last year's Prix Vermeille-winner Mandesha, owned by the Aga Khan IV's daughter Princess Zahra and ridden by Christophe Soumillon, arrived on the back of three second places – in the Grand Prix de Saint-Cloud, Nassau Stakes and Prix Foy.

The other French-trained runners were Prix Niel-second Sagara, and Getaway, the runner-up in the Prix Gladiateur.

Les Visiteurs: The Irish quartet was comprised of Dylan Thomas and Soldier of Fortune, along with Gordon Stakes-winner Yellowstone, and Ulster Derby-second Song of Hiawatha, who were the pacemakers for the first two. England's trio were: Authorized; the King George VI and Queen Elizabeth Stakes-second Youmzain; and the Prix Foy-third, Dragon Dancer, who'd been second to Sir Percy in the previous year's Derby. Germany was represented by Saddex, who was unbeaten in his three outings this year, including landing a Group 1 at Cologne.

Betting

1/1 Authorized, 6.1/1 Dylan Thomas & Soldier Of Fortune & Song Of Hiawatha & Yellowstone (all coupled), 6/1 Zambezi Sun, 6.5/1 Mandesha, 20/1 Saddex, 27/1 BAR

British Industry Prices
1.1/1 Authorized, 3.33/1 Soldier Of Fortune, 5.5/1 Dylan Thomas, 5.5/1 Zambezi Sun, 12/1 Mandesha, 25/1 BAR.

Three-year-old form lines
Prix du Jockey Club: 1st Lawman, 2nd Literato, 3rd Shamdinan, 7th **Sagara**
Grand Prix de Paris: 1st **Zambezi Sun**, 2nd Axxos, 3rd **Sagara**
Prix Niel: 1st **Soldier of Fortune**, 2nd **Sagara**, 3rd **Zambezi Sun**, 6th/last **Song Of Hiawatha**

Fillies only
Prix de Diane: 1st West Wind, 2nd Mrs Lindsay, 3rd Diyakalanie
Prix Vermeille: 1st Mrs Lindsay, 2nd West Wind, 3rd Passage of Time

Older horses and inter-generational races
Grand Prix de Saint-Cloud: 1st Mountain High, 2nd **Mandesha**, 3rd Prince Flori
Grand Prix de Deauville: 1st Irish Wells, 2nd Poet Laureate, 3rd Champs-Élysées, 5th **Sagara**
Prix Foy: 1st Manduro, 2nd **Mandesha**, 3rd **Dragon Dancer**

Abroad
In England
Derby Stakes: 1st **Authorized**, 2nd Eagle Mountain, 3rd Aqaleem, 5th **Soldier of Fortune**
King George VI and Queen Elizabeth Stakes: 1st **Dylan Thomas**, 2nd **Youmzain**, 3rd Maraahel

In Ireland
Irish Derby: 1st **Soldier of Fortune**, 2nd Alexander of Hales, 3rd Eagle Mountain
Irish Champion Stakes: 1st **Dylan Thomas**, 2nd Duke Of Marmalade, 3rd Red Rock Canyon

In Germany
Grosser Preis von Baden: 1st Quijano, 2nd Adlerflug, 3rd Egerton, 4th **Youmzain**

The race

The Aidan O'Brien-trained pacemakers, Song Of Hiawatha and Yellowstone, set off at a furious gallop. Dragon Dancer was third and Soldier Of Fortune, in the pink alternative Magnier colours, fourth with Authorized settled in rear.

The order was maintained until entering the straight, when Soldier Of Fortune joined his stablemates to momentarily make a three-wide O'Brien wall on the inner. Then Soldier Of Fortune pushed on, with Saddex and Dylan Thomas setting off in pursuit.

Authorized, who'd initially moved up ominously on the outside, found nothing when coming off the bridle, but Dylan Thomas, in the dark blue Magnier silks, was making ground in leaps and bounds – but was also drifting towards the rail.

Dylan Thomas joined battle with Soldier Of Fortune at the 300-metre pole, but in the process crossed Zambezi Sun and squeezed Saddex. Dylan Thomas also crossed Soldier Of Fortune as he took the lead and grabbed the rail. It wasn't over though, and he had to pull out all the stops to repel the storming challenge of Youmzain in the dying strides, which he did by a head.

There was a further one and a half lengths to the fast-finishing pair of Sagara – who'd had nowhere to go in the last few strides – and Getaway, with Soldier Of Fortune and Saddex fifth and sixth respectively.

Post-race

A lengthy stewards' inquiry was held but the placings remained unaltered. Dylan Thomas had caused interference but was the best horse on the day and deserved to keep the race. There is still much debate about the way the rules of racing are enforced and attempts have been made to unify their application across the racing world.

The rules themselves have been updated over the years and the difference between the interference Sagace caused to Rainbow Quest in 1985, which resulted in a disqualification, compared to that generated in the wake of Dylan Thomas, which didn't, is certainly marked.

Dylan Thomas was the first Arc winner to carry the dark blue colours of Sue Magnier, the daughter of trainer Vincent O'Brien, who had won with Ballymoss in 1958, and Alleged in 1977 and 1978.

He also opened the account of Aidan O'Brien – no relation to Vincent – who'd been champion jumps trainer in Ireland for five seasons in a row, starting with the 1993/1994 season, before taking over Ballydoyle from Vincent in 1996. Aided and abetted by his wife Anne-Marie – herself a former champion jumps trainer – the O'Briens were to figure prominently in future Arcs.

It was a second win for Kieren Fallon who'd ridden Hurricane Run in 2005. At the end of the season Dylan Thomas was retired and has produced winners in both hemispheres, especially in Japan. Some of the most notable include Nymphea, who won the 2013 Grosser Preis von Berlin, and Dylan Mouth, who won the Gran Premio di Milano on two occasions.

Result

2007 Prix de l'Arc de Triomphe Lucien Barrière
Longchamp. Sunday, 7 October 2007
Weights: 3yo c: 56kg, 3yo f: 54.5kg, 4yo+ c: 59.5kg, 4yo+ f: 58kg

1st Dylan Thomas (IRE)   4yo c   59.5kg   **6/1** (coupled*)
by Danehill out of Lagrion (Diesis). Sue Magnier / Aidan O'Brien / Kieren Fallon

2nd Youmzain (IRE)   4yo c   59.5kg   **80/1**
by Sinndar out of Sadima (Sadler's Wells). Jaber Abdullah / Mick Channon / Richard Hughes

3rd Sagara (USA)   3yo c   56kg   **32/1**
by Sadler's Wells out of Rangoon Ruby (Kingmambo). Famille Niarchos / Jonathan Pease / Thierry Gillet
*with Soldier Of Fortune, Song Of Hiawatha & Yellowstone

Runners: 12 (FR 4, IRE 4, GB 3, GER 1). Distances: hd, 1½. Going: good to soft. Time: 2m 28.50s

Stewards' Inquiry: result stands after an inquiry into the interference caused by the winner

Also ran: 4th **Getaway** (GER) 4yo c, 5th **Soldier Of Fortune** (IRE) 3yo c, 6th **Saddex** (GB) 4yo c, 7th **Mandesha** (FR) 4yo f, 8th **Zambezi Sun** (GB) 3yo c, 9th **Dragon Dancer** (GB) 4yo c, 10th **Authorized** (IRE) 3yo c, 11th **Yellowstone** (IRE) 3yo c, 12th **Song Of Hiawatha** (GB) 3yo c.

After a stumbling start
Zarkava zooms in

The new Allez France is all class as prize money doubles

Background and fancied horses

The Arc had a new sponsor in the form of the Qatar Racing and Equestrian Club (QREC). Led by the Emir of Qatar, Sheikh Tamim bin Hamad Al Thani, the organisation signed up for a five-year deal. The primary purpose was to promote Arabian racing, and the Arc meeting would now include events for Arabian horses, including the inauguration of the Qatar Arabian World Cup.

However, QREC was also keen to extend its interests in the thoroughbred sphere, a project that would be very successful. It wouldn't be too long before the Emir's brother, Sheikh Joaan bin Hamad Al Thani, made an impact – firstly in his own colours and then via Al Shaqab Racing – to become a major force in the sport. The sponsorship started with a bang as the prize money was doubled to €4m.

Favourite to win the money was the Alain de Royer-Dupré-trained Zarkava, who had a perfect record approaching the Arc. Last backend she'd won a newcomers' race in eye-catching fashion before taking the Prix Marcel Boussac.

This term the Aga Khan IV's daughter of Zamindar had obliged in the Prix de La Grotte on seasonal debut, and then gone on to win the three big fillies' races – the Poule d'Essai des Pouliches, the Prix de Diane and, after a slow start, the Prix Vermeille – all in the style of a champion. It was no wonder that she was a warm order to add the Arc.

Duke Of Marmalade – not to be confused with the horse that was unplaced in 1975 and 1976 – was one of three runners for Aidan O'Brien. He'd been second to Dylan Thomas in last year's Irish Champion Stakes and this term had won five in a row, including the Prix Ganay and the King George VI and Queen Elizabeth Stakes, where he beat Michael Stoute's Papal Bull with Youmzain in third.

O'Brien also ran the returning Soldier Of Fortune. He'd only been seen twice this season, firstly winning the Coronation Cup and then finishing second to Youmzain in the Grand Prix de Saint-Cloud. Red Rock Canyon was also in the line-up in order to ensure a fierce pace.

The Jacques Détré-owned Vision d'État was the best French colt in the field. He'd won the Prix du Jockey Club and after a break returned to score in the Prix Niel. In addition to Soldier Of Fortune, the previous year's second, fourth and eighth – the already-mentioned Youmzain, Getaway and Zambezi Sun – were all back and in total 16 went to post.

Les Visiteurs: England had four Runners: Youmzain and Papal Bull; the King George VI and Queen Elizabeth Stakes-fifth Ask; and Prix Foy-second Schiaparelli. Ireland had the previously mentioned Aidan O'Brien trio. The first and third in the Grosser Preis von Baden, Deutsches Derby-winner Kamsin and It's Gino, were there for Germany. Italy had the Derby Italiano-winner Cima de Triomphe, and Japan ran Meisho Samson, who'd won two Grade 1s last year and had been placed in two this campaign.

Betting
1/1 Zarkava, 5/1 Duke Of Marmalade & Soldier of Fortune & Red Rock Canyon (all coupled), 7.3/1 Vision d'État, 14/1 Youmzain, 17/1 Getaway, 23/1 BAR

British Industry Prices
1.625/1 Zarkava, 4/1 Duke Of Marmalade, 4.5/1 Soldier Of Fortune, 7/1 Vision d'État, 11/1 Getaway, 12/1 Youmzain, 16/1 Papal Bull, 25/1 BAR.

Three-year-old form lines
Prix du Jockey Club: 1st **Vision d'État**, 2nd Famous Name, 3rd Natagora, 13th **Blue Bresil**
Grand Prix de Paris: 1st Montmartre, 2nd Prospect Wells, 3rd Magadan, 7th **Cima De Triomphe**
Prix Niel: 1st **Vision d'État**, 2nd Ideal World, 3rd Centennial

Fillies only
Prix de Diane: 1st **Zarkava**, 2nd Gagnoa, 3rd Goldikova
Prix Vermeille: 1st **Zarkava**, 2nd Dar Re Mi, 3rd Michita

Older horses and inter-generational races
Grand Prix de Saint-Cloud: 1st **Youmzain**, 2nd **Soldier of Fortune**, 3rd Doctor Dino, 4th **Zambezi Sun**, 5th **Getaway**
Grand Prix de Deauville: 1st **Getaway**, 2nd Doctor Dino, 3rd Poseidon Adventure
Prix Foy: 1st **Zambezi Sun**, 2nd **Schiaparelli**, 3rd Light Green

Abroad
In England
Derby Stakes: 1st New Approach, 2nd Tartan Bearer, 3rd Casual Conquest
King George VI and Queen Elizabeth Stakes: 1st **Duke Of Marmalade**, 2nd **Papal Bull**, 3rd **Youmzain**, 4th **Red Rock Canyon**, 5th **Ask**

In Ireland
Irish Champion Stakes: 1st New Approach, 2nd Traffic Guard, 3rd Mores Wells, 6th **Red Rock Canyon**

In Germany
Grosser Preis von Baden: 1st **Kamsin**, 2nd Adlerflug, 3rd **It's Gino**

The race

As the stalls opened on what was a rainy, wet day, Zarkava, drawn on the rail, pitched dramatically and nearly unseated Christophe Soumillon. Conversely, It's Gino was fast away and led from Red Rock Canyon and the hard-pulling Blue Bresil. Zarkava was last, but still in the race.

Soon afterwards, Red Rock Canyon crossed to the rails to become the outright leader, extending the advantage to six lengths at the Petit Bois. He came under pressure on the false straight, but still had a few lengths on the field. However, on the home turn Red Rock Canyon drifted, or was purposely taken, to the outside and was quickly undertaken by the whole field.

It's Gino inherited the lead from Schiaparelli, with Youmzain and Vision d'État just behind. Out wide, Soldier of Fortune started to challenge, a rank ahead of Zambezi Sun, Duke Of Marmalade and Cima De Triomphe.

Zarkava, though, was full of running and making ground, and quickly cruised into the gap between Vision d'État and Blue Bresil – who was in a cul-de-sac and just about to run into the horse in front of him. Then Soumillon edged left, starting to make his own gap on the inner of Vision d'État.

Passing the 300-metre pole, obligingly Soldier Of Fortune started to hang towards the rails presenting Zarkava with a clear passage; she devoured the ground. From being three lengths behind It's Gino, she was now half a length in front at the 100-metre mark, and at the line had two lengths to spare over Youmzain.

He'd been snatched up with 200 metres to go but, after being switched round Soldier Of Fortune, had finished fastest of the rest to claim the berth reserved for the runner-up for the second year. Half a length behind, Soldier Of Fortune and It's Gino dead-heated for the minor honour ahead of Vision d'État and Ask, who had been the debut Arc ride for Ryan Moore.

Zarkava had overcome adversity to score in unforgettable style and became the first to add the Arc to the Prix de Diane and Prix Vermeille since Nikellora in 1945. It was a great achievement and in a few repeated gestures Soumillon summed up it up. He pointed to Zarkava, patted his heart, and then pointed and blew kisses at the crowd.

Post-race

Hailed as the new Allez France, Zarkava was the fourth Arc winner for the Aga Khan IV, adding to Akiyda, Sinndar and Dalakhani. The last-named had been the first Arc winner for trainer Alain de Royer-Dupré and jockey Christophe Soumillon, who now both doubled their scores.

Zarkava retired to the paddocks and, as befits her ability, has been covered by the some of the top sires including the aforementioned Dalakhani, as well as Galileo, Frankel and the 2009 Arc winner. So far her best offspring has been Zarak, by Dubawi, who won the 2017 Grand Prix de Saint-Cloud before running in that year's Arc.

Result

2008 Qatar Prix de l'Arc de Triomphe

Longchamp. Sunday, 5 October 2008
Weights: 3yo c: 56kg, 3yo f: 54.5kg, 4yo+ c: 59.5kg, 4yo+ f: 58kg

1st Zarkava (IRE)   3yo f   54.5kg   **1/1 fav**
by Zamindar out of Zarkasha (Kahyasi). HH Aga Khan IV / Alain de Royer-Dupré / Christophe Soumillon

2nd Youmzain (IRE)   5yo h   59.5kg   **14/1**
by Sinndar out of Sadima (Sadler's Wells). Jaber Abdullah / Mick Channon / Richard Hills

DH3rd It's Gino (GER)   5yo h   59.5kg   **102/1**
by Perugino out of Imelda (Lomitas). Stall 5-Stars / Pavel Vovcenko / Thierry Thuillez

DH3rd Soldier Of Fortune (IRE) 5yo h   59.5kg   **5/1** (coupled*)
by Galileo out of Affianced (Erins Isle). Sue Magnier & Michael Tabor & Derrick Smith / Aidan O'Brien / Seamie Heffernan

*with Duke Of Marmalade & Red Rock Canyon

Runners: 16 (FR 5, GB 4, IRE 3, GER 2, ITY 1, JPN 1). Distances: 2, ½. Going: good to soft. Time: 2m 28.80s

Also ran: 5th **Vision d'État** (FR) 3yo c, 6th **Ask** (GB) 5yo h, 7th **Duke Of Marmalade** (IRE) 4yo c, 8th **Getaway** (GER) 5yo h, 9th **Cima De Triomphe** (IRE) 3yo c, 10th **Meisho Samson** (JPN) 5yo h, 11th **Kamsin** (GER) 3yo c, 12th **Papal Bull** (GB) 5yo h, 13th **Schiaparelli** (GER) 5yo h, 14th **Blue Bresil** (FR) 3yo c, 15th **Zambezi Sun** (GB) 4yo c, 16th **Red Rock Canyon** (IRE) 4yo c.

Sea The Stars is out of this world

Youmzain is runner-up for the third time

Background and fanced horses

To paraphrase the old saying about buses, you wait for one superstar and then two come along in quick succession. After Zarkava last season, this year was the turn of Sea The Stars.

The son of Cape Cross out of Urban Sea had won two of his three starts at two before landing his first Group 1 on seasonal debut in the 2000 Guineas when an 8/1 chance.

Then the fun really started as he took the Derby from Fame And Glory, followed by wins in the Eclipse Stakes and the Juddmonte International Stakes. Each time being held up before unleashing his finishing run. Sometimes it looked as though he was a little sluggish to get going but he always did once Mick Kinane really asked.

Next up in the Irish Champion Stakes he was better than ever beating Fame And Glory by further than in the Derby. Trained by John Oxx, who'd won with Sinndar in 2000, Sea The Stars was odds-on to win a sixth Group 1 in a row.

Fame And Glory, who'd won the Irish Derby in between his two defeats to Sea The Stars, was joint second favourite along with the home team's main chance Stacelita. Jean-Claude Rouget's Prix de Diane-winner added to her tally when awarded the race in what was a controversial running of the Prix Vermeille.

She'd finished second to the John Gosden-trained Dar Re Mi, but the latter was demoted to fifth after being adjudged to have interfered with the fifth-past-the-post Soberania. A decision that served to emphasise the continuing lack of harmonisation between the rules in France and England.

The runner-up for the last two years, Youmzain, was back for another try. Vision d'État also returned, and this term he'd won the Prix Ganay and Prince of Wales's Stakes before finishing second in the Prix Foy.

Others with chances included the 2008 St Leger and Breeders' Cup Turf-winner Conduit, who'd come out on top in this season's King George VI and Queen Elizabeth Stakes.

Godolphin had Cavalryman, who'd won the Grand Prix de Paris and Prix Niel. In the latter he'd beaten the Aga Khan IV's Beheshtam, who would be renamed Carthage when racing in Hong Kong later in his career.

Les Visiteurs: Youmzain, Conduit, Dar Re Mi, and longshot Steele Tango for England. Ireland had Sea The Stars plus Fame And Glory and his pacemakers Grand Ducal and Set Sail, the latter of which was called Cornish when racing in Australia afterwards. Hot Six, who won a Group 1 in São Paulo in March, raced for Brazil. Tullamore, who hadn't won since his debut in June 2008, represented the Czech Republic. And Germany had the winner of the Grosser Preis von Baden, Getaway, who'd previously been trained by André Fabre.

Betting
0.8/1 Sea The Stars, 10/1 Fame And Glory & Grand Ducal & Set Sail (all coupled), 10/1 Stacelita, 14/1 Conduit, 16/1 Vision d'État, 17/1 Cavalryman, 21/1 Youmzain, 23/1 Beheshtam, 23/1 Dar Re Mi, 24/1 Getaway, 76/1 BAR

British Industry Prices
0.67/1 Sea The Stars, 6/1 Fame And Glory, 8/1 Conduit, 12/1 Cavalryman, 14/1 Vision d'État, 16/1 Beheshtam, 20/1 Stacelita, 20/1 Youmzain, 25/1 Dar Re Mi, 33/1 BAR.

Three-year-old form lines
Prix du Jockey Club: 1st Le Havre, 2nd Fuisse, 3rd Westphalia, 4th **Beheshtam**, 15th **Set Sail**
Grand Prix de Paris: 1st **Cavalryman**, 2nd Age of Aquarius, 3rd Mastery, 6th **Beheshtam**
Prix Niel: 1st **Cavalryman**, 2nd **Beheshtam**, 3rd Aizavoski

Fillies only
Prix de Diane: 1st **Stacelita**, 2nd Tamazirte, 3rd Plumania
Prix Vermeille: 1st **Stacelita**, 2nd Plumania, 3rd **Board Meeting**, 4th (5th ptp) Soberania, 5th **Dar Re Mi** (1st ptp, demoted for causing interference to Soberania), 9th **Tangaspeed**

Older horses and inter-generational races
Grand Prix de Saint-Cloud: 1st Spanish Moon, 2nd Alpine Rose, 3rd **Youmzain**, 5th **Magadan**
Prix Foy: 1st Spanish Moon, 2nd **Vision d'État**, 3rd Crossharbour

Abroad
In England
Derby Stakes: 1st **Sea The Stars**, 2nd **Fame And Glory**, 3rd Masterofthehorse, 9th/last **Beheshtam**

King George VI and Queen Elizabeth Stakes: 1st **Conduit**, 2nd Tartan Bearer, 3rd Ask

In Ireland
Irish Derby: 1st **Fame And Glory**, 2nd Golden Sword, 3rd Mourayan
Irish Champion Stakes: 1st **Sea The Stars**, 2nd **Fame And Glory**, 3rd Mastercraftsman, 9th/last **Set Sail**

In Germany
Grosser Preis von Baden: 1st **Getaway**, 2nd Eastern Anthem, 3rd **Youmzain**, 4th Wiener Walzer

The race

Set Sail was quickly away in the centre of the course, with Grand Ducal and the keen Sea The Stars prominent on the inner, although Mick Kinane soon steadied him back a few spots. At the Petit Bois, Set Sail's lead had increased to five lengths and he continued in front until being joined by Grand Ducal on the turn for home.

They were still eight lengths to the good over the peloton, albeit starting to reach the end of their tethers. At the same time, Sea The Stars was making some ground on the inner and wasn't far off the pace of the chasing group.

Soumillon on Stacelita quickly ate into the leaders' advantage, and moved off the rail to come around them, in doing so presenting a clear channel for Sea The Stars on the inner. With daylight in front of him, Sea The Stars had his chance and took off, but with the better part of four lengths to make up he seemingly had plenty to do.

Stacelita still had a two-length lead inside the final 300 metres, followed by Conduit, Dar Re Mi and Cavalryman, who was racing in the beige colours of Godolphin's French operation, Godolphin SNC. Just behind Cavalryman, Sea The Stars was finishing two to the others one. It only took a few strides for him to catch and pass Stacelita and he then motored clear to enter the last 100 metres with a margin of three lengths on the field.

At the line that advantage had been cut to two by Youmzain who, for the third year in a row, had come from a different county to take second place. There was a further head to Cavalryman and Conduit, with Dar Re Mi and Fame And Glory coming home in fifth and sixth.

Post-race

It was a breathtaking performance by Sea The Stars, who had now won eight times in a row. Owner Christopher Tsui had replicated his father's achievement with Urban Sea in 1993, and furthermore with a son of that great mare, who became the eighth former winner to parent another.

Trainer John Oxx added to his win with Sinndar in 2000. The yellow and maroon silks were worn by Mick Kinane who, having won on Carroll House in 1989 and Montjeu in 1999, made it '999' as again his winning year ended in that number.

Sea The Stars is generally seen as one of the best ever Arc winners and was given a rating of 140 by Timeform, which meant he was the equal eighth best horse since their records began in 1948. He remains the co-fourth highest-rated Arc winner, after Sea Bird 145, Ribot 142, Mill Reef 141, sharing the same mark as Vaguely Noble and Dancing Brave.

He was also the fifth Derby winner to score in the Arc after Sea Bird, Mill Reef, Lammtarra and Sinndar.

Sea The Stars didn't race again and was retired to stud where he has continued his good work. Among his many successes are: Derby-winner Harzand, Oaks-winner Taghrooda, the Prince of Wales's Stakes-winner Crystal Ocean, the 2019 Irish Oaks and British Champions Fillies & Mares Stakes-heroine Star Catcher, and the excellent stayer Stradivarius. Others, including Cloth Of Stars and Sea Of Class, will feature in this chronicle in due course.

Result

2009 Qatar Prix de l'Arc de Triomphe
Longchamp. Sunday, 4 October 2009
Weights: 3yo c: 56kg, 3yo f: 54.5kg, 4yo+ c: 59.5kg, 4yo+ f: 58kg

1st Sea The Stars (IRE)   3yo c   56kg   **0.8/1 fav**
by Cape Cross out of Urban Sea (Miswaki). Christopher Tsui / John Oxx / Mick Kinane

2nd Youmzain (IRE)   6yo h   59.5kg   **21/1**
by Sinndar out of Sadima (Sadler's Wells). Jaber Abdullah / Mick Channon / Kieren Fallon

3rd Cavalryman (GB)   3yo c   56kg   **17/1**
by Halling out of Silversword (Highest Honor). Godolphin SNC / André Fabre / Frankie Dettori

Runners: 19 (FR 8, GB 4, IRE 4, CZE 1, GER 1, ITY 1). Distances: 2, hd. Going: good. Time: 2m 26.30s

Also ran: 4th **Conduit** (IRE) 4yo c, 5th **Dar Re Mi** (GB) 4yo f, 6th **Fame And Glory** (GB) 3yo c, DH7th **La Boum** (GER) 6yo m, DH7th **Stacelita** (FR) 3yo f, 9th **Magadan** (IRE) 4yo c, 10th **Vision d'État** (FR) 4yo c, 11th **Tangaspeed** (FR) 4yo f, 12th **Beheshtam** (FR) 3yo c, 13th **Getaway** (GER) 6yo h, 14th **The Bogberry** (USA) 4yo c, 15th **Hot Six** (BRZ) 4yo c, 16th **Tullamore** (USA) 4yo c, 17th **Grand Ducal** (IRE) 3yo c, 18th **Set Sail** (IRE) 3yo c, 19th **Steele Tango** (USA) 4yo c.

2010
Workforce wows

Stoute's substitute avoids carnage as Planteur runs amok

Background and fancied horses

The Qatar sponsorship had proved to be very successful and so, in what was year three of the original five-year deal, the partnership was duly extended for another ten years, ensuring backing until 2022.

The Aga Khan IV had a strong hand with Sarafina and Behkabad. The last-named, who was wearing the second colours with a distinguishing red sash, was the most fancied.

Trained by Jean-Claude Rouget, Behkabad had been beaten by André Fabre's Poule d'Essai des Poulains-winner Lope De Vega and Planteur in the Prix du Jockey Club. But he then overcame the latter when landing the Grand Prix de Paris on Bastille Day. After a break, Behkabad confirmed those placings in the Prix Niel, and was marginally the punters' pick in an open renewal of the Arc.

Sarafina had shown speed and resolution when landing the Prix de Diane, after meeting trouble in running, on what was only her third racecourse appearance. However, she took too long to get going in the Prix Vermeille and had to be content with third place, despite making ground hand over fist in the closing 100 metres.

The other main French contender was the Ecurie Wildenstein-owned, and previously mentioned, Planteur, who'd been runner-up in all three of the top colts' trials.

The Irish challenge was comprised of three horses from Ballydoyle. The returning Fame And Glory had won the Coronation Cup, while Irish Derby-winner Cape Blanco – who'd been beaten out of sight when second to the ill-fated Harbinger in the King George VI and Queen Elizabeth Stakes – had recently taken the Irish Champion Stakes.

Both ran in the Derrick Smith purple with white seams and striped sleeves colours, while Midas Touch, runner-up in the Irish Derby and St Leger, was in Sue Magnier's dark blue. All three, though, were part-owned by Michael Tabor, as well as Smith and Magnier, with Fitri Hay and Denford Stud also involved.

The main English hope was Khalid Abdullah's impressive Derby-winner Workforce, who'd broken the Epsom course record. However, like Cape

Blanco and Youmzain, he'd subsequently been slaughtered by his stablemate Harbinger at Ascot when odds-on.

With the former Arc-favourite Harbinger now retired after fracturing a leg on the gallops, Sir Michael Stoute had to rely on what was to have been his second string.

The hardy-perennial Youmzain was back for a fourth try, after being runner-up three times. Also returning was Grosser Preis von Baden-third Cavalryman, now sporting the royal blue Godolphin silks.

Les Visiteurs: Workforce, Cavalryman, Youmzain, and Prix Foy-winner Duncan for England. Ireland's Fame And Glory, Cape Blanco, and Midas Touch. The Group 3-winner Liang Kay and Wiener Walzer, who'd won the 2009 Deutsches Derby, for Germany. While Japan was represented by Takarazuka Kinen-winner – and Prix Foy-second – Nakayama Festa, and Victoire Pisa, who'd won the Japanese 2000 Guineas and finished fourth in the Prix Niel.

Betting
4.5/1 Behkabad & Sarafina (coupled), 5.5/1 Fame And Glory & Cape Blanco & Midas Touch (all coupled), 6.3/1 Planteur & Pouvoir Absolu (coupled), 7.6/1 Workforce, 11/1 Youmzain, 15/1 Cavalryman, 17/1 Lope De Vega, 23/1 BAR

British Industry Prices
3.5/1 Behkabad, 4.5/1 Fame And Glory, 5.5/1 Planteur, 6/1 Workforce, 11/1 Cape Blanco, 12/1 Sarafina, 12/1 Youmzain, 20/1 BAR.

Three-year-old form lines
Prix du Jockey Club: 1st **Lope De Vega**, 2nd **Planteur**, 3rd Pain Perdu, 4th **Behkabad**, 10th **Cape Blanco**
Grand Prix de Paris: 1st **Behkabad**, 2nd **Planteur**, 3rd Jan Vermeer
Prix Niel: 1st **Behkabad**, 2nd **Planteur**, 3rd Kidnapping, 4th **Victoire Pisa**

Fillies only
Prix de Diane: 1st **Sarafina**, 2nd Rosanara, 3rd Sandbar
Prix Vermeille: 1st Midday, 2nd **Plumania**, 3rd **Sarafina**

Older horses and inter-generational races
Grand Prix de Saint-Cloud: 1st **Plumania**, 2nd **Youmzain**, 3rd Daryakana, 5th **Pouvoir Absolu**
Grand Prix de Deauville: 1st **Marinous**, 2nd Redwood, 3rd La Boum
Prix Foy: 1st **Duncan**, 2nd **Nakayama Festa**, 3rd **Timos**

Abroad
In England
Derby Stakes: 1st **Workforce**, 2nd At First Sight, 3rd Rewilding, 5th **Midas Touch**
King George VI and Queen Elizabeth Stakes: 1st Harbinger, 2nd **Cape Blanco**, 3rd **Youmzain**, 4th **Workforce**

St Leger: 1st Arctic Cosmos, 2nd **Midas Touch**, 3rd Corsica

In Ireland
Irish Derby: 1st **Cape Blanco**, 2nd **Midas Touch**, 3rd Jan Vermeer
Irish Champion Stakes: 1st **Cape Blanco**, 2nd Rip Van Winkle, 3rd Twice Over

In Germany
Grosser Preis von Baden: 1st Night Magic, 2nd Quijano, 3rd **Cavalryman**, 6th **Wiener Walzer**

The race

Planteur's pacemaker, Pouvoir Absolu, had to be shoved along vigorously to make it to the front ahead of Planteur, who was readily to the fore. Midas Touch joined Pouvoir Absolu on the descent, followed in pairs by Planteur and Duncan, Fame And Glory and Sarafina, with Lope De Vega wide, followed by Behkabad and Nakayama Festa, and then Workforce on the inside.

Turning into the false straight, Pouvoir Absolu opted for lane two, giving Planteur the opportunity to come up on his inside. In an unconnected, and unplanned, manoeuvre, Duncan veered out from behind Midas Touch, going violently left and causing interference to Lope De Vega and Cape Blanco.

Despite that, Lope De Vega, who quickly recovered his equilibrium, was the first to challenge Planteur as they entered the home run. Behind them the pacemakers got in the way as they fell back through the field, with most noticeably Masayoshi Ebina, on Nakayama Festa, having to sit still for a moment to avoid a collision.

Five rows off the pace, Ryan Moore angled Workforce off the rails in order to find racing room between Cape Blanco and Nakayama Festa in the centre of the track.

He got through in the nick of time, as on the inner, Planteur suddenly swerved left, setting off a domino effect that took out Lope De Vega, Fame And Glory, Cape Blanco, and Liang Kay. He then proceeded to come back to the rail, in the process blocking Cavalryman.

Into the final 250 metres it was Nakayama Festa and Workforce, who in unison forged to the lead and then engaged in a battle royal. The Epsom Derby-winner just took the upper hand in the final 150 metres and held on to the line, winning by a head.

Out wide, two and a half lengths back, Sarafina came from the clouds to grab third, followed by the Aga Khan's other runner, Behkabad, then Fame And Glory and Marinous.

Post-race

With Planteur jinking left and then right it was not surprising that a stewards' inquiry was called, and even less surprising that he was disqualified.

Workforce was lucky as he'd only just squeezed past before the interference started.

But the margins between success and failure are perilously thin, and Workforce was on the right side this time to give owner Khalid Abdulla a fourth Arc after Rainbow Quest, Dancing Brave, and Rail Link. He also became the sixth Derby-winner to capture the Arc and the second in a row after Sea The Stars.

Trainer Sir Michael Stoute, who'd been third with Opera House and runner-up twice with Pilsudski, opened his account, as did jockey Ryan Moore. Ryan is one of the four children of former jump jockey and current trainer Gary Moore and had been champion jockey in 2006, 2008, and 2009. Workforce was kept in training and would return the following October.

Result

2010 Qatar Prix de l'Arc de Triomphe
Longchamp. Sunday, 3 October 2010
Weights: 3yo c: 56kg, 3yo f: 54.5kg, 4yo+ c: 59.5kg, 4yo+ f: 58kg

1st Workforce (GB)   3yo c   56kg   **7.6/1**
by King's Best out of Soviet Moon (Sadler's Wells). Khalid Abdulla / Sir Michael Stoute / Ryan Moore

2nd Nakayama Festa (JPN) 4yo c   59.5kg   **26/1**
by Stay Gold out of Dear Wink (Tight Spot). Shinichi Izumi / Yoshitaka Ninomiya / Masayoshi Ebina

3rd Sarafina (FR)   3yo f   54.5kg   **4.5/1** (coupled with Behkabad)
by Refuse To Bend out of Sanariya (Darshaan). HH Aga Khan IV / Alain de Royer-Dupré / Gérald Mossé

Runners: 19 (FR 8, GB 4, IRE 3, GER 2, JPN 2). Distances: hd, 2½. Going: very soft. Time: 2m 35.30s

Stewards' Inquiry: Planteur, who finished seventh, was disqualified for causing interference

Also ran: 4th **Behkabad** (FR) 3yo c, 5th **Fame And Glory** (GB) 4yo c, 6th **Marinous** (FR) 4yo c, 7th **Victoire Pisa** (JPN) 3yo c, 8th **Cavalryman** (GB) 4yo c, 9th **Liang Kay** (GER) 5yo h, 10th **Youmzain** (IRE) 7yo h, 11th **Lope De Vega** (IRE) 3yo c, 12th **Wiener Walzer** (GER) 4yo c, 13th **Cape Blanco** (IRE) 3yo c, 14th **Timos** (GER) 5yo h, 15th **Duncan** (GB) 5yo h, 16th **Plumania** (GB) 4yo f, 17th **Midas Touch** (GB) 3yo c, 18th **Pouvoir Absolu** (GB) 5yo h, disq (7th ptp) **Planteur** (IRE) 3yo c.

Danedream comes true in record time

First German-bred winner is partly owned in Japan

Background and fancied horses

Last year's first, second, and third – Workforce, Nakayama Festa and Sarafina – were back. But it was the last-named that was favourite at 3.5/1. In the summer the Aga Khan IV's filly had won the Prix Corrida before adding the Grand Prix de Saint-Cloud in great style.

After a break, she came from last to first off a dawdling pace to win the Prix Foy. In the process she beat three who would re-oppose in the Arc, including both of the Japanese entries. She was accompanied to post by Prix Vermeille-third Shareta, whose guide price was 71/1, and who was wearing the distinguishing red sash.

Workforce had won the Brigadier Gerard Stakes on his reappearance, but was then beaten by the New Zealand-bred So You Think in the Eclipse Stakes. He took the same berth behind Nathaniel – who will play his own part in our story as the sire of Enable – in the King George VI and Queen Elizabeth Stakes on his last run before the Arc.

He was a 12/1-shot, with the horse he beat last year, Nakayama Festa – who was having his first run for ten months when last of four in the Prix Foy – returned at 21/1. Nakayama Festa's compatriot, Hiruno D'Amour, had won a Grade 1 in Kyoto in May before coming to Europe and was 8.3/1 after his good showing when runner-up in the aforesaid Prix Foy.

The Wertheimer's Galikova had finished second to Golden Lilac in the Prix de Diane, before easily despatching the intriguingly named Testosterone, and Shareta, in the Prix Vermeille. Trained by Freddy Head and ridden by Olivier Peslier, she was joint-second favourite along with Méandre.

André Fabre's representative had completed a hat-trick, started in the Prix Comrade, when a cosy winner of the Grand Prix de Paris. That day Méandre had beaten Prix du Jockey Club-winner Reliable Man, but the tables were turned in the Prix Niel when the Gérald Mossé-ridden steel grey produced the better turn of foot.

The previously mentioned So You Think headed the Aidan O'Brien-trained trio. He'd won two Cox Plates before coming to the northern hemisphere, and had made an immediate impact, winning by ten lengths on his first appearance before adding the Group 1 Tattersalls Gold Cup by four and a half.

He was seen by some as a certainty at Royal Ascot for the Prince of Wales's Stakes, but was collared in the closing strides by Godolphin's ill-fated Rewilding, before resuming winning ways in the Eclipse Stakes and Irish Champion Stakes. In the latter he'd beaten the 2010 English and Irish Oaks-winner Snow Fairy, who would also line up at Longchamp.

O'Brien's other two were: Irish Derby-winner Treasure Beach, who'd most recently been seen winning the Secretariat Stakes in America, and St Nicholas Abbey. The latter, who was to be ridden by the trainer's son Joseph, had won the Coronation Cup and then been third in both the King George VI and Queen Elizabeth Stakes and Prix Foy.

Les Visiteurs: Workforce, Snow Fairy, and St Leger-winner Masked Marvel for England. Ireland's So You Think, Treasure Beach, and St Nicholas Abbey. Hiruno d'Amour and Nakayama Festa for Japan. And Germany's Oaks d'Italia and Grosser Preis von Baden-winner Danedream.

Betting

3.5/1 Sarafina & Shareta (coupled), 6.8/1 Galikova, 6.8/1 Méandre, 7.8/1 So You Think & Treasure Beach & St Nicholas Abbey (all coupled), 8.3/1 Hiruno D'Amour, 8.8/1 Reliable Man, 12/1 Workforce, 15/1 Snow Fairy, 21/1 Nakayama Festa, 21/1 Masked Marvel, 27/1 Danedream, 39/1 BAR

British Industry Prices
4/1 Sarafina, 4.5/1 So You Think, 7/1 Galikova, 10/1 Hiruno D'Amour, 10/1 Workforce, 12/1 Méandre, 12/1 Reliable Man, 14/1 Masked Marvel, 14/1 Snow Fairy, 20/1 Danedream, 28/1 BAR.

Three-year-old form lines
Prix du Jockey Club: 1st **Reliable Man**, 2nd Bubble Chic, 3rd Baraan
Grand Prix de Paris: 1st **Méandre**, 2nd Seville, 3rd **Reliable Man**, 4th **Treasure Beach**
Prix Niel: 1st **Reliable Man**, 2nd **Méandre**, 3rd Vadamar

Fillies only
Prix de Diane: 1st Golden Lilac, 2nd **Galikova**, 3rd Glorious Sight, 7th **Shareta**
Prix Vermeille: 1st **Galikova**, 2nd **Testosterone**, 3rd **Shareta**

Older horses and inter-generational races
Grand Prix de Saint-Cloud: 1st **Sarafina**, 2nd Cirrus Des Aigles, 3rd **Silver Pond**
Grand Prix de Deauville: 1st Cirrus Des Aigles, 2nd **Silver Pond**, 3rd Marinous
Prix Foy: 1st **Sarafina**, 2nd **Hiruno D'Amour**, 3rd **St Nicholas Abbey**, 4th/last **Nakayama Festa**

Abroad

In England

Derby Stakes: 1st Pour Moi, 2nd **Treasure Beach**, 3rd Carlton House, 8th **Masked Marvel**

King George VI and Queen Elizabeth Stakes: 1st Nathaniel, 2nd **Workforce**, 3rd **St Nicholas Abbey**

St Leger: 1st **Masked Marvel**, 2nd Brown Panther, 3rd Sea Moon

In Ireland

Irish Derby: 1st **Treasure Beach**, 2nd Seville, 3rd Memphis Tennessee

Irish Champion Stakes: 1st **So You Think**, 2nd **Snow Fairy**, 3rd Famous Name

In Germany

Grosser Preis von Baden: 1st **Danedream**, 2nd Night Magic, 3rd Joshua Tree

The race

The Irish Derby-winner Treasure Beach broke smartly and moved across to the inside rail. At the Petit Bois he had a four-length lead over the Prix Vermeille-third Shareta, who in turn was two lengths clear of the remainder.

The classy pacemaking combination led to the false straight where Treasure Beach was joined by St Nicholas Abbey. Shareta was still there half a length back, followed by Hiruno D'Amour and the filly Testosterone, with Masked Marvel and Danedream sixth and seventh.

Joseph O'Brien took St Nicholas Abbey to the front at the head of the straight, but was challenged at once by Shareta. Meanwhile Andrasch Starke steered Danedream, who was racing three off the rail, into a share of fourth.

As St Nicholas Abbey and Shareta duelled, they drifted towards the rail, which invitingly presented Danedream with a clear track. The daughter of Lomitas responded and was soon alongside the leaders. She then galloped away, opening up a five-length advantage at the line to win in record time – beating the mark set by Peintre Célèbre in 1997.

In behind, Shareta finally got the better of St Nicholas Abbey to take second. The fast-finishing Snow Fairy and So You Think also stormed home taking third and fourth, which in turn demoted St Nicholas Abbey to fifth ahead of Méandre. The favourite Sarafina was seventh while Workforce didn't pick up in the straight and came home an eased-down 12th, just behind last year's runner-up Nakayama Festa.

Post-race

Danedream was the first German-bred winner of the Arc, and she had done it in style beating a field packed with champions. Star Appeal had created a shock in 1975 when becoming the first German-trained winner and many at Longchamp were equally stunned this time.

But it was no fluke; she'd won the Oaks d'Italia by six and a half lengths and was completing a hat-trick in the Arc. Her only poor performance of the year had been in the Prix de Malleret on her sole outing in France prior to the Arc, and many punters may have judged her on that race alone.

For trainer Peter Schiergen, who'd been third with Tiger Hill behind Sagamix, and jockey Andrasch Starke, whose previous best was fifth place on Caitano also in 1998, it was a moment to savour.

Owned jointly by the breeding enterprise Gestüt Burg Eberstein and Teruya Yoshida. Danedream's win was not only a triumph for German breeding but also meant a share in a winner for a Japanese owner. Teruya is the son of the late Zenya Yoshida, who was runner-up with White Muzzle in 1993. Together with his brothers, Katsumi and Haruya, they run the dominant Shadai Stallion Station and Northern Farm operations in Japan.

Last year's winner, Workforce, had run his last race and was retired to the aforementioned Shadai Stallion Station, where he has sired a few winners but no champions as yet.

Danedream was kept in training and the plan was to return, but as we shall see matters beyond her control intervened.

Result

2011 Qatar Prix de l'Arc de Triomphe
Longchamp. Sunday, 2 October 2011
Weights: 3yo c: 56kg, 3yo f: 54.5kg, 4yo+ c: 59.5kg, 4yo+ f: 58kg

1st Danedream (GER)　　3yo f　54.5kg　**27/1**
by Lomitas out of Danedrop (Danehill). Gestüt Burg Eberstein & Teruya Yoshida / Peter Schiergen / Andrasch Starke

2nd Shareta (IRE)　　3yo f　54.5kg　**3.5/1 fav*** (coupled with Sarafina)
by Sinndar out of Shawara (Barathea). HH Aga Khan IV / Alain de Royer-Dupré / Thierry Jarnet

3rd Snow Fairy (IRE)　　4yo f　58kg　**15/1**
by Intikhab out of Woodland Dream (Charnwood Forest). Anamoine Limited / Ed Dunlop / Frankie Dettori

* the individual PMU guide price for Shareta was 71/1, Sarafina was the favourite

Runners: 16 (FR 7, GB 3, IRE 3, JPN 2, GER 1). Distances: 5, nk. Going: good. Time: 2m 24.49s

Also ran: 4th **So You Think** (NZ) 5yo h, 5th **St Nicholas Abbey** (IRE) 4yo c, 6th **Méandre** (FR) 3yo c, 7th **Sarafina** (FR) 4yo f, 8th **Silver Pond** (FR) 4yo c, 9th **Galikova** (FR) 3yo f, 10th **Hiruno D'Amour** (JPN) 4yo c, 11th **Nakayama Festa** (JPN) 5yo h, 12th **Workforce** (GB) 4yo c, 13th **Testosterone** (IRE) 3yo f, 14th **Treasure Beach** (GB) 3yo c, 15th **Reliable Man** (GB) 3yo c, 16th **Masked Marvel** (GB) 3yo c.

2012
Orfevre succumbs to Solemia
Favourite forges to the front but loses lustre in final strides

Background and fancied horses

Danedream had fulfilled German breeders' wishes when winning last year. She was partly Japanese-owned, but the quest for a Japanese-bred winner continued. The big hope was Orfevre – which means goldsmith – and with him the Japanese hoped to strike, well, gold.

Orfevre had won the Japanese Triple Crown in 2011 and had added to his Grade 1 haul in June before leaving for France. Ridden by Christophe Soumillon on his European debut, he comprehensively beat Méandre in the Prix Foy. In Paris he was backed into favouritism.

In England, though, the market leader was Camelot. Trained by Aidan O'Brien, he'd won the 2000 Guineas, the Epsom Derby, and the Irish Derby. He then only failed by three parts of a length in the St Leger, which went to the subsequently controversial Encke, in his bid to become the first English Triple Crown-winner since Nijinsky in 1970.

Camelot was to be ridden by the soon-to-be-freelance Frankie Dettori at Longchamp, while his previous pilot, Joseph O'Brien, was aboard St Nicholas Abbey. He'd won the Breeders' Cup Turf after last year's Arc, and this term had been third in both the King George VI and Queen Elizabeth Stakes and the Irish Champion Stakes. The O'Brien-trained quartet was completed by Ernest Hemingway and Robin Hood, who were to act as pacemakers.

Next in the betting came the recent winner of the Prix Niel, the Jean-Pierre Gauvin-trained Saonois – who'd won the Prix du Jockey Club as a 25/1-chance – and John Gosden's Lancashire and Irish Oaks-winner Great Heavens, owned by Lady Serena Rothschild.

The Aga Khan IV had three runners with Shareta the flag bearer. Last year's runner-up had just lost out in a good battle with Méandre in the Grand Prix de Saint-Cloud, before winning the Yorkshire Oaks and then the Prix Vermeille.

In the latter she'd accounted for the Wertheimer's Solemia and Yellow And Green – who'd recently been purchased by Sheikh Fahad bin Abdulla Al Thani, a cousin of Sheikh Joaan, who was already having a major impact on the sport.

Both Solemia and Yellow And Green were to re-oppose in the Arc. The other two Aga Khan horses were Prix Niel-second Bayrir, and Kesampour, who'd won the Prix Greffulhe.

André Fabre was doubly represented with the previously mentioned Méandre and Godolphin's Grand Prix de Deauville-winner Masterstroke, while Khalid Abdullah ran the Breeders' Cup Turf runner-up and Hardwicke Stakes-winner Sea Moon.

The reigning champion Danedream was also due to be there. She'd just nosed out Nathaniel in a thrilling finish to the King George VI and Queen Elizabeth Stakes, before winning the Grosser Preis Von Baden for a second time.

But then her chances of a second Arc victory evaporated when she – along with 300 others – was quarantined for three months after a horse in a veterinary clinic near to her Cologne training centre tested positive for equine infectious anaemia, known colloquially as swamp fever. With Danedream confined to barracks, there would be a new name on the trophy.

Les Visiteurs: Camelot, St Nicholas Abbey, Ernest Hemingway, and Robin Hood for Ireland. Great Heavens and Sea Moon for England. Orfevre and Aventino representing Japan. And the former Ballydoyle inmate Mikhail Glinka, who'd won a Group 3 in Baden-Baden at the end of August for his latest trainer, the Czech Republic-based Arslangirej Savujev.

Betting
3.5/1 Orfevre, 3.8/1 Camelot & St Nicholas Abbey & Ernest Hemingway & Robin Hood (all coupled), 5.5/1 Saonois, 7.5/1 Great Heavens, 11/1 Shareta & Bayrir & Kesampour (all coupled), 13/1 Masterstroke, 14/1 Méandre, 15/1 Sea Moon, 22/1 BAR

British Industry Prices
2/1 Camelot, 5/1 Orfevre, 6/1 Great Heavens, 9/1 Saonois, 9/1 Sea Moon, 11/1 Masterstroke, 14/1 St Nicholas Abbey, 14/1 Shareta, 14/1 Yellow And Green, 20/1 BAR.

Three-year-old form lines
Prix du Jockey Club: 1st **Saonois**, 2nd Saint Baudolino, 3rd Nutello, 4th **Kesampour**
Grand Prix de Paris: 1st Imperial Monarch, 2nd Last Train, 3rd Saint Baudolino
Prix Niel: 1st **Saonois**, 2nd **Bayrir**, 3rd Last Train, 5th **Kesampour**

Fillies only
Prix de Diane: 1st Valyra, 2nd Beauty Parlour, 3rd Rjwa
Prix Vermeille: 1st **Shareta**, 2nd Pirika, 3rd **Solemia**, 4th **Yellow And Green**

Older horses and inter-generational races

Grand Prix de Saint-Cloud: 1st **Méandre**, 2nd **Shareta**, 3rd Galikova, 4th/last Danedream

Grand Prix de Deauville: 1st **Masterstroke**, 2nd Gatewood, 3rd Ok Coral

Prix Foy: 1st **Orfevre**, 2nd **Méandre**, 3rd Joshua Tree, 5th/last **Aventino**

Abroad

In England

Derby Stakes: 1st **Camelot**, 2nd Main Sequence, 3rd Astrology

King George VI and Queen Elizabeth Stakes: 1st Danedream, 2nd Nathaniel, 3rd **St Nicholas Abbey**, 5th **Sea Moon** 19th/last **Robin Hood**

St Leger: 1st Encke, 2nd **Camelot**, 3rd Michelangelo

In Ireland

Irish Derby: 1st **Camelot**, 2nd Born To Sea, 3rd Light Heavy

Irish Champion Stakes: 1st Snow Fairy, 2nd Nathaniel, 3rd **St Nicholas Abbey**

The race

After a lot of rain, the ground was heavy and it was Ernest Hemingway, in the pink Magnier colours, who set a medium pace from Mikhail Glinka. Just behind them, Solemia was prominent with Robin Hood out wide. The latter was pushed up into second at the Petit Bois, and then the order remained pretty much unchanged down the hill and on to the false straight, with Camelot in the midfield and Orfevre at the back.

Colm O'Donoghue kicked Ernest Hemingway on, and they extended the lead to six lengths as Solemia and Mikhail Glinka overtook the fading Robin Hood. But turning in, Ernest Hemingway also started to empty out and was tackled by Solemia. Orfevre was still at the back but was being angled out for a run by Soumillon.

Solemia took it up at the 400-metre pole from Great Heavens and Masterstroke, who was in the beige Godolphin silks. Meanwhile, out wide, Orfevre was scything through the field, his speed carried him into second and he then overtook Solemia to take what looked like an unassailable lead, despite the fact that he was hanging across to the rail.

Once passed, though, Solemia accelerated again and gradually started to eat into Orfevre's advantage. There wasn't much in it entering the last few strides, but then Orfevre ducked right and made contact with the running rail. Soumillon had to stop riding for a stride, and in doing so lost some momentum and the race.

Solemia prevailed by a neck, with the pair seven lengths clear of Masterstroke, who was followed in by Haya Landa, a never-nearer Yellow And Green and Great Heavens with Camelot seventh.

Post-race

In a sensational renewal the Wertheimer colours – blue, with white seams, sleeves and cap – had been carried to victory again, this time for Gérard and Alain, the sons of Jacques who had won with Ivanjica in 1976.

It was also another winner for the Head family, as trainer Carlos Laffon-Parias is married to Christiane Head-Maarek's daughter, Patricia.

For Olivier Peslier, it was his first win of the new century after his hat-trick with Peintre Célèbre, Hélissio, and Sagamix in the 1990s. He therefore became the fifth jockey in the four-winners club with Jacques Doyasbère, Freddy Head, Yves Saint-Martin, and Pat Eddery.

Orfevre had come so close but had lost out in an epic duel with a mare who had found an extra gear in the final 100 metres. He comprehensively beat Solemia the following month in the Japan Cup on firm ground, when he was second to Gentildonna, who ran in the same ownership and bumped him on the way through. Solemia could only finish 13th that day on what was her swansong.

Solemia's first two offspring both won on debut, and she has subsequently been covered by Sea The Stars and Dubawi. Danedream, who'd had to miss the race, was also retired to the paddocks and Faylaq, her colt by Dubawi, has won a few races. Subsequently she's been covered by Frankel.

Both Solemia and Danedream are only in the infancy of their stud careers and time will tell if they can produce horses who are as good on the track as they were.

Result

2012 Qatar Prix de l'Arc de Triomphe

Longchamp. Sunday, 7 October 2012
Weights: 3yo c: 56kg, 3yo f: 54.5kg, 4yo+ c: 59.5kg, 4yo+ f: 58kg

1st Solemia (IRE)   4yo f   58kg   41/1

by Poliglote out of Brooklyn's Dance (Shirley Heights). Wertheimer & Frere / Carlos Laffon-Parias / Olivier Peslier

2nd Orfevre (JPN)   4yo c   59.5kg   3.5/1 fav

by Stay Gold out of Oriental Art (Mejiro McQueen). Sunday Racing Co Ltd / Yasutoshi Ikee / Christophe Soumillon

3rd Masterstroke (USA)   3yo c   56kg   13/1

by Monsun out of Melikah (Lammtarra). Godolphin SNC / André Fabre / Mickael Barzalona

Runners: 18 (FR 9, IRE 4, GB 2, JPN 2, CZE 1). Distances: nk, 7. Going: heavy. Time: 2m 37.68s

Also ran: 4th **Haya Landa** (FR) 4yo f, 5th **Yellow And Green** (GB) 3yo f, 6th **Great Heavens** (GB) 3yo f, 7th **Camelot** (GB) 3yo c, 8th **Sea Moon** (GB) 4yo c, 9th **Shareta** (IRE) 4yo f, 10th **Bayrir** (FR) 3yo c, 11th **St Nicholas Abbey** (IRE) 5yo h, 12th **Méandre** (FR) 4yo c, 13th **Kesampour** (FR) 3yo c, 14th **Mikhail Glinka** (IRE) 5yo h, 15th **Saonois** (FR) 3yo c, 16th **Ernest Hemingway** (IRE) 3yo c, 17th **Aventino** (JPN) 8yo h, 18th **Robin Hood** (IRE) 4yo c.

1988: Tony Bin and John Reid receive the plaudits of the crowd after holding on from Mtoto

2006: Rail Link and Stéphane Pasquier (pink cap) beat Pride (number 4) with Deep Impact (yellow cap) third past the post

1995: Frankie Dettori's first Arc winner, Lammtarra, remains unbeaten on his swansong

Owner Jean-Luc Lagardère is delighted as Sagamix scores in 1998 to complete Olivier Peslier's three-timer

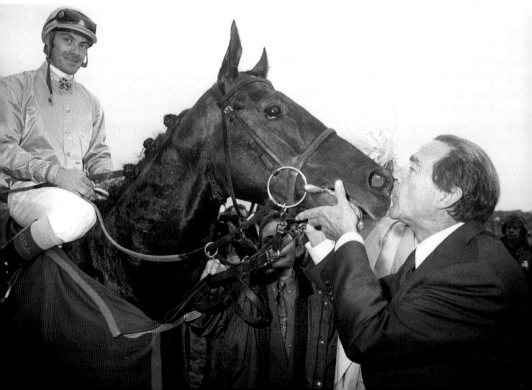

1991: Cash Asmussen enjoys the post-race celebrations after Suave Dancer's slick success

2000: Sinndar in the winner's enclosure with jockey Johnny Murtagh and owner the Aga Khan IV

Kieren Fallon and Hurricane Run after storming home in the driving rain in 2005

2012: Solemia retakes Orfevre to prevail in a sensational running

Sea The Stars (left) caps his stellar career at Longchamp in 2009. Also pictured: Stacelita (orange), Dar Re Mi (pink), Fame And Glory (purple), La Boum (yellow cap), and Cavalryman in Godolphin SNC beige

2014: Thierry Jarnet celebrates as Trêve wins for the second time

2018: Enable just holds Sea Of Class's late surge to add to her win at Chantilly, Cloth Of Stars is third

2016: Ryan Moore and Found lead home a one-two-three for Aidan O'Brien at Chantilly. Highland Reel (purple) is second with Order Of St George (white cap) third

2015: Golden Horn is roared home by Frankie Dettori

2019: Waldgeist (red and green) hunts down Enable (pink cap) to become André Fabre's record-breaking eighth Arc winner, Sottsass (green) is third and Japan (purple) fourth

Unbeaten Trêve
avec beaucoup de vitesse

Jarnet regains mount after Dettori injury

Background and fancied horses

Last year's runner-up, Orfevre, won on his seasonal reappearance at Hanshin at the end of March before returning to France. His next mission was the Prix Foy in mid-September, which he took comfortably by three lengths, beating Very Nice Name, Pirika, and Haya Landa, all of whom would renew rivalry in the Arc.

With the huge Japanese contingent present at Longchamp lumping on Orfevre again, he was sent off a warm order at 1.3/1, however 2/1 was available in England.

The leading French candidate was the only filly in the field, Trêve at 4.8/1, who was unbeaten after four races. Thierry Jarnet was in the saddle for her first three outings, which culminated in an emphatic four-length victory in the Prix de Diane.

After that success she was sold to Sheikh Joaan bin Hamad Al Thani, with the mount going to the Sheikh's retained rider, Frankie Dettori. The new pairing duly obliged in the Prix Vermeille. However, Dettori subsequently broke his ankle in a fall at Nottingham and Jarnet was back in the saddle for the Arc.

The other Japanese-raider, Kizuna, who had won the Tokyo Yushan (Japanese Derby) and then the Prix Niel on his French debut, was third favourite at 6.5/1.

The French and English Derby winners, Intello and Ruler Of The World, were 10/1 and 12/1 respectively. After finishing third to Moonlight Cloud in a strong renewal of the Jacques Le Marois, Intello had regained the winning thread in the Prix du Prince d'Orange.

Ruler Of The World, on the other hand, could only finish fifth in the Irish Derby and although in the Prix Niel he beat the first and third home in the Grand Prix de Paris, Flintshire and Ocovango, he'd had to play second fiddle to Kizuna.

Leading Light, who won the St Leger in testing conditions, and Irish Champion Stakes-second Al Kazeem were next best.

They were all racing for a purse that had increased from €4m to €4.8m to the winner.

Les Visiteurs: Al Kazeem and last year's Prix Foy-third Joshua Tree from England. Ireland's Ruler Of The World and Leading Light. Orfevre and Kizuna for Japan. Méandre again for the Czech Republic, and the Alban de Mieulle-trained Very Nice Name for Qatar, running in the colours of Sheikh Fahad.

Betting
1.3/1 Orfevre, 4.8/1 Trêve, 6.5/1 Kizuna, 10/1 Intello, 12/1 Ruler Of The World & Leading Light (coupled), 19/1 Al Kazeem, 20/1 Flintshire, 53/1 BAR

British Industry Prices
2/1 Orfevre, 9/2 Trêve, 7/1 Kizuna, 7/1 Ruler Of The World, 9/1 Intello, 10/1 Leading Light, 12/1 Flintshire, 16/1 Al Kazeem, 28/1 BAR.

Three-year-old form lines
Prix du Jockey Club: 1st **Intello**, 2nd Morandi, 3rd Sky Hunter
Grand Prix de Paris: 1st **Flintshire**, 2nd Manndawi, 3rd **Ocovango**
Prix Niel: 1st **Kizuna**, 2nd **Ruler Of The World**, 3rd **Ocovango**, 4th **Flintshire**

Fillies only
Prix de Diane: 1st **Trêve**, 2nd Chicquita, 3rd Silasol
Prix Vermeille: 1st **Trêve**, 2nd Wild Coco, 3rd Tasaday

Older horses and inter-generational races
Grand Prix de Saint-Cloud: 1st Novellist, 2nd Dunaden, 3rd **Haya Landa**, 6th **Pirika**, 10th **Joshua Tree**
Grand Prix de Deauville: 1st Tres Blue, 2nd **Penglai Pavilion**, 3rd Slow Pace, 4th **Very Nice Name**
Prix du Prince d'Orange: 1st **Intello**, 2nd Morandi, 3rd Zhiyi
Prix Foy: 1st **Orfevre**, 2nd **Very Nice Name**, 3rd **Pirika**, 6th **Haya Landa**

Abroad
In England
Derby Stakes: 1st **Ruler Of The World**, 2nd Libertarian, 3rd Galileo Rock, 5th **Ocovango**
King George VI and Queen Elizabeth Stakes: 1st Novellist, 2nd Trading Leather, 3rd Hillstar, 7th **Very Nice Name**
St Leger: 1st **Leading Light**, 2nd Talent, 3rd Galileo Rock

In Ireland
Irish Derby: 1st Trading Leather, 2nd Galileo Rock, 3rd Festive Cheer, 5th **Ruler Of The World**
Irish Champion Stakes: 1st The Fugue, 2nd **Al Kazeem**, 3rd Trading Leather

In Germany
Grosser Preis von Baden: 1st Novellist, 2nd Seismos, 3rd **Méandre**

The race

The early skirmishes involved the Brazilian-bred Going Somewhere, Penglai Pavilion – in the Godolphin SNC beige – and Joshua Tree. Trêve, who was pulling hard, and Orfevre raced in tandem towards the rear. By the Petit Bois it was Joshua Tree, with his tongue lolling, who was in the lead, setting a modest pace from a closely packed field.

On the descent, Méandre was noticeably short of space on the rail in midfield, and with only seven lengths covering the entire field as they turned into the *faux ligne droite*, racing room was at a premium – and for the time being Orfevre couldn't get out.

Jårnet on Trêve, though, was in the clear on the outside, and started to make progress into fifth. Ocovango challenged Joshua Tree, just ahead of Penglai Pavilion, as they entered the straight, with Trêve just behind, followed by Kizuna, Intello, the now-in-the-clear Orfevre and Flintshire. Then Trêve made her move, mastering Joshua Tree and quickly opening up a two-length gap to Intello, who followed her through, with Orfevre and Kizuna next.

Without duly being put under pressure, Trêve stormed away in brilliant style, extending the advantage at the line to five lengths over Orfevre, who finished best of the rest to take second place again. He in turn was just ahead of Intello, with Kizuna a further two lengths back in fourth and similar distances to Penglai Pavilion and then Al Kazeem.

Post-race

Although the Head clan had won last year's race with Solemia, it had been more than three decades since Criquette Head-Maarek had won in her own right with Three Troïkas in 1979.

Bred at Haras du Quesnay, Trêve had been bought back at auction by her father, Alec, for the relatively paltry sum of €22,000. It proved a good investment as after her Prix de Diane victory Sheikh Joaan purchased her for €8m. Time showed that both parties had made a shrewd deal.

With the Qatar brand having sponsored the Arc since 2008, it was fitting that Sheikh Joaan, a prominent member of the Qatari royal family, had won back some of his family's money.

For Thierry Jarnet it was a third success overall and his first in the 21st century, after Subotica in 1992 and Carnégie in 1994. Trêve was retired for the season and would return.

Result

2013 Qatar Prix de l'Arc de Triomphe
Longchamp. Sunday, 6 October 2013
Weights: 3yo c: 56kg, 3yo f: 54.5kg, 4yo+ c: 59.5kg, 4yo+ f: 58kg

1st Trêve (FR)　　　　3yo f　54.5kg　**4.8/1**
by Motivator out of Trévise (Anabaa). Sheikh Joaan bin Hamad Al Thani / Christiane Head-Maarek / Thierry Jarnet

2nd Orfevre (JPN)　　　5yo c　59.5kg　**1.3/1 fav**
by Stay Gold out of Oriental Art (Mejiro McQueen). Sunday Racing Co Ltd / Yasutoshi Ikee / Christophe Soumillon

3rd Intello (GER)　　　3yo c　56kg　**10/1**
by Galileo out of Impressionnante (Danehill). Wertheimer & Frere / André Fabre / Olivier Peslier

Runners: 17 (FR 9, GB 2, IRE 2, JPN 2, CZE 1, QAT 1). Distances: 5, nk. Going: soft. Time: 2m 32.04s

Also ran: 4th **Kizuna** (JPN) 3yo c, 5th **Penglai Pavilion** (USA) 3yo c, 6th **Al Kazeem** (GB) 5yo h, 7th **Ruler Of The World** (IRE) 3yo c, 8th **Flintshire** (GB) 3yo c, 9th **Going Somewhere** (BRZ) 4yo c, 10th **Méandre** (FR) 5yo h, 11th **Sahawar** (FR) 3yo c, 12th **Leading Light** (IRE) 3yo c, 13th **Joshua Tree** (IRE) 6yo h, 14th **Ocovango** (GB) 3yo c, 15th **Pirika** (IRE) 5yo m, 16th **Very Nice Name** (FR) 4yo c, 17th **Haya Landa** (FR) 5yo m.

No truce as Trêve repeats success

First dual winner since Alleged

Background and fancied horses

The prize money rose further, reaching €5m to the winner. Favourite to win it was Taghrooda, who had been the best filly in England. Trained by John Gosden, the daughter of Sea The Stars had won her first four races, including The Oaks and the King George VI and Queen Elizabeth Stakes. Most recently, though, she'd been beaten by Aidan O'Brien's Tapestry when 1/5 in the Yorkshire Oaks.

At 5.5/1 she was marginally the favourite on the PMU, with only half a point to Poule d'Essai des Pouliches and Prix de Diane-winner Avenir Certain, who'd won all of her six starts. Only fractions behind her was Ectot, who'd been purchased by Al Shaqab Racing just prior to his win in the Prix Niel – one of three interests they had in the Arc.

The most fancied of the three Japanese runners, Harp Star, had won the Japanese 1000 Guineas and been runner-up in the Japanese Oaks. Just A Way, at 8/1, had romped home by more than six lengths in the Dubai Duty Free in Meydan. He'd then taken the Grade 1 Yasuda Kinen back in Tokyo, before venturing to Europe. Making up the trio was the 2012 Japanese 2000 Guineas and St Leger-winner, Gold Ship, who had won the Grade 1 Takarazuka Kinen in June and was a 12/1-shot.

Last year's winner, Trêve, was yet to score in 2014 having finished second to Cirrus Des Aigles in the Prix Ganay, third in the Prince of Wales's Stakes in her sole race outside of France, and then only fourth when odds-on in the Prix Vermeille. As such, her guide price was 14/1.

She'd also moved from Sheikh Joaan's sole ownership to that of Al Shaqab Racing. They also had a share in the returning Ruler of the World, and, together with the previously mentioned Ectot, the most fancied of the trio, they were coupled on 6.8/1.

Ruler of the World, one of three horses trained by Aidan O'Brien, had won the Prix Foy and would be partnered by Frankie Dettori. O'Brien also ran Tapestry, who was to be ridden by Ryan Moore. She was on 16/1, while last season's Prix de Diane runner-up, Chicquita, who had gone on to win the Irish Oaks, was 45/1.

The last two weren't coupled, even though both were owned to varying degrees by Michael Tabor, Sue Smith and Derrick Smith – with Flaxman Stables also owning part of Tapestry. The first three also retained their interests in Ruler of the World.

Others of note included the Aga Khan IV's Prix Vermeille-third Dolniya on 18/1, and the returning Flintshire, who'd been runner-up in the Prix Foy, who was 20/1, and it was 26/1 bar.

Les Visiteurs: England's Taghrooda, St Leger-winner Kingston Hill, and returnee Al Kazeem. Tapestry, Ruler of the World, and Chicquita from Ireland. Harp Star, Just A Way, and Gold Ship representing Japan. And Germany's Ivanhowe, who'd won the Grosser Preis von Baden.

Betting

5.5/1 Taghrooda, 6/1 Avenir Certain, 6.8/1 Ectot & Trêve & Ruler Of The World (all coupled), 7/1 Harp Star, 8/1 Just A Way, 12/1 Gold Ship, 16/1 Tapestry, 18/1 Dolniya, 20/1 Flintshire, 26/1 BAR

British Industry Prices

4.5/1 Taghrooda, 6/1 Ectot, 7/1 Just A Way, 8/1 Avenir Certain, 8/1 Harp Star, 11/1 Trêve, 12/1 Gold Ship, 12/1 Ruler Of The World, 14/1 Tapestry, 16/1 Dolniya, 16/1 Flintshire, 25/1 BAR.

Three-year-old form lines

Prix du Jockey Club: 1st The Grey Gatsby, 2nd Shamkiyr, 3rd **Prince Gibraltar**, 14th **Free Port Lux**

Grand Prix de Paris: 1st Gallante, 2nd **Prince Gibraltar**, 3rd Teletext, 4th **Free Port Lux**

Prix Niel: 1st **Ectot**, 2nd Teletext, 3rd Adelaide

Fillies only

Prix de Diane: 1st **Avenir Certain**, 2nd Amour A Papa, 3rd Xcellence

Prix Vermeille: 1st Baltic Baroness, 2nd Pomology, 3rd **Dolniya**, 4th **Trêve**, 7th **Siljan's Saga**

Older horses and inter-generational races

Grand Prix de Saint-Cloud: 1st (2nd ptp) Noble Mission, 2nd **Siljan's Saga**, 3rd Narniyn, 4th **Flintshire**, disq (1st ptp tested positive for banned substance) **Spiritjim**

Prix du Prince d'Orange: 1st **Free Port Lux**, 2nd Bodhi, 3rd Calling Out

Prix Foy: 1st **Ruler Of The World**, 2nd **Flintshire**, 3rd **Spiritjim**

Abroad

In England

Derby Stakes: 1st Australia, 2nd **Kingston Hill**, 3rd Romsdal

Oaks Stakes: 1st **Taghrooda**, 2nd Tarfasha, 3rd Volume

King George VI and Queen Elizabeth Stakes: 1st **Taghrooda**, 2nd Telescope, 3rd Mukhadram

St Leger: 1st **Kingston Hill**, 2nd Romsdal, 3rd Snow Sky

In Ireland
Irish Champion Stakes: 1st The Grey Gatsby, 2nd Australia, 3rd Trading Leather, 5th **Al Kazeem**

In Germany
Grosser Preis von Baden: 1st **Ivanhowe**, 2nd Sea The Moon, 3rd Night Wish

The race

Ruler Of The World was the first to show but he was quickly reined back and Montviron came past to take it up. At the top of hill, he still had the advantage from Kingston Hill, Avenir Certain, Ruler Of The World and Taghrooda, with Ivanhowe on the outside and the sweating-up Trêve on the inner.

Entering the straight, Montviron drifted off the rail into lane three with Kingston Hill going even wider. This left plenty of room for Trêve, Avenir Certain and Prince Gibraltar to come up on the inner. Trêve cruised through on the bridle and quickly opened up a three-length gap.

The dangers were out wide, with Flintshire and Taghrooda making ground fast, and from the back Harp Star was finishing best of all. But, although Flintshire and Taghrooda ultimately cut the gap to two lengths and one and a quarter, the race was over.

Jarnet rode out hands and heels to the line, allowing himself the luxury of punching the air and saluting the crowd in the last couple of strides as Trêve retained her crown. Kingston Hill and Dolniya came through in fourth and fifth, with Harp Star a fast-finishing sixth. Moments later, after a handshake with Christophe Soumillon, the full impact of Trêve's achievement hit home and Jarnet wiped away a tear.

Post-race

Trêve, whose name means truce, had refused to surrender her title and became the first since Alleged in 1977 and 1978 to win twice, and the seventh in all. It was officially a first win for Al Shaqab Racing. However, as previous owner Sheikh Joaan was instrumental in the organisation, it was in reality a second win for the bourgeoning Qatari interests in European racing.

Sheikh Joaan's cousin, Sheikh Fahad, had shown the way in the thoroughbred sphere. Initially he ran horses in the name of Pearl Bloodstock – notably winning the Melbourne Cup with Dunaden in 2011 – but, with his brothers on board, created Qatar Racing which is run by the Qatar Investment and Projects Development Holding Company (QIPCO). Their horses run in the maroon colours with gold braiding and maroon cap with a gold tassel.

Inspired by their success, Sheikh Joaan expanded his thoroughbred interests through Al Shaqab Racing, which is the racing and breeding wing of the centre for equine excellence that had previously concentrated solely on Arabian-bred horses. Al Shaqab runners sport the grey silks with gold braiding and maroon cap with a gold tassel. And with Trêve they had just witnessed a landmark success.

Trêve was a third winner for trainer Criquette Head-Maarek and a fourth for Thierry Jarnet, who joined Jacques Doyasbère, Freddy Head, Yves Saint-Martin, Pat Eddery, and Olivier Peslier as the sixth jockey in the four-winners club. Trêve was kept in training and would be the first to attempt a hat-trick.

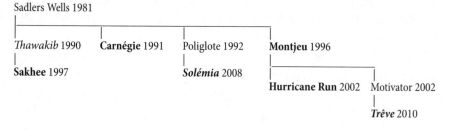

Result
2014 Qatar Prix de l'Arc de Triomphe
Longchamp. Sunday, 5 October 2014
Weights: 3yo c: 56kg, 3yo f: 54.5kg, 4yo+ c: 59.5kg, 4yo+ f: 58kg

1st Trêve (FR)　　4yo f 58kg　**6.8/1*** (coupled with Ectot & Ruler Of The World)
by Motivator out of Trévise (Anabaa). Al Shaqab Racing / Christiane Head-Maarek / Thierry Jarnet

2nd Flintshire (GB)　4yo c 59.5kg **20/1**
by Dansili out of Dance Routine (Sadler's Wells). Khalid Abdullah / André Fabre / Maxime Guyon

3rd Taghrooda (GB)　3yo f 54.5kg **5.5/1 fav**
by Sea The Stars out of Ezima (Sadler's Wells). Hamdan Al Maktoum / John Gosden / Paul Hanagan

* the individual PMU guide price for Trêve was 14/1 with Ruler Of The World 17/1, Ectot was the most fancied of the trio

Runners: 20 (FR 10, GB 3, IRE 3, JPN 3, GER 1) Distances: 2, 1¼. Going: good. Time: 2m 26.05s

Also ran: 4th **Kingston Hill** (GB) 3yo c, 5th **Dolniya** (FR) 3yo f, 6th **Harp Star** (JPN) 3yo f, 7th **Prince Gibraltar** (FR) 3yo c, 8th **Just A Way** (JPN) 5yo h, 9th **Ruler Of The World** (IRE) 4yo c, 10th **Al Kazeem** (GB) 6yo h, 11th **Avenir Certain** (FR) 3yo f, 12th **Siljan's Saga** (FR) 4yo f, 13th **Tapestry** (IRE) 3yo f, 14th **Gold Ship** (JPN) 5yo h, 15th **Chicquita** (IRE) 4yo f, 16th **Spiritjim** (FR) 4yo c, 17th **Ectot** (GB) 3yo c, 18th **Ivanhowe** (GER) 4yo c, 19th **Free Port Lux** (GB) 3yo c, 20th **Montviron** (FR) 3yo c.

Golden Horn for the golden boy

Flintshire second again, first hat-trick bid foiled

Background and fancied horses

In contrast to last year's campaign, Trêve was unbeaten this term winning the Grand Prix de Saint-Cloud on her second outing – beating Flintshire, the Aga Khan IV's Dolniya and Manatee – and then demolishing her rivals in the Prix Vermeille. The first Arc hat-trick bid was on, Shahah was entered to ensure the pace, and in Paris, Trêve was odds-on to do it.

The main danger appeared to be Khalid Abdullah's three-year-old colt, New Bay, ridden by former jump jockey Vincent Cheminaud. They'd won the Prix du Jockey Club and more recently the Prix Niel, beating among others Silverwave and the Grand Prix de Paris-winner Erupt.

The leading candidate *outre-Manche* was Anthony Oppenheimer's Golden Horn. He'd won the Derby, the Eclipse Stakes and the Irish Champion Stakes. His only defeat had come in the Juddmonte International Stakes, when he'd gone down by a neck to 50/1-shot Arabian Queen.

It was double figures bar the three in England, with Dermot Weld's Prince of Wales's Stakes-winner Free Eagle next, followed by last year's runner-up Flintshire, who'd won the Grade 1 Sword Dancer Stakes at Saratoga on his latest outing.

In addition to the Khalid Abdullah pair, New Bay and Flintshire, André Fabre also ran Godolphin's Manatee. While Aidan O'Brien saddled two runners: last year's Prix Marcel Boussac-winner Found, who'd been second in some of the top races this year including the Irish Champion Stakes; and Tapestry, who was back but had only been seen once, when runner-up in the Blandford Stakes in mid-September.

Although the Al Shaqab and Khalid Abdullah horses were coupled on the PMU, the dual interests of Michael Tabor, Sue Smith and Derrick Smith weren't, seemingly based on the fact that they were wearing different colours to each other.

Les Visiteurs: Ireland's Free Eagle, Found, and Tapestry. Golden Horn, and King George VI and Queen Elizabeth Stakes-second Eagle Top for England.

Betting

0.9/1 Trêve & Shahah (coupled), 5/1 New Bay & Flintshire (coupled), 5.3/1 Golden Horn, 17/1 Free Eagle, 27/1 Dolniya, 28/1 Found, 29/1 Erupt, 42/1 BAR

British Industry Prices

1/1 Trêve. 4.5/1 Golden Horn, 5/1 New Bay, 14/1 Free Eagle, 18/1 Found, 20/1 Flintshire, 25/1 Erupt, 33/1 BAR.

Three-year-old form lines

Prix du Jockey Club: 1st **New Bay**, 2nd Highland Reel, 3rd War Dispatch, 9th **Silverwave**

Grand Prix de Paris: 1st **Erupt**, 2nd Ampere, 3rd Storm The Stars, 4th **Silverwave**

Prix Niel: 1st **New Bay**, 2nd **Silverwave**, 3rd Migwar, 4th **Erupt**

Fillies only

Prix de Diane: 1st Star Of Seville, 2nd Physiocrate, 3rd Little Nightingale

Prix Vermeille: 1st **Trêve**, 2nd Candarliya, 3rd Sea Calisi 4th **Frine**

Older horses and inter-generational races

Grand Prix de Saint-Cloud: 1st **Trêve**, 2nd **Flintshire**, 3rd **Dolniya**, 4th **Manatee**

Grand Prix de Deauville: 1st **Siljan's Saga**, 2nd Cocktail Queen, 3rd Loresho

Prix Foy: 1st Postponed, 2nd **Spiritjim**, 3rd Baino Hope, 4th **Dolniya**

Abroad

In England

Derby Stakes: 1st **Golden Horn**, 2nd Jack Hobbs, 3rd Storm The Stars

King George VI and Queen Elizabeth Stakes: 1st Postponed, 2nd **Eagle Top**, 3rd Romsdal

In Ireland

Irish Champion Stakes: 1st **Golden Horn**, 2nd **Found**, 3rd **Free Eagle**

In Germany

Grosser Preis von Baden: 1st **Prince Gibraltar**, 2nd Nightflower, 3rd Sirius

The race

Shahah was away fast on the rail with New Bay in lane three. Dolniya raced in the middle of the track and was angling across to the inner, but Golden Horn on the wide outside stayed straight for the time being *en isolation splendide*. However, approaching the Petit Bois, he gradually moved across towards the inner, taking up second place.

On the descent there was interference in midfield as Manatee, who became short of room, blocked Tapestry who in turn knocked into Eagle Top. Golden Horn was clear of the trouble and going very comfortably and, despite running a little wide on the turn, took it up early in the straight.

New Bay, on his inner, and Flintshire on the outer started their challenges, with Erupt and Siljan's Saga just behind. They were followed by Dolniya, Free Eagle and Trêve, who was out wide and starting to move through the gears. Further back, Found lost all chance after becoming entangled and knocked sideways in an altercation with Eagle Top.

The Khalid Abdullah pair tried their best but couldn't get on terms, and in the final 200 metres Golden Horn extended the advantage. Under an ecstatic Dettori, who was already celebrating as he passed the line, Golden Horn won by two lengths, with Flintshire just beating his younger stablemate by a neck for second spot.

Trêve, who finished fastest of all, just failed by a nose to make the podium. The hat-trick bid may not have succeeded but she had run another big race. Erupt and Free Eagle were one and a half lengths further back in fifth and sixth.

Post-race

The image of Frankie Dettori crossing the line with his whip aloft in the Anthony Oppenheimer silks – black and white halved colours with a red cap – will live long in the memory. Dettori had suffered a few reverses in the preceding years but was enjoying the start of what would be a sensational renaissance, and was very much the golden boy again.

The Oppenheimers had been synonymous with diamonds for generations through the company De Beers, who sponsored the King George VI and Queen Elizabeth Stakes from the early 1970s until 2006. Anthony's father, Philip, had also passed on the fascination of owning and breeding racehorses.

It was John Gosden's first Arc winner – he'd been third with Taghrooda last year – and his current base, Clarehaven in Newmarket, provides a link to the inaugural Arc, as it was from there that Comrade, who won that race, was prepared.

After Lammtarra, Sakhee, and Marienbard, Frankie Dettori became the seventh jockey to ride four winners, emulating the feats of Jacques Doyasbère, Freddy Head, Yves Saint-Martin, Pat Eddery, Olivier Peslier, and last year's new entrant Thierry Jarnet.

Jarnet's fourth on Trêve turned out to be his last ride in the Arc, and he retired with a knee injury in February 2017 – a month before his 50th birthday. It was also the last appearance for Trêve, who retired to the paddocks.

Golden Horn, who was the seventh horse to win the Derby and the Arc, had one more race before he went to stud, being beaten half a length by Found in the Breeders' Cup Turf at the end of the month. It was some recompense for Aidan O'Brien's filly, who had been knocked all over the shop in the Arc.

Found would return for the 2016 Arc, but not to Longchamp. The whole show would be moving 50km up the road to Chantilly, while a radical overhaul of Longchamp's main grandstand and the surrounding areas took place.

Golden Horn sired his first Group winner when West End Girl scored in the Group 3 Sweet Solera Stakes in August 2019.

Result

2015 Qatar Prix de l'Arc de Triomphe

Longchamp. Sunday, 4 October 2015
Weights: 3yo c: 56kg, 3yo f: 54.5kg, 4yo+ c: 59.5kg, 4yo+ f: 58kg

1st Golden Horn (GB)   3yo c   56kg   **5.3/1**
by Cape Cross out of Fleche d'Or (Dubai Destination). Anthony Oppenheimer / John Gosden / Frankie Dettori

2nd Flintshire (GB)   5yo h   59.5kg   **5/1*** (coupled with New Bay)
by Dansili out of Dance Routine (Sadler's Wells). Khalid Abdullah / André Fabre / Maxime Guyon

3rd New Bay (GB)   3yo c   56kg   **5/1** (coupled with Flintshire)
by Dubawi out of Cinnamon Bay (Zamindar). Khalid Abdullah / André Fabre / Vincent Cheminaud

* the individual PMU guide price for Flintshire was 18/1

Runners: 17 (FR 12, IRE 3, GB 2). Distances: 2, nk. Going: good. Time: 2m 27.23s

Also ran: 4th **Trêve** (FR) 5yo m, 5th **Erupt** (IRE) 3yo c, 6th **Free Eagle** (IRE) 4yo c, 7th **Prince Gibraltar** 4yo c, 8th **Siljan's Saga** (FR) 5yo m, 9th **Found** (IRE) 3yo f, 10th **Silverwave** (FR) 3yo c, 11th **Manatee** (GB) 4yo c, 12th **Spiritjim** (FR) 5yo h, 13th **Dolniya** (FR) 4yo f, 14th **Frine** (IRE) 5yo m, 15th **Eagle Top** (GB) 4yo c, 16th **Tapestry** (IRE) 4yo f, 17th **Shahah** (GB) 3yo f.

2016
Found is fantastic
as O'Brien dominates
Ballydoyle trio shine at Chantilly

Background and fancied horses

Chantilly is a fantastic, picturesque course with the Grand Ecurie on the back straight and the château on the home turn. However, the last bend is quite tight, and it pays to be no more than three wide until entering the straight. The start of the 2,400-metre course is a mirror image of Epsom's Derby course, with a left turn to start with on what is a right-handed track.

The favourite for the first of what would be two Arcs at Chantilly, while Longchamp was being upgraded, was Postponed. He'd made his reputation under the tutelage of Luca Cumani, winning the King George VI and Queen Elizabeth Stakes and the Prix Foy in 2015.

This term, now trained by Roger Varian, he'd further enhanced his *palmarès,* scoring twice in Meydan, including the Dubai Sheema Classic, before adding the Coronation Cup and the Juddmonte International Stakes. Ridden by Andrea Atzeni in the yellow with black spots of Mohammed Obaid Al Maktoum, Postponed was 2/1 to win the Arc.

The second favourite on the PMU, Makahiki, had finished runner-up in the Japanese 2000 Guineas before going one place better in the Japanese Derby in May. After settling in France, he reappeared in the Prix Niel, which was also run at Chantilly, coming fast and wide to score by a neck.

The Japanese hope was heavily backed at the course, but in England it was the Aga Khan IV's Harzand who followed Postponed in the betting. Trained by Dermot Weld, the son of Sea The Stars won the Derby and then added the Irish version. He was accompanied to post by Vedevani, who was to act as a pacemaker.

André Fabre had two representatives, last year's third, New Bay, who'd won the Prix Gontaut-Biron, and Godolphin's flashy Talismanic, who was fourth home in the Prix du Jockey Club.

That race had been won by Almanzor, who'd put up one of the performances of the year when taking the Irish Champion Stakes from Found, with New Bay, Highland Reel and Harzand, in third, fourth and fifth.

Found had won the Group 3 Mooresbridge Stakes on her second outing of the year, and since then had been runner-up five times. She was the choice of Ryan Moore, while the globe-trotting Highland Reel, who'd triumphed in the King George VI and Queen Elizabeth Stakes, would be partnered by Seamie Heffernan.

Together with the Ascot Gold Cup-winner Order Of St George, with Frankie Dettori booked, they made up an impressive Ballydoyle trio. They were again left uncoupled by the PMU despite being largely owned by the same people.

Others worthy of note included the Wertheimer's Prix Vermeille-winner Left Hand, and Silverwave, who was back having won the Grand Prix de Saint-Cloud and the Prix Foy.

Les Visiteurs: the Irish quartet of Harzand, Found, Order Of St George, and Highland Reel. England's Postponed, and the returning The Grey Gatsby. And Makahiki for Japan.

Betting
2/1 Postponed, 4/1 Makahiki, 6.5/1 Harzand & Vedevani (coupled), 9/1 Found, 9/1 New Bay, 13/1 Left Hand, 14/1 Order Of St George, 16/1 Silverwave, 24/1 Highland Reel, 41/1 BAR

British Industry Prices
1.875/1 Postponed, 5.5/1 Harzand, 6/1 Found, 6.5/1 Makahiki, 12/1 New Bay, 14/1 Order Of St George, 16/1 Left Hand, 16/1 Silverwave, 20/1 Highland Reel, 40/1 BAR.

Three-year-old form lines
Prix du Jockey Club: 1st Almanzor, 2nd Zarak, 3rd Dicton, 4th **Talismanic**
Grand Prix de Paris: 1st Mont Ormel, 2nd Red Verdon, 3rd Cloth Of Stars, 5th **Talismanic**
Prix Niel: 1st **Makahiki**, 2nd Midterm, 3rd Doha Dream

Fillies only
Prix de Diane: 1st La Cressonniere, 2nd **Left Hand**, 3rd Volta
Prix Vermeille: 1st **Left Hand**, 2nd Endless Time, 3rd The Juliet Rose

Older horses and inter-generational races
Grand Prix de Saint-Cloud: 1st **Silverwave**, 2nd Erupt, 3rd **Siljan's Saga**, 6th **One Foot In Heaven**
Grand Prix de Deauville: 1st **Savoir Vivre**, 2nd **Siljan's Saga**, 3rd Erupt
Prix Foy: 1st **Silverwave**, 2nd Ito, 3rd Elliptique, 4th/last **One Foot In Heaven**

Abroad
In England
Derby Stakes: 1st **Harzand**, 2nd US Army Ranger, 3rd Idaho, 8th Cloth Of Stars, 12th Ulysses
King George VI and Queen Elizabeth Stakes: 1st **Highland Reel**, 2nd Wings of Desire, 3rd Dartmouth

In Ireland
Irish Derby: 1st **Harzand**, 2nd Idaho, 3rd Stellar Mass
Irish Champion Stakes: 1st Almanzor, 2nd **Found**, 3rd Minding, 4th **New Bay**, 7th
Highland Reel, 8th **Harzand**

The race

Postponed was quickly to the fore but after they'd turned left then right, Vedevani emerged as the new leader from Highland Reel and Order Of St George.

The order was maintained passing the Grand Ecurie, and turning out of the back straight Vedevani was still there on her own. Then came the second rank of The Grey Gatsby on the inner of Order Of St George, Highland Reel and Postponed. They in turn were followed by Found, Harzand, Left Hand and Makahiki in the third row.

The Grey Gatsby dropped back entering the *ligne d'arrivée*, and soon afterwards, Found came through between Postponed and Order Of St George to take it up as Vedevani finally capitulated. Meanwhile, Siljan's Saga moved into the front six, who were clear of the remainder.

In the closing stages Found ran on strongly, opening up a clear gap, while stable companions Highland Reel, in the centre, and Order Of St George, on the rail, stayed on to take the other places on the podium. At the line the distances were one and three quarters and one and a half with three parts to Siljan's Saga, then two and a half to the favourite Postponed and One Foot In Heaven.

Team O'Brien had dominated proceedings and the jockeys celebrated in their own ways, with the reserved winning-jockey Ryan Moore not being the most willing recipient of a Dettori kiss.

Post-race

The Michael Tabor silks had been carried to a third Arc victory, adding to Montjeu and Hurricane Run. Derrick Smith's colours were on the second horse, while Order Of St George, was in the very dark blue, white armlets and cap of Lloyd Williams. However, Tabor, Smith, and Sue Magnier – who'd won with Dylan Thomas – had shares in all of the first three.

Coolmore had monopolised the podium and they were all sired by their flagbearer Galileo. Urban Sea's superstar son had first been champion sire in Britain in 2008 and had won each year since 2010. However, he still needs a few more titles to equal his own father, Sadler's Wells, who topped the list on 15 occasions.

Found's time was the fastest in Arc history, but impressive as it was, it took place at Chantilly rather than Longchamp so is somewhat of an anomaly as it doesn't involve comparing like with like.

Aidan O'Brien moved his Arc score on to two, as he had trained Dylan Thomas, and Ryan Moore also doubled his tally having opened his account on Workforce.

Found raced twice more, firstly coming second again to Almanzor in the Champion Stakes two weeks later. She then finished her career with third place behind Highland Reel and Flintshire in the Breeders' Cup Turf.

Result

2016 Qatar Prix de l'Arc de Triomphe

Chantilly. Sunday, 2 October 2016
Weights: 3yo c: 56kg, 3yo f: 54.5kg, 4yo+ c: 59.5kg, 4yo+ f: 58kg

1st Found (IRE)   4yo f   58kg   **9/1**
by Galileo out of Red Evie (Intikhab). Michael Tabor, Derrick Smith & Sue Magnier / Aidan O'Brien / Ryan Moore

2nd Highland Reel (IRE)   4yo c   59.5kg   **24/1**
by Galileo out of Hveger (Danehill). Derrick Smith, Sue Magnier & Michael Tabor / Aidan O'Brien / Seamie Heffernan

3rd Order Of St George (IRE)   4yo c   59.5kg   **14/1**
by Galileo out of Another Storm (Gone West). Lloyd Williams, Sue Magnier, Michael Tabor & Derrick Smith / Aidan O'Brien / Frankie Dettori

Runners: 16 (FR 9, IRE 4, GB 2, JPN 1). Distances: 1¾, 1½. Going: good. Time: 2m 23.61s

Also ran: 4th **Siljan's Saga** (FR) 6yo m, 5th **Postponed** (IRE) 5yo h, 6th **One Foot In Heaven** (IRE) 4yo c, 7th **New Bay** (GB) 4yo c, 8th **Savoir Vivre** (IRE) 3yo c, 9th **Harzand** (IRE) 3yo c, 10th **Vedevani** (FR) 3yo c, 11th **Talismanic** (GB) 3yo c, 12th **Left Hand** (GB) 3yo f, 13th **Silverwave** (FR) 4yo c, 14th **Makahiki** (JPN) 3yo c, 15th **Migwar** (IRE) 4yo c, 16th **The Grey Gatsby** (IRE) 5yo h.

Willing Enable stars in second Chantilly Arc

Dettori becomes winning-most rider

Background and fancied horses

Khalid Abdullah's Enable first came to prominence when winning The Oaks during a torrential thunderstorm at Epsom. Trained by John Gosden and ridden by Frankie Dettori, she'd been sent off joint second favourite after winning the Cheshire Oaks, however it was the way she pulled five lengths clear of the odds-on favourite Rhododendron that marked her out as a filly to watch.

After adding the Irish Oaks in effortless style, she faced her first real test when up against the older horses and colts in the King George VI and Queen Elizabeth Stakes. She came through in style, accounting for the Eclipse Stakes-winner Ulysses by four and a half lengths.

As expected, her next engagement, the Yorkshire Oaks, proved to be a formality and she readily pulled five lengths clear of her stable companion Coronet when sent off at 1/4. Enable was also odds-on for her first outing in France – the Arc – and on the PMU it was 11/1 bar one.

That brought in Aidan O'Brien's own star filly, Winter, who wore Sue Magnier's colours. The grey daughter of Galileo had won the English and Irish 1000 Guineas, before adding the Coronation Stakes at Royal Ascot and the Nassau Stakes at the Qatar Festival at Goodwood. However, in her latest start, the Matron Stakes, she'd lost out by a head to her stablemate Hydrangea.

Winter had plenty of team mates at Chantilly as the O'Brien battalion numbered five, all owned in part by Magnier, Michael Tabor and Derrick Smith. Last year's third, Order Of St George, who was the second favourite in England, had been beaten by Big Orange when trying to defend the Ascot Gold Cup, before winning the Irish St Leger.

He was to be the first Arc ride for Joseph O'Brien's younger brother Donnacha, and back in the Tabor colours this year, he was coupled with Hardwicke Stakes-victor Idaho, who was also in blue and orange. St Leger-winner Capri, and last year's Irish Oaks-heroine, Seventh Heaven, completed the Ballydoyle team, and were coupled separately at 37/1, as they both sported Smith's purple and white silks.

The previously mentioned Ulysses, who in the interim had added the Juddmonte International Stakes, was third favourite, followed by the most fancied of the German pair Dschingis Secret. Markus Klug's charge had beaten Godolphin's Arc hope, Cloth Of Stars, as well as Japan's two entries and Silverwave, in the Prix Foy.

The André Fabre-trained Cloth Of Stars, by Sea The Stars, had won all three of his early-season starts before the Prix Foy, which was his first run since May. Fabre also fielded Grand Prix de Deauville runner-up Doha Dream in the Al Shaqab first colours and the Wertheimer representative Plumatic, who'd been second in the Prix du Prince d'Orange.

The two most supported home runners were the Aga Khan IV's Grand Prix de Saint-Cloud victor, Zarak, who'd finished second in last year's Prix du Jockey Club, and this year's winner of that race, Brametot.

Owned in partnership by Al Shaqab Racing and Gérard Augustin-Normand, Brametot had also won the Poule d'Essai des Poulains and was wearing the gold-capped second colours of Al Shaqab. Last season's Arima Kinen and Japanese St Leger-winner, Satono Diamond, led the Japanese challenge and was accompanied by Satono Noblesse, who'd won two Grade 3s in 2016.

Les Visiteurs: Winter, Order Of St George, Idaho, Capri, and Seventh Heaven representing Ireland. Enable and Ulysses for England. Germany's Dschingis Secret and 2016 Grosser Preis von Baden-winner Iquitos, who'd been second in that race this year. Plus Satono Diamond and Satono Noblesse for Japan.

Betting
0.8/1 Enable, 11/1 Winter, 12/1 Ulysses, 14/1 Dschingis Secret, 14/1 Order Of St George & Idaho (coupled), 15/1 Zarak, 17/1 Brametot & Doha Dream (coupled), 20/1 Cloth Of Stars, 21/1 Satono Diamond & Satono Noblesse (coupled), 35/1 BAR

British Industry Prices
0.91/1 Enable, 8/1 Order Of St George, 9/1 Ulysses, 9/1 Winter, 14/1 Dschingis Secret, 20/1 Brametot, 20/1 Capri, 20/1 Cloth Of Stars, 25/1 BAR.

Three-year-old form lines
Prix du Jockey Club: 1st **Brametot**, 2nd Waldgeist, 3rd Recoletos, 12th/last **Plumatic**
Grand Prix de Paris: 1st Shakeel, 2nd Permian, 3rd Venice Beach
Prix Niel: 1st Cracksman, 2nd Avilius, 3rd Finche

Fillies only
Prix de Diane: 1st Senga, 2nd Sistercharlie, 3rd Terrakova
Prix Vermeille: 1st Bateel, 2nd Journey, 3rd Left Hand

Older horses and inter-generational races

Grand Prix de Saint-Cloud: 1st **Zarak**, 2nd **Silverwave**, 3rd Armande

La Coupe de Maisons-Laffitte: 1st Garlingari, 2nd **One Foot In Heaven**, 3rd Haggle

Grand Prix de Deauville: 1st Tiberian, 2nd **Doha Dream**, 3rd Travelling Man

Prix du Prince d'Orange: 1st Recoletos, 2nd **Plumatic**, 3rd Afandem

Prix Foy: 1st **Dschingis Secret**, 2nd **Cloth Of Stars**, 3rd Talismanic, 4th **Satono Diamond**, 5th **Silverwave**, 6th/last **Satono Noblesse**

Abroad

In England

Derby Stakes: 1st Wings of Eagles, 2nd Cliffs of Moher, 3rd Cracksman, 6th **Capri**, 13th Salouen

Oaks Stakes: 1st **Enable**, 2nd Rhododendron, 3rd Alluringly

King George VI and Queen Elizabeth Stakes: 1st **Enable**, 2nd **Ulysses**, 3rd **Idaho**

St Leger: 1st **Capri**, 2nd Crystal Ocean, 3rd Stradivarius, 10th Defoe

In Ireland

Irish Derby: 1st **Capri**, 2nd Cracksman, 3rd Wings of Eagles

In Germany

Grosser Preis von Baden: 1st Guignol, 2nd **Iquitos**, 3rd Colomano

The race

Idaho and Satono Noblesse were immediately prominent, while Cloth Of Stars, who'd pinged the stalls, was reined back. Iquitos was bumped by Winter at the point where the left turn ends and the right turn begins.

Passing the Grand Ecurie, Idaho still led from Order Of St George, Brametot and Enable and on the turn for home Enable came alongside Brametot to dispute third. With 400 metres to run, Idaho drifted off the rails and Brametot was blocked as he tried to come between him and Order Of St George.

Meanwhile Enable was still cruising on the outside, with Dschingis Secret and Ulysses not far behind.

When Dettori galvanised Enable she quickened in style to take the lead and then rapidly opened up a four-length advantage. Idaho dropped out, while Ulysses challenged Order Of St George for second place. Behind them Cloth Of Stars had racing room and was starting to charge.

Enable, though, was never in danger and won in emphatic style. Behind her, Cloth Of Stars moved into second and had reduced the margin to two and a half lengths on the line, albeit the winner was already being eased down. Ulysses was just over a length behind Cloth Of Stars, then came Order Of St George, Brametot and Dschingis Secret.

Post-race

After the recent placings of Flintshire and New Bay, Khalid Abdullah had found another winner, taking his score to five after Rainbow Quest, Dancing Brave, Rail Link, and Workforce.

John Gosden doubled his tally, adding to Golden Horn two years ago, while Frankie Dettori, left the seven-strong four-winner club to take the record outright, and with the hope of more to come as Enable was kept in training.

Result

2017 Qatar Prix de l'Arc de Triomphe
Chantilly. Sunday, 1 October 2017
Weights: 3yo c: 56.5kg, 3yo f: 55kg, 4yo+ c: 59.5kg, 4yo+ f: 58kg

1st Enable (GB)   3yo f   55kg   **0.8/1 fav**
by Nathaniel out of Concentric (Sadler's Wells). Khalid Abdullah / John Gosden / Frankie Dettori

2nd Cloth Of Stars (IRE)   4yo c   59.5kg   **20/1**
by Sea The Stars out of Strawberry Fledge (Kingmambo). Godolphin SNC / André Fabre / Mickael Barzalona

3rd Ulysses (IRE)   4yo c   59.5kg   **12/1**
by Galileo out of Light Shift (Kingmambo). Flaxman Stables Ireland Ltd / Sir Michael Stoute / Jim Crowley

Runners: 18 (FR 7, IRE 5, GB 2, GER 2, JPN 2). Distances: 2½, 1¼. Going: soft. Time: 2m 28.69s

Also ran: 4th **Order Of St George** (IRE) 5yo h, 5th **Brametot** (IRE) 3yo c, 6th **Dschingis Secret** (GER) 4yo c, 7th **Iquitos** (GER) 5yo h, 8th **Idaho** (IRE) 4yo c, 9th **Winter** (IRE) 3yo f, 10th **Zarak** (FR) 4yo c, 11th **One Foot In Heaven** (IRE) 5yo h, 12th **Doha Dream** (FR) 4yo c, 13th **Plumatic** (GB) 3yo c, 14th **Seventh Heaven** (IRE) 4yo f, 15th **Satono Diamond** (JPN) 4yo c, 16th **Satono Noblesse** (JPN) 7yo h, 17th **Capri** (IRE) 3yo c, 18th **Silverwave** (FR) 5yo c.

Enable doubles up as Arc returns to Longchamp

Khalid Abdullah equals Boussac haul

Background and fancied horses

The reappearance of Enable was gradually put further and further back as the season progressed. There was talk of her running in the Prix Ganay, for which the prize money had been doubled to celebrate the official reopening of the renovated and rebranded ParisLongchamp, featuring the new autumn-coloured grandstand.

In the end, John Gosden ran Anthony Oppenheimer's Cracksman instead, who proved to be an able deputy. Eventually, the news came through that Enable had picked up an injury and wouldn't be seen until at least August. It turned out to be the first week of the following month when she lined up for what was effectively a match in the September Stakes on the all-weather at Kempton Park.

She came through in good style, beating the King George VI and Queen Elizabeth Stakes-second Crystal Ocean by three and a half lengths, with a further 17 lengths to the two outsiders who'd lined up. Deemed to be 80 per cent fit, and therefore open to improvement, Enable was even money to pull off the Arc double.

The main French hope was Waldgeist running in the red with green accoutrements of Gestüt Ammerland and Newsells Park. One of three trained by André Fabre, he'd been second to Brametot in last year's Prix du Jockey Club. This season he'd won the Grand Prix de Saint-Cloud and Prix Foy, in the latter beating his stable companions – the 2017 Breeders' Cup Turf-winner Talismanic and last year's Arc runner-up Cloth Of Stars, who were both owned by Godolphin.

Waldgeist shared second favouritism with another English raider Sea Of Class, who, like Cloth Of Stars, was sired by Sea Of Stars. A late developing sort, she debuted in mid-April and had won four of her five races, including the Irish and Lancashire Oaks, each time finding good late speed.

Aidan O'Brien had his usual quiver of high-class ammunition, with Grand Prix de Paris and St Leger-winner Kew Gardens the choice of Ryan Moore. Capri, who'd been fifth in the Prix Foy on his first run since April, was back, while Magical had also been rested for an autumn campaign after winning a Group 2 at the Curragh in July. These three wore Derrick Smith's colours and were grouped together in one coupling by the PMU on 11/1.

Prix Niel-second Hunting Horn and pacemaker Nelson were in the Sue Magnier colours – the former in dark blue, the latter in pink – and were coupled separately at 70/1. Needless to say, Michael Tabor, along with Smith and Magnier, owned bits of all five.

The Prix du Jockey Club first and second, Study Of Man and Patascoy, were among the longer shots, with the latter at a shorter price after the former had disappointed in the Irish Champion Stakes. Neufbosc, who'd been placed in the Grand Prix de Paris and Prix Niel, was the only other horse under 40/1.

Les Visiteurs: Kew Gardens, Capri, Magical, Hunting Horn, and Nelson for Ireland. Enable, Sea Of Class, Grosser Preis von Baden-second Defoe, and Salouen – who'd been third in the Grand Prix de Saint-Cloud and Grand Prix de Deauville – for England. Italy had Prix Foy-fourth Way to Paris. And Clincher, the runner-up in the 2017 Kikuka Sho (Japanese St Leger) represented Japan.

Betting

1/1 Enable, 5.5/1 Sea Of Class, 5.5/1 Waldgeist, 11/1 Kew Gardens & Capri & Magical (all coupled), 24/1 Talismanic & Cloth Of Stars (coupled), 29/1 Patascoy, 32/1 Neufbosc, 32/1 Study Of Man, 41/1 BAR

British Industry Prices

1/1 Enable, 6/1 Sea Of Class, 6/1 Waldgeist, 8/1 Kew Gardens, 25/1 Capri, 25/1 Talismanic, 28/1 Cloth Of Stars, 40/1 BAR.

Three-year-old form lines
Prix du Jockey Club: 1st **Study Of Man**, 2nd **Patascoy**, 3rd **Louis D'Or**, 6th **Hunting Horn**
Grand Prix de Paris: 1st **Kew Gardens**, 2nd **Neufbosc**, 3rd Dee Ex Bee, 5th **Nelson**
Prix Niel: 1st Brundtland, 2nd **Hunting Horn**, 3rd **Neufbosc**, 6th/last **Louis D'Or**

Fillies only
Prix de Diane: 1st Laurens, 2nd Musis Amica, 3rd Homerique
Prix Vermeille: 1st Kitesurf, 2nd Magic Wand, 3rd Zarkamiya

Older horses and inter-generational races
Grand Prix de Saint-Cloud: 1st **Waldgeist**, 2nd Coronet, 3rd **Salouen**, 4th **Cloth Of Stars**
Grand Prix de Deauville: 1st Loxley, 2nd Master's Spirit, 3rd **Salouen**, 5th **Tiberian**, 6th **Way To Paris**
Prix Foy: 1st **Waldgeist**, 2nd **Talismanic**, 3rd **Cloth Of Stars**, 4th **Way To Paris**, 5th **Capri**, 6th/last **Clincher**

Abroad

In England

Derby Stakes: 1st Masar, 2nd Dee Ex Bee, 3rd Roaring Lion, 9th **Kew Gardens**

King George VI and Queen Elizabeth Stakes: 1st Poet's Word, 2nd Crystal Ocean, 3rd Coronet, 4th **Salouen**

St Leger: 1st **Kew Gardens**, 2nd Lah Ti Dar, 3rd Southern France, 7th **Nelson**

In Ireland

Irish Champion Stakes: 1st Roaring Lion, 2nd Saxon Warrior, 3rd Deauville, 5th **Study Of Man**

In Germany

Grosser Preis von Baden: 1st Best Solution, 2nd **Defoe**, 3rd Iquitos

The race

Nelson took it up straight away from the grey Capri and Clincher, followed by Enable and Patascoy. On the descent, Defoe slotted into third, but he tired on the false straight and as they entered the home run Capri collared Nelson. Cloth Of Stars had made progress into a share of fifth with Salouen, while Sea Of Class, who'd been last, had been switched wide and was two lengths further back.

And then Dettori, who'd been sitting motionless just behind the leaders, asked Enable to quicken. She found plenty and moved to the front just after the 300-metre pole. Last year's winner was clear entering the final 200 metres, however the children of Sea The Stars were both finishing to good effect. Cloth Of Stars nosed into second for a moment before being engulfed by Sea Of Class, who was flying home.

It had looked as though it was going to be easy for Enable, but now her advantage was being eaten into by Sea Of Class. What was two lengths with 100 metres to run became half that in the final 50 metres, and Sea Of Class was still coming. In the last few strides she lunged at the line forcing a photo.

But Enable had just done enough, holding on by a short neck, with three parts further back to Cloth Of Stars – in the frame for the second year – followed by Waldgeist, and then a length and a half to the staying-on Capri and Salouen.

Post-race

It was later revealed that Enable had suffered a further setback between Kempton and Longchamp, that even Dettori was unaware of. Thus a fabulous performance was made even more remarkable.

La reine de Chantilly was now also *la reine de Longchamp* and received the plaudits of the crowd. James Doyle, though, received some criticism for coming so late on Sea Of Class – others countered that she had to be ridden that way – and although the mare had to take one side-step she was granted a fairly clear run by Longchamp standards.

Khalid Abdullah equalled Marcel Boussac's achievement of owning six Arc winners, a record set in 1949.

Le recordman Frankie Dettori also took his score to six, celebrating with his trademark flying dismount or *fameux saut de l'ange* (famous angel jump) as it's known in France. And it was a third Arc in four years for John Gosden, bettering Charles Semblat's achievement in winning three in five years between 1942 and 1946.

As Enable's season had started late, she was sent to Churchill Downs for the Breeders' Cup Turf. Running wide on the tight circuit, she held Magical by three parts of a length with the pair drawing nine lengths clear of the third.

The queen of the world was then put away for the winter, with the aim being to go three places better than Trêve did in 2016 and land the elusive Arc hat-trick.

Result
2018 Qatar Prix de l'Arc de Triomphe
ParisLongchamp. Sunday, 7 October 2018
Weights: 3yo c: 56.5kg, 3yo f: 55kg, 4yo+ c: 59.5kg, 4yo+ f: 58kg

1st Enable (GB) 4yo f 58kg **1/1 fav**
by Nathaniel out of Concentric (Sadler's Wells). Khalid Abdullah / John Gosden / Frankie Dettori

2nd Sea Of Class (IRE) 3yo f 55kg **5.5/1**
by Sea the Stars out of Holy Moon (Hernando). Sunderland Holding Inc / William Haggas / James Doyle

3rd Cloth Of Stars (IRE) 5yo c 59.5kg **41/1**
by Sea The Stars out of Strawberry Fledge (Kingmambo). Godolphin SNC / André Fabre / Vincent Cheminaud

Runners: 19 (FR 8, IRE 5, GB 4, ITY 1, JPN 1). Distances: sh nk, ¾. Going: good. Time: 2m 29.24s

Also ran: 4th **Waldgeist** (GB) 4yo c, 5th **Capri** (IRE) 4yo c, 6th **Salouen** (IRE) 4yo c, 7th **Kew Gardens** (IRE) 3yo c, 8th **Nelson** (IRE) 3yo c, 9th **Study Of Man** (IRE) 3yo c, 10th **Magical** (IRE) 3yo f, 11th **Way To Paris** (GB) 5yo h, 12th **Tiberian** (FR) 6yo h, 13th **Talismanic** (GB) 5yo h, 14th **Patascoy** (FR) 3yo c, 15th **Defoe** (IRE) 4yo c, 16th **Hunting Horn** (IRE) 3yo c, 17th **Clincher** (JPN) 4yo c, 18th **Neufbosc** (FR) 3yo c, 19th **Louis D'Or** (IRE) 3yo c.

Waldgeist is wunderbar

Monsieur Arc's record-breaking eighth winner

Background and fancied horses

When ParisLongchamp reopened in 2018 there were several successful experiments using *l'open stretch*, a false rail and cutaway which had already been used at several racecourses, notably Chester in England. This directs horses into the home straight several lanes off the main rail, enabling challengers to come on both sides of the leaders and reduce the number of horses who don't get a clear run. This year *l'open stretch* was to be used in the Arc for the first time.

On the betting front, the coupling system had finally been terminated, so horses in the same ownership would now be individually priced. In England the industry prices had also come to an end, with each bookmaker offering their own prices or taking the PMU dividends. Not surprisingly the horse topping all the markets was last year's winner Enable, who'd enjoyed a great season.

After her trip to America she'd been given plenty of time before making her seasonal reappearance in the Eclipse Stakes at the start of July. Enable confirmed the Breeders' Cup Turf form with Magical at Sandown, winning comfortably, again by three quarters of a length.

Later in the month, in the King George VI and Queen Elizabeth Stakes, she met Crystal Ocean again, along with the Derby-winner, Anthony Van Dyck, and last year's Arc-fourth, Waldgeist, who'd won the Prix Ganay.

It turned into an epic duel, with Enable, having been forced to race wide, eventually taking the measure of Crystal Ocean after a great battle. Waldgeist finished third but Anthony Van Dyck ran no sort of race and was tailed off in 10th place.

Enable's only other run was effectively a lap of honour in the Yorkshire Oaks, where she beat Magical again, this time by two and a quarter lengths. With an uninterrupted preparation under her belt, Khalid Abdullah's fabulous filly was odds-on to win the Arc for the third time.

Magical subsequently won the Irish Champion Stakes with Anthony Van Dyck in third. The latter was entered in the Arc but was taken out four days before the race. Magical, though, did line up, and was accompanied by Japan, who was seen as Aidan O'Brien's first string with Ryan Moore taking the mount.

After finishing third in the Derby to his stable companion, Japan had won the King Edward VII Stakes at Royal Ascot, the Grand Prix de Paris, and the Juddmonte International Stakes, in which he beat Crystal Ocean by a head. It proved to be the last race for Crystal Ocean, who injured a leg on the gallops in mid-September.

Waldgeist had a mid-season break, after his third in the King George VI and Queen Elizabeth Stakes, returning to action in the Prix Foy. He won comfortably by two lengths and took his place as André Fabre's sole representative in the Arc.

The best three-year-old colt in France had been the Jean-Claude Rouget-trained Sottsass, named after the Italian architect Ettore Sottsass. He was owned by the American polo-player Peter Brant, who had recently returned to racing after a 30-year hiatus. Running in the colours of his White Birch Farm outfit, Sottsass had hosed up in the Prix de Suresnes at Chantilly, before coming from off the pace to land the Prix du Jockey Club in great style.

Returning after 70 days off, Sottsass had shown plenty of speed to extricate himself from a less than ideal position in the Prix Niel and win going away, and was sent off second favourite for the Arc.

Godolphin's Ghaiyyath had been a promising two-year-old, but had only been seen once at three when taking the Prix du Prince d'Orange in September 2018. This April he'd won the Prix d'Harcourt, and finished third to Waldgeist in the Prix Ganay, before being put away again. Resuming in September he'd run away with the Grosser Preis von Baden, turning the race into a procession, coming home 14 lengths to the good.

The Japanese challenge was three-strong, with Fierement representing the owners of Orfevre the most fancied at 36/1. He'd won the Grade 1 Kikuka Sho last October with Blast Onepiece in fourth, but had been beaten by the latter in this year's Grade 2 Sapporo Kinen in mid-August when sent off favourite.

Both horses had subsequently made the journey to Europe to join the 2017 Japanese St Leger-winner Kiseki, who'd had to make his own running in the Prix Foy when eventually finishing third of four to Waldgeist.

Japanese-bred but Czech-owned Nagano Gold had won the Prix Lord Seymour at Longchamp in mid-April. He'd then made a daring raid on Royal Ascot, only going down by half a length to Defoe in the Hardwicke Stakes when a 25/1-shot with Christophe Soumillon in the plate. Next time, though, he didn't find so much off the bridle, and had to be content with third when favourite for the Grand Prix de Deauville.

The runner-up that day was Soft Light, who'd previously been fifth in the Grand Prix de Paris. Like Sottsass, he was trained by Jean-Claude Rouget and had been supplemented for the Arc, but was among the longshots.

Completing the round dozen who went to post was French King, owned by Sheikh Fahad's father, Sheikh Abdulla bin Khalifa Al Thani. He'd won the Amir Trophy in Doha in February and since then had added three Group races in Germany, most recently the Group 1 Grosser Preis von Berlin at Hoppegarten in August.

Betting
0.5/1 Enable, 6.5/1 Sottsass, 9/1 Japan, 13/1 Ghaiyyath, 13/1 Waldgeist, 19/1 Magical, 36/1 Fierement, 41/1 French King, 44/1 Kiseki, 58/1 BAR.

Three-year-old form lines
Prix du Jockey Club: 1st **Sottsass**, 2nd Persian King, 3rd Motamarris
Grand Prix de Paris: 1st **Japan**, 2nd Slalom, 3rd Jalmoud, 5th **Soft Light**
Prix Niel: 1st **Sottsass**, 2nd Mutamakina, 3rd Mohawk

Fillies only
Prix de Diane: 1st Channel, 2nd Comme, 3rd Grand Glory
Prix Vermeille: 1st Star Catcher, 2nd Musis Amica, 3rd Ligne d'Or

Older horses and inter-generational races
Grand Prix de Saint-Cloud: 1st Coronet, 2nd Ziyad, 3rd Lah Ti Dar
Grand Prix de Deauville: 1st Ziyad, 2nd **Soft Light**, 3rd **Nagano Gold**
Prix Foy: 1st **Waldgeist**, 2nd Way To Paris, 3rd **Kiseki**

Abroad
In England
Derby Stakes: 1st Anthony van Dyck, 2nd Madhmoon, 3rd **Japan**
King George VI and Queen Elizabeth Stakes: 1st **Enable**, 2nd Crystal Ocean, 3rd **Waldgeist**

In Ireland
Irish Champion Stakes: 1st **Magical**, 2nd Magic Wand, 3rd Anthony Van Dyck

In Germany
Grosser Preis von Baden: 1st **Ghaiyyath**, 2nd Donjah, 3rd Laccario

The race

With plenty of rain in the days leading up to the race, the ground was soft and cloying. The weather, though, was bright and sunny as they careered away from the stalls. Fierement was immediately in the vanguard against the rail, with Blast Onepiece and Sottsass close behind. Out wide Magical was also prominent followed by Enable, with Ghaiyyath widest of all.

Ghaiyyath gradually angled across to lead at the Petit Bois, while Enable had to be rousted for a few strides in order to take up a share of fourth position, racing three wide.

At the top of the hill, Ghaiyyath, tongue lolling, led by two to Magical and Fierement, with a gap to Enable now in a clear fourth just ahead of Sottsass. Meanwhile, at the back, Soft Light was struggling and Nagano Gold was in danger of being tailed-off.

On the false straight Enable closed in and was going well, while Waldgeist moved into sixth. Turning in, Ghaiyyath ran out of petrol, handing the lead to Magical by *l'open stretch* as her stable companion, Japan, made headway round the outside.

Enable ranged alongside Magical and took it up with 350 metres to go, Sottsass and Japan were looking menacing just behind, followed by Waldgeist. The winner for the previous two years gamely fought off Sottsass and Japan, and extended her advantage to two lengths at the 200-metre pole. But behind them, and switched to the outside, Waldgeist was still coming, albeit with four lengths to make up.

Enable, though, was tiring, and in the last 100 metres she started to slow. Waldgeist cut the deficit in leaps and bounds to draw level in the last 50 metres, and then opened up a margin of nearly two lengths at the line to become the first French-trained winner since Trêve.

Sottsass was the same distance back in third with half a length to Japan, then six more to the remainder, headed by Magical and Soft Light.

After the post, Pierre-Charles Boudot, aka PCB, stood bolt upright in the stirrups and celebrated the triumph by blowing kisses to his late father Marc.

Post-race

Enable – who has been kept in training with the aim of lining up for the 2020 Arc – lost nothing in defeat, as she was clearly unsuited by the ground which blunted her finishing effort. But that was to take nothing away from Waldgeist, who had outstayed the dual winner on the holding ground, to win handsomely in the red, green chevron, red cap with a green star silks of co-owners Gestüt Ammerland and Newsells Park.

Both institutions have a rich history in racing with the Ammerland stud in Germany having produced high-calibre horses like Borgia and Lope de Vega as well as previous Arc-winner Hurricane Run. Going further back, Newsells Park in England was once owned by Sir Humphrey de Trafford, who bred the 1958 St Leger-winner Alcide, and the 1959 Derby-winner Parthia. Their current roster of stallions includes Enable's sire Nathaniel.

PCB, who'd been in the top three in the *cravache d'or* every year since 2013 – including being joint-champion with Christophe Soumillon in 2015 and outright champion in 2016 – had delivered Waldgeist at the telling moment to open his Arc account.

Waldgeist became the seventh five-year-old colt to win the great race, and in doing so doubled Galileo's Arc score as a sire, adding to Found who won in 2016. Having reached the summit, Waldgeist was retired to Ballylinch Stud in Ireland to stand alongside Lope de Vega. He now lives in the stall formerly occupied by The Tetrarch.

In winning the 2019 Prix de l'Arc de Triomphe, André Fabre not only extended his own Arc training record to eight wins, but became the winning-most person in Arc history – a record he had previously shared with Charles Semblat. Fabre's successes have all come in his role as trainer, while Semblat won three times as a jockey before training four winners for Marcel Boussac.

All hail Monsieur Arc, we salute you.

Galileo 1998

Nathaniel 2008   *Found* 2012   **Waldgeist** 2014

Enable 2014

Result

2019 Qatar Prix de l'Arc de Triomphe

ParisLongchamp. Sunday, 6 October 2019
Weights: 3yo c: 56.5kg, 3yo f: 55kg, 4yo+ c: 59.5kg, 4yo+ f: 58kg

1st Waldgeist (GB)   5yo h   59.5kg **13/1**
by Galileo out of Waldlerche (Monsun). Gestüt Ammerland & Newsells Park / André Fabre / Pierre-Charles Boudot

2nd Enable (GB)   5yo m   58kg   **0.5/1 fav**
by Nathaniel out of Concentric (Sadler's Wells). Khalid Abdullah / John Gosden / Frankie Dettori

3rd Sottsass (FR)   3yo c   56.5kg **6.5/1**
by Siyouni out of Starlet's Sister (Galileo). White Birch Farm / Jean-Claude Rouget / Vincent Cheminaud

Runners: 12 (FR 4, JPN 3, GB 2, IRE 2, CZE 1). Distances: 1¾, 1¾. Going: very soft. Time: 2m 31.97s

Also ran: 4th **Japan** (GB) 3yo c, 5th **Magical** (IRE) 4yo f, 6th **Soft Light** (FR) 3yo c, 7th **Kiseki** (JPN) 5yo h, 8th **Nagano Gold** (GB) 5yo h, 9th **French King** (GB) 4yo c, 10th **Ghaiyyath** (IRE) 4yo c, 11th **Blast Onepiece** (JPN) 4yo c, 12th **Fierement** (JPN) 4yo c.

Prix de l'Arc de Triomphe
Race Records

Most winners: Overall
Eight wins
André Fabre, trainer
Trempolino 1987, Subotica 1992, Carnégie 1994, Peintre Célèbre 1997, Sagamix 1998, Hurricane Run 2005, Rail Link 2006, Waldgeist 2019

Seven wins
Charles Semblat, jockey/trainer
As a jockey: Mon Talisman 1927, Pearl Cap 1931, Motrico 1932
As a trainer: Djébel 1942, Ardan 1943, Caracalla 1946, Coronation 1949

Six wins
Marcel Boussac, owner
Corrida 1936 & 1937, Djébel 1942, Ardan 1944, Caracalla 1946, Coronation 1949

Khalid Abdullah, owner
Rainbow Quest 1985, Dancing Brave 1986, Rail Link 2006, Workforce 2010, Enable 2017 & 2018

Frankie Dettori, jockey
Lammtarra 1995, Sakhee 2001, Marienbard 2002, Golden Horn 2015, Enable 2017 & 2018

Most winners: Owners
Six wins
Marcel Boussac
Corrida 1936 & 1937, Djébel 1942, Ardan 1944, Caracalla 1946, Coronation 1949

Khalid Abdullah
Rainbow Quest 1985, Dancing Brave 1986, Rail Link 2006, Workforce 2010, Enable 2017 & 2018

Four wins
Daniel Wildenstein
Allez France 1974, All Along 1983, Sagace 1984, Peintre Célèbre 1997

Aga Khan IV
Akiyda 1982, Sinndar 2001, Dalakhani 2003, Zarkava 2008

Three wins
Robert Sangster
Alleged 1977 & 1978, Detroit 1980

Michael Tabor
Montjeu 1999, Hurricane Run 2005,
Found (with Derrick Smith & Sue Magnier) 2016

Two wins
Marthe Blanc
Ksar 1921 & 1922

Max de Rivaud
Motrico 1930 & 1932

Evremond de Saint-Alary
Comrade 1920, Samos 1935

Édouard de Rothschild
Brantôme 1934, Éclair au Chocolat 1938

François Dupré
Tantième 1950 & 1951

Aga Khan III
Migoli 1948, Nuccio 1952

Marchese Mario Incisa della Rocchetta
Ribot 1955 & 1956

Jacques Wertheimer
Ivanjica 1976, Gold River 1981

Bruce McNall
Trempolino 1987, Saumarez 1990

Godolphin
Sakhee 2001, Marienbard 2002

Sue Magnier
Dylan Thomas 2007, Found (with Michael Tabor & Derrick Smith) 2016

Most winners: Trainers

Eight wins
André Fabre
Trempolino 1987, Subotica 1992, Carnégie 1994, Peintre Célèbre 1997, Sagamix 1998, Hurricane Run 2005, Rail Link 2006, Waldgeist 2019

Four wins
Charles Semblat
Djébel 1942, Ardan 1944, Caracalla 1946, Coronation 1949

Alec Head
Nuccio 1952, Saint Crespin 1959, Ivanjica 1976, Gold River 1981

François Mathet
Tantième 1950, 1951, Sassafras 1970, Akiyda 1982

Three wins
Frank Carter
Mon Talisman 1927, Pearl Cap 1931, Samos 1935

Étienne Pollet
La Sorellina 1953, Sea Bird 1965, Vaguely Noble 1968

Vincent O'Brien
Ballymoss 1958, Alleged 1977 & 1978

Saeed Bin Suroor
Lammtarra 1995, Sakhee 2001, Marienbard 2002

Christiane Head-Maarek
Three Troikas 1979, Trêve 2013 & 2014

John Gosden
Golden Horn 2015, Enable 2017 & 2018

Two wins
Walter Walton
Ksar 1921 & 1922

Maurice d'Okhuysen
Motrico 1930 & 1932

Jack Watts
Corrida 1936 & 1937

Lucien Robert
Brantôme 1934, Éclair au Chocolat 1938

Ugo Penco
Ribot 1955 & 1956

René Pelat
Nikellora 1945, Soltikoff 1962

Willie Head
Le Paillon 1947, Bon Mot 1966

Mick Bartholomew
Puissant Chef 1960, Topyo 1967

Angel Penna
San San 1972, Allez France 1974

Patrick Biancone
All Along 1983, Sagace 1984

John Hammond
Suave Dancer 1991, Montjeu 1999

Alain de Royer-Dupré
Dalakhani 2003, Zarkava 2008

John Oxx
Sinndar 2000, Sea the Stars 2009

Aidan O'Brien
Dylan Thomas 2007, Found 2016

Most winners: Jockeys

Six wins
Frankie Dettori
Lammtarra 1995, Sakhee 2001, Marienbard 2002,
Golden Horn 2015, Enable 2017 & 2018

Four wins
Jacques Doyasbère
Djébel 1942, Ardan 1944, Tantième 1950 & 1951

Freddy Head
Bon Mot 1966, San San 1972, Ivanjica 1976, Three Troikas 1979

Yves Saint-Martin
Sassafras 1970, Allez France 1974, Akiyda 1982, Sagace 1984

Pat Eddery
Detroit 1980, Rainbow Quest 1985, Dancing Brave 1986, Trempolino 1987

Olivier Peslier
Hélissio 1996, Peintre Célèbre 1997, Sagamix 1998, Solemia 2012

Thierry Jarnet
Subotica 1992, Carnégie 1994, Trêve 2013 & 2014

Three wins
Charles Semblat
Mon Talisman 1927, Pearl Cap 1931, Motrico 1932

Charlie Elliott
Corrida 1936 & 1937, Caracalla 1946

Roger Poincelet
Coronation 1949, Nuccio 1952, Prince Royal 1964

Enrico Camici
Ribot 1955 & 1956, Molvedo 1961

Lester Piggott
Rheingold 1973, Alleged 1977 & 1978

Mick Kinane
Carroll House 1989, Montjeu 1999, Sea the Stars 2009

Two wins
Frank Bullock
Comrade 1920, Ksar 1922

Charles Bouillon
Brantôme 1934, Éclair au Chocolat 1938

Rae Johnstone
Nikellora 1945, Sica Boy 1954

Bill Williamson
Vaguely Noble 1968, Levmoss 1969

Kieren Fallon
Hurricane Run 2005, Dylan Thomas 2007

Christophe Soumillon
Dalakhani 2003, Zarkava 2008

Ryan Moore
Workforce 2010, Found 2016

Prix de l'Arc de Triomphe
Horse Statistics

Winners by country trained
France 67
Great Britain 15
Ireland 8
Italy 6
Germany 2

Winners by country born
France 46
Ireland 19
Great Britain14
USA 14
Italy 4
Germany 1

Winners by age/sex
3yo colts: 47
3yo fillies: 13
4yo colts: 19
4yo fillies: 10
5yo horses: 7
5yo mares: 1
7yo horses: 1

Dual Arc winners
Ksar 1921, 1922
Motrico 1930, 1932
Corrida 1936, 1937
Tantième 1950, 1951
Ribot 1955, 1956
Alleged 1977, 1978
Trêve 2013, 2014
Enable 2017, 2018

Arc winners who produced further Arc winners

Biribi (Le Pacha 1941)
Djébel (Coronation 1949)
Ribot (Prince Royal 1964, Molvedo 1961)
Sea Bird (Allez France 1974)
Rainbow Quest (Saumarez 1990)
Detroit (Carnégie 1994)
Montjeu (Hurricane Run 2005)
Urban Sea (Sea The Stars 2009)

Disqualifications

Cadum 1925, in favour of Priori
Midnight Sun 1959, in favour of fellow dead-heater Saint Crespin
Sagace 1985, in favour of Rainbow Quest

Fastest times

2min 23.61s   Found at Chantilly in 2016
2min 24.49s   Danedream at Longchamp in 2011

Prix du Jockey Club winners who added the Arc

Ksar 1921
Mon Talsiman 1927
Le Pacha 1941
Verso II 1943
Ardan 1944
Sassafras 1970
Suave Dancer 1991
Peintre Célèbre 1997
Montjeu 1999
Dalakhani 2003

Derby winners who added the Arc

Sea Bird 1965
Mill Reef 1971
Lammtarra 1995
Sinndar 2000
Sea The Stars 2009
Workforce 2010
Golden Horn 2015

Breeding diagrams

Simplified breeding charts showing some of the connections between the winners of the Prix de l'Arc de Triomphe, and their heritage dating back to the Darley Arabian. There are other more complex but equally valid relationships between some of the horses. Those illustrated are the most straightforward using both the sire and dam lines. KEY: The year that follows the horse's name is its year of birth. Names in brackets link back to previously mentioned horses

Darley Arabian 1700
Bartlett's Childers 1716
Squirt 1732
Marske 1750
Eclipse 1764
Pot8os 1773
Waxy 1790
Whalebone 1807
Sir Hercules 1826
Birdcatcher 1833
The Baron 1842
Stockwell 1849

Uncas 1865 — *Celerrima* 1862 — Doncaster 1870
War Paint 1878 — *Chaff* 1880 — Bend Or 1877 *see below* — *Thora* 1878
War Dance 1887 — *Satirical* 1891 — *Bijou* 1890
Perth 1896 — *Rabelais* 1900 *see below* — *Basse Terre* 1899
Alcantara 1908 — Brûleur 1910 *see below*
Kantar 1925 — Pinceau 1925
Verso II 1940

390

Bend Or 1877 (by Doncaster)

- Kendal 1883
- Tredennis 1898
  - Bachelor's Double 1906
    - Wet Kiss 1913
    - Coronach 1923
    - **Comrade** 1917
    - **Corrida** 1932
- Ormonde 1883
  - Orme 1889
    - Flying Fox 1896
      - Ajax 1901
      - Teddy 1913 *see below*
- Bona Vista 1889 *see below*
  - Sea Shell 1908
    - Pearl Maiden 1918
    - **Pearl Cap** 1928
  - Radium 1903
    - Clarissimus 1913
    - Vitamine 1924
    - **Brantôme** 1931
  - Console 1895
    - Consols 1908
    - **Massine** 1920

Bona Vista 1889 (by Bend Or)

- Cyllene 1895
  - Polymelus 1902 *see below*
    - Captivation 1902
    - Kircubben 1918
    - Honey Sweet 1927
    - **Eclair au Chocolat** 1935
  - Maid of the Mist 1906
    - Craig An Eran 1918
    - **Mon Talisman** 1924
  - Vahren 1897
    - The Tetrach 1911
    - Mumtaz Mahal 1921
    - Mah Mahal 1928
    - Mah Iran 1939
    - **Migoli** 1944

Rabelais 1900 (out of *Satirical*)

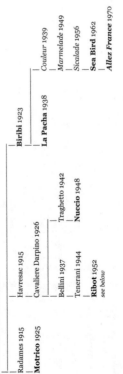

- Radames 1915
- **Motrico** 1925
- Havresac 1915
- Cavaliere Darpino 1926
  - Bellini 1937
  - Tenerani 1944
  - **Ribot** 1952 *see below*
  - Traghetto 1942
  - **Nuccio** 1948
- **Biribi** 1923
- **La Pacha** 1938
  - *Couleur* 1939
  - *Marmelade* 1949
  - *Sicalade* 1956
  - **Sea Bird** 1962
  - ***Allez France*** 1970

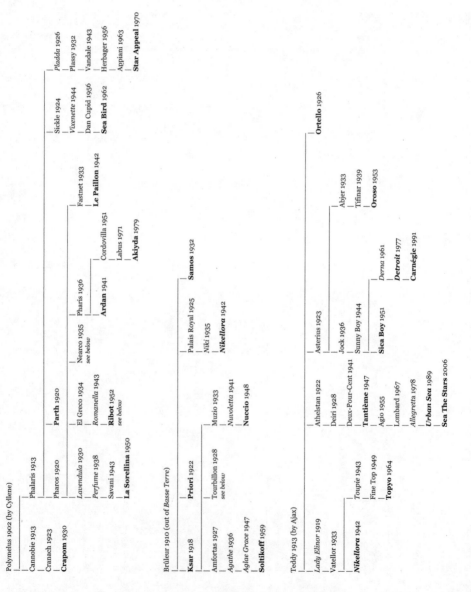

Tourbillon 1928 (by Ksar)

Djébel 1937   **Caracalla** 1942

Le Lavandou 1944
  Le Lavanstell 1957
    Levmoss 1965
Clarion 1944
  Klairon 1952
    Luthier 1965
      Sagace 1980
      Saganeca 1988
      Sagamix 1995
Djefou 1945
  Puissant Chef 1957
Djebe 1945
  Glamour 1960
    Glaneuse 1966
      Gold River 1977
Coronation 1946
Djebellica 1948
Djebel Idra 1957
Bon Mot 1963

Brantôme 1931 (out of *Vitamine*)

Vieux Manoir 1947

Le Haar 1954
  Mourne 1954
  Snob 1959
    Glaneuse 1966
      Gold River 1977
  Astuce 1964
    Ivanjica 1972
  Val de Loir 1959
    see below
  Aguita 1966
    All Along 1979
Exbury 1959
  Plencia 1968
  Petroleuse 1978
  Peinture Bleue 1987
    Peinture Célèbre 1994

Nearco 1935 (by Pharos)

Nasrullah 1940
  see below
Royal Charger 1942
  Turn-To 1951
  Sir Gaylord 1959
    Sir Ivor 1965
      Lord Gayle 1965
    Ivanjica 1972
      Carroll House 1985
Neocracy 1944
  Saint Crespin 1956
Mossborough 1947
  Ballymoss 1947
    Greensward 1953
      Exbury 1959
    Feemoss 1960
      Levmoss 1965
Noorani 1950
  Sheshoon 1956
    Sassafras 1967
Nearctic 1954
  Northern Dancer 1961
    see below
Noble Lassie 1956
  Vaguely Noble 1965
    Empery 1965
    Golden Alibi 1978
    Dockage 1984
    Docklands 1989
      Rail Link 2003

Nasrullah 1940 (by Nearco)

- _Thicket_ 1947
  - _Princely Gift_ 1951
    - Hornbeam 1953
      - _Nashua_ 1952
        - _Severn Bridge_ 1965
          - _Bold Ruler_ 1954
            - _Faberge_ 1961
              - **Rheingold** 1969
            - _Gold Digger_ 1962
              - _Mr Prospector_ 1970 _see below_
            - _Matriarch_ 1964
              - Targowice 1970
                - **Tony Bin** 1983
                - **All Along** 1979
- _Red God_ 1954
  - Yellow God 1967
    - Pampapaul 1974
      - Pampabird 1979
        - **Subotica** 1988
  - Blushing Groom 1974 _see below_
- Bald Eagle 1955
  - **San San** 1969
- Never Bend 1960 _see below_

Ribot 1952 (by Tenerani out of _Romanella_)

- **Molvedo** 1958
  - **Prince Royal** 1961
    - _Quiriquina_ 1966
      - Tom Rolfe 1962
        - _Trephine_ 1977
          - His Majesty 1968
            - Hoist The Flag 1968
              - _Razzana_ 1981
                - Tobira Celeste 1971
                  - **Trempolino** 1984
                  - **Alleged** 1974
                    - Danehill 1986
                      - Thawakib 1990
                  - _Suavite_ 1981
                    - **Dylan Thomas** 2003
                      - **Sakhee** 1997
                  - **Suave Dancer** 1988

Val de Loir 1959 (by Vieux Manoir)

- Chaparral 1966
  - _Green Valley_ 1967
    - _Seneca_ 1973
      - Green Dancer 1972
        - **Sagace** 1980
          - **Suave Dancer** 1988
            - _Saganeca_ 1988
              - Tennyson 1970
                - **Sagamix** 1995
                  - _Toute Cy_ 1979
                    - _Floripedes_ 1985
                      - **Montjeu** 1996
                      - **Hurricane Run** 2002
                    - _Hirondelle_ 1981
                      - _Helice_ 1988
                        - **Hélissio** 1993

Never Bend 1960 (by Nasrullah)

- **Mill Reef** 1968
  - Shirley Heights 1975
    - Darshaan 1981
      - Lashkari 1981
      - *Sinntara* 1989
        - **Sinndar** 1997
      - Doyoun 1985
      - *Zarkana* 1992
        - **Zarkava** 2005
      - *Marienbad* 1991
      - **Marienbard** 1997
      - **Dalakhani** 2000
  - Riverman 1969
    - ***Detroit*** 1977 *see below*
      - **Carnegie** 1991
    - ***Gold River*** 1977
      - *Dockage* 1984
        - *Docklands* 1989
          - **Rail Link** 2003
      - Bahri 1992
        - **Sakhee** 1997

Northern Dancer 1961 (by Nearctic)

- Viceregal 1966
- *Trephine* 1977
  - **Trempolino** 1984
- Nijinsky 1967 *see below*
- Lyphard 1969 *see below*
  - The Minstrel 1974
  - *Zaizafon* 1982
  - Zamindar 1994
    - **Zarkava** 2005
  - Nureyev 1977 *see below*
  - Danzig 1977 *see below*
  - Sadler's Wells 1981 *see below*
  - Fairy King 1982
    - **Hélissio** 1993

Nijinsky 1967 (by Northern Dancer)

- Green Dancer 1972
- **Suave Dancer** 1988
- Ile de Bourbon 1975
- Kahyasi 1985
  - *Hasili* 1991
    - *Zarkasha* 1999
    - Dansili 1996
    - **Zarkava** 2005
    - **Rail Link** 2003
  - Niniski 1976
  - Lomitas 1988
    - **Danedream** 2008
  - Caerleon 1980
  - **Marienbard** 1997
  - *Wasnah* 1987
  - Bahri 1992
    - **Sakhee** 1997
  - **Lammtarra** 1992

Lyphard 1969 (by Northern Dancer)
- **Three Troïkas** 1976
- Bellypha 1976
  - Mendez 1981
  - Linamix 1987
    - **Sagamix** 1995
- **Dancing Brave** 1983

Mr Prospector 1970 (by Raise A Native out of *Gold Digger*)
- Miswaki 1978
  - *Urban Sea* 1989
  - *Daltawa* 1989
    - **Dalakhani** 2000
  - **Sea The Stars** 2006
  - *Coup de Genie* 1991
    - *Moonlight's Box* 1996
      - **Bago** 2001

Blushing Groom 1974 (by Red God)
- **Rainbow Quest** 1981
- **Saumarez** 1987
  - *Snow Bride* 1986
    - **Lammtarra** 1992
  - Nashwan 1986
  - **Bago** 2001

Nureyev 1977 (by Northern Dancer)
- Theatrical 1982
- *Docklands* 1989
  - **Rail Link** 2006
  - Kingmambo 1990
  - King's Best 1997
    - **Workforce** 2007
  - **Peintre Célèbre** 1994
    - Moonlight's Box 1996
      - **Bago** 2001

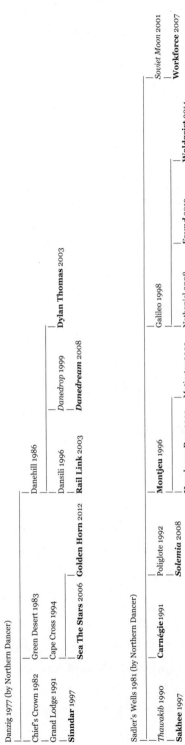

Danzig 1977 (by Northern Dancer)

Chief's Crown 1982
Green Desert 1983
Grand Lodge 1991
Cape Cross 1994
Sinndar 1997

Danehill 1986
Dansili 1996
Rail Link 2003
Danedrop 1999
Danedream 2008
Dylan Thomas 2003
Sea The Stars 2006
Golden Horn 2012

Sadler's Wells 1981 (by Northern Dancer)

Thawakib 1990
Carnégie 1991
Sakhee 1997
Poliglote 1992
Solemia 2008
Montjeu 1996
Hurricane Run 2002
Motivator 2002
Trêve 2010
Galileo 1998
Nathaniel 2008
Enable 2014
Found 2012
Waldgeist 2014
Soviet Moon 2001
Workforce 2007

Bibliography

Black, R., *Horse-Racing in France* (London: Sampson Low, Marston, Searle & Rivington, 1886)

Bowen, E. L., *Legacies of the Turf: A Century of Great Thoroughbred Breeders, Volume 1* (Eclipse Press, 2003)

Bowen, E. L., *Legacies of the Turf: A Century of Great Thoroughbred Breeders, Volume 2* (Eclipse Press, 2004)

Caro, I., *Paris to the Past: Traveling through French History by Train* (New York: W. W. Norton, 2012)

Desan, S. M, *Living the French Revolution and the Age of Napoleon* (Audible Audio, The Great Courses, 2013)

Downie, D., *Paris, Paris: Journey Into the City of Light* (Broadway Books, 2005)

Fitzgerald, A. & Seth-Smith, M., *Prix de L'Arc de Triomphe 1920-1948* (J. A. Allen, 1980)

Fitzgerald, A., *Prix de L'Arc de Triomphe 1949-1964* (J. A. Allen, 1982)

Fitzgerald, A. *Prix de L'Arc de Triomphe 1965-1982 The Official History* (Sidgwick & Jackson, 1983)

Kirkland, S., *Paris Reborn: Napoléon III, Baron Haussmann, and the Quest to Build a Modern City* (St Martin's Griffin, 2013) or (Picador USA, 2014)

Lee, H., *Historique des courses de chevaux, de l'antiquité à ce jour* (Paris: Charpentier et Fasquelle, 1914)

Longrigg, R., *The History of Horse Racing* (Stein and Day, 1972)

McGrath, C., *Mr Darley's Arabian* (John Murray, 2016)

Nicholson, J. C., *Never Say Die: A Kentucky Colt, the Epsom Derby, and the Rise of the Modern Thoroughbred Industry* (University Press of Kentucky, 2013)

Norwich, J. J., *France: A History: from Gaul to de Gaulle* (John Murray, 2018)

Reid, J., *Monsieur X: The incredible story of the most audacious gambler in history* (Bloomsbury Sport, 2018)

Roberts, A., *Napoleon the Great* (Penguin, 2015)

Taunton, T. W., *Famous horses* (London: Sampson Low, Marston, 1901)

Regarding 1972:

Batthyány, S., *A Crime in the Family: A World War II Secret Buried in Silence – And My Search for the Truth* (Da Capo Press, 2017)

Index